The Handmade Life

DEDICATION

We dedicate this book to the
extraordinary global craft community
we are lucky enough to call home.
You inspire us every day.

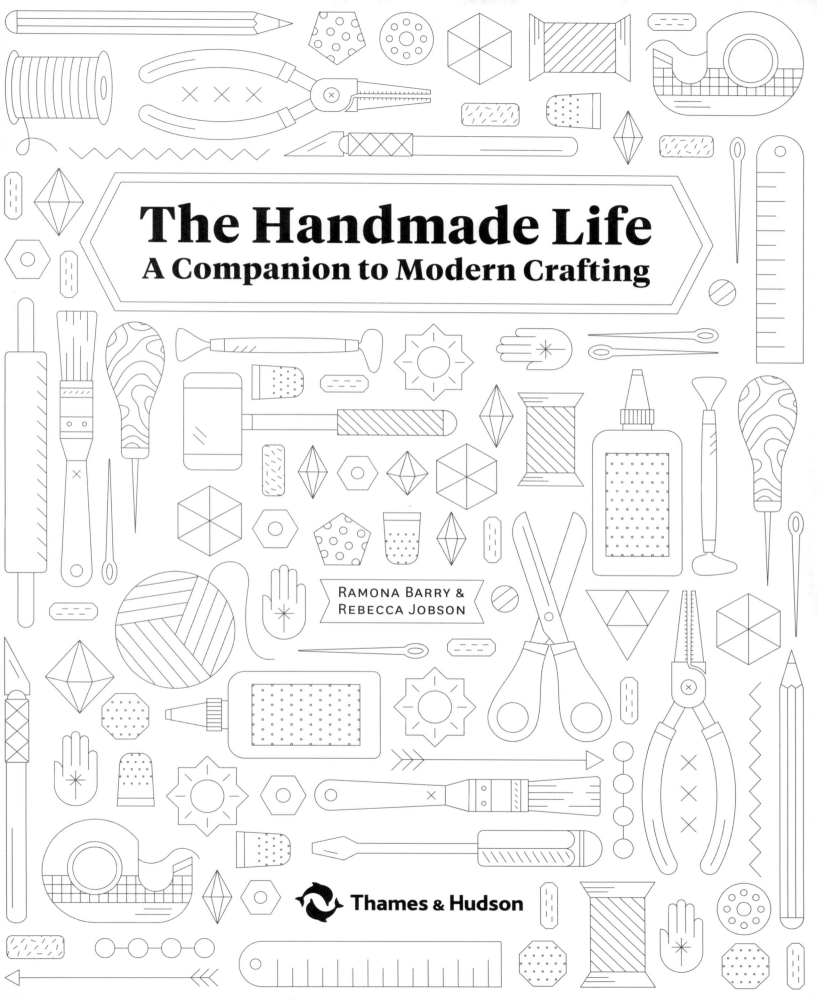

The Handmade Life
A Companion to Modern Crafting

Ramona Barry &
Rebecca Jobson

Thames & Hudson

First published as *The Craft Companion* in Australia
in 2015 by Thames & Hudson Australia Pty Ltd

First published in 2016 in hardcover in the United States
of America as *The Handmade Life* by Thames & Hudson
Inc., 500 Fifth Avenue, New York, New York 10110

www.thameshudson.com.au

Editing: Lucy James
Proofreading: Susie Ashworth
Design: Spencer Harrison
Photography: Hilary Walker
Illustrations: Oslo Davis

thamesandhudsonusa.com

Library of Congress Catalog Card Number 2015959501

ISBN: 9780500518922
Printed and bound in China by Everbest Printing Co. Ltd

CONTENTS

Introduction

◇◇◇

Welcome to *The Handmade Life*. We wrote this book for you. Making is at the heart of what it means to be human. It allows us to be curious, clever, dextrous, and useful. It forces us to solve problems creatively, think laterally, and ponder both the biggest picture and the tiniest microcosm. It slows us down and quickens our pulse, it's expressive and expansive, and it brings us closer to who we are. Our best selves are often found while sitting at the bench focused absolutely on the task at hand — magically melding mind and body in the process.

If you picked up this book, chances are you're already a keen crafter or know someone who is — you may be a crochet champ, marbling maestro or felt fanatic, or you may just be an enthusiastic novice itching to learn more. Well, this book is for you — all of you. We've discovered that the more we craft, the more ideas we have, and the more ideas, the more techniques we need to learn. With this in mind we designed this book as both instructional sampler and degustation menu, and offer you a delectable taste of key processes, materials, and contemporary artists.

There are many ways you can use *The Handmade Life*. Flip through and see what catches your eye; head straight to your favorite craft and dig deep; or work through it meticulously in order. Any way you slice it up you're bound to find something to chew on. Each chapter is divided into seven sections: introduction, contemporary artists, design notes, tools list, techniques, ideas, and project. Collectively these sections weave together the many aspects of craft: history, design, process, concept, and outcome. Whatever technique you fall for, you're part of a long craft continuum.

We are so excited to share the genius of contemporary artists, designers, and makers choosing to revisit and revolutionize craft practice — and inspire you to think big and work hard. Makers that made us turn to each other and say "WOW, have you seen this? AMAZING!" If they excite us, we suspect they will excite you too.

The techniques and tools are designed to keep it simple, encourage sustainable making, enable what we call "cross-craft projects" and confound the common misconception that to make things you need a lot of highly specialized equipment. The general tool kit is a basic go-to full of great multi-taskers to get you started. We also recommend re-purposing, borrowing, and sharing with fellow crafters, and engaging in neighborhood foraging whenever possible. We've broken down the techniques to the bare bones because we firmly believe that if you nail the simple building blocks well, you create the best foundation for future learning and making. Many of the projects were born from the adage that you need 10,000 hours of practice to master a skill. But don't sweat it — there's something for even the most time-poor maker. Some will take a weekend, some a couple of hours, and others will see you crafting into the wee hours for months on end. Whether you choose a snack or main course approach, all the projects are designed to teach you techniques that will take you to new places.

We have a lot to say about craft. It's what energizes and excites us. It is how we engage with the world and how we celebrate and commemorate our lives. Craft is the glue that binds us. Craft provides an almost magical link to the history of the world and is embedded in the everyday. It often takes place between other activities: at the kitchen table, and around kids, jobs, illness, relationships, study, and travel. As you'll learn, craft is not about the endgame; it's about the process. It can be frustrating, challenging, exhilarating, and sustaining — simultaneously, your best friend and worst enemy. But we'd never give it up. Craft will be with you in good times and bad, and will be, as we hope this book is, your companion for life.

Beck and Ramona

Each craft has its own specialist tools, but a basic tool kit is something that you'll return to again and again, regardless of what materials you're playing with. We suggest starting out with these and then allowing your tool kit to grow as you explore different techniques.

ADHESIVE

You'll want different types for different jobs. PVA glue (also called white glue) is our favorite all-rounder. Mod Podge is what we call the "craft industry standard." Fabric, wood, and jewelry glue are medium-specific. Double-sided tape and dimensional glue dots are useful for everything from card making to collage and are a no-mess option. Art cement is great for fine work.

AWL

Doubling as an ice pick, this lethal-looking spike helps you create holes in paper, cardboard, balsa wood, leather, fabric, and rubber.

BONE FOLDER

Don't panic, it's not made of bone (anymore), but this handy flat resin tool helps put perfect creases and scores in any paper project.

BRAYER

A hard rubber roller, this tool is infinitely useful for printing, collage and papercrafts.

BUCKETS

You'll be surprised how many crafts require one, from dyeing fabric to making clay pinch pots to collage (where it doubles as a wastebasket). Buy a few and keep them new because the one festering in the laundry is not going to cut it!

CRAFT KNIFE

Also called a retractable, Stanley or utility knife, they usually come with replaceable blades, which is great because we have a "new project equals new blade" policy.

CUTTING MAT

We usually have three cutting mats: a super-clean one for fabric cutting, a large one for papercrafts, and a dirty one for wet crafts. Self-healing mats are the best kind.

DISPOSABLE GLOVES

These are a crafter's best friend. They're not the most environmentally friendly product but are a must-have when handling chemicals, or when you don't want to transfer colors inadvertently with paint projects or have blue hands from the indigo vat for a week.

FABRIC

Once you start crafting, your stash of fabrics builds up over time. Even if you buy fabric for specific projects you always have bits left over that are worth keeping. We sort ours into colors but you may choose to categorize by weight or type. Don't rule out your old clothing or soft furnishings as top fabric choices. We go with natural fibers whenever possible.

FABRIC MEDIUM

This may seem like an odd item in a general toolbox but we LOVE this stuff. Add it to acrylic paint and it becomes fabric paint, able to be washed and ironed. Genius.

HOLE PUNCH

Invest in an adjustable hole punch for everything from paper to leather craft. Sharpen it by punching holes through fine-grit sandpaper.

HOT GLUE GUN

You get what you pay for, so invest wisely. This tool comes in both high and low temperatures. We prefer to go hot or go home.

IRON

We hear people use this to flatten clothes. We use it constantly in sewing, quilting and patching, heat-setting printed fabric, fusing plastic, and fixing transfers.

LIDDED CONTAINERS

You'll need these for buttons, beads, natural dye baths, needles and pins, and embellishments. You can't have enough storage for craft supplies.

MEASURING CUPS & SPOONS

We advise investing in a large glass jug with easy-to-read numbers, preferably with metric, imperial and cup sizes, as well as a standard set of measuring spoons, plastic or stainless steel. Everything from dyeing and marbling to indigo and printing needs them. Remember to keep them for craft only to avoid ingesting something other than cake batter.

NEEDLES AND PINS

It's good to invest in a variety for sewing — for the machine, embroidery, yarn, upholstery, doll making, leather and quilting. Store them in a pincushion or sewing box to keep them sharp and safe. Buy as you need and your collection will build fast.

NOTEBOOK

For any creative endeavor you'll want to keep all your ideas and inspiration in an easy-to-access place. We always have several small ones on the go but you may prefer a fat hardcover one for record keeping.

PAINT

You get what you pay for, even with basic acrylic and watercolor paint. Craft, art and hardware stores all have great paint options. We like sample pots of house paint, spray paint, good-quality acrylic, and artist's gouache.

PAINTBRUSHES

Your basic white nylon brush is the most versatile for craft projects but it's wise to invest in some natural bristle brushes too. Our holy grail of brushes is the sable size 6 tapered watercolor brush. It's expensive but worth every penny. We also go through foam brushes by the truckload.

PAINTER'S TAPE

We prefer this to masking tape as it's purpose-made so as not to lift paint off projects. This low-tack tape is usually a bright color so it's easy to spot and remove when you're finished.

PAPER

Drawing, watercolor, bank paper, card stock, crepe, tissue, origami, artist rag, kraft, butcher and scrapbook papers are the ones we like to have on hand.

PAPER TRIMMER

This handy guillotine-type tool is great for papercraft of all types.

PENCILS

We recommend you invest in a nice box of 48 colored pencils. They're invaluable for working out designs in your notebook. You also need a selection of soft and hard gray lead pencils for sketching. Watercolor pencils are very useful for designing.

PENS

Permanent markers, gel pens, paint pens, fiber tip, and calligraphy pens are our favorites.

PINKING SHEARS

These create a zigzag edge that stops fabric from fraying or adds a decorative edge to paper.

PUNCHES

There is an endless array of decorative punches on the market. We found the star, circle, and tag shapes to be the most useful.

ROTARY CUTTER

Aligned with a ruler, this is used for long straight cuts in fabric. Invest in a good-quality one that has replaceable blades.

RULER

This is a trusty staple. It's worth investing in a metal one as the weight means it won't shift when measuring or tearing. Buy standard and yard lengths.

SANDPAPER

You can often buy a mixed pack with different grit sizes. Sometimes it is just referred to as coarse/medium/smooth or has a number, system. The higher the number the smoother the sandpaper. Most jobs will require you to start out with a rougher sandpaper and work your way up to the smooth stuff.

SCALPEL

This is a precision tool finer than your basic craft knife and necessary for cutting stencils, curved lines and delicate papercraft work. The blades are detachable and blunt quickly, so stock up on a few for your kit.

SCISSORS

This is where we recommend investment. Good heavy-duty fabric, small embroidery, paper, extra fine and decorative-edge scissors are the cornerstone of any crafter's arsenal. Buy the best you can afford, and keep them sharp for years of service.

SEWING MACHINE

We are big proponents of "slow" sewing by hand but nothing beats a trusty machine for expediency and accuracy. Invest in a basic sewing machine and befriend it. Don't be put off by vintage; sometimes the simplest straight stitchers are the best (and the most reliable).

STAMPS AND INK PADS

Use these for customizing stationery, cards, wrapping paper and fabric. We suggest starting off with a good alphabet set.

STATIONERY SUPPLIES

String, adhesive dots, shipping tags, envelopes and copy paper are just some of the crafter's treasure to be found in the stationery store.

TAPE MEASURE

A fabric measure and a retractable metal measure are endlessly useful.

THREAD

Collect basic sewing threads in cotton and polyester. White, cream, black, and navy are the most commonly used colors.

WASHI TAPE

A newcomer to the toolbox, this beautiful and decorative paper tape comes in an endless array of designs and colors.

WIRE CUTTERS

Don't ruin your scissors by cutting even the finest of wires. Flush cutters are the best as they don't leave a burr on your wire end.

· Fiber ·

Felt

◇◇◇

Felt is probably the most primitive and flexible of all textile construction processes. It's the perfect all-purpose fiber — able to protect against cold, insulate against heat, absorb moisture and be cut without fraying. It's kind of a super-powered fabric. The simplicity of its construction makes it a fantastic entry-level activity for novice crafters.

While many cultures around the globe lay claim to being felt's first creators, the earliest evidence of felted "fabric" stems from the Neolithic era in the form of matted animal hair, and it's pretty safe to assume it was discovered as an accidental by-product of daily life. Unlike many other textile crafts, a large number of historical specimens of felt have survived in good condition. Examples of highly decorated, thick, ceremonial felt caps have been found in prehistorical Jutland in burial mounds that date back to the Bronze Age around 3,500 years ago.

The nomadic Mongol tribes under the rule of Genghis Khan were called "people of felt" and they used it for everything from shelter to saddlery. To this day Mongolian yurts are still constructed using felt for the protective outer wall. The Industrial Revolution delivered innovations in the 1700s that provided a more economical, consistent and durable fabric, which infiltrated all areas of mass production. In the mid-20th century artists began using unconventional materials and craft techniques in their work. Felt, with its long history and almost endless design capacity, was a perfect medium of exploration. The 1960s German Fluxus artist Joseph Beuys appropriated felt as his own, creating iconic works such as his now famous *Felt Suit* (1970).

Most recently, technologies such as laser cutting have reinvigorated the aesthetic possibilities of felt, pairing oppositional post-modern juxtapositions of "hard technology" with "soft edges" in both industrial design and domestic interiors. Today, the industrial uses of felt cover everything from floor underlay to pen tips.

Amazingly, hand-felting techniques remain virtually unchanged from ancient times. New developments stem from the inclusion of contemporary materials such as bubble wrap or, as with needle felting, the adoption of new tools inspired by industrial machinery.

Needle felting rose to prominence in the mid-1980s as artists realized they could use the barbed needles of industrial felting to create neater, more manageable 3-D objects than was possible with wet felting, which involves massaging the wool in water to create felt. Ironically, the newest felting technique — known as nuno — also comes with the most ancient sounding name. Developed in the early 1990s by Australian textile artist Polly Stirling, nuno combines woolen felt with a more delicate fabric (usually silk) to create a lighter, more wearable fabric suited to warm climates and fine projects.

Today, contemporary artists and object designers are creating hand-felted works to inject new hipness into the direct tactility and "wonky" finish of felt. Wet or dry, felting is an almost ideal domestic craft that only requires basic supplies, easily acquired skill and minimal space. The process may be simple, but as you can see, the possibilities are endless.

CONTEMPORARY ARTISTS

SONYA YONG JAMES
United States

Maker, educator and curator Sonya Yong James's connection to the source and cultural associations of her raw materials is deftly exemplified within her work. From wall art to domestic furnishings, Yong James makes uniquely tactile works that are so textural that the finished pieces often look more found than manufactured.

⌨ sonyayongjames.com

CAT RABBIT
Australia

Melbourne-based illustrator, softie maker and textile artist Cat Rabbit has carved out a niche within indie circles as the definitive go-to artist for gorgeously melancholic oddness. Managing to consistently hit the mark, her felt creations are as well considered as they are crafted. Funny, sad, clever and always excellently outfitted, the creatures of Cat Rabbit redefine the genre in her own eccentric image.

⌨ catrabbit.com.au

KIYOSHI MINO
United States

The mind-blowing realism of Kiyoshi Mino's needle-felted birds and animals is a spectacular example of the precision and control possible through the simplest of processes and materials. Both humorous and gentle, these creatures are bursting with personality and are a testament to the skill and kindness of their maker.

 kiyoshimino.com

FELT MISTRESS
Britain

Wielding scissors, needle and thread, Britain's Felt Mistress uses commercial felt like an illustrator uses vector curves. Often working side-by-side with some of the best graphic artists in the business, she creates pop cultural iconography as sharp as her wit.

 feltmistress.com

DESIGN NOTES

BASE NOTES

Handmade felt is a brilliant base fabric for a whole range of embellishing techniques, offering you the option of adding details to the finished product or embedding them into the fabric itself during the making process. It also dyes beautifully in flat or object form and can be hand-painted, carved or cut as well, allowing you almost endless possibilities to transform your base unit into something completely unique and utterly spectacular.

CAN YOU VS. SHOULD YOU

The materials for felting are very seductive. A rainbow of carded wool is totally swoon-worthy but remember, just because it can be felted doesn't mean it should be. Riotous color may be your thing but don't forget that a little can go a long way. You don't necessarily want your work looking like a Mardi Gras float that's been left out in the rain. Sometimes less is more, and the textural possibilities of felt come into their own in monochromatic and tonal palettes.

CHEAT SHEET

If you want some of the benefits of felt without having to pick up a carder or needle, you can go for what we call "cheat's felting." This technique is especially useful for cut-and-sew projects. You just throw everything your mother taught you about hand-washing woolens out of the window and instead throw 100 percent wool sweaters or blankets into the washing machine with loads of hot water and soap and then tumble-dry the bejeezus out of them. The finer the knit, the better the end result.

DRY VS. WET

Both dry and wet techniques have their pros and cons. Dry felting is fantastic for making 3-D objects — you can shape your work as you go and it's a no-mess, no-fuss process that is perfect for when time and space are limited and you want a sharper edge. The organic, soft-edged results of wet felting reflect the process beautifully, and once begun, it's highly addictive. It's also much less dangerous than needle (dry) felting and therefore a great option for children and klutzes alike. Think about which technique will convey your idea best and make your choice accordingly.

OUT OF THE BOX

Felt is often thought of as a soft medium, but its density means that it can become an exercise in high contrast. Think of it as the closest to wood that a fabric can get and sharpen up your design ideas. Take cues from industrial use — boxes, baskets, even furniture can be created in felt. Ask yourself where soft can replace hard and a slew of new possibilities will open up to you.

Whether specifically designed for wet or dry techniques, all felting tools have one common purpose — to manipulate the scaled surface of pure wool to firmly lock fibers together in a solid mass.

WET FELTING

- **Water:** Has to be warm, has to get sudsy. Tap water is fine.

- **Soap:** Pure soap flakes are best but adding a few drops of ordinary dishwashing liquid will also do the trick.

- **Sushi mat:** This is used as a backing for your felting process. Remember to check first that it fits into your felting tray or is long enough to accommodate projects like scarves.

- **Unbleached muslin, broadcloth or netting:** This sits between the sushi mat and your felt project. Any lightweight cotton will do but you'll need something un-dyed so the color doesn't run into your work.

- **Assorted silk, cotton, wool threads:** These can be embedded into your project as a textural or color design feature.

- **Felter's tray:** Essentially a shallow, broad plastic tub that can sit firmly on your work surface. We use an under-the-bed storage tub. Wet felting outside is a great option as you can slosh around a bit, but a kitchen table will work too, if you don't mind mopping up. These tubs are also great for marbling paper.

- **Rubber gloves:** Long ones are great for keeping out the water, but shorter surgical versions give you greater feel. Choose what works best for you.

- **Wool roving:** Prepared sheep's wool, known as roving, which has been washed to remove excess lanolin (grease) and carded or combed to orient all the individual fibers in the same direction. Alternatively, you can buy roving uncarded and invest in your own carding comb.

DRY FELTING

- **Needles:** These terrifying things come in a variety of gauges from coarse to fine but essentially all do the same thing: by repeatedly stabbing the wool fibers, these barbed wonders transform the carded sliver into a solid section of felt. Just watch your fingers! Every dry felter knows the pain of stabbing themselves. Thankfully, after a couple of accidental incidents your body installs an in-built warning system.

- **Multi-needle tool:** These are even more lethal than regular needles but certainly work like speed demons on large sections of felting. Definitely an investment tool, so try the craft before purchasing one.

- **Dense foam block:** The block works to protect both your work surface and you. You can get craft-specific foam block but we like the dense industrial foam as you can get it cut to size and it tends to last a lot longer.

- **Wool:** Carded wool or sliver is the basic cornerstone of all felt construction. This soft "combed" and cleaned wool comes natural, bleached or dyed in a rainbow of colors ready for transformation. What you choose is up to you! Synthetic fibers do not behave at all well when you attempt to felt them: they simply refuse to hold hands! Take note that merino wool is best for wet felting but not for dry. When dry felting, go for Romney Southdown or Corriedale wool instead.

SURE-FIRE WET FELTING

This basic method for wet felting is incredibly simple. Make sure you follow the steps in the right order to ensure that you end up with fabric and not just soggy wool.

WHAT YOU NEED

- Wool roving

- Large, round-stick sushi mat

- Piece of netting fabric such as tulle (like a tutu), around 3" wider than the sushi mat on all sides

- Shallow plastic tub

- Pure soap flakes

- Hot water

- Rubber gloves

WHAT YOU DO

1. Pull a fine tuft of wool from your roving and put it onto the sushi mat, starting at the top. Continue the process across the whole surface until you have a rectangle shape. Make sure all the wool fibers are running the same way, and that the tufts overlap. The layer must be fine enough that you can still see the sushi mat.

2. Make a second layer with the fibers running in the opposite direction. Use either the same color or a different one, depending on the effect you're after. Make a third layer, reversing the direction of your fiber again.

3. Place netting on top of your felt and place the whole lot (sushi mat, wool, and net) in a tub of very warm soapy water.

4. Using a gentle circular motion, massage the wool through the netting. After a couple of minutes, carefully lift up your netting to make sure you're not trapping wool in it and turn your felt 90 degrees. Replace the net and keep rubbing for 2–3 more minutes.

5. You'll feel the wool getting firmer as it turns into felt. Once it has shrunk by around 25 percent, it's done. Gently rinse the felt in tepid water until the water clears of soap. Squeeze out excess water. Dry the felt flat in a warm place.

DRY NEEDLE FELTING

The trick with needle felting is not speed but rhythm. Steady pokes with the needle will yield the best (and safest) results. It is a very simple technique but inevitably you will incur injury, so it's not one to try with little kids.

WHAT YOU NEED

- Wool roving

- Thick foam block

- Barbed needle or multi-needle handle

WHAT YOU DO

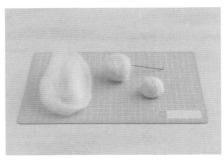

1. Take a section of wool roving about five times the size you want the finished ball to be.

2. Roll the wool tightly into a compact shape, then tuck the ends in underneath. The more compact the starting shape, the shorter the felting time will be.

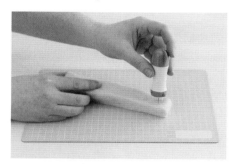

3. Place the compacted wool on top of the foam. Begin piercing with a barbed needle. Poke the wool with repetitive downward strokes. Be careful to exit the needle at the same angle as entered, as the needles are fragile and will break easily if bent. As the shape takes form, rotate it frequently to maintain an even shape. The wool will become denser the more you poke it.

PROJECT IDEAS

→ Wet felting lends itself to easy shaping. Match a thick sack of handmade felt with upcycled leather handles and bold embroidery stitching for a designer carry-all.

→ Cheat your way to a new woolen bedspread by felting pre-existing knits, cutting them into patchwork squares and sewing them together.

→ Needle-felted balls can be used for loads of projects. String them together to make decorative chains — upsize for room-sized garlands or downsize for person-sized neckpieces. Incorporate needle-felted balls as beads into other projects such as macramé and weaving, or use en masse in a rug or wreath.

→ Use a zoo visit or children's drawings to create a miniature menagerie of needle-felted monsters or a barnyard full of animals.

→ Combine references from organic shapes such as nests or boulders to create your own felted light coverings, vessels, or furnishings using shaped wet or dry techniques. Decorate them with embroidery, print, or paint in patterns that reference their inspiration source.

Felt Town

WHAT YOU NEED

- Wool roving — white (approx. 100 g/3½" for the whole town), small amounts of red, orange, terracotta, pale blue, mint green, pale yellow, baby pink, black and gray

- Leather thimble (don't laugh)

- Felting needles (we went through five of them for this project)

- Felting-needle holder (holds up to four needles at once, great for making the main blocks)

- Foam block

- Plastic adhesive bandages (trust us)

- PVA (white) glue

- Craft knife

- Balsa wood

HOT TIP

The key to selecting the right amount of roving is remembering that it shrinks to around one quarter of its original size once felted. It's a forgiving medium, so if you feel your building shape is too small simply add more and continue felting. Our largest building (the pink arched Art Deco number) took approximately 16" of white roving.

Apart from the inherent dangers of impaling yourself, needle felting is a really simple craft. It's basically sculpting with wool. To build our town we first created simple white block shapes — square, rectangle, arch, and triangle — in different sizes, then added color to the sides and architectural details to the front. You could make one building or fifty. Add toy cars, fake grass, and cardboard trees, put them in a dry terrarium or string them from the Christmas tree. Be warned though — felt architecture is highly addictive!

WHAT YOU DO

1. Take a length of white roving and tease it out to a long strip. Fold it tightly over and over until you have a fairly compact rectangle. This is the beginning of your first building.

2. With the needle holder, start jabbing at the wool, using your thimble hand to hold it in place on your foam block. Soon you will feel the wool start to firm up and felt. Keep turning the work as you felt to create an even density.

3. Remember, you're sculpting with wool so use your thimble hand to push the wool into shape as you felt. Keep on felting until you have a small, firm building block.

4. Pull out a small amount of colored roving and place it on the facing edge of the white block, making sure you have a long enough piece to cover the whole edge. Again, using the needle holder, attach the colored roving to your felted block.

5. Switch to a single needle to add the architectural details. Windows only need the tiniest amounts of wool. Use your needle to manipulate it into shape as you felt it to the front facing of your block.

6. For extra stability, apply PVA glue to the base and allow it to dry, then cut balsa strips to size and glue to the base of your felt building.

7. You are now ready to play town planner.

Knit

◇◇◇

When most people think of craft they think of knitting. So pervasive is its association with handmade items it can pretty much be considered craft royalty. It's a testament to the ingenuity of humans that one simple technique can be so widely reinterpreted, from the complex Fair Isle knitwear of Scotland, to traditional Icelandic lopapeysa, the heavy cables of the Aran Isles, and the amazing outfits of West African masquerade. Knitting techniques, practices, and garments are deeply embedded in almost all cultures, while its amazing versatility has readily lent itself to practical and decorative solutions for warmth, strength, movement, and ceremony.

As with so many textile crafts, accurately pinning down the origins of knitting is difficult. Many early civilizations, from Egypt to Persia, depict figures wearing garments that appear knitted. Most histories of the craft refer to North African shepherds 1,500 years ago making socks from wool spun by their wives. This simple technology lent itself perfectly to nomadic life and fabric production on the run. Part of the confusion stems from the existence of similar techniques, such as sprang and naelbinding (both single needle-looping techniques), which create fabric almost identical to knitting. Although the exact origins may be obscure, knitting is generally dated back to the Middle East from around 200 C.E.

Initially knitting was very much men's business. Spreading quickly through the Mediterranean via trade routes to Europe in the mid-1500s, a network of trade knitting guilds sprang up, with young men serving lengthy apprenticeships before being sufficiently skilled to be called a "master knitter." The looping system made knitting ideal for the production of stretch fabrics such as socks and hosiery, and by the middle of the 16th century the island of Jersey had a thriving hand-knitting industry with the skills of master knitters much in demand.

As fashions changed and the demand for stretch fabrics grew, so did the impetus for a cheaper, faster way of production. The invention of the first knitting machine in 1589 had its patent denied by Queen Elizabeth I, but by the 18th century, machine knitting was commonplace and quickly shifted the craft of hand-knitting to a useful but nonessential pastime.

As with many domestic crafts, knitting saw a resurgence in the 19th century, becoming both moral duty and one of the expected skills of well-bred ladies. It emerged as a parlor craft (a much more refined version of today's Stitch 'n Bitch sessions) and written patterns began to be published for the first time. The post-Second World War re-domestication of women saw knitting increasingly used as a tool to encourage them out of the workforce and back into the home. Patterns for projects such as sweetheart sweaters were intended to show potential beaux what wonderful wives they would make. Seriously!

Knitting's deep associations with women's roles and domestic work have also made the craft a favorite technique for artists from first-wave feminists to Riot Grrrls looking to disrupt and subvert hegemonic discourse on gender, race, and identity. Contemporary knit advocates range from superstar endorsers to gender-bending socio-political activists, visual artists, designers, hobbyists, grandmothers, bearded hipsters, and kids, all making wonderful works using two sticks and a piece of string.

FREDDIE ROBINS
Britain

Multimedia artist Freddie Robins's practice is a sophisticated, subversive exploration of meaning and making that fuses multiple textile techniques into pieces that reveal the traditional categories of art, craft, and design for the outmoded definitions they are. Meticulously crafted, there is both wit and terror in the work as Robins continues a long history of artists disrupting hegemonic gender bias and value-based assumptions regarding domestic vs. gallery craft by using soft materials and techniques in hard ways.

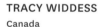 freddierobins.com

TRACY WIDDESS
Canada

Inspired by B-grade 1950s cult sci-fi, Tracy Widdess is an artist after our own geek hearts. Creating outstanding wearable and object-based works bordering on mad genius, her brilliant "brutal knitting" project has been running for nearly a decade. Driven by both her own imagination and the illustrations of outsiders, her pieces are equal parts creepy and hilarious. By cleverly manipulating the best of both hand- and machine-knitting techniques, she brilliantly brings these "creatures from the dark side" to life in the most tactile of ways.

▢ brutal-knitting.tumblr.com

ISABEL BERGLUND
Denmark

Textile designer and artist Isabel Berglund confounds categorization, creating a range of knitted works from isolated objects to immersive installations. Her bricolage-based, mixed-media pieces result in strangely anthropomorphic objects. Her use of monochromatic color is regally architectural and her smaller-scale exhibition works, placed within the context of the clinical gallery space, disturbingly alien. Berglund produces pieces that are brilliant in both conception and execution.

🖥 **isabelberglund.dk**

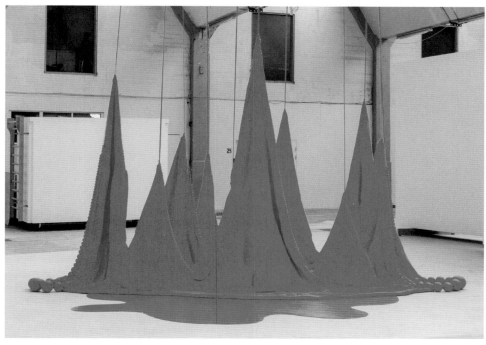

MANDY MCINTOSH
Britain

Highly skilled, politically charged, and socially engaged artist Mandy McIntosh is a multimedia artist and knitter whose work is site specific — either geographically or anatomically. Her diverse artistic output playfully confounds cultural traditions through skewed and oversize use of surface patterning and structures such as intarsia and cabling, while her insertion of subcultural vernacular as graphic text make possible poignant high/low contrasts between notions of public art and wearable design.

🖥 **ham-and-enos.org.uk**

DESIGN NOTES

ATTENTION PLEASE

Knitting patterns can be notoriously difficult to read, especially for a beginner. Fear not. Good knitting books and magazines should have a clear legend at the beginning of each pattern, and many also have illustrated instructions on how to execute the required stitches. The key is to start simple and work your way up. Follow our golden rules: when in doubt, Google; when confused, YouTube; and when tired, stop knitting because it's nap time.

DON'T DRINK THE KOOL-AID

There is not a single color in the Pantone library that is not reproduced in yarn somewhere, but if you can't find it, dye it. You can use everything from onions to Kool-Aid and experiment with commercial yarns or spin your own. The options are virtually endless. Dark colors are notoriously hard to "read," especially for night-time knitters, so if you're starting out, keep it light and you'll find it easier to pick up dropped stitches, count your rows and remember where you are.

CAN YOU FEEL IT?

This is where knit really shines. From the bulkiest cables to the finest baby booties, knitting is a completely tactile craft with amazing versatility. Combine different yarn weights and styles, play with stitch varieties and alter your needle size to create amazing textural effects. The yarn you love to touch will be the knit you love to wear.

HANDLE ME WITH CARE

Every knitter has a horror story of the hand knit that went into the wash and ended up doll-sized and felted beyond recognition. Pure wool, even when labeled "washable," needs a little special love and attention in the laundry. Gently hand-wash, lie flat in the shade to retain the shape and wait an eternity for it to dry. Watch out for synthetic fibers too. Sometimes the color can run if treated too roughly. Most yarn labels include washing instructions — be alert but not alarmed.

SIZE MATTERS

By changing the scale we change perception. Use the "wrong" needles with yarn, combine strands from multiple balls into one yarn for extra bulk, arm knit with lightly twisted wool tops for an ultra-bulky knit. Variations are also going to alter your end product so do a tension gauge swatch before you set out. A sweater with 6-foot arms might be a great exhibition piece, but if you're knitting it for nan it's just crazy town.

HAVE A YARN

Yarn comes in endless natural and synthetic varieties. Beautiful cottons, cashmeres, wools and mohair all come in drool-worthy colors. We, however, wouldn't touch acrylic with a 10-foot pole. Assorted twine, leather cord and neon bricklayer's string are all also exciting possibilities for the adventurous knitter. You can even knit with spun pet hair or paper!

SUBSTITUTE

Every pattern will call for a particular weight of yarn, often a specific brand of yarn, some of which are very expensive. Most yarns fall into similar weight and/ or ply categories. As long as your gauge swatch matches up, substituting one yarn for another is totally fine. That being said, the drape and feel of a silk cashmere 4-ply blend is remarkably different from its acrylic counterpart.

FASHION FORWARD

Top designers often feature artisanal craft details in their couture that offer great inspiration for domestic knitters. Whip up your own wearables to suit the season — gray sweater with a neon neckband one year, monochrome midnight shades the next. Of course, if you are a slow knitter you can either do a little fashion forecasting or try working on smaller accessories such as scarves, wraps and hats to stay ahead of the game.

- **Needles:** They come in wood, bamboo, steel, plastic and aluminum. Plastic and steel are a bit slippery, which is good for fast knitters, but not such fun for new knitters, who tend to drop stitches. We favor bamboo as it's beautiful, warm to hold and holds yarn nicely.

- **Double-pointed needles:** Primarily for making socks.

- **Circular needles:** For circular and tubular knitting.

- **Cable needles:** These may be notched or U-shaped and are used to hold stitches to the front or back of the work while knitting adjacent stitches.

- **Stitch holders:** These look like large safety pins and are used for holding stitches to be worked later.

- **Row counter:** Fits close to the knob of the needle. You can move a dial to keep track of your rows. It only helps if you remember to turn it, which we never do.

- **Needle gauge:** A handy tool for checking the size of random needles. Very helpful if you're picking needles up from secondhand shops and they're sans a size label.

- **Yarn**

- **Scissors**

- **Pins**

- **Tape measure**

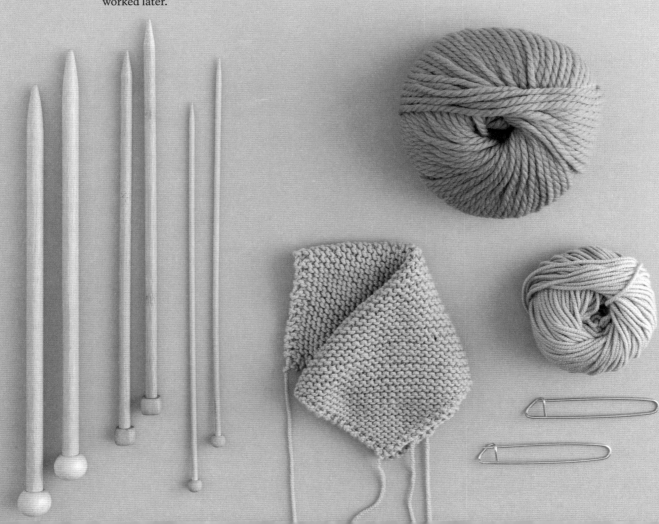

The first thing you need to learn is how to hold your yarn and needles. So persuade a knit-savvy friend or family member to cast on some stitches for you so that you can literally get to grips with your materials and learn the two basic stitches: knit and purl.

There are two basic ways to knit: the "English" or "throwing" method and the "Continental" or "picking" method.

"ENGLISH" METHOD

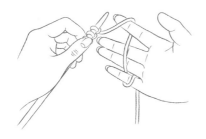

1. Holding the needle with cast-on stitches in your left hand, wrap the working yarn over the fingers of your right hand as shown. Pick up the free needle in your right hand. (Experienced knitters will do this first.)

2. To form a knit stitch, insert the free needle through the first stitch on the left-hand needle from front to back, then use the index finger of your right hand to loop the yarn around the point of the working needle. Complete the stitch as shown opposite.

"CONTINENTAL" METHOD

1. Holding the needle with the cast-on stitches in your right hand, wrap the yarn around the fingers of your left hand as shown. Transfer the needle with the stitches to your left hand.

2. To form a knit stitch, insert the free needle into the first stitch from front to back. Raise the index finger of your left hand to tension the yarn and bring this finger forward to wrap it around the needle. Complete the stitch as shown opposite.

SLIP KNOT

1. Form a loop with your yarn, then catch the yarn with the needle.

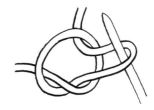

2. Pull the needle through the loop to create a stitch.

3. Pull the yarn to tighten.

CASTING ON

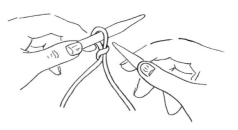

1. Make a slip knot on one needle and hold it in your left hand.

2. Push your right needle through the slip knot loop, then wind your yarn over the right needle behind the slip knot.

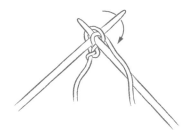

3. Draw your right needle and the loop through the loop on the left needle.

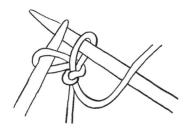

4. You will now have a loop on each needle.

5. Use your left needle to catch the loop on the right needle. You now have two stitches on your left needle.

6. Continue forming stitches this way until you have the desired number. Easy!

KNIT STITCH

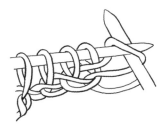

1. Push the right needle through the back of the first stitch on your left needle.

2. Wrap the yarn over the right needle from the back and then bring that loop through the stitch.

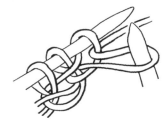

3. Allow the first stitch to slide off the left needle.

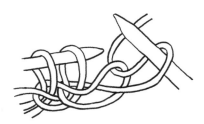

4. Your new stitch remains on the right needle.

PURL STITCH

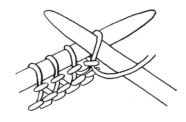

1. With your yarn at the front of your work, push the right needle through the front of the first stitch on the left needle.

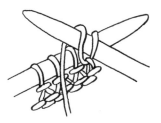

2. Wrap your yarn around from front to back.

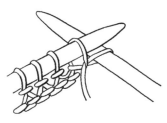

3. Bring the loop of your yarn through the stitch so that you have a stitch sitting on your right needle.

4. Allow the first stitch on the left needle to slide off and leave your new stitch on your right needle.

BINDING OFF

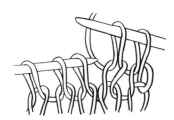

1. Knit the first two stitches of your row.

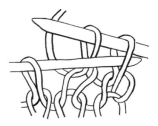

2. Using the left needle pick up the first stitch and lift it over the second stitch, dropping it off the right needle once it's over.

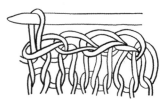

3. Repeat the first two steps along your row until you have only have one stitch left on the needle.

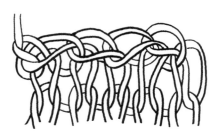

4. Gently take the needle out of the loop. Cut the end of your yarn and feed it through the loop, then pull gently to tighten. You're done!

I-CORD

Knitting doyenne Elizabeth Zimmerman named this the "idiot cord" in honor of stumbling on the technique.

WHAT YOU NEED

- Pair of double-pointed needles (8 mm/US 11)

- Ball of 8-ply yarn

WHAT YOU DO

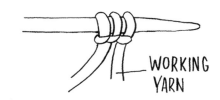

1. Cast on three stitches.

2. Slide the three stitches to the other end of the needle. Your working yarn will now be at the end rather than the beginning of your stitches. Take your working tail firmly from the end, ready to start stitching.

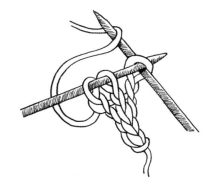

3. Knit three stitches and again slide to the opposite end.

4. Repeat steps 2 to 3 to create a cord to your desired length, then bind off and sew in the tail ends.

MATTRESS STITCH

Somewhat counter-intuitively, this seaming stitch is done on the outside of the garment. It virtually disappears into the fabric and makes a lovely flat seam.

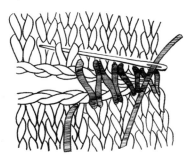

Take a tapestry needle and thread it with the same yarn used for your project. Starting at one end of your knitted piece, thread the needle in and out of the stitches on either side of the seam. Double back on your stitch and tie off to finish.

NEEDLE CONVERSION CHART

MM	USA	UK
2	0	14
2.25	1	13
2.75	2	12
3	3	11
3.25	3	10
3.5	4	4
3.75	5	9
4	6	8
4.5	7	7
5	8	6
5.5	9	5
6	10	4
6.5	10.5	3
7	7	2
7.5	7.5	1
8	11	0
9	13	00
10	15	000

PROJECT IDEAS

→ Try a 365 throw rug. Knit one row a day for a year, changing colors to suit season, mood or available material. Use crochet (see p. 37) to create a unifying solid color border and you'll have a beautiful blanket/textile diary ready for next year's winter.

→ Pure cotton yarns make beautiful hand towels that will last for years. Try knitting up some simple striped ones to match your bathroom, or coordinate with handmade soap or scrub for a spa-themed present.

→ Give old furniture a thoroughly modern makeover by re-covering it in hand-knitted upholstery. Pick a range of yarn colors to work with and knit a selection of patches in different textures and patterns. Sew them together patchwork style to cover your favorite chair and whip up the leftover patches into snuggly cushions for winter reading sessions.

→ Knitting has been a political act since the French Revolution. Instead of using complex intarsia to create text, re-fashion an existing sweater with an embroidered slogan and craft like you mean it.

→ Using string or hemp twine can be tough on the hands but the results are amazing. Knit five squares of the same size and either sew or crochet them together to make a storage box for your softer yarns.

Space-Dyed Sweater

This cool slouchy knit could well be the easiest version of a sweater you will ever find. Knit two identical square panels and sew them together. Yep, that's it. It doesn't even take an eternity to knit, although you'll get plenty of stitch practice and confidence by the time you're done.

WHAT YOU NEED

- 10-12 x 50 g (2 oz.) balls of cotton
- Pair size 7 knitting needles
- Ruler or tape measure
- Tapestry needle

SPECIFICATIONS

Sizing: When laid flat it measures approx. 18" x 20".

Tension (gauge): For this pattern you need to first knit a tension (gauge) square 22 stitches x 28 rows = 10 cm. This is an important step to confirm your garment will fit like it says it does in the pattern.

WHAT YOU DO

1. To make your front panel, cast on 100 stitches for small, medium 110, large 120, x-large 130, xx-large 140.

2. Knit stockinette stitch (row 1 knit, row 2 purl, repeat) until your knitted square measures generously from hip to shoulder.

3. Bind off.

4. Repeat steps 1 to 3 to create your back panel.

5. To sew the shoulder seams, lay your two squares flat on top of each other with right sides showing. Measure approx. 8" from the outside top edges (this will vary due to cranial uniqueness) and mattress stitch the shoulder seams. Then mark the desired depth of each armhole and mattress stitch the side seams together, being sure you leave a generous enough hole to fit your head.

HOT TIP

We space-dyed (see Dye chapter) cotton yarn indigo blue to add interest to this super-simple design, but this sweater would work equally well in commercially dyed or plain yarn.

Crochet

◇◇◇

Crochet seems almost too simple to be true — a hook, a piece of string and human ingenuity. Given this, you could easily assume that it's one of the ancient crafts that Neanderthals used to whip up codpieces out of reeds. Surprise! Turns out that although it may have evolved from more traditional practices there's no physical evidence to back this up. Crochet as it's defined today has a far more recent but relatively nebulous history, not officially coming into focus until the 1800s. Early references in pattern books from Denmark, Sweden and France are vague and certainly not conclusive. The 1840 publication of the delightfully titled *The Lady's Assistant for Executing Useful and Fanciful Designs in Knitting, Netting and Crochet Work* gives us as good a starting point as any from which to chart the course of the craft's history.

The Irish Famine (1845–52) saw a surge in skill sharing as nuns encouraged local women to learn the craft so they could sell "Irish lace" in Europe and America. This domestic production is said to have kept many families alive during this terrible time. It is one of those examples where craft as "women's work" was actually a form of grass-roots activism and should be celebrated as an important moment in crochet's history. Queen Victoria was instrumental in raising the profile of crochet/Irish lace when she became not only a collector but also a practitioner of the craft. Formerly seen as a lesser version of fine lace-making and knitting, it was given a substantial boost in profile by this royal recommendation. This established crochet as a significant textile craft, proving that in Victorian England, at least, celebrity endorsement could be a good thing.

These days you are just as likely to see crochet on the runway or red carpet as you are on the end of the bed. From the granny square dresses of Australian avant-garde darlings Romance Was Born to the elegant womenswear of British designer Paul Smith, crochet is experiencing a real resurgence in popularity and innovation. The ease with which 3-D work can be formed in crochet has hooked contemporary visual artists as they push it in unlimited directions, as well as spawning new subcultural tribes, from the super kawaii amigurumi clan with their cute stuffed animals to the sci-fi-obsessed Tardis-making geek crafters.

CONTEMPORARY ARTISTS

JO HAMILTON
United States

Jo Hamilton is an artist who successfully employs paint, drawing and crochet in equal measure in her prolific practice. Hamilton's approach to yarn is the same as a painter's approach to paint, and her skill in selecting a tonal palette allows her to create both detailed portraits and sprawling landscapes. Distinctively she leaves the edges of her works tangled and unfinished, simultaneously showcasing the process and origin of the artwork alongside the finished work.

⌨ **johamiltonart.com**

PHIL FERGUSON
AKA CHILIPHILLY
Australia

Wearing his art on his head and his heart on his sleeve, Chiliphilly mashes up culture, gaming, fashion, food, humor and headgear. A kind of whole body amigurumi artist who incorporates himself into the work, Chiliphilly creates a kind of performance that endears and entertains. This, combined with a high level of technical wizardry, makes him a master of crochet as cultural reference.

⌨ **instagram.com/chiliphilly**

NATHAN VINCENT
United States

Knuckledusters, guns, gas masks and dynamite are not what you'd expect from what is often considered "the gentle art of crochet." Nathan Vincent is part of a fraternity of male artists employing traditionally female craft technologies to produce well-executed, socially conscious works, and his output is particularly slick and well placed. Vincent is bang on, not just in his selection of the loaded aesthetics and cultural positioning of crafts such as doily lace and amigurumi, but in the ease with which he conveys his commentary on the cultured divide between women's work (in this case crochet) and men's work (war, destruction, trouble).

🖵 **nathanvincent.com**

CÉCILE DACHARY
France

French textile artist Cécile Dachary uses all manner of textile traditions to create soft sculptures that represent the body and the home in equal measure. She is technical master of crochet and her lace installation works are particularly seductive, whether floating in suspended animation or in amorphous shapes.

🖵 **ceciledachary.com**

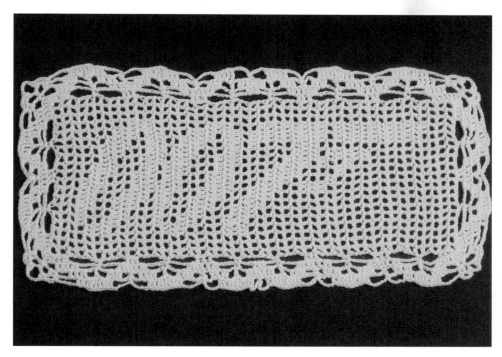

DESIGN NOTES

DRESSED IN RAGS

Any fabric can be turned into a yarn for crochet. Salvage a much-loved quilt cover or sheet, or spot a bargain at a secondhand store and transform it into a fantastic rag rug for your hallway or bathroom. Create the yarn first by cutting the fabric into strips; sew together and wind it up into a ball ready for use. Don't worry about fraying, it's a "textural effect" that will add to the charm of the finished object. However, if you're more of a neat freak you might want to try old t-shirts or sweatpants, as these will maintain their sharp edges.

ON THE EDGE

Crochet is a fantastic edging technique. Finish off knitting and sewing projects with a row of decorative crochet to add that extra zing. Yes, zing! With fabric you normally make the crochet edge first and then attach it by hand-sewing. With knitting you can dive right in and use each stitch as a "chain" for a crochet edge. Crochet is also a brilliant way to piece knitted squares together into a large patchwork rug or bed cover.

BEYOND THE GRANNY SQUARE

Pre-hipster revolution, crochet had the unfair reputation of being an old-fashioned and conservative craft. Perhaps the roots of this belief lay in the ubiquitous granny square — the building block of so many of the afghans that populate vacation houses, op-shops and old people's homes. This limited view is unfair. Crochet AND granny squares are as relevant and modern as you want to make them — think feisty not fusty.

TOUCH ME

If you have the time and the inclination, we recommend the process of hooking up a series of identical swatches using different yarns to get a feel for how much variety is possible. Getting the texture of your work right is so important. It's all very well to knit up a cushion in leather string but, my goodness, it's going to be uncomfortable to nap on. The same goes for working up a shopping bag in fluffy mohair. God help you when you try to put anything heavier than a box of teabags in it. That doesn't mean that you can't play with perceptions and mix up your media. By all means subvert the dominant paradigm — just don't use your experiment to carry home your milk.

PRACTICE MAKES ... BETTER

Just between friends, we aren't afraid to admit that crochet, as old-school as it is, was one craft we hadn't attempted in any serious way before writing this book. They say that people either knit or crochet and we are both knitters. It was with trepidation that we took up the hook and our first attempts were indeed quite dire. But with a couple of weeks of consistent practice we were, you guessed it, hooked.

IN THE ROUND

The great thing about crochet is that its production grammar is so much looser than knitting or weaving. Fashioning a fully formed object in the round can be intuitive or planned, and you don't have to switch to a complex pattern or extra set of tools to get the job done. It's one of the many reasons why artists and hobbyists alike choose crochet so often to make everything from tiny amigurumi figurines to massive room-sized installations.

There are so few tools needed for crochet. All you really need is a hook, scissors and yarn. However, there are some hot tips on variants of these that will make your crafting easier and more awesome.

- **Crochet hooks:** They come in a variety of materials but bamboo, plastic and steel are the most common. Bamboo will "hold" your yarn, while plastic and steel are more slippery. Some yarns respond better to certain hooks so experiment to find your own groove. Hooks range in size, typically from 0.6 mm to 16 mm. Use the small ones for very fine lace and the ones that resemble sharpened broomsticks for floor cushions or vampire staking.

- **Cotton yarn:** The best yarn to start with, it produces well-defined stitches that are easy to see. It also looks and feels beautiful.

- **Wool yarn:** The traditional choice, it comes in an almost unlimited range of colors, weights, prices and textures. Work out how much is required for your project (patterns will tell you this up front) and buy three extra balls. This ensures that if you get caught making afghans over years rather than weeks (guilty as charged), you'll still have enough of the same yarn left to finish your project.

- **Leather cord:** A great but expensive option. Tricky to wrangle when cold, so find a sunny spot or an open fire to cozy up to before you start work.

- **String:** Comes in such a wide variety of weights and finishes and it's fun to experiment with. Be warned though — it's quite rough on your hands, so start small or work out a way of crocheting in gloves.

- **Fine wire:** Super-fine wire can be transformed into delicate lace jewelry with patience and skill. Try copper or rubber-coated wire for an inexpensive starter and make your way to fine silver once you've nailed the technique.

- **Notepad and pencil:** For keeping track of your stitches.

- **Scissors**

- **Tape measure**

- **Tapestry needle**

STITCHES

Basically, crochet is made up of a series of loops. You push the hook through a loop — sometimes first wrapping the yarn around the hook one or more times — then you pull another loop through.

CHAIN STITCH

This is the starting point for all crochet projects. Every pattern will tell you how many stitches should be in your foundation chain as this determines the length of your first row.

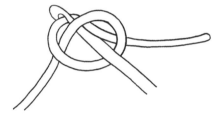

1. Start with a slip knot.

2. Tighten the knot by pulling on both ends. Now you are ready to start your chain.

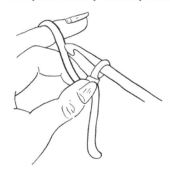

3. Hold the knot and let the short tail hang out of the way.

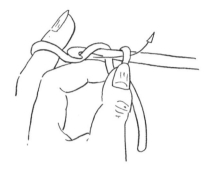

4. Bring the long tail of your yarn over the hook from back to front.

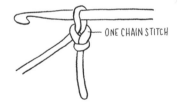

ONE CHAIN STITCH

5. Slip your first loop over and off your hook to create the first stitch.

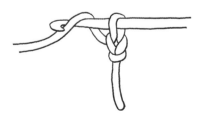

6. Repeat steps 1 to 5 to create a chain.

SINGLE CROCHET (SLIPSTITCH)

If worked in rows, single crochet makes a very dense fabric with little drape. For this reason it's not commonly used.

1. Take your hook through the first stitch of your chain, then bring your yarn from the back to the front over the hook.

2. Draw that loop and the hook through the first two loops, leaving one, and you've got your first stitch done. Follow this to the end of your row, make one chain, turn the work and repeat.

TURNING CHAINS

When finishing a row of crochet, you need to work one or more extra stitches, called a turning chain, to start the next row at the right level. For single crochet just one chain is required, but deeper stitches will need more chains. The same applies to working in rounds (see opposite, step 4).

DOUBLE CROCHET (SINGLE CROCHET)

Double crochet is the bee's knees when it comes to basic yardage in crochet. It has more movement and drape than single slipstitch and makes a beautiful, smooth fabric. It's also super fast, which is great for big projects.

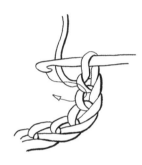

1. Make your chain and then start your "single" by taking your hook back through the second chain link.

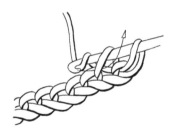

2. Wrap the yarn over your hook as shown and draw that loop through the middle loop, leaving two loops on your hook.

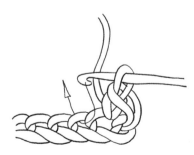

3. Bring your yarn over again and draw it through both loops to leave one.

4. Repeat this stitch along the rest of your chain.

WORKING IN ROUNDS

This satisfying and simple technique is easy to master and gives impressive results. Aim for a coaster and end up with a floor rug. Once you've mastered chain stitch and single crochet, rounds are a simple proposition.

1. To form a ring, first crochet a chain. The length of your chain will determine the initial diameter of your circle.

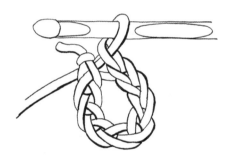

2. Put your hook through the first chain link, wrap your yarn around the hook and draw it through the two loops, leaving one loop on the hook.

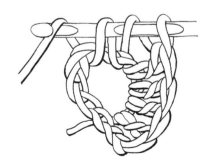

3. To work single crochet into the ring, start with one chain, then work your single crochet stitches around your initial circle.

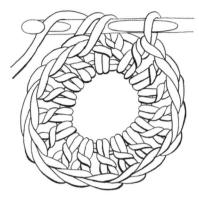

4. Once you get back to the beginning of this first round, repeat step 2 and then continue stitching around in double crochet. When you reach the starting point, join your last single crochet to the first with a slip stitch. Now make one chain (this is the equivalent of the turning chain required when working in rows).

5. When your piece is finished, cut the long thread and draw it through the remaining loop. Finish by sewing in your end.

LONGER STITCHES

To produce a softer fabric, you can make taller stitches. You do this by wrapping the yarn more times around the hook to make more loops. We show you two longer stitches here.

HALF-DOUBLE CROCHET

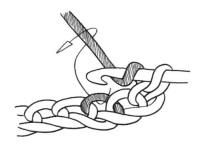

1. Bring your yarn from back to front around the hook and insert it into the third chain link.

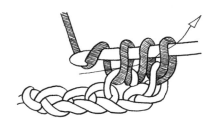

2. Draw a loop through the chain. You now have three loops on your hook. Now wrap the yarn around your hook to form another loop and draw that one through the other three loops to complete the half-treble stitch.

TREBLE CROCHET (DOUBLE CROCHET)

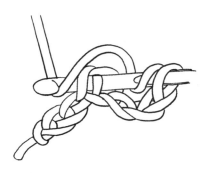

1. Wrap the yarn around your hook, then insert the hook into the fourth chain and wrap it around the hook again as shown. Pull the new loop through so that you have three loops on your hook.

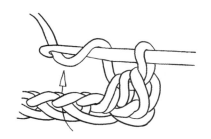

2. Wrap the yarn around the hook again, as shown, and draw it through two loops. You now have two loops on your hook. Wrap the yarn around the hook again and draw it through these last two loops to complete the treble stitch.

JOINING SQUARES

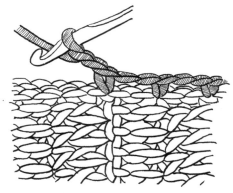

Joining crochet squares is a strong and sure-fire way to quickly build up a rug-sized work in no time. The method couldn't be simpler (and works just as well for joining knitting too). Place your two edges together and insert your crochet hook through two stitches. Draw your working yarn through to create a loop, work a single crochet stitch and continue along your edge. Use a contrasting yarn to create a more decorative edge, or keep the same yarn to hide it from sight. Note that this creates a pretty robust seam so although it's perfect for blankets, it's less than ideal for garments.

DECORATIVE EDGES

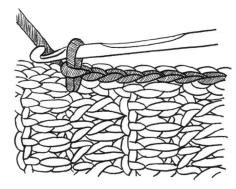

Once you get the hang of it, a whole new world of decorative edges opens up to you that can be applied to all manner of crafts. Start out by practicing a simple method of creating chains between stitches. This gives you more flex in the fabric but also creates a nice foundation for more decorative stitches. Knitting, embroidery, needlepoint and sewing are all obvious picks for crochet pimping but you can also add punch holes in ceramics, paper, leather and wood and work crochet into those. As always, we ask you to live on the edge — see what we did there?

PROJECT IDEAS

→ Crochet is the perfect medium for working in 3-D, which is why amigurumi enthusiasts the world over are so drawn to the technique. Although it looks incredibly complex, even the most detailed work is still fashioned from the basic stitches. Try starting with simple animals or plants, such as worms or peas, then get busy creating a super-cute face with embroidered detailing — it's all about personality. Once you've nailed the technique, you'll quickly be able to take on more complex animals, foods and, yes, even *Star Wars* characters.

→ Learning how to make a granny square is a craft rite of passage. They are also the perfect pick-up and put-down project. Keep your scrap yarn handy and stock up on balls of a single unifying color for edges. If you start making one square per week in January you'll have enough for a bed throw by the start of December.

→ Think outside the craft box and work your crochet in less traditional fibers. Hit the hardware store for neon cords or fishing line and work them in different spiral motifs to create a stunning "all-weather" garland for your backyard or balcony.

→ Circle crochet techniques are a breeze and give you plenty of scope to freestyle without a pattern. Super-size your crochet hook and raid your rag-bag to make a floor-sized circular cushion for you or your four-legged friend.

→ Make a custom footstool by fashioning six dense crochet squares big enough to put your feet on. Chain them together in a contrasting yarn, leaving a hole large enough for your stuffing, and finish by sealing it up with a few more stitches. Make a drink, get a good book and put your feet up — you've earned a break!

Double-Duty Backpack

WHAT YOU NEED

- Size J/10 crochet hook
- 4 x 50 g (1¾ oz.) balls of black double knitting yarn
- 2 x 50 g (1¾ oz.) balls of green double knitting yarn
- 2 x 50 g (1¾ oz.) balls of cream double knitting yarn
- Tapestry needle
- Pins
- Double-pointed knitting needles

This sturdy backpack makes light work of goods on the go. Keep it handy for weekend farmers' markets, urban odd jobs or park-time parenting duties. Custom-fit your straps for the perfect portable transporter of everything from baguettes to baby toys.

WHAT YOU DO

1. Using two strands of black yarn as one, make your foundation chain 28" long.

2. Crochet 16 rows of 70 single crochet stitches. This will make a panel 4¾ x 24".

3. Change to green and repeat step 2.

4. Change to cream and repeat step 2.

5. Change to black and repeat step 2.

6. Slip the last stitch and tie off. You should now have a rectangle of striped fabric measuring 19 x 24".

7. Fold your fabric in half width-wise. Sew along the back seam using mattress stitch (see the Knit chapter), remembering to change color as you hit each stripe for a completely hidden stitch.

8. To make your two arm straps, start with a foundation chain five stitches long using two black strands of yarn held together. Single-crochet rows until your strap is long enough to go around your shoulders. (Just pin it and check before finishing.)

9. Hand-sew your straps to the back of your bag using the black yarn to hide your stitches. Don't be shy in this process; you need to use many stitches to keep it secure.

10. Using a pair of double-pointed needles, create a pull closure by knitting a three-stitch i-cord with black yarn (check out the Knit chapter for instructions). Alternatively, thread cotton rope or ribbon in and out through the holes in your crochet about 1" from the top of your backpack. For a decorative finish, attach a pom-pom to each end of the i-cord, as we've done here (see the Stitch chapter), or tie a knot to stop it from sliding out of the holes.

HOT TIP

This simple backpack is a great way to use up leftover yarn or to seasonally update your wardrobe. If you use pure wool you can throw it in the wash for felting. Don't like color or wool? Transform this transporter by working the project in natural jute or cotton string for a totally utilitarian look, and switch out the crochet straps to leather or canvas webbing for a sturdy, non-stretch option.

Weave

◇◇◇

Weaving, perhaps more than any other, is the craft that tells our story. There is evidence of woven cloth from as early as the Neolithic era 10,000 years ago. As soon as we cracked the code of interlocking threads, we set in motion a chain of events that would lead not only to industrialization, but also to empiricism and even computer technology. It is a fundamental craft that continues to be integral to civilization today. Through warp and weft, each and every civilization from ancient to modern times has utilized weave.

The development of the loom runs parallel with the development of mechanization. The universal need for cloth for shelter, clothing and utility has acted as a spark for the creation of a diverse range of weaving systems perfectly matched to the materials, landscape and culture of the people using them. All manner of looms — warp-weighted, card, backstrap, draw, freestanding, peg, inkle, pit, tapestry, table and floor — mark key points of change. Images of women and children weaving have been found in the archeological ruins of ancient Egypt. In China they were harnessing the beauty of silk as early as 500 B.C.E. By 700 C.E. vertical looms could be found across Asia, Europe and Africa. Andean and North American tribes and nation states had also fully embraced the technique, each adding their own unique twist.

It is impossible to discuss weaving and not speak about Indian textiles. There is archeological evidence of a cotton textile industry in the Indus Valley that dates back to 3000 B.C.E. Alexander the Great wrote of fine gold-embroidered fabric he had seen in India, and there was even a formal weaving guild and manufacturing industry for weavers and spinners working from home that dated back to the 3rd century B.C.E. A community of fine silk weavers, the Ansari of Varanasi, still work from the family home to this day, their skills passed through the generations from father to son.

As is so often the case, there are two histories of weaving. Women working in or around the home made a small income from the cottage industry while the term "master weaver" was restricted to groups of men forming guilds with strict guidelines and a rigid hierarchy. By the 11th century, weaving was a central craft in medieval Europe.

The jacquard head, named after its inventor Joseph-Marie Jacquard, revolutionized cloth production in the early 1800s. When attached to a loom the jacquard head gave weavers a mechanized capacity to weave complex brocade patterns through a system of hole-punched cards that allowed threads to be lifted and lowered individually. Anyone who has used a punch-card knitting machine will recognize this technology. Charles Babbage, father of modern computing, was not only aware of the jacquard head but based his binary system around its punch-card technology.

The mechanization of weaving in the 18th and early 19th centuries caused massive social change. Cottage industries all but disappeared as the labour force moved away from family business and into factories, which were under enormous pressure to produce vast quantities of cloth. Not everyone was happy about this development. The Luddites of the early 19th century were predominantly a group of English textile workers protesting the replacement of people with labour-saving machinery. This paralleled the philosophy of the Arts and Crafts movement spearheaded by William Morris in the 1860s, which also espoused the value of home production. Weaving was seen as central to this. If you could weave your own cloth, you could be truly independent of a system thriving on the exploitation of a poor workforce.

The counterculture of the 1960s and early 1970s saw a huge resurgence of domestic hand weaving within the West, part of a movement of people rejecting mass production and industrialization. While fine hand weaving retained a level of popularity as a studio craft and hobby, it fell off the kids' cool radar until relatively recently. A new appreciation for the mastery, skill and aesthetics of ethnic handcraft has also led the masses back to antediluvian technologies, and today a new generation of crafters and designers are rediscovering something many of us have known for years. Weaving rocks.

JESS FEURY
United States

Jess Feury has a knack for combining materials. Her keen eye for color is manifested in the subtle tonal gradations and soft palettes she uses to create harmonious yet surprising works full of charm and sophisticated restraint. Varied loom widths inform the construction of Feury's simple boxy garments, which also take full advantage of both color and texture weft patterning to create lively surface patterns. Feury cleverly blends naturally dyed fibers into innovative patchworked jewelry, apparel and textile pieces that honor the craft's traditions while remaining steadfastly modern in outlook.

🖥 jess-feury.com

JUSTINE ASHBEE/NATIVE LINE
United States

The polished geometry of Justine Ashbee's woven wall works is a testament to technical mastery and aesthetic restraint. Using soft, minimal palettes accented with black and metallic threads, Ashbee creates striking works that play with light and transparency. In these textile meditations, harmony and balance are key. Referencing design influences from tribal rugs to 1960s sci-fi, she often operates multiple warps using both yarn and construction to conceal and reveal in a kind of fabric peekaboo.

🖥 nativeline.com

HIROKO TAKEDA
Japan/United States

Textile designer Hiroko Takeda's approach to weaving is eloquently calculated. Artfully playing with texture, structure and scale, her diverse practice spans architectural collaborations through to contemporary fashion and homewares design. Takeda displays a rich technical and cultural understanding of the history of weave and a fearless technical curiosity that pushes her work to the craft's outer limits. Employing a variety of experimental materials, from metal to string, she utilizes traditional weave constructions such as overshot, waffle and honeycomb to create deliberate, exquisite works that both surprise and confound.

🖥 hirokotakeda.com

JOHN BROOKS
Australia

Combining weaving, soft sculpture, casting techniques and video, John Brooks takes us on a wild ride through textile technology hybrids that explore the Darwinian concept of difference and mutation. His bejeweled pelts are one part Tom Baker-era Dr. Who and two parts Mighty Boosh. His training as a studio weaver gives him a deep understanding of construction textiles and the material properties of fiber, allowing for a level of control in the cosmic chaos.

🖥 loom-ing.tumblr.com

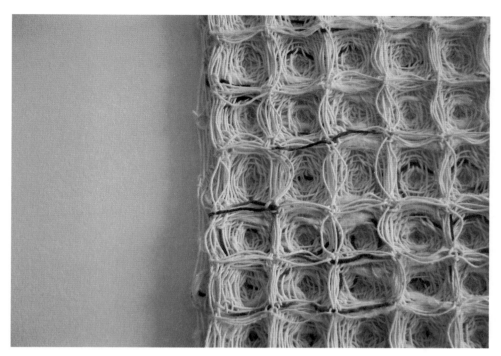

CAROLINE ROSE KAUFMAN
United States

Caroline Rose Kaufman comes from a long line of crafters. This personal history and intimate familiarity with everyday making might go some way to explaining the fearlessness with which she inserts multiple textile techniques into her high-pop fashion collections. Traditional weave patterns and structures are turned on their heads in super-craft mash-ups that read like fairytale samplers on acid, joyously bold and confidently executed with skill that belies her young age.

🖥 carolinerosekaufman.com

MARYANN TALIA PAU
Australia

Artist and weaver Maryann Talia Pau respectfully maintains the traditional techniques, culture and spirituality of Samoan basket weaving while producing characteristically urban works she calls Pasifika bling. Blending material combinations that include raw and dyed raffia, beads, plants, shells, plastic, feathers and discarded fabric, her work is both bricolage and bird of paradise. Underpinning this is an ongoing commitment to public engagement through craft and a conceptual framing that is strongly political and speaks directly to the complex nature of Islander identity within contemporary white Australia.

🖥 maryanntaliapau.net

SUMMER MOORE/LESH
United States

Summer Moore's lateral approach to weaving sees her create highly unique, wearable works that draw as much from the art of adornment as they do from the traditions of fiber art. Moore has first-hand experience of the power of handcraft derived from her immediate family and experiences traveling and working in Turkey and Peru. This tactile history, combined with her photographic background, provides Moore with an innate understanding of color, form and texture that results in works that appear both effortless and complex. Striking color contrasts and clever combinations of warp and weft patterns intermingle with hand-dyed cord in neckpieces and cuffs that showcase technical dexterity and strong design skills.

 leshloom.com

LUCIA CUBA
Peru

Fashion designer, artist and social scientist Lucia Cuba uses handcrafted garments and cloth as metaphor and tactile aesthetic device in her interventions and political actions. Reaching back into a long history of makers who identify cloth production as a key vehicle for political change, her works act both as a mechanism of transformative autonomy and as a way of bringing issues of social significance dramatically to the forefront of public discourse.

🖥 **luciacuba.com**

READY SETT GO

We won't lie, there's a lot of pre-thinking that goes into weaving. When it comes to the all-important sett (the number of warp threads per inch) you'll have to consider your end use before making your warp. There are different setts for different cloths for a reason, and getting your sett right is key to a successful project. The sett you use for a draping scarf will be lower than the one you make for a length of fabric. The latter needs to be firm enough to be cut and sewn back together, to stand up to wear and tear and to survive repeated cleaning over time. Measure twice, warp once and sett yourself up for success.

BEAT IT

While the sett of your cloth determines the warp threads per inch, the density of your weft is determined partly by a process called beating in (or up). After inserting a weft thread through the warp threads, you need to pull it close to the weaving, using the reed (or on simple looms, a rigid heddle), which separates the warp threads. Normally you want to keep a steady, even beat to create consistent cloth. However, you can play around with the beat to make interesting variations that can provide great textural interest to non-functional work. Heavy beating will result in a dense and sturdy weft-faced cloth, while lighter beating will produce a floaty but less stable fabric. Learn how to beat it and you won't be defeated.

SHRINKY DINKS

You can use washing shrinkage to your design advantage. Felt open weaves for a denser finish by washing them in high temperatures and hard detergents. Or create textural striping in either direction by mixing natural and synthetic fibers in stripes in your warp and weft. As the fabric is washed the natural fibers will matte and shrink while the synthetic areas will stay the same, creating gathered stripes or bubbles in the surface of your weave, such as in seersucker.

FRINGE DWELLER

Cutting your work off the loom is the perfect time to add extra detailing. Loose warp threads can easily be twisted, braided, knotted or beaded into fringed features that add extra design oomph to the simplest tabby (plain) weave. Add pom-poms or tassels in complementary yarns, or dip-dye the ends in a darker shade or contrasting color for a stunning finish.

OLD DOG, NEW TRICKS

Traditional patterns can have new life breathed into them with the use of clever threading and unexpected materials or color palettes. Reversing your threading will create mirror-image patterns, while including a row of tabby weave on opposite rows will scale up a pattern. Try creating highlights or lowlights that exploit the structural texture of the weave by adding one electrifying tone of the same color. Simple patterns are all excellent starting points ripe for experimentation.

CHECKMATE

One of the easiest ways to create all-over patterning is to use checks or plaids. Most of you will be familiar with traditional tartans, which duplicate stripes in warp and weft in equal measure. However, there are other ways to use this technique that are less obvious. Use space-dyed yarns to create gradients that add unexpected dimension to regimented checks or combine textured and smooth yarns to create subtle surface patterning in monochromatic work. Remember, you'll be creating regular intervals of both solid and blended blocks of "third" color, so keep your palette in check.

REED IT AND WEEP

Ambitious beginners often try putting a variety of fancy yarns into their warp, forgetting that these threads have to regularly pass cleanly through the reed. With consideration this can be achieved, but it's perhaps more prudent to leave the super-crazy additions, such as plastic bags, metal filament, plastic tubing and straw, to the weft. While you're at it, you might also remember to check your warp yarns' snap and snag factor. Warp threads are held under tension and take a pounding from both the shed lifts and the beating in. If they tangle easily or snap in your fingers, you're in for a very bumpy ride. Don't say you weren't warned.

TOOLS

- **Calculator:** Weaving involves a lot of math, so make it easy on yourself by having a calculator handy.

- **Tape measure:** Keep one handy as there's a lot of measuring that goes with the math.

- **Embroidery or tapestry needle:** For finishing techniques such as hemming.

- **Heddle hook:** A thin metal hook with an easy-grip handle that lets you pull the yarn through the holes in your heddle.

- **Reed hook:** A flat plastic S-curve that helps feed the yarn through the slits in the reed.

- **Stick shuttles:** Go for flat, finished wood and keep a range of different lengths for different projects.

- **Warping sticks:** Thick cardboard, folded newspaper and thin timber can all be used between your layers of rolled warp to help maintain tension.

- **Warping peg:** Rigid heddle weaving really only requires one that can be clamped onto a bench, table or chair. These are used to measure and organize the warp, getting it ready for threading onto the loom.

- **Clamps:** For holding your loom onto the table to assist you to dress and weave on the loom.

- **Rigid heddles:** These come in a variety of lengths and "dents." The width cannot be wider than your loom, while the dent refers to the number of threads per inch that can be threaded. If you want to weave in different yarn weights you'll need a few different heddles.

- **Rigid heddle loom:** A number of loom manufacturers produce rigid heddle looms in a variety of sizes that usually come flat-packed ready for assembly. Buy online or from craft stores. We use Schacht and Ashford looms and we love them.

- **Yarn:** Generally speaking, the best yarns for weaving are the ones you want to wear, such as silk, cotton, wool and flax. Warp yarns need to be strong, while weft yarns can be anything you want them to be.

- **Wooden ruler**

- **Notebook and pen**

- **Scissors**

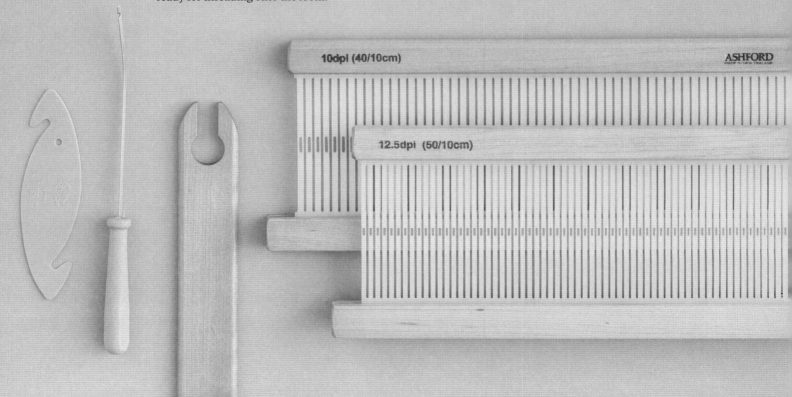

Like most crafts, weaving has its own special vocabulary and equipment. Some looms are very complex, but as a beginner you can start with a simple heddle loom and learn the basics. A heddle is a small wire or piece of plastic containing a loop or hole through which a single warp thread passes. The warp threads are lifted up and passed through this in a pre-set sequence to enable the weft thread to pass through. On complex looms the heddles can be organized on several shafts in different sequences to create different weaves. On a rigid heddle loom they are fixed to a single shaft and moved up and down together.

LOOM ANATOMY

Learning the basic anatomy of a rigid heddle loom and some technical terms will allow you to dive head first into this craft. This diagram shows you a bird's-eye view of a typical rigid heddle loom. It's worth noting that different manufacturers have slightly different ways of resolving the same function.

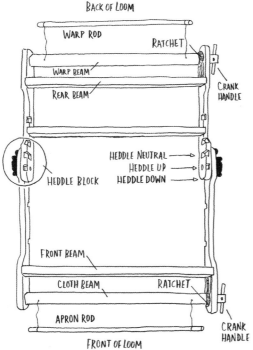

- Rigid heddle: A solid plate with alternating slits and holes that serves multiple functions. It determines the sett like a regular reed, creates the shed for weaving when lowered or raised, and beats the weft into place. These come in a variety of dents, which refer to the number of slits and holes per inch.

- Heddle blocks or notches: These hold the rigid heddle in the up, down or neutral position. The up and down positions create the shed (open space) for inserting the weft thread. Lifting the heddle raises the warp threads in the holes, while lowering it raises the threads in the slits. In the neutral position all the warp threads are aligned between the up and down positions.

- Cloth beam: Holds the woven cloth at the front of the loom.

- Warp beam: Holds the warp threads at the back of the loom.

- Apron rod: Where the warp is tied and tensioned at the front of the loom.

- Warp rod: Where the warp is tied onto the back of the loom.

- Shuttle: A tool for holding and passing weft yarn while weaving.

- Brake or crank handle: The active gear that both locks the warp in tension and allows it to be released and tightened.

WEAVING TERMS

- Balanced weave: Plain-weave fabric in which the warp and weft threads are of the same weight and evenly spaced.

- Beating: Process of pushing the weft threads down into place.

- End: One warp thread.

- EPI: Ends per inch. EPI refers to the number of warp threads or ends per inch of woven fabric. In a rigid heddle loom this is determined by the number of slits and holes per inch on the heddle. This is used to calculate the sett of your fabric. More ends per inch equals dense fabric, while fewer ends per inch equals a more open fabric.

- Heddle block: Notches on a rigid heddle loom that hold the heddle in its upper, lower and neutral position.

- Loom waste: Ends of the warp thread that are tied to your apron rod and back beam that you cannot weave. "Waste" is a bit of a misnomer as you can use this wastage for fringes.

- PPI: Picks per inch. PPI refers to the number of weft ends per inch of woven fabric.

- Plain weave: Often called tabby weave, the most basic of weaves, in which the weft thread travels over and under each warp thread.

- Selvage: Outer edges of a woven fabric.

- Sett: Number of warp ends per inch, which determines the density of your fabric.

- Shed: Space created between warp threads, according to a pre-set pattern, through which the weft travels.

- Warp: A word that's both a noun and a verb (we love this). As a noun it describes the vertical group of threads held in place by your loom and as a verb (warping up) it describes the process of threading the warp onto the loom.

- Weft: Yarn that travels horizontally over and under your warp threads.

BEFORE YOU WEAVE

There is quite a bit of setting up and planning for weaving, but really no more than for screen printing.

SETT

The sett for each project will be different. To work out the right number of ends per inch (EPI) for plain weave, first wrap your yarn of choice firmly around a ruler, with the threads touching each other, for one inch. Then count the number of threads across and divide that number by two; this number is your EPI. The number you get will determine how many warp ends you will need per inch of fabric you want to create.

For example, if your EPI count is 15 and you want to make a cloth 20" across, multiply 15 x 20 to get 300 ends or warp threads.

Your EPI also gives you your reed size; work to the closest reed available and expect a little variation in the density of your finished fabric as a result.

WARP LENGTH

To determine your warp length, first work out what you want your cloth length to be. Then add some extra to account for loom waste. Add another 20" as loom waste for tying on and fringing.

MAKING A WARP

The best thing about making a warp for your rigid heddle is you just need one warping peg and a clamp. It's virtually idiot-proof.

1. Once you've determined your warp length, set up a space where you can make it. Clamp the back of the loom to a table and measure the distance from the warp beam to the warping peg.

2. Clamp your warp peg to another surface at the same height as your loom. This is important, as varying the height will distort the warp length.

3. You're now ready to start warping up. Put your heddle into the neutral position on your loom. First, you'll need to center your warp. Look at your reed and mark the center with a pencil. Halve your warp number and count the number of slots out to the left side of your center mark. Tie a little bit of waste yarn at that point. This is where you will start your warp.

4. Bring your warp rod up over the back beam. With your ball of yarn on the floor, bring the end of your yarn up between the back beam and warp rod and tie the end to the warp rod. Make sure your warp rod is locked in place by your ratchets.

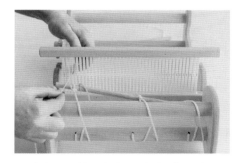

5. Feed the reed hook through the first slit, then use it to pull the yarn through. Notice that you now have two threads through the one slit.

6. Drag it up, out and over the top of the warp peg. You have your first two warp ends on the loom!

7. Make the next two warp ends by taking another loop of yarn under the warp beam and then through the heddle and onto the warp peg. Continue this, taking your warp yarn through the heddle and alternating over and under the warp beam. Maintain an even and firm tension. Keep count as you go, and when you have reached your warp width, cut your yarn, leaving 6" (15 cm) to tie it securely to the warp rod.

8. Tie a piece of waste yarn around the warp about 8" (20 cm) from the end of the warp peg, then cut it off with scissors. These cut ends will be what you thread through the heddle.

9. Time to wind the warp back onto your loom. Get a friend to help you maintain tension while you do this. You'll need them to hold your warp out firmly in a straight horizontal line while you use the ratchets to wind it onto the warp beam.

10. Place sheets of paper or warping sticks between the layers of warp as you wind it on to help keep tension even across the warp. A roll of brown craft paper works a treat. As you are winding, you should be hearing the click of the ratchets and feel tension against the locked brakes.

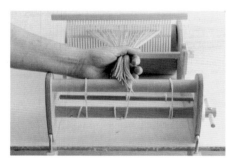

11. Stop winding once the end of your warp reaches the cloth beam, so you have enough length in your ends to start threading them through the holes in the heddle.

THREADING THE LOOM

1. Turn your loom around and clamp it onto the table facing you. You'll see that you have two threads in each slit. Leave one thread and use the heddle hook to pull the other yarn through the adjacent hole. Continue this process right across the heddle so you end up with yarns alternating, one in a slit and the next in a hole.

2. Pay close attention while doing this as the order must be maintained. We're not joking. Taking care with your threading is a lesson you need to learn for all weaving projects.

TYING ON

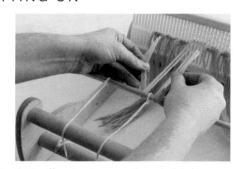

1. Once all your yarns are threaded, take your ends and make them into little bundles of between six and eight ends ready to be tied onto the apron rod.

2. Take your apron rod up and over the front beam and make sure your crank handle is locked into place. Starting in the center, wrap your first bundle over the apron rod then split it in half.

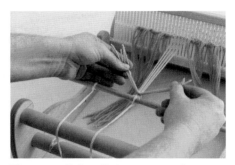

3. Tie your split bundle into a secure bow. You are aiming for a bouncy but firm tension right across your warp. To do this you'll most likely need to re-tie some of the bundles. Using a bow allows you to keep your ends secure but makes it easy to tighten where needed.

WINDING A SHUTTLE

Before you start weaving (yes, you're nearly ready to start!), you'll need to get your weft yarns onto the shuttles. While you can wind straight down the center between the notches, you can also wind on the sides, which gives you the benefit of another color on the other side. Super handy.

WEAVING

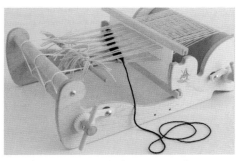

At its heart, weaving is the process of alternately lifting and lowering the heddle while passing the shuttle through the shed each time. This effectively traps the weft yarn to make an interlocked woven fabric.

1. First you need to weave a waste yarn "header." You do this by weaving a few rows of waste yarn. This creates an evenly spaced warp. This is called weaving a header. Put your heddle into the up position and pass a shuttle with waste yarn from the right to the left side. Change the heddle into the down position and pass the shuttle through the shed from left to right. Lift the shuttle back into the up position and pass the shuttle back through the shed to the left.

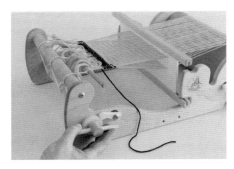

2. Once you've made three passes use the heddle to beat down the weft yarns until they are touching.

3. Continue to weave rows of waste yarn for another four rows and so that your warp is sitting evenly in line with the reed holes and slits.

4. Now it's time to start with your real weft yarns. Start on the right and leave a length of around 4" (10 cm) to weave back into your work once you're done. If you're planning on finishing your work with hemstitching, leave a length four times the width of your warp.

5. Pass the shuttle through the shed at a 45-degree angle and leave a loop so that when you beat it down with your heddle it sits flush with the selvage. If little loops appear it means you are leaving too much yarn on the warp between beats, and if it's pulling in at the sides you are pulling your weft yarn too tightly between beats.

ADVANCING THE WARP

As your fabric grows, you will get closer and closer to the heddle and it will become increasingly difficult to pass the shuttle or beat the weave. When this happens, it's time to advance your warp.

1. Put the heddle into the neutral position and release the tension on the warp by unlocking the brakes at the front and back of the loom.

2. Turn the crank handle or wheel at the front of your loom to wind the fabric around the cloth beam, leaving a couple of inches of fabric in front of you.

3. Re-engage the brakes on the front and then on the back ones to bring the warp back into tension. Keep on weaving until you need to advance the warp again.

ADDING NEW WEFT

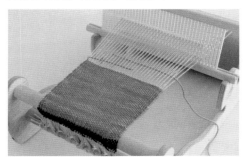

As you weave, the shuttle is going to run out of yarn. It's annoying but inevitable so you need to get used to it.

1. To add new weft you just overlap the old and new yarn ends for about 2" (5 cm) in the middle of the fabric.

2. Continue weaving and trimming off excess threads. You can also use this same process for color changes.

GETTING OFF THE LOOM

The most basic way to finish is by weaving a few rows of waste yarn to keep "real" rows in place, and either cutting or untying your warp from the back of the loom, then unrolling the fabric at the front of the loom and repeating the process. If you want a decorative fringe, be sure to leave enough warp at the end to make it. If you are going to hemstitch your edges it's best to do it while your fabric is still on the loom.

HEMSTITCH

This is a simple, neat and effective way of finishing your woven edges, which allows you to either leave long-fringed tassels or cut close to the edges with style and security. It's a little like blanket stitch (which you could also use) so if you're confident with blanket stitch you'll find this a breeze.

1. When you have finished weaving, cut the end of your weft yarn three to four times the width of your warp and thread it into a tapestry needle. Use hemstitch to create secure bundles of warp threads. The bundles of yarn you join with hemstitch can vary, but we find that groups of three, four or five stitches work for most of our projects. Here we used four. Take the needle over the first thread and under the next three.

2. Now pull the yarn back to the left over all four threads.

3. Bring the needle up four thread ends to the left and four weft threads down. Pull the thread gently to form the first bundle.

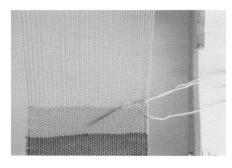

4. Take your needle under the next four thread ends.

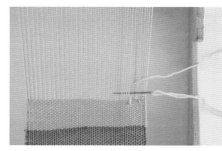

5. Wrap the yarn around these four thread ends and bring it up four weft threads down, as in step 3. Again, pull the thread ends together.

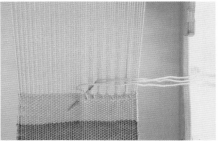

6. Continue to repeat this across the width of your fabric.

7. When you get to the end, bring your yarn back through the wrapping loop rather than through the fabric, secure the tail with a knot and either cut it off or weave it back through the fabric.

8. Your weaving is now secure enough to cut off the loom. The warp threads will become your fringe.

FRINGES

Two great off-the-loom decorative fringes are the braided fringe and the twisted fringe. Both are simple to create and very hardwearing. Braids are good for heavy yarn and rugs, while twisted edging works particularly well on finer woolen fabric.

For a braided fringe, create bundles of ends in groups of three. Braid them together, then tie them at the end in an overhand knot.

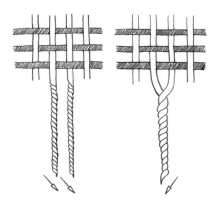

For a twisted fringe, twist each separate end in line with its natural twist, then take two ends and twist them together in the opposite direction. Tie the end in an overhand knot. Once washed you can cut off the knot if you like, as the ends will have felted together slightly during the wash.

WASHING

Hand-woven fabric will shrink a little with the first wash. Expect this and, when planning your project, adjust your warp width and length to accommodate it. Use cool water and a gentle wool wash as you would for all delicate fabrics. After washing you will need to block the woven fabric. This process re-aligns your warp and weft at a perpendicular angle to each other. The slightly sticky surface of a yoga mat is ideal to help secure the scarf into a regular shape while drying.

PROJECT IDEAS

→ Paper weaving can deliver seriously sophisticated results. Cut your own strips from favorite papers or re-fashion tinsel for a metallic edge. It's a great way to trial patterns and color combinations and you will also get some great artwork.

→ Shortcut traditional ikat weaving by dip-dyeing hanks of yarn in high-contrast colors for a simple tabby weave scarf. Use the yarn for both your warp and your weft, and watch as it creates beautiful random patterns as you weave.

→ Off-loom projects are a great way to get kids involved in weaving. You can warp up anything from a hula-hoop to a portable clothes rack. Use t-shirt yarn or stripped sheeting for these big-scale projects and make it simple for little fingers to work the basic under-and-over technique.

→ Make up a bunch of little cardboard looms for long-haul car trips. Using a tabby weave and a plastic yarn needle, you can fashion yourself a smartphone cover before you reach your destination. Double bonus points if you have small people traveling — you can also use this simple craft to keep them occupied while the digital technology recharges!

→ Weaving an entire garment from scratch is a beautiful but laborious task. If you don't have the loom width or patience to do it, try using hand-woven cloth in combination with commercial fabrics of a similar weight. Woven bag straps, pockets and patches add texture and detailing to ready-made or hand-sewn clothing and accessories.

Balmoral Scarf

WHAT YOU NEED

- 4 x 200g (8 oz.) balls of black wool double knitting yarn
- 4 x 200g (8 oz.) balls of ecru wool double knitting yarn
- Double knitting waste yarn
- 8-dent rigid heddle
- 2 wooden shuttles
- Rigid heddle loom
- Tapestry needle
- Scissors
- Iron and press cloth

SPECIFICATIONS

- Warp length 3 yards
- Warp ends: 80
- EPI: 10
- PPI: 10
- Finished length (washed including fringe) 2¼ yards

HOT TIP

While we've gone with a high-contrast check there's no reason you can't be subtle and choose two shades of the same tone. If you use the same weight of yarn for both, you'll have a smooth fabric surface and seamless transition between shades. Create a more textured surface by choosing the same shade in a more hand-spun or a finer yarn.

One of the oldest, most sophisticated and simplest woven patterns, gingham check is made from equal squares worked into the warp and weft to make solid and blended blocks of color. Perfect for winter corgi walking or cold-weather cuddles with your Highland fling.

WARPING PLAN

Devising a warping plan is imperative if you are making fabric with different warp threads. While multi-harness warp plans follow a more complex structure, this simple one is perfect for a tabby weave project on a rigid heddle loom. Imagine yourself sitting in front of this chart and use it as a guide to show you the order for threading your warp ends into your reed.

black	ecru	black	ecru	black	ecru	black	ecru
10 ends	10 ends	10 ends	10 ends	10 ends	10 ends	10 ends	10 ends

WHAT YOU DO

1. Warp up 80 ends following the order of the warping plan above.

2. Weave in eight rows of waste yarn using the instructions in the Techniques section.

3. Fill one shuttle with black and one with ecru yarn.

4. Leaving a tail four times the width of your warp, start weaving 10 rows of the ecru yarn.

5. Swap to the black yarn and weave another 10 rows.

6. Keep on weaving in this pattern, alternating rows of black and ecru, until you have made 28 rows of each. Make sure to weave your last row in ecru.

7. Make your last pass through the shed from left to right, and leave a tail of the weft yarn four times the width of the warp.

8. Now work your hemstitch right to left. Leaving a fringe of 5", cut the warp off the warp rod.

9. Unroll your fabric and hemstitch using your tail of weft yarn left from the start.

10. Pull out your waste yarn, leaving 5" for the fringe, and cut the warp off the apron rod.

11. Wash the scarf in warm water and dry flat. When dry, steam press, keeping a press cloth between your work and the iron.

Tapestry

Tapestry weaving distinguishes itself as an "artist's craft." It is essentially painting with thread and it is this pictorial tradition that distinguishes it from other weaving. In *The Odyssey*, Homer describes Penelope working on a tapestry as she waits for the return of Odysseus. Fragments of tapestry have been found dating back to ancient Egypt and Greece. The pottery of native Andean cultures of ancient Peru depicted women working at simple looms. In other words, tapestry has been with us for thousands of years as a way of marking events, recording history and displaying wealth.

Acting as decoration, insulation and information, tapestry was a must-have craft for the status seekers of the Middle Ages. Family crests, battle scenes and Bible excerpts were all ripe sources for tapestry design. Two of the oldest surviving tapestries are the Överhogdal tapestries and "The Cloth of St. Gereon." The latter is a classic example of its time, a simple mural tapestry featuring a repeated motif worked in seven colors of wool, made in Cologne, Germany, in 1050. The Överhogdal tapestries of Sweden, dated at around 800 C.E., depict aspects of both Christian and Norse religion, which makes them both an incredible textile artifact for that date and an important record of Viking history. Yes, people, tapestry is a Viking craft.

Translation of images into yarn was ideal as tapestries were both portable and useful displays of wealth and grandeur, embraced by the Church and wealthy patrons alike. The Renaissance master Raphael was commissioned by Pope Leo X to draw cartoons (designs) for a tapestry to be hung in the Sistine Chapel. It is said that up to 300 different yarn colors were used to create the intricate "Apostles of the Chapel" series. The cartoons themselves are held in the collection of the Victoria and Albert Museum, while the tapestries now only make an appearance on special occasions. The fact that both the original artwork by a master painter and woven tapestry created by artisans are equally prized demonstrates perfectly the symbiotic relationship between art and craft.

The 17th century saw the Flanders region of Europe become the center of tapestry weaving. Political turmoil in the region created a diaspora of master weavers whose skills were highly sought after throughout Europe. Louis XIV is said to have had more than 250 artisans beavering away at the tapestry looms of the Gobelins at any given time, such was the fashion for large-scale interior wall coverings. Known as the Royal Factory of Furnishings to the Crown, the Gobelins operates to this day, albeit in a less grandiose manner.

Modern tapestry owes more than a nod to the Arts and Crafts Movement headed by William Morris in the late 19th century. Morris himself was so committed to reinvigorating tapestry that he had a loom built in his bedroom and taught himself the craft from an 18th-century French instruction book. As a parlor craft, however, tapestry weaving never became as popular or widespread as other textile crafts such as needlepoint or quilting, perhaps partly because its function beyond decoration was so limited.

With the resurgence of interest in fiber arts, and upright loom weaving in particular, the time is right for the next renaissance of tapestry weavers. There are still well-established tapestry workshops and organizations around the globe, most notably Dovecot Studios in Britain, the American Tapestry Alliance in the United States and the Australian Tapestry Workshop. These have become important cultural centers for contemporary practice. Today, fine artists are again being drawn into the craft, using it as a "slow" methodology that adds a textural interface between their paintings, drawings, photography and the viewer, and one that explores the ongoing connections between art, craft and technology.

SOLA FIEDLER
Canada

Imagine Google Maps in the hands of a tapestry weaver and this goes some way to describe the cityscape tapestries of Sola Fiedler. Each piece takes up to 5,000 hours of finely detailed work, making Fiedler commit to both time and place. Using wool sourced from discarded sweaters and blankets, Fiedler brings as much accuracy, variation and texture into her palette as the cities themselves. Skylines are recreated with as much geographic accuracy as the medium allows. Enough time passes from beginning to end that, upon completion, the city represented no longer exists in that form, tapping into the traditional role of tapestry as social record.

🖥 **solafiedler.com**

ERIN M. RILEY
United States

Erin M. Riley's woven interpretations of "sexy selfies" are like loaded guns. Confrontational in their apparently blasé attitude, the works (which feature images of Riley herself) are radical interruptions to the seemingly mindless consumption of sexualized images of women's bodies — blurring lines between public and private, object and subject, exploitation and power. The considered conceptual framing and extensive research behind the works are matched by the laborious process of their production, posing even more questions about the digital longevity of these seemingly instantaneous throwaway images of exchange. Riveting stuff.

🖥 **erinmriley.com**

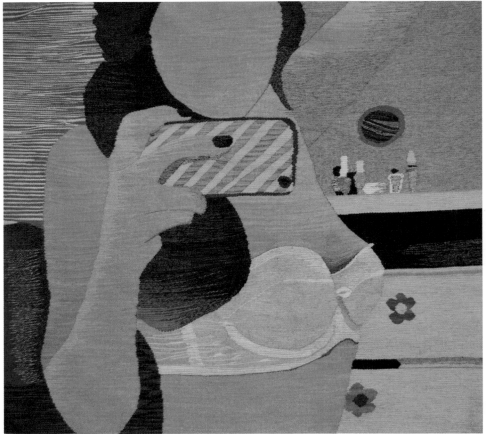

MARGO WOLOWIEC
United States

There seems to be a digital glitch informing the work of Margo Wolowiec. Combining tapestry weaving, sublimation printing and dyeing, her time-consuming technique sits at odds with its subject matter. The constant barrage of digital images is layered, filtered and then frozen. These textile versions of an interrupted news feed force us to hit the pause button. Wolowiec examines the impact of more screen time than down time and our capacity to absorb endless amounts of digital information as we increasingly live online.

🖥 margowolowiec.com

DANIEL EDWARDS
Australia

Daniel Edwards's series of bearded men could now be considered a benchmark of proto-hipsterism. This collection of portrait tapestries is an ambitious series with multiple purposes. Edwards utilizes folk's universal symbol of masculinity as a unifying motif for works that articulate the vindication of craft practice as legitimate art to celebrate the numbers of men now skillfully participating in craft methodologies. His work acts as a tactile homage to the textile craft movement of the 1970s.

DESIGN NOTES

DONE AND DUSTED

Like most things worth doing, tapestry takes time to get to the finish line. The good news is this will allow you to put some thought into what you're going to do with it once you're done! If you've thought ahead and made a D.I.Y. frame like ours to work on, you'll be ready to hang almost as soon as you've finished weaving. If not, think laterally about what you can attach your work to — anything from branches to painted broomsticks can work! Just tie ends onto a rod or weave extra length to hem by machine or hand and remember to ALWAYS weave several rows of stitches before you finish to keep your work secure.

FLIP IT GOOD

Tapestry is what we call a weft-faced form of weaving because the warp is generally obscured in the finished piece. This creates a dense textile made up of horizontal ridges. Often tapestries are woven with the image on its side, rather than upright, as this makes it easier to weave in shapes and details. Whether or not you decide on this technique, it's worth considering it during the design process to make sure you make the most of the process and avoid potential pitfalls.

STORY TIME

Tapestry has often been used as a narrative craft form. Tapping into this story-telling tradition can add an extra level of personal engagement with the process that will help you reach the finish line. Try using significant events that interest you as inspiration for your designs, be they domestic or global, current or historical, real or imagined.

PICTURE THIS

As a beginner it can be hard to know exactly what images will work best, which makes it hard to decide what you want to use as a starting point. If you don't have a slew of original sketches or images ready to go, you can always look to existing source material. Magazines, picture books and kids' art are great places to start, but so is your Instagram or phone photo feed. Start snapping details, colors or textures that inspire you and use them as the basis for new works.

EXPAND AND CONTRACT

Although you aren't making cloth in the same way as you do on a horizontal loom, you are still creating a fabric that can have a life beyond the frame. Think of your tapestry as a placement print or the feature material for accessories, pockets, patches, bags, and cushions.

PAINTER'S PALETTE

One of the great tricks a tapestry weaver has up their sleeve is the ability to have multiple bobbins on the go at any given time. While this does allow for intricate patterning it's especially effective if applied to varied shades of the same color. When used in blocks of solid color these subtle gradients deliver a dynamic painterly touch that can really bring a tapestry to life.

CRAFTERS GO WILD

As with any craft, once you have mastered the basics you can push the boundaries. Take your tapestry into fiber art territory by adding embellishments, experimenting with different yarns, dyeing or even adding paint to your tapestry surface. Whether you get it right first time or not, you might stumble across an amazing idea for another piece. You might run the risk of ruin, but we're all for living on the edge every once in a while.

- **Warp yarn:** This needs to be very strong as it carries a lot of tension. Heavy cotton thread is recommended for the beginner, but any strong yarn can be used.

- **Weft yarn:** Some things need to be considered when translating your design into a tapestry. We'd love to say "anything goes" but that isn't quite the case. By using different types and weights of yarn you can get a great deal of surface texture but it can also look like a hot mess. Tapestry artists tend to use one type of yarn throughout a project and concentrate more on color. If you can't easily access tapestry weaving yarn we recommend substituting with 4- or 6-ply knitting yarn.

- **Tapestry bobbins:** For holding small amounts of yarn, these are used to "beat" down the weaving, making it sit evenly.

- **Shed stick:** A flat wooden stick that's inserted into the warp to make a "shed" for you to pass the bobbin through (optional).

- **Colored pencils and pens:** For designing.

- **Indelible marker:** For drawing your design onto your warp.

- **Looms:** These come in many shapes, sizes and price points. Start your tapestry weaving with an inexpensive frame loom or table loom. A frame loom is just that: a simple frame with either nails at each end to wind the warp around, or notches that hold the warp threads in place. A table loom can be clamped upright to the table and is closest to the vertical looms used by expert tapestry weavers.

- **Needle and thread**

- **Cardboard**

- **Clamps**

- **Masking tape**

- **Ruler**

- **Tape measure**

- **Notebook**

- **Scissors**

We'll be talking a lot in this section about warp (vertical threads) and weft (horizontal threads). Remember, the warp is what you attach to the loom, and the weft is what you weave into the warp. In tapestry weaving, the warp is hidden by the weft, which is why it's referred to as weft-faced weaving.

BOBBINS VS. BUTTERFLIES

There is no denying that tapestry bobbins are beautiful objects but they aren't essential. Some tapestry weavers prefer to work with small bunches of yarn known as butterflies, pushing them through the warp with their fingers. This can be rough on the hands after a while but is pretty satisfying. You'll also need a tool to push down ("beat") the yarn — a fork will do nicely. When using a bobbin it helps not to overload it; just take your yarn up to the ridge or you'll find it too big to move smoothly over and under your warp threads.

CARTOONS

Translating your design from drawing to tapestry weaving is an art in itself. The trick is to break the design down into simple shapes that can be expressed with an outline. What you are trying to capture is your composition. You can use tracing paper placed over drawings, photographs or paintings. Once you've got this sorted, hold your sketch behind your warp and use it as a guide to copy it directly onto your warp, using an indelible marker. This is called a cartoon. Some weavers skip this step, preferring to use the cartoon as a reference without marking up their warp. It's up to you.

WARPING UP

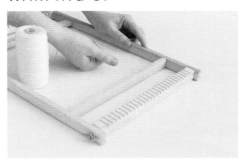

The all-important first step. Warp threads must be stretched tightly in even tension across the loom. Traditional tapestry looms require you to wind your warp around the top and bottom bars of the loom in a figure 8 pattern. Frame looms with notches or nails let you tie your warp thread to the bottom bar and then go up, over the first nail or notch, down and under the corresponding nail or notch on the bottom bar, repeating the process across the face of the loom.

Your warp should always be centered on your loom. Mark the center of the loom with a pencil and warp up an equal number of threads on either side of the center point.

FLOOR AND BEDDING (HEM)

Before starting to weave you will need to provide your work with a "floor" and "bedding" to sit on, also known as a hem. This hem spaces your warp threads evenly and gives you a solid foundation to work on. It's usually removed when the tapestry comes off the loom. Use a thread that contrasts with your main tapestry so you can easily see it when you've finished.

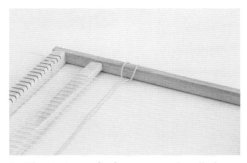

1. The starter weft of your weave is called the floor. Cut a length of yarn three times the width of the frame. Loop it around the bottom left side, creating two starter threads. Pass one of your starter threads under the first warp thread, then work it across the loom, over and under each warp thread. Repeat the process with the second start thread, this time beginning by passing it over the first warp thread, then working it across the loom under and over each warp thread. You'll now have two threads on the right-hand side. Tie these securely to the loom.

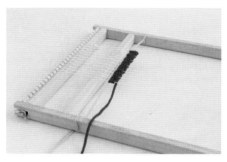

2. To create the bedding, take a weft butterfly of yarn in a contrasting color under the first warp thread, then work your way across over and under. Keep your weft thread quite "relaxed." If you pull too tightly you'll distort the edges of your warp.

3. The trick to this is to create a "hill" before beating down. Use your bobbin tip (or fork) to "beat down" your stitches into place every couple of rows. Do this for about six rows so you have a nice visible hem.

HITCH KNOT ROW

For a tapestry that won't slide down your warp, we recommend doing a row of hitch knots before you begin.

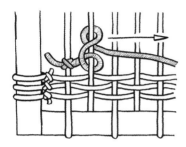

This step may feel like overkill, but it will ensure your tapestry won't end up on the floor after a few years. This step is especially important if you're tying your work to a dowel for finishing. We also recommend a row of hitch knots to finish off your tapestry to really lock it in place for when you cut it off the loom. To make your hitch knot row, tie the end of your weft thread to the first warp thread and then make a figure 8 around the next warp thread as shown in the diagram. Continue repeating this same knot across all of your warp threads, then you're ready to start weaving back the other way. Easy.

HITCHING ON

You are now ready to begin weaving. The first thing to do is to "hitch on." This is done by bringing up your weft thread from the back to the front at least two warp threads in before starting your first row. To start a new thread, hitch on as usual but mirror the last row to hide your thread in the weave.

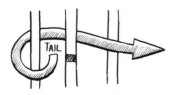

HALF PASSING AND PASSING (WEFT-FACED TABBY WEAVING)

Basic over-and-under rows are the backbone of tapestry weaving. One row across is a half pass, go back the other way and it's a full pass. These days, you'll find that it's often referred to as tabby weave or plain weave.

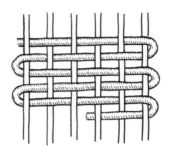

SOUMAK

Soumak is a super-fast and secure stitch that is looped over one or more warp threads at a time. This adds a decorative raised line across the warp, handy for outlining shapes.

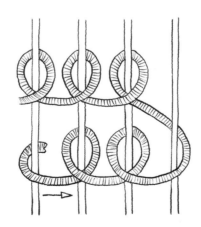

RYA

Rya is a tufting stitch that is used sparingly in traditional tapestry weaving but is great for adding surface texture. It should be wedged between a couple of tabby rows to secure it. It can be used en masse to create shag effects and decorative edging to hide your hem.

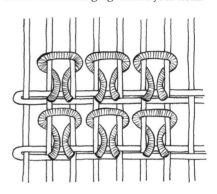

HATCHING

Hatching is a horizontal single-line patterning technique that intermixes two colors. It is very useful for blending and shading areas. Two colors are worked simultaneously so that they dovetail together in overlapping rows.

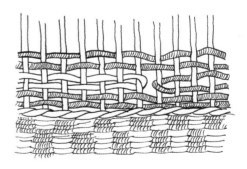

SLIT

Where you want to make a vertical color change, you can simply bring each color up to the changing point, then take it back in the opposite direction. This leaves a slit in the weaving. Some weavers choose to hand-sew these slits together as a finishing and strengthening process.

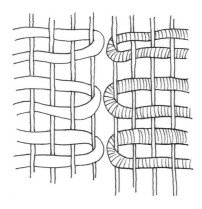

INTERLOCKING

Interlocking creates a strong vertical line between two areas of weaving and avoids the slit in the warp. Two weft threads are worked simultaneously and wrap around each other before going back in the opposite direction.

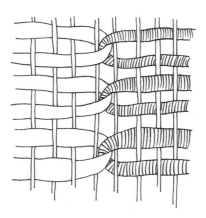

SHAPES

As soon as you get the hang of simple passes and tabby weaving you can start incorporating shapes into your work. It's a relatively simple process, but there are some rules. Weave shapes first, then weave around them. Always weave one row at a time, bottom to top. Don't go crazy weaving all over the place. It will end in tears. Trust us.

TRIANGLES

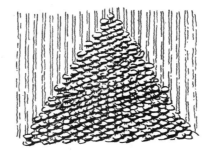

If you want it to hit a single stitch point at the top of your triangle, start with an odd number of weft threads at the bottom of your triangle. Use the interlocking technique to work around the triangle.

CIRCLES

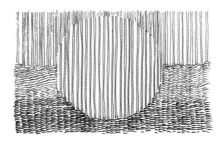

1. When weaving a circle, first draw it on your warp, then weave around the shape up to its widest diameter.

2. Fill in the bottom half of the circle using the interlocking technique. Fill in the rest of the circle before weaving the rest of the perimeter, again using interlocking.

FINISHING

There is nothing more exciting than the moment you cut the tapestry off the loom. Before you do, you will need to decide what finishing technique you want to go with. You can either insert a rod through the warp for hanging, or hem your work and frame it. If you decide on the rod, weave the rod in and out of your warp threads before you cut and tie them to avoid unraveling.

Carefully remove your floor and bedding hem by snipping between your warp threads and then use the stitch ripper from your sewing kit to gently unpick your threads.

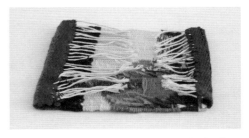

Stitching down your edges onto the back of your tapestry is a popular option to achieve a neat finish. Instead of removing the hem, use it to your advantage. Fold it to the wrong side and use whip stitch (see p. 114) to secure it.

To frame your work, stitch the hemmed tapestry onto a base cloth such as linen. Stretch the linen over canvas stretcher bars or glue it to a mat board cut to fit your frame.

PROJECT IDEAS

→ Traditionally tapestries served as insulation on stone walls. Why not turn your room into a cozy cave by tricking out your bedroom door with a full-length tapestry worked in neutral tones? Make several small tapestries and sew them together, or build your own vertical loom and make like a medieval craft master.

→ Keep a unique travel diary. Record your next trip in a series of snapshot tapestries — small works that evoke perhaps the color or light of your surrounds. Pin looms travel well and are a nice way to take a craft breather, or as a diversionary accompaniment to second-rate, in-house hotel movies.

→ Use tapestry to create a personal accessories collection. The technique makes such a sturdy textile that once it's backed and seamed you can use it to create snappy clutches, smartphone covers, stylish waist cinchers and natty brooches. Working small scale also gives you quick results, so little projects like this are perfect for impatient weavers.

→ Tapestry weaving can be a little laborious, as the many half-finished pieces languishing in secondhand stores attest. If you're open to sharing you can always work on a craft co-lab. Take turns week to week with a friend. The hard part will be deciding whose house it ends up in. You may need to draw a formal "time-share" agreement.

→ Create a tapestry based on a painting. Fine art has always offered great source material for tapestry, but you can just as easily be inspired by lowbrow or outsider art. Look at a favorite artwork, be it a cubist Picasso or one of Tretchikoff's dames, and find encouragement in its elements, shape, color, composition or scale to create your own original work.

Dark Side of the Loom Tapestry

WHAT YOU NEED

- 7⅞ x 7⅞" frame
- Staple gun
- Pencil
- Ruler
- 120 x ¹/₁₀" flat-head nails
- Hammer
- Cotton warp thread
- Scissors
- Tapestry bobbins
- 2 balls of double knitting yarn in four shades of gray
- 2 balls of bulky variegated yarn in black and silver
- Scrap yarn in a contrasting color
- Cardboard
- Permanent marker

HOT TIP

You can just as easily use a picture frame as stretcher bars; you just need to go for something sturdy with a wide molding. Cheap wood will split when you try to hammer in the nails, or warp once it comes under pressure from the warp yarns.

One of the easiest ways to get started on tapestry weaving is to make your own loom. Using a frame and some nails, you'll be warping up in no time. We took inspiration from one of our favorite childhood albums to make a ready-to-hang wall work.

WHAT YOU DO

1. Reinforce your frame at all four back corner joins using a staple gun.

2. Now mark up your frame. Using your pencil and ruler, mark your nail spots in a zigzag formation at ¼" intervals.

3. Hammer in your nails along your marked line. This will take some time. Take it slow and steady so you don't split the wood. Once all the nails are in, your loom is complete and ready for weaving.

4. Tie your warp thread to the far-left bottom nail, then take it up and around the corresponding nail at the top of your loom. Bring the warp thread back down to the next nail on the bottom and wind back up to the top. Continue across the frame at each nail, maintaining a firm tension as you go, and tie your warp thread off on the last nail on the bottom right.

5. Load your tapestry bobbins with your yarn for weaving.

6. Make your floor and bed using your scrap yarn (see Techniques section).

7. Make a row of double hitch knots in your darkest shade of gray yarn.

8. Cut a 8"-diameter "moon" template from your cardboard. Position it in the center of your frame and trace around it onto your warp threads with a permanent marker.

9. Start weaving your striped rows in order of darkest to lightest, with each row around ½" wide.

10. When you reach the bottom point of your circle, continue to build up the sides of the circle's perimeter to the mid-point of the circle.

11. Fill in the bottom half of your circle with the black yarn, making sure to interlock with the stripes around it. Then continue to fill in the rest of your circle in black.

12. Build up the rest of the circle perimeter in stripes following the same order. Then continue working the stripes until you almost reach the top of your frame. Finish with another row of double hitches in the same color as your last row.

13. Hang that sucker up and wait for the compliments to roll on in.

Macramé

◇◇◇

Probably more than any other craft, macramé has a history of reinvention to rival Bowie. While many cultures can claim their own version of knot craft, macramé as we know it can be traced back to 13th-century Arab weavers, who used it to create decorative fringes for loom work. Over the next 200 years it meandered its way around the Western world via missionaries, Arabian trade routes and eventually sailors, who developed their own utilitarian seafaring knots into more complex, decorative adaptations that remain the fundamentals of the craft today.

In the 16th century a specialist style of fine macramé developed in Genoa, Italy, where a kind of fine knotted lace was created. This regional specialty was called *punto a groppo* and the craft's delicate patterning became highly sought after. The technique created a blueprint for bobbin lace-making, utilizing twisting and knotting to make lace entirely by hand. The desirability of the product and accessibility of the process laid the groundwork for the prevalence of fine macramé as a key decorative device for fringing and edging textiles.

The Victorian era saw the first real popular resurgence of macramé. Firmly embedded within the domestic arts, it found favor as one of the expected accomplishments of gentlewomen, with examples decorating numerous Victorian garments and most Victorian homes. Fine macramé continued to be employed for ornamental purposes but also came to be used as a social activity. The development of Cavandoli macramé, most commonly seen today in the form of friendship bracelets, is a more recent evolution of *punto a groppo*. This micro-macramé was named after schoolteacher Valentina Cavandoli, who used it as a recovery technique for sick children in her care in the aftermath of World War I, so perhaps it's no accident that it has since also become so familiar as a fun camp craft activity for generations of children.

After 50 years in the cultural wasteland, macramé became a popular leisure activity during the 1970s craft revival. This is the version of macramé with which most of us are familiar: fringed bags, hammocks, knotted vests, beaded neckpieces and experimental fiber art. Many of us have fond memories of sitting with our mothers and their circle of craft friends as they whipped up plant hangers over instant coffee, gossip and cookies.

Until relatively recently macramé was still pretty uncool, so uncool in fact that the iconic macramé owl of the 1970s was almost universally used as a benchmark of all that was wrong with craft. Not so anymore. Fashion's constant recycling of historical style and technique has met the new millennium's D.I.Y. movement, resulting in crafters picking up the rope again and knotting in new ways. Today you can find the same simple half hitch and lark's heads used by sailors and Arab weavers, reinterpreted everywhere from catwalk to hipster bar. And, sure, the owls are still here, but now they're 35 feet tall and neon.

SALLY ENGLAND
United States

Fiber artist Sally England uses macramé technique to create oversize wall hangings that range from the elegantly simple to the remarkably complex. England successfully built a practice that operates more as design studio, taking on large commissions for a variety of commercial and domestic spaces. She has now extended her practice outward to site-specific installations. Finding inspiration and solace in nature, she keeps her palette muted, utilizing the natural color of the rope to bring the outside in. In doing so, she makes sure the knots are well and truly the stars of the show.

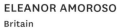 sallyengland.com

ELEANOR AMOROSO
Britain

Designer Eleanor Amoroso utilizes the fine knotting of macramé as both a signature decorative element and a formative shaping mechanism throughout her elegantly tribal fashion collections. Worked primarily in monochromatic palettes, the knotwork provides textural weight and surface decoration, catching the light to create modern shapes, dimensionality and movement while remaining just kitsch enough to evoke memories of Princess Leia in Jabba the Hut's den.

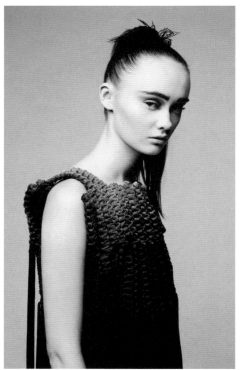 eleanoramoroso.com

NATALIE MILLER
Australia

The complex macramé hangings of fiber artist Natalie Miller are epically weighty and monumental. Dense with shag and complex knots, they hang like strung pelts from prehistoric beasts. Miller's emphasis on materiality and simple, natural and monochromatic color palettes delivers in spades as the viewer's eye is caught in the web of her dexterous construction.

 nataliemillerdesign.com

SARAH PARKES
Australia

By applying commercial design imperatives to large-scale macramé, Sarah Parkes refreshes our view of a craft normally associated with domestic spaces. With a background in graphic design and jewelry making, Parkes scales up her work to create super-sized hangings and installations for public venues and business locations. Her creations perform as tactile focal points in otherwise austere architectural spaces.

smalltown.net.au

DESIGN NOTES

STRUNG OUT

The best thing about macramé is that you can pretty much use any kind of "string" to create works. While jute and cotton string may be the more traditional options, there's nothing stopping you from using neon industrial rope, wool, monofilament, leather, hemp, linen, filler cord, raffia, copper wire, embroidery floss, shoelaces or plain string — hell, you can even cut up a t-shirt and use that. The only real limitation is that you need your knotting material to be relatively smooth, firm enough to prevent excessive stretching, and able to hold the knots without slipping. The finer the fiber, the harder it is to unpick, so we recommend starting with something pretty chunky.

ALL HANDS ON

As in all "soft crafts," texture is a key component in design. Remember that macramé is really tactile and people will not be admiring from afar, so use texture to your advantage — silk embroidery floss for jewelry, heavy nylon for outdoor furniture. You'll also be spending a lot of time with your hands working the material so it helps to think about how something is going to feel while you're making it — stiff or rough fibers will be rough on your hands during knotting.

SUIT YOURSELF

You can go from micro to macro when it comes to projects. One of the magical elements of macramé is that it lends itself to both intricate jewelry and whole-room installations. Think about what suits you best. Are you more interested in creating a wearable masterpiece or a statement room divider? Sculptural or practical? Simple or complex? The only limitations are your imagination and perhaps the size of your living room.

ABSOLUTE BEGINNERS

Macramé is one of those fantastic crafts that everyone can attempt with a fair degree of success. There are really only four basic knots that underpin everything. We've learned the hard way that it's best to start simple, sort out the basics and THEN move your way up to more complicated structures — otherwise, you end up in more knots than your project.

ADD-ONS

Macramé offers makers a raft of opportunities to showcase other craft skills. It's a great base for adding other fiber-based techniques into the mix — from dyeing your raw materials to the inclusion of felted balls or sewn-in pom-poms or sequins. Raid your "hard" craft basket and add handcarved wooden beads, ceramic bells or metal clips. There are really no rules.

KNOTS LANDING

Once you've mastered the basic knots, start experimenting with different combinations, sampler-style. It's really worth spending time working through your repertoire in a range of different materials as the twist (or lack thereof) and sheen of different materials will have a strong impact on how the knots look on your finished piece. Simple ropes will take complex knotting well while you can let fancy fibers do most of the work for you and employ the most basic techniques.

FOLLOW THE LEADER

Designing your own projects can seem daunting at first. It can be really hard to work out how much or what kind of cord you need and even more tricky to write out the steps to follow before you begin. While trial and error might be great teachers, following patterns from craft books or online sources is a really great way of learning how different knots intersect and interact, as well as how to combine them in order in the context of a project. Take cues from the masters and practice your skills on a project from start to finish and soon you'll be designing your own.

TOOLS

- **Cord:** Jute, cotton, string, satin, rope, leather and hemp are all good workable options for most macramé. Our favorite is woven nylon cord. It's readily available at hardware stores and comes in all sorts of colors, patterns and widths. It's relatively cheap, smooth to work with and shows off your knotting skills superbly.

- **T-pins:** Use these to separate your cord and keep spacing even while you work. They are available in the quilting section of any good fabric store.

- **Over-door hook:** This makes an excellent moveable hook that acts as a securing anchor for larger works. A great help when you're short on space.

- **Project board:** This is great if you are working on a small scale, for instance making a necklace or bracelet. You can purchase purpose-made project boards for macramé but they can be hard to find. A flat piece of fabric covered in Styrofoam, cork or mounting board is perfectly fine as a more readily available alternative. One measuring 11 x 17" is an ideal size to start with.

- **Finishing extras:** PVA (white) glue can be used for coating outdoor projects made from non-waterproof materials. Use a jar candle for dipping the ends of natural fibers to prevent fraying, and a lighter for sealing the end of Polycord.

- **Accessories:** Metal rings, wooden, plastic, glass or handmade polymer beads, bag handles, dowel, driftwood and found branches are all useful decorative items. Think about multicolored embroidery floss or yarn. Even colored duct or washi tape can be used for wrapping cords.

- **Scissors**

- **Bulldog clips**

- **Rubber bands**

- **Tape measure or ruler**

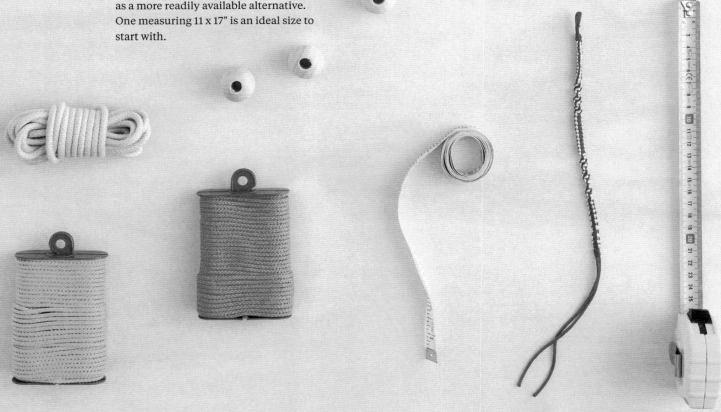

All macramé stems from combining knots in repetition to create pattern and form. While there are a multitude of knots to explore, here we've given you the essentials and the terminology that comes with them.

LARK'S HEAD KNOT

This is used to mount strands for most macramé projects. It attaches your cords onto an anchor rod, which holds your project in place while you work. You can also use these knots as a decorative feature.

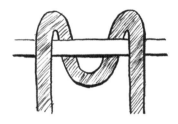

1. Fold cord in half. Place it over your support with the loop behind the support.

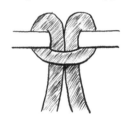

2. Pull the loop forward and feed the two cord ends through it.

3. Pull down on your cord ends to tighten.

GATHERING KNOT

This knot is perfect for binding your macramé cords together. First cut a spare length of cord, long enough to wrap around the other cords several times, leaving a long end.

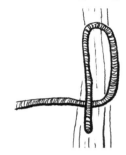

1. Form the cord into a loop and place it on top of the grouped cords, with the short end hanging down and working end on top. With the loop in place, wrap the cord around the others from the bottom up.

2. Once the cord is wound to the top of the loop, poke the end through the loop.

3. Pull the bottom cord end until the loop has been pulled down about halfway into the "noose." To tighten, pull both ends in opposite directions at the same time.

SENNITS

A sennit is a string of knots tied one after another, and these babies form the basis of nearly every linear project from plant hanger to headband. They can be worked vertically, horizontally or diagonally.

SQUARE KNOT

The basic macramé knot — essentially it's two half knots facing opposite directions, usually worked in groups of four using the outside strands only.

1. Begin by tying two lark's head knots onto your support. Take the left cord over your two interior filler cords and under the right-hand cord, like a number 4.

2. Next, bring the right cord under the inside fillers and up through the space on the left.

3. Tighten the first half of the knot by pulling both ends, then take what is now the right cord over the two center fillers and under the left one.

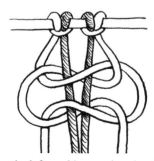

4. Bring the left working cord under the fillers and through the space on the left side. Tighten the knot by pulling on both ends. Voilà — a finished square knot! Repeat steps 1 to 4 to make a flat sennit.

HALF SQUARE KNOT

This is a magic knot that gives you a ladder-shaped spiraling sennit. Work this knot by repeating steps 1 and 2 of a square knot. The sennit chain will start to twist around itself naturally as long as you keep making knots using the cord on the left-hand side.

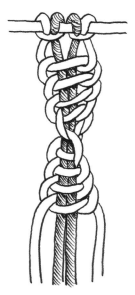

To stop your sennit from twisting, complete steps 3 and 4 of a square knot and you'll straighten yourself out again.

INTERLOCKING SQUARE KNOTS

These interlocking squares are great for creating large widths of open and lace-like mesh macramé, and are most often employed in wall works, hammocks and the baskets of plant hangers.

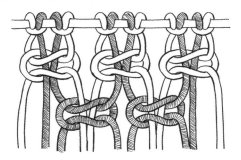

HITCHES

The half hitch and its sister, the double half hitch, create ridged effects, just like the ones you see in old-school owls and wall hangings. Use them to create horizontal, vertical and angled details and form symmetrical shapes. Super easy to make, all hitches are worked by using one cord (filler) to bear the knot, while the next (working) cord in your row wraps around it.

HALF HITCH

Start by looping your working cord under your filler cord, then take it up, over and through the loop to tighten it up.

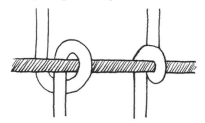

DOUBLE HALF HITCH

Work a half hitch, then bring the working cord up and over the filler cord and then through the loop, pulling it tight to finish.

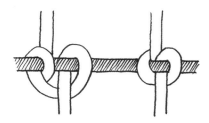

WORKING A DOUBLE HALF HITCH RIDGE

To work this horizontal ridge technique you need to work from left to right. Start with the cord at the far left and place it horizontally across your other knotting cords. Using the next cord to the right, tie a double half hitch over this horizontal filler cord. Repeat with the remaining cords to the end of the row. To turn back and make a second horizontal

row underneath, take your filler cord back around under the first row and work the same knotting process in reverse, working from right to left.

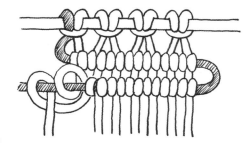

WORKING A DOUBLE HALF HITCH DIAGONAL RIDGE

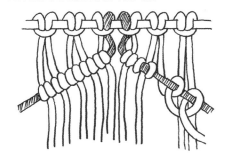

Working diagonal double half hitch rows is a very similar process to working horizontally; the only difference is that you position your filler cord diagonally instead of horizontally. You can work from one side to another or outward from a central point to make symmetrical shapes as shown.

To work a right-sloping diagonal, take the cord on the far left and place it across the front of the other cords, pointing downwards toward the far right edge at your chosen angle.

Pick up the next cord on the left and use it to start knotting double half hitches across your diagonal cord. Continue knotting along the diagonal until you reach the last right-hand cord. Make a left-facing diagonal by starting on the far right instead and work the same steps across to the left-hand side.

BASIC POT HANGER

Second only to the macramé owl in the nostalgia stakes is the potted-plant hanger, and making one is a rite of passage for any budding macramé enthusiast. We may not have green thumbs but we LOVE hanging gardens so we've made a lot of these over the past few years. This one is super easy and uses just three knots—gathering, square and half square. Let's just say, if you can tie your shoes you can make this.

WHAT YOU NEED

- 40 yards of ⅛" Polycord — cut into 8 equal lengths
- 1 x wooden curtain ring
- 1¾ yards of ⅛" Polycord in a contrasting color
- 4 x bulldog clips
- 8 x ¼" wooden beads with a ¼" hole
- Tape measure
- Ceramic or plastic pot
- Scissors
- Lighter

WHAT YOU DO

1. Take your eight cords and feed them through the wooden ring; pull all the cords until they're the same length. You now have 16 cords to make your hanger.

2. Take your contrasting cord and tie a gathering knot underneath the ring around all cords.

3. Divide the cords into two groups of eight and secure them with your bulldog clips.

4. Take one group of eight and make 20 half square knots to create a twisting sennit. You should have two working cords on each side and four in the center as you do this.

5. Feed two of the beads onto the four filler cords you are working on and knot underneath with one square knot to secure them.

6. Repeat steps 4 and 5 on the other group of eight cords.

7. Split each of your sennits into two groups of four cords each. You now have four groups of four cords. Tie ten square knots on each group to create four sennits. These four sennits will sit at the top of the basket that holds your pot.

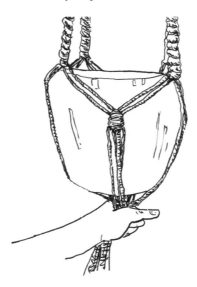

8. To turn your sennits into a basket, use interlocking square knots. Take two adjacent sennits. Use the two right cords from the sennit on your left and the two left cords from the sennit on your right; leave a space of 6" of cord. Then tie two square knots (as shown). Repeat this on the other two sennits. Finally, join the remaining four loose cords from two adjacent sennits with square knots as before. You now have 16 cords that can be joined to secure the pot.

9. Trim and heat-seal your hanging ends with a lighter. Pop your plant in, hang it up and step back to admire your handiwork.

ADDING BEADS

Bead detailing is as central to macramé as the owl, and it's an easy way to add decorative detailing to the simplest sennit. You do this by threading your beads onto the two floating center cords and securing their position with knots on the working cords.

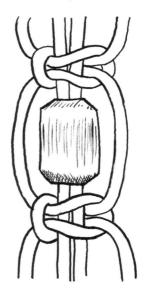

To add beads using square knots, tie a full square, thread your bead onto the two center cords and then tie a second square knot below to secure. Great for sennits on hangers or linear projects.

You can add bead detailing into the center of concentric shaping using double half hitches. Work your upper knots in the ridge, then slip your bead onto the center filler cords and start knotting the bottom rows underneath to secure the bead.

PROJECT IDEAS

→ Beads are a classic addition to macramé work. Make your own from paper, wood, ceramics or polymer clay, or recycle leftovers from beading projects. Don't be limited to regular beads either. If you can drill a hole through it, you can thread a rope through it. Think about stones, shells, plastic bottle lids — if it looks good, use it.

→ Miniature macramé makes for beautifully textured accessories. Use silk threads to create fine macramé neckpieces or use oversize rope to make super-scale showstoppers.

→ Update your macramé wall hanging by highlighting sections of natural rope with colored accents. Spray the ends of your work with cold-water reactive dyes, dip them in indigo when finished or paint sections of your rope with flexible acrylic wall paints before knotting.

→ The decorative knotting of macramé can be used in any setting where cord or rope is used. You can gussy up an outdoor swing by using twisted sennits of industrial rope and oversize beads to hang it from a tree in the back garden.

→ Introduce macramé into other craft projects in unexpected ways. Poke holes in the top of handmade ceramic vessels before firing, so you can add macramé detailing once it's glazed. Make it a purely decorative edge or turn your vessel into a mini hanging planter.

Super-fly flyscreen

Let's face it, summers often mean uninvited guests, and we're not talking about your flaky second cousins. Keep your home classy and insect-free with this super-fly flyscreen, which uses knots and weatherproof cord to keep unwanted visitors to a minimum.

WHAT YOU NEED

- 153 yards of weatherproof woven cord
- Scissors
- Ruler or tape measure
- Wooden dowel or broom handle cut to fit your door frame
- Washi tape
- Hammer
- 4 large nails
- Stepladder

HOT TIP

If you don't have an outside door that you need to screen, you can still work this project to make a super-hot room divider or window dressing.

WHAT YOU DO

1. Cut your cord into 5 m lengths.

2. Make 24 neat lark's head knots across your dowel, leaving a small bare edge of dowel on each side of the knotted section. This will make 12 working groups of four cords for you to start making into your interlocking square knots.

3. Start at the left and work a full square knot 3" down from the dowel, using the first four ropes. Then continue this process across the other 11 groups of four ropes.

4. Move down another 3" and, leaving the first two ropes from the left edge free, start making your next row of square knots. You'll notice that these will sit between your original row.

5. Go back to the left edge, moving another 3" down. Make another row of square knots starting with the first four ropes just as you did in the first row.

6. Go back to the far left, pick up the first four cords and make a sennit of four square knots. Then take your two filler cords to the outside of the working cords, leave a space of 4" and make another five square knots. Repeat this sennit on the last four cords on the far right. Push these sennits aside as they will not be knotted again.

7. Now make another two rows of interlocking square knots on the ropes that sit between your two sennits 3" below the row above.

8. Leave the first two ropes on the left, make a square knot 3" below the row above, then do the same on the right-hand edge.

9. Finish off the knotting pattern by tying one final square knot on either side with the four cords next to the sennit.

10. Finish off the ends with washi tape and cut the rope under the tape. We used a red tape to match our rope.

11. To hang, hammer four long nails into the top of the door frame for the dowel to sit on. Stand on a small stepladder and get a friend to help you put your masterpiece up and onto the nails (safety first, people). Then stand back and open that door to the world!

Yarn

◇◇◇

It's impossible to imagine what might have become of humanity if we hadn't learned how to make yarn. In order to make cloth you have to first make yarn, and communities that learned to turn the fibers from plants and animals into yarn had a distinct advantage over those that had not yet mastered its production. Cotton, flax, silk and fleece were all embraced by ancient civilizations for yarn production. Depictions of string skirts that date back to the Palaeolithic era have been found on wall paintings — proof of a tradition of yarn making that stretches almost as far back in time as we do.

The histories of yarn and spinning are inextricably linked. The most basic techniques came from rolling fibers by hand along the thigh, but people quickly developed more sophisticated tools such as the straight spindle, a simple and highly effective device for producing longer lengths of finer yarn. Images of women using drop spindles adorn Greek vases from 490 B.C.E. So necessary was spinning to everyday life, it peppers the origin stories of cultures worldwide, from the story of Arachne in ancient Greece to the Norns of Norse mythology. The word "spinster" derives from the name given to an unmarried daughter who was responsible for spinning a family's yarn.

It would be a long time before the technology advanced, but with the introduction of the spinning wheel the craft took a great leap forward. This extraordinary piece of equipment is referred to in texts and paintings in the Middle East and China dating back to the mid-11th century. Imported from Iran in the 13th century, the spinning wheel was widely popular throughout India. Perhaps most famous of all modern spinners was the religious leader and political activist Mahatma Gandhi, who spun daily, not only as a meditation aid but also as a tacit rejection of imperialism. He understood that to make your own cloth for your back was a mark of independence, a gentle but pointed act of defiance.

In keeping with the shift to industrialization, spinning quickly turned from cottage industry to big business. The multi-spool "spinning jenny" was invented by James Hargreaves in 1764, while around the same time a water-wheel-powered spinning system was invented by Richard Arkwright. In 1779 Samuel Crompton created the spinning mule, joining elements from both jenny and water wheel to produce a machine that created stronger thread, which made production on a grand scale possible. This change was fundamental to the mechanization of fabric production in Britain and the broader Industrial Revolution worldwide. After this, spinning in the Western world would be relegated to domestic craft, although it remains important to yarn production in traditional societies to this day.

Creating your own yarn is empowering for a number of reasons, both obvious and profound. It has low environmental impact and is able to be achieved entirely without fossil fuels. It allows you to disengage with consumerist culture, endowing you with both the skills and the technology for home production, and it allows you to design and manufacture textile projects from beginning to end. With the current resurgence in fiber art, it is no surprise that many makers are now looking to create their own yarn. Whether you choose a drop spindle, a spinning wheel or a twining technique, or plan to upcycle old clothing, this fundamental building block offers the ultimate craft credo of creating something beautiful and useful from whatever you have at hand.

CONTEMPORARY ARTISTS

SPIDERTAG
Spain

The geometric yarn and nail interventions of Spidertag flip the old-school kitsch of 1970s string art into an unexpectedly self-assured and convincing form of geometric street art. Spidertag is a "true" street artist working within a craft paradigm — graduating from Krylon cans to yarn, nails and hammer to create temporary illegals on the margins. Captivated by process and lured by thrill, he works his freestyle forms as a spider makes its web. His ephemeral works inhabit the city's unseen corners and deserted spaces, playing all kinds of mind games with viewers lucky enough to discover them.

 spidertag.wordpress.com

NIKKI GABRIEL
New Zealand

Fashion-knit designer Nikki Gabriel has created a unique practice by developing an aesthetic and philosophical framework, encompassing pattern design and custom-made-yarn manufacture. Gabriel has cleverly developed simple modular "construction" patterns for beginners that can be built piece by geometric piece into complex fashion-forward garments. Key to the success of these garments is the use of her own super-light and super-chunky yarns — created using 100 percent recycled factory fiber remnants, mixed together and re-spun into a bulky roving yarn that packs a visual punch but leaves minimal environmental impact.

nikkigabriel.com

IVANO VITALI
Italy

By making the conscious decision to use only newspaper, Ivano Vitali was an eco-artist long before it became a buzzword. In the tradition of the Arte Povera movement of the early 1970s, Vitali embraces what is commonly discarded. He creates knitted and woven works that range from the wearable to the fantastical, and uses a twisting technique that eschews the need for glue or machinery. The variety of the yarn's color and ply is as endless as the source it is drawn from.

 artnest.eu/casina/casina.html

JAY MOHLER
United States

Jay Mohler has taken the Mexican folk art tradition of the Ojo de Dios (God's eye mandala) and made it his own. His practice began humbly in the 1970s when the craft was at the height of its domestic popularity in the American Southwest. Over decades his work developed above and beyond these folksy roadside roots as he focused on a singular craft object, and his skill is now unparalleled. With a natural instinct for color, pattern and balance, Mohler creates work that is kaleidoscopic in design and epic in scope.

ojos-de-dios.com

DESIGN NOTES

STRING THEORY

Just about anything can be turned into a usable "yarn." Take a fresh look at the clothes you wear, the bedding you sleep under and the ribbon you wrap with and you'll see that there is a wealth of materials ready to be transformed. T-shirts can be cut without fraying into a brilliantly flexible yarn perfect for knitting and crochet. Sheeting and shirts can be cut and twined ready for rag rugs or weaving, while ribbons, string and baker's twine come in ready-made lengths that can add texture and interest to all textile-based projects.

DYEING FOR IT

While the choices of yarn may seem inexhaustible, you can struggle to find the right shade in the fiber you need. If you want to dictate the project rather than the yarn dictating it, we recommend dyeing as an excellent way of ensuring the perfect palette or making plain yarns fancy with minimal expense. Check your fiber content and end use and get the right dye for the job. Regular crafters will also be well aware of the impact of vat variations in commercial yarns so we advise dyeing more than you need every time.

STRUNG OUT

We love string art. Maybe it's because we coveted the outlandish metallic thread on blackboard pieces from the 1970s, but it could just as easily be the simplicity of the process and the brilliant geometry of the outcome. Contemporary crafters seem similarly hooked and are taking this old-school gem into new territory, using it to create outdoor installations and indoor artworks. Using a hammer, nails and your favorite yarns, you can quickly translate text into unique wall works or use color as your inspiration and create simple shapes in gradient rainbows. A great way to use up yarn ends, and a simple way of incorporating color and texture into a room.

UNRAVELED

Unraveling old sweaters and blankets is a great way to source yarn for new projects. Both thrifty and full of eco-cred, these offer makers unusual options in texture and color that are no longer commercially available. While the unraveling can be a little fiddly and take time, it's a perfect activity to do while watching TV or having a conversation. The only downside is that the amount of yarn you collect is finite, and old knitwear doesn't always come with handy fiber-content specifications. Consider your end use carefully and flame-test a sample before starting out. You don't want to spend hours unraveling an acrylic mix for a pure-wool project.

HANDLE IT

The key to understanding the implications of yarn selection on project outcome is an understanding of weight, flex, drape and stability of certain yarns and yarn combinations. Whether you're weaving or knitting, you do have to think carefully about the intersection of process and product and the consequences of flouting convention. We're all for pushing boundaries but you don't want to spend more time unraveling than crafting. Sample early and sample often.

FULL OF FIBER

The resurgence in fiber arts has put the focus firmly back on fancy and super-sized yarns. Monochromatic works can be amazingly dynamic and complex by taking advantage of the contrasting textures and weights, finishes and content. Think big wool tops next to monofilament, metallic threads next to raw linen, t-shirt yarn and mercerized fine cotton. Needlepoint and weaving give you a blank canvas to work your surface through patterning and texture, which makes them great vehicles for this kind of fiber play.

The tools for small-scale domestic yarn production could not be simpler. When it comes to which commercially manufactured yarns you should include in your tool kit, well, that's a more complicated question. They fall into two categories: natural and synthetic. Both serve a purpose. The range of colors, sizes and textures is almost endless. We encourage you to use what you love, whether it's the finest angora, sturdiest linen or shiniest metallic filament.

- **Drop spindle:** A circle of timber with a notched stick stuck through the center.

- **Fibers:** Plant fibers such as cotton and flax, animal hair such as angora, wool and cashmere, and animal fibers such as silk.

- **Wool roving:** Prepared sheep's wool, known as roving, which has been washed to remove excess lanolin (grease) and carded or combed to orient all the individual fibers in the same direction. Alternatively, you can buy roving uncarded and invest in your own carding comb.

- **Natural yarns:** Wool, silk, cotton, linen, jute, hemp, hair.

- **Synthetic yarns:** Rayon, acetate, polyester, nylon, acrylic.

- **Alternative yarns:** Paper, grasses, reeds, raffia, upcycled clothing.

- **Bobbins**

- **Cardboard yarn cones**

- **Wool carders**

- **Scissors**

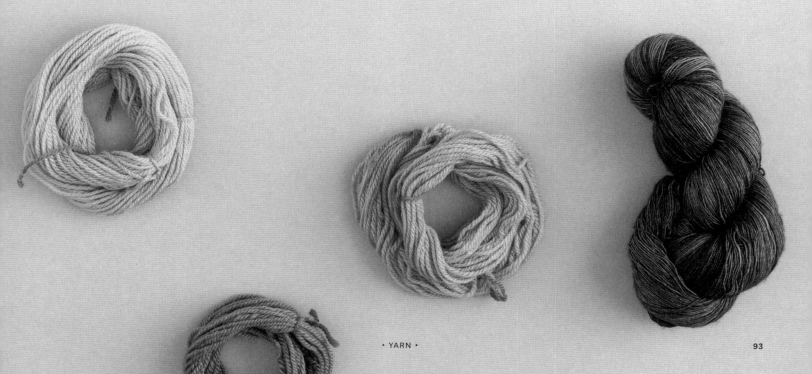

DROP SPINDLE SPINNING

One of the oldest spinning traditions, drop spindle is also one of the simplest. It's said that women would make yarn this way while riding sidesaddle on long journeys. That's some medieval multi-tasking if you ask us!

WHAT YOU NEED

- A yard of yarn
- Drop spindle
- Wool rovings

WHAT YOU DO

1. Tie a piece of leader yarn onto the spindle above the disc, and wrap it around once, bringing it under the disc, looping it around the bottom of the spindle and then back up around to the top.

2. Holding the end of the leader yarn in one hand and your rovings in the other, tease out the yarn fibers and wrap them around the leader yarn above your spindle.

3. Hold a length of around 6" of teased yarn fibers in one hand and the top of your spindle in the other. Gravity and continuous motion will form the yarn as it spins. Drop the spindle and spin the disc in the direction you want your twist.

4. Keep feeding in your yarn to the spinning thread, maintaining the rotation by giving your spindle a quick turn as you go. Trust us, it's easier than it sounds! Just think of it as a vertical version of wheel spinning and you'll quickly get your head around the motion.

5. As your yarn grows you will periodically need to stop and wind it onto your spindle. Stop the spinning and wind the long yarn around your fingers in a figure 8. Then hold the stick and turn it to wind the yarn back onto the spindle frame. Simple.

TWINING

Use up scraps to create unique and strong yarns that can be used in a million different ways.

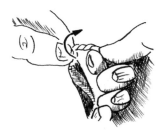

1. Take two narrow strips of fabric and tie them together in a knot. You might like to tape them to your workbench before you start.

2. Twist one strip tightly away from yourself, then fold it over the second.

3. Then twist the second strip away from yourself and fold it back over the first. The twisting-away motion makes it twist back on itself, creating the entwined yarn.

4. To add more strips to your length, wrap the tail end of your working strip around your new strip and twist together before continuing.

T-SHIRT YARN

You can buy t-shirt yarn commercially as an upcycled product of the fashion industry or you can easily make it.

1. Lay an old t-shirt on a flat surface. Cut off the bottom seam and the top half just above the bottom of the sleeve. Then fold one side of your t-shirt almost to the other side, seam to seam.

2. Cut the fabric into strips 1" thick, stopping before you reach the end.

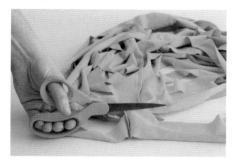

3. Unfold your cut t-shirt. To turn it into continuous yarn, cut through the uncut section diagonally across to the next strip.

4. Pull the yarn out and it will roll around itself and turn tubular.

PROJECT IDEAS

→ Keeping yarn safe from moth damage is an ongoing mission so it's worth making your own anti-moth bags using lemon and herbs such as lavender, mint, thyme and cloves. Not only will you keep your yarn safe, it will smell good too.

→ You should keep your spare bits of yarn, but how do you keep all those little bits in order? You can bag and tag them so you know what their fiber content is, but another great way is to use wooden clothespins. Open the clothespin and pinch the end of the yarn, then wrap the remainder around the middle, pop your other end into the clothespin and, voilà, problem solved.

→ Turn your old tin cans, glass jars, wooden blocks and ceramic pots into cool new vessels for pencils, cooking utensils and plants. Apply glue or double-sided tape to your surface and wind your yarn around, using a range of colored stripes. Use yarn to decorate twigs and tree branches for celebrations, or customize your smartphone cord so you always know who's got your charger!

→ Temari are traditional Japanese ornaments given as gifts to represent friendship and loyalty. These intricately wound and stitched yarn balls are incredibly beautiful and highly complex. They also make amazing decorations.

→ Wool yarns are fantastic absorbers of natural dyes. Make up a batch of food-based dyes and distribute them between a dozen mason jars. Wind off small skeins of scoured white yarn, and put one into each of the jars of dye, sealing the lids and leaving them in the sun to cure. You'll have a pitch-perfect palette for a woven wall hanging within 48 hours.

Hanging Herb Garden

We have to admit we are in love with the Japanese craft of Kokedama. These mossy plant yarn balls are known as "poor man's bonsai," but for us they combine two passions perfectly — yarn and gardening. When hung together by a kitchen window they create a beautiful herb garden that not only increases your bench space but also showcases a beautiful collection of colored yarns.

WHAT YOU NEED

- Newspaper
- Peat moss
- 2 buckets
- Peat soil
- Good-quality potting mix (bonsai soil works well)
- Slow-release fertilizer
- Selection of small herb plants (such as basil, coriander, thyme, parsley)
- Sphagnum moss
- Cotton thread
- Scissors
- Acrylic yarn in a variety of colors (we used pink, red and blue)
- 3 S-hooks

WHAT YOU DO

1. Put newspaper on your work surface. You are about to make a mess.

2. Take a generous amount of peat moss and soak it in one of the buckets with water to soften it. In your other bucket, mix one part peat soil to five parts potting mix and toss in a tablespoon of slow-release fertilizer.

3. Add a small amount of water to your potting mix so it just comes together as a ball. Do not make it too mushy!

4. Form your mix into balls the size of an orange. Make one for each plant and make sure they're big enough to contain tender roots.

5. Remove most of the soil from the roots of your small herb plants. Then gently wrap some soaked sphagnum moss around the roots of each plant and secure with cotton thread, being careful not to damage the roots in the process.

6. Make small holes in your soil balls and gently push each plant into a hole. Compact the soil back into a ball shape.

7. Using the peat moss, cover each ball well.

8. Now take your yarn and start wrapping. This process can feel awkward at the start, but persevere, being careful to replace any moss to fill in the gaps in the process. There is no right or wrong way, so use as much or as little as you want. Your aim is to secure the moss and make a pretty ball.

9. Once you're done wrapping, attach a longer loop for hanging the ball.

10. Use an S-hook to suspend balls from a rod. You'll need to take your Kokedamas down once a week to give them a good soak. Between soakings a nice mist of water is always welcome.

HOT TIP

We used bright acrylic yarns for a pop of color but Kokedama is also a beautiful way to showcase handspun yarns and natural jute. These more organic options will encourage moss growth and become more embedded into the ball with age — BONUS! Just between us, Kokedamas also look just as gorgeous and stay just as healthy sitting in small bowls on your dining table or kitchen bench.

Baskets

◇◇◇

Practical, decorative or ceremonial — the basket is the ultimate craft utility object. The history of basket making reaches well beyond recorded history. We suspect baskets were invented about the same time as people realized life would be much easier if we could carry more than one thing at a time. Imprints of baskets have been found on ancient Egyptian pottery dating back 10,000 years but it is safe to assume there were much earlier examples long since lost. Basket making is a true foundation craft with a global history and a continuing contemporary currency.

Indigenous cultures the world over developed basket making in different ways depending on the materials available. The split grass coiled pots of Native Americans are as diverse in style and design as the many tribes who produce them. The English willow baskets, New England splint baskets and the spinifex grass work of Arnhem Land in Australia are all prime examples of enduring traditions of basket making that are as vibrant today as when they were first conceived.

The availability of source material has consistently determined style and design. As with many crafts, over time decorative practices develop that are highly specific both to cultural groups and to geographical regions. In this way it's not just food, water, trade goods, fish and fowl that are transported but social history as well. In Africa, coiling techniques and bold geometric patterning ruled the day, while in China formal symmetrical lacquered baskets were used as both an everyday item and a highly prized trade material. In 16th-century Japan, a new rustic style of ikebana and the tea ceremony were heavily influential in the development of a unique approach to basket design that has dictated traditions ever since.

Regional isolation and the varying availability of raw supplies have also meant that as materials become scarce or new materials arrive, techniques and designs adjust to accommodate them. The Zulu telephone wire baskets of South Africa are a spectacular case in point. Watchmen used the colored wire to weave patterns around their sticks during long night shifts. The flexible wire was a perfect replacement for the increasingly scarce palms that were traditionally used for basket making and so it was quickly adopted by local makers. This simple change modernized an established practice, ushering in a new cottage industry and financial independence for an entire community. Today, material selection is limited only by your imagination. Any pliable material can be used, from packing tape to hand-harvested wicker.

Contemporary practice stretches basket-making techniques to their limits, pushing scale, material and application in challenging directions. The essential "usefulness" is up-ended as technique is used to create more sculptural or conceptual work. Synthetic fibers provide an endless source of base material, and with natural resources still being utilized there is a basket-making style to suit every crafter.

TIM JOHNSON
Britain

From creating basket "costumes" and hosting workshops to installing large-scale outdoor sculptural pieces, artist and basket maker Tim Johnson combines old-world technique with contemporary edge. Harnessing styles and source materials that span the globe, Johnson engages with basket making with an investigative eye and a commitment to learning both old and new approaches to the craft.

🖥 timjohnsonartist.com

MICHELE MORCOS
Australia

Artist Michele Morcos brings her painter's understanding of both color and composition to creating baskets and wall works that play with negative and positive space. Her multidisciplinary practice draws its inspiration from sources as diverse as the "God particle" to the Quantum Theory of the Universe. Using the colored binding thread almost like a pencil, Morcos explores a tactile way of mark-making.

🖥 michelemorcos.com

DOUG JOHNSTON
United States

We refer to Doug Johnston as "The Man of all Awesome." Since we first saw images of his rope baskets way back in 2010 we've followed the stratospheric trajectory of his broad practice with great delight. The stitched rope coil technique he employs allows for a perfect marriage between his architecture background and curious exploration of craft process and production. These elements solidly underpin his practice and create a conceptual and tactile equilibrium manifested in his skilled hand and highly refined aesthetics, spatial awareness, deft construction and form.

🖵 **dougjohnston.net**

CORDULA KEHRER
Germany

Designer Cordula Kehrer partnered with the Aeta people of the Philippines to create half-plastic, half-wicker baskets for American brand Areaware. They elegantly comment on ideas of tradition, collaboration, waste, design and mass production vs. handmade. This fair trade project brought together two seemingly disparate worlds of design and produced an object both practical and charming, the joke cleverly not at the expense of either point of view.

🖵 **cordulakehrer.de**

DESIGN NOTES

WALLFLOWERS

Don't be bound by end-use traditions. Basket-making techniques can be applied just as successfully to wall art, light fittings and wearable works. By using the fundamental woven construction, you can push the technique in surprising shapes and directions to create pieces that go way beyond the fruit bowl.

CUSTOM JOB

Whether your basket is handmade or prefab there's no reason you can't play around. Alter or add to your basket to create a unique statement piece. Dip-dye, spray-paint, attach pom-poms, sew in colored yarn details or line with fabric. There are a multitude of ways you can customize your basket to great effect to ensure that it's both functional and fabulous.

TIP THE SCALE

Basket-making techniques can be translated up and down in scale without too much drama. Once you have a method nailed, go ahead and experiment with material and application and confound expectations of both. Theoretically, the method for making a firewood basket is essentially the same as for a basket brooch, although you will need to consider the malleability of up-sized materials and your own ability to manipulate them in order to guarantee a successful outcome and your own sanity.

CHOOSE YOUR OWN ADVENTURE

While there are no hard and fast rules about what you can use to make baskets, there is one fundamental design rule that can't be ignored: choose the right material for the job. This is true for most crafts where form and function collide, but especially true of basket making. Stick with sturdy materials for heavy-duty end use or, if you're feeling adventurous, mitigate potential problems by choosing finishing processes such as varnishing or waterproofing to extend the life of your masterpiece.

MASH-UP

One of the quickest ways to transform and update a craft is through the injection of contemporary materials. Both necessity and aesthetics can drive brilliant innovation. Try throwing neon-bound cord, plastic bags, newspaper and wrapping raffia into the mix as alternative supplies for traditional coil and woven constructions. Each will leave its own distinctive aesthetic imprint on the end product and give a new twist to an old standard.

DESIGN DELIBERATION

The coiled and woven surfaces of baskets give crafters enormous scope for deliberate design and decorative elements. Intentional striping, fiber inter-mixing and surface pattern play are all literally at your fingertips. Think about the construction process and plan out where to bring these options into play for the greatest impact. Going backwards to try to even out crooked stripes, weave in a missing bead or add metallic thread can be a messy and frustrating business.

There is a long list of specialist tools needed for the creation of traditional reed and wicker baskets. However, beginners who want to build up skills before making major investments can get away with the following tools and still be able to make coiled and woven baskets from everyday materials.

- **Pliers:** Good for dealing with stubborn ends and for pulling needles through tough coiled work.

- **Scissors and hand pruners:** Scissors for softer materials and pruners for gathering tougher ones.

- **Binding thread:** Important for coiling. Embroidery thread, crochet cotton, woolen yarn and raffia are all great for this purpose.

- **Yarn needles:** Wide-eyed needles with blunt ends in metal (preferable) or plastic (average) used to construct coiled baskets. Keep them around 3", as they get difficult to maneuver if longer or shorter.

- **Embellishments:** Beads, pom-poms, washi tape and shells are all great options.

- **Masking tape:** Incredibly useful for holding fraying ends together at the start of coiled baskets.

- **Natural materials:** Includes farmed willow, center cane, raffia, garden leaves, dry grasses, lavender stalks, rushes and straw. Be intuitive with natural materials, as their pliability and strength will vary depending on growing and storage conditions.

- **Manmade materials:** Can be pretty much anything from plastic bags and clothesline cord to telephone wire and climbing rope. Look for length and flex to ensure optimum manageability.

- **Ruler**

- **Craft knife**

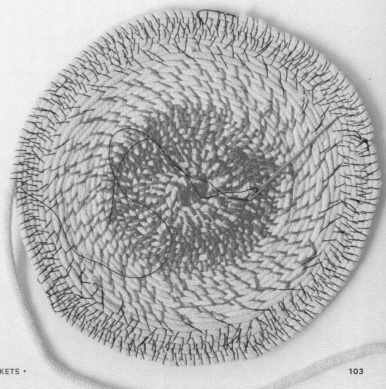

There are a few variations of coiling techniques used by different cultures to make baskets. Ostensibly, however, they all follow the same basic rules. One fiber is used as the filler and one as the binder.

WRAP

In this version, we show you how to develop a thread-faced basket.

WHAT YOU NEED

– 3 50g (2 oz.) balls of double knitting yarn in complementary colors

– 2 yards of ⅛" woven cord

– Masking tape

– Scissors

– Yarn (tapestry) needle

WHAT YOU DO

1. Wind off three 1-yard lengths of each yarn color and loosely bundle.

2. Wrap one end of your cord in tape to stop it fraying and cut at an angle through this.

3. Lay your cord out flat with the tapered end facing left and place your first yarn color beside it, around 3" from the end. Start wrapping the yarn back toward the end of your cord, wrapping closely and neatly so the yarn completely covers the cord.

4. Bend the wrapped section inwards and continue wrapping so the cut end is entirely covered. Keep wrapping down the leading edge of your cord for another 2", then thread the end of your wrapping yarn through your yarn needle.

5. Take your wrapped cord and very carefully start coiling it to create the base of your basket. Getting this right will set you up for success. Hold the coil tightly with one hand.

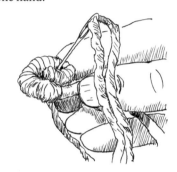

6. Using your other hand, take your yarn needle and stitch through the coil from above, then pull the stitch tight to anchor it.

7. Continue this process of wrapping, coiling and anchoring with stitches until you get close to running out of your yarn. As your basket coil increases in size you'll also need to increase the number of times the yarn wraps around the cord between stitches. Keep the number of wraps between stitches relatively small to help keep your basket holding together.

8. Once you're nearly out of yarn, make one last anchoring stitch and pass it through the last row of wrapped stitches. Cut the end off.

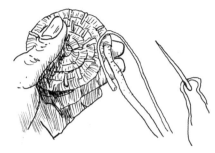

9. Lay your new yarn strand next to your cord, starting 1½" out from your coil. Wrap the yarn around both its own end and the cord seven times. Thread the other end of your yarn through your needle and use a stitch to anchor both the coil and your new thread. Continue as for step 5.

10. Once you're happy with your basket base you can start building the sides. This is actually really simple; just position your new coil right above the old one instead of next to it and proceed as before.

11. Adjust the shape with your hands as you coil and keep on going until you're happy with the size.

12. Finishing up is just like starting out. Cut the end of the cord on a diagonal and tape it. Wrap your yarn around it and stitch down into the last coil of your basket, then pull your yarn through the last few wraps and cut it off.

BLANKET STITCH

In this version, a binding thread is used to trap the filler and connect the coils of your basket. Use t-shirt yarn, cord or raffia as filler; raffia, wool yarn or crochet cotton for a binder; and a yarn needle, scissors and patience.

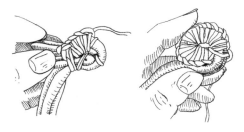

1. Make a small loop with your filler, thread your needle with binding thread and tie the end tightly around your loop so you have a little doughnut shape. Use your thread to make the first blanket stitch around the filler, making sure you push the needle from the front through to the back, through the thread loop and back out firmly, away from your body.

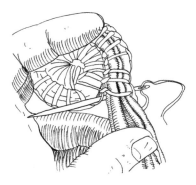

2. Make blanket stitches right around the circle with the straight part of the stitch sitting on the outside. Keep your stitches firm, neat and closely spaced.

3. To start the next row take your threaded needle through the top of the blanket stitch on the outside instead of through the center. Repeat this process right around the outside, forming a parallel second row.

PROJECT IDEAS

→   If you're anything like us it's likely you have at least three projects on the go at any given time. Instead of leaving said projects lying randomly around the house, whip yourself up a swathe of coiled or woven baskets for the living room or studio, specifically sized to house them. You'll keep your projects safe and your spaces stylish.

→   Apply your coiling techniques on a micro level. Use some indigo-dyed fabric and stripped raffia and embroidery thread to make statement earrings, bangles or neckpieces that are fun and fashion-forward.

→   Plastic bags are a scourge of our time. Even when you take your own tote you can still end up with loads of them sitting listlessly in a kitchen drawer. Upcycle those bags into an all-weather clothespins basket by using them as filler for a coil construction with a banging bright nylon cord as your binder.

→   Neighborhood walks are a great time to collect plant-based materials for basket making. Take a bag with you and look out for reeds, branches, grasses and vines that could be bent and shaped into basket frames ready for colorful yarns or fiber finishes.

→   Coiling is just the first step in a long list of traditional techniques. Use a basic woven technique (see Upcycle chapter). Keep your stakes stiff and you can apply this simple technique to anything from veneer strips to willow stakes, and weave through paper, fabric strips, plastic tubing or natural grasses depending on what's available and what effect you're after.

Tisket Tasket T-shirt Basket

WHAT YOU NEED

- 33 yards of natural raffia

- Large tapestry needle

- 22 yards of t-shirt yarn

- Scissors

This will make a basket approx. 12" wide and 6" high.

HOT TIP

We like to make balls of t-shirt yarn in advance so we have a variety to choose from. Striped or printed t-shirts make great random patterns along your basket as you weave. Woven fabrics will also work, but for beginners the natural curl that comes from jersey knits makes the process much easier.

Upcycled coil fabric baskets are a breeze to make and are a great way of turning worn-out clothes into useful containers. We made ours from old t-shirts but you can also use any light woven scrap fabric. The start is a little fiddly, but with practice you'll soon be churning these puppies out with gay abandon.

WHAT YOU DO

1. Thread your needle with one strand of raffia. You may want to strip your raffia in half to make it finer for this first stage, as you will be making fine stitches to secure the base.

2. Make a loop with your t-shirt yarn filler just big enough to fit your needle through and tie the bottom of your raffia securely around the loop to hold it in a circular shape.

3. Make your first blanket stitch and pull it tight. Continue blanket-stitching around the circle, working clockwise, until you come back to the tail of your loop. Once your stitches join up, you're ready to start the second row.

4. This time, as you work around the circle, take your raffia through the top of the last blanket stitch instead of through the hole of your fabric loop.

5. Hold the coil toward you as you work and keep your raffia on the right-hand side in these initial rows — it will make it easier to keep things moving clockwise and the base flat.

6. When your raffia is nearly used up, simply tie on another piece with a knot, tuck the leftover ends into the coil of the yarn and keep making your blanket stitches.

7. To add another color, cut the end of the old t-shirt yarn on a diagonal and wrap the new piece around it. Remember to make sure you have enough raffia left on your needle to make a good five or six stitches before doing this, as you want a secure line of stitches to cover the join and keep it in place. Keep working until your flat coil reaches a diameter of 12".

8. To turn the sides of the basket, start pulling the blanket stitches while moving the next row of t-shirt yarn so it sits on top rather than beside the previous one. As your stitches tighten and the yarn moves, the basket will naturally start turning up.

9. Keep coiling in this fashion until your walls reach a basket height of around 4".

10. Time to finish up! Leave around 6" of raffia on your needle, then cut your t-shirt yarn at an angle with a tail of around 2". Continue blanket stitching right over this cut tail, then work the raffia back into the vertical stitches of the row below. Cut, knot and weave through a couple more stitches to hide your ends and you're done.

Leather

◇◇◇

Humans have long relied on the unwitting generosity of animals to serve our most basic needs. Hides have been scraped for shelter and clothing, furs used for warmth, and meat eaten for sustenance. Nearly all nations have developed techniques for tanning, piercing and sewing that have enabled them to utilize the strength and durability of the animal skins that came as the by-product of hunting for food. Our complicated love affair with leather continues unabated. Today the number of animals needed to meet demand far outstrips what is used in food production. Leather sits as a curious relic, both luxury item and tactile link to our prehistoric past.

In the Neolithic period animal husbandry developed, allowing people a regular source of hides. These were useful in the short-term but were quick to stiffen and rot. Eventually communities developed rudimentary tanning techniques, using plant and fecal matter as well as smoke and grease drying to use leather more effectively. The world's oldest surviving leather shoe was made in Armenia around 3500 B.C.E. Other leather artifacts exist from 1300 B.C.E. The production and use of leather are extensively recorded in written texts, including Homer's *Iliad*.

The ancient civilizations of Rome, Egypt and Greece used leather as innovatively as possible, for everything from footwear to dresses, belts, vessels and boats. The Phoenicians even used leather to develop water-pipe systems. Leather developed as a textile that could protect the body in battle as well as transporting food and water; the impact of these developments was felt worldwide.

Mastery over leather is probably no better exemplified than in the deer or buckskin garments of North America and Alaska, in particular those worn by the Iroquois and Cherokee. They developed elaborate and exceptionally efficient garments and footwear. Their techniques for garment construction utilized well-resolved decorative solutions for functional issues; for example, heavy fringe was used to deflect rain rather than absorb it. Traditional native dress continues to be a dominant aesthetic influence on modern fashion, even when not appropriately acknowledged.

The Middle Ages saw the formation of European leather guilds, and the skills of their members were highly sought after in the production of saddles, boots and capes. Leatherwork was seen as a profession akin to blacksmithing, and tanneries could be found on the outskirts of every village. Up until the mid-19th century vegetable tanning, utilizing naturally occurring tannins of tree barks, was the predominant method. Hides were soaked for weeks in vats of increasingly strong tannin solutions. The introduction of chrome cut this process to less than a day and is still the method of choice for leather manufacturing. Chrome tanning, however, is certainly not for the squeamish, and it's important to recognize how much toxic waste is involved in its creation. It's a multi-step process that involves soaking, liming, pickling, tanning and crusting. Many parts of the world still tan leather with chrome and there are areas indelibly stained by the extensive damage to the environment and health risks associated with the process.

An understanding of these risks has seen a recent return to vegetable tanning. Leather's prevalence within the super-luxe end of the car, luggage and fashion industries attests to its continued appeal. Increasingly, people are unable to disconnect from its source or the impact of its production. New, more environmentally sustainable options are being developed, including kelp and cork and "micro suede" textiles. These materials improve every year and are now barely distinguishable from the "real deal."

As contemporary makers, artists, fashion and industrial designers continue to use this incredible material, they are also upcycling existing leather or exploring alternatives. Leather's rich history is inspiring a new generation of makers to investigate construction techniques and reference age-old aesthetic traditions from sources as varied as Roman sandals and samurai armor.

CLAIRE MCARDLE
Australia

Artist Claire McArdle has a highly conceptual and process-oriented practice, often with a component of audience participation. In her "Identity Fair" series McArdle asked what it meant to be Australian through the creation of a series of native animal totemic heads from hand-pieced leather. These are national representatives recreated in monotones using a range of fringing, cutting and layering techniques to recreate feathers, furs and faces. These could be worn as oversize neckpieces by exhibition visitors, posing the question, "Which animal are you?"

 clairemcardle.com

SIMON HASAN
Britain

The leather vessels of Simon Hasan are perfect examples of where industrial design and traditional craft meet. Utilizing a boiled leather technique originally used to make armor matched by a decidedly minimalist design aesthetic, his vessels become an almost archeological mirror image of the ubiquitous soft-drink bottle. After the stripping back of the object and removal of all commercial branding, we are left to admire the perfect curve for the hand to grip. Hasan makes the disposable desirable.

simonhasan.com

ÚNA BURKE

Britain

The leather accessories of Úna Burke function as both fetish item and armory. Burke's capacity to straddle the complex power relations between the cultural functions of these associations shows a confidence and surety that defy the limitations of both. Drawing inspiration from the long history of battle gear, she uses intricate interlocking systems via lacing and metal studs to create an ornate exoskeleton, both protective and consuming. Her choice of material, the most ancient of coverings, literally ties us back to our primitive beginnings using hide to cover skin.

🖳 **unaburke.com**

ATSUSHI KITAZAKI

Japan

Combining elements of rockabilly, heavy metal, traditional Japanese mythology and tattoo flash could be a recipe for disaster. However, in the hands of super cool and super-skilled leatherworker Atsushi Kitazaki they hang together perfectly. Handsomely rendered on belts, bags and the most ubiquitous of Japanese geisha wear, the platform sandle, or "geta," these perfect cultural mash-ups are handcarved and colored in Kitazaki's signature style.

🖳 **chelsea-leather-art-work.com**

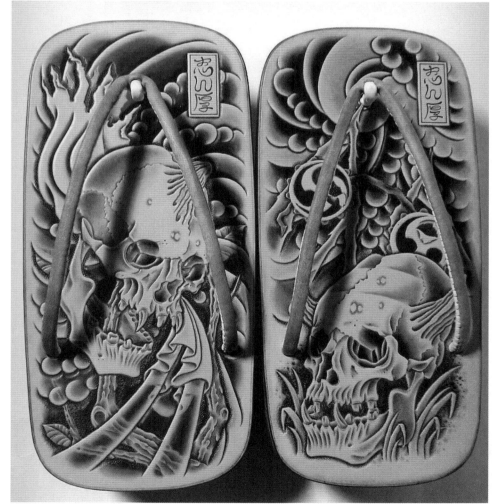

DESIGN NOTES

CREATURE FEATURE

A key thing to remember about working with leather is that you are working with a creature's skin. Animal hides, just like our own skin, are full of flaws. As you'll normally be buying whole hides, you'll need to either work around these or build them into your design. Personally, we're all for embracing imperfection (and not just because we're over 40). Flaws act as a salient reminder of the material's origins as well as adding incidental "realness" to the work.

MAKING THE GRADE

There are so many fabulous finishes available in leather that you may be tempted to opt for the embossed crocodile red patent leather when you really need some sturdy cowhide. Think carefully about the construction, wear and end use, and make sure you match the right material with the right job for best results. And then buy the patent leather anyway — you know you're going to find a use for it.

FLEXI-TIME

The flexibility of leather as a construction material is extraordinary. It is unique in that you can shape leather into 3-D forms as well as carve, cut, burn, dye, stamp and print its surface. Print onto the face, then carve around the prints to make a relief surface or stamp repeat designs into damp leather and then highlight details with dye. Consider the options in isolation or combination for maximum impact.

SECOND SKIN

If you're a vegetarian as well as an avid crafter you'll no doubt be confronted by the use of leather — on one hand, it's a brilliantly sturdy and versatile material, but on the other, a living creature has died for your use. Today, you have the option to go faux. There is a brilliant array of synthetic options that will give you the look without the guilt (although often their production is less than eco-friendly), or you can choose to upcycle existing leather products destined for landfill and make sure you make work to last.

INTO THE FRAY

One of leather's most endearing qualities is that, for the most part, it doesn't fray when cut. This means you can cut and sew to your heart's content without needing to consider hemming or finishing. However, as with most things, there is a catch. Soft, fine leathers DO need to be treated with the same amount of care as fabric. Kid goat and fine kangaroo will tear along the grain and the sewn edges, so if you're a slapdash crafter, steer clear of the soft stuff and head straight for the sturdy.

HEAVY DUTY

Leather has strong associations with both serious utility and super high-end luxe, offering product designers enormous scope by playing oppositional aesthetics and functions against each other. However, even domestic makers can use this idea — think foiled gold leather tool belts or bike panniers as a playful way of mixing materials and metaphors.

- **Leather groover:** Cuts out straight grooves for stitch lines.

- **Hole spacer:** Creates even marks for holes to be made with your awl.

- **Rivet set:** Comes with both front and back sections of the rivets.

- **Rivet setter:** Sits between the hammer and the rivet top when setting rivets.

- **Stamp set:** For embossing leather.

- **Stamp setter:** Sits between the hammer and the stamp when embossing.

- **Leather thonging:** For threading through holes and decorative stitches.

- **Leather sewing needles:** Longer and stronger than standard needles.

- **Electric burnisher:** For burnishing designs into your leatherwork.

- **Leather stitching pony:** A wooden stand that helps to hold the leather in place while saddle stitching.

- **Leather dye**

- **Gilding foil**

- **Soft cloth**

- **Low-tack masking tape**

- **Awl**

- **Rubber mallet**

- **Leather cement glue**

- **Hammer**

- **Scissors**

- **Craft knife**

- **Metal ruler**

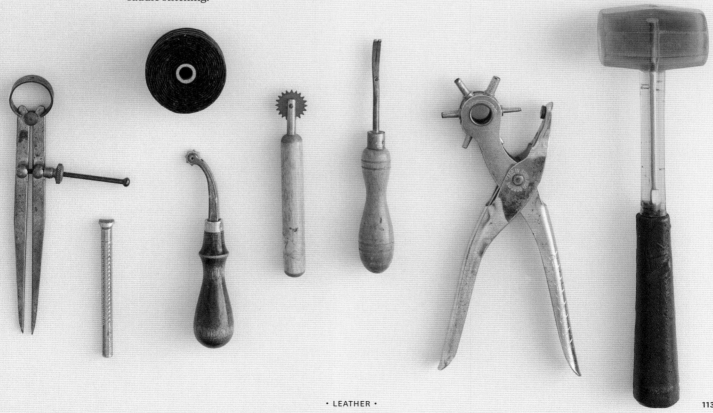

Leather is generally sold in packs of mixed small sections or in single hides. It comes in its natural state, colored or foiled. Cowhide is the most common leather and is readily available and relatively inexpensive. Lamb, kid and deer are somewhat harder to come by and pricier. All have their own qualities. Lambskin is super soft and perfect for clothing, while deer is more commonly used for coin purses and wallets.

The process of tanning leather is both complex and toxic so its implications do bear thinking about. There are many fantastic alternatives that imperceptibly mimic the look and feel of natural leather. Pleather, ultra-suede and vegan microfiber are all sterling switch outs if you aren't comfortable with the natural option.

MACHINE STITCHING

If your sewing machine can cope with heavy denim it can cope with a hide. You'll have to use heavy-duty needles and protect the leather surface from marks by laying a sheet of paper between the leather and the presser foot. Use polyester or nylon thread for strength and durability.

PRE-MAKING HOLES

Whether you want a fine saddle-stitched edge or a blanket stitch design detail, you will have to make holes for your thread to pass through.

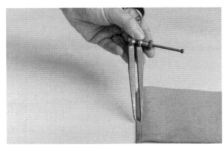

1. First, use a leather groover to carve out a straight valley for stitching. This is a super-useful tool with an excellent name.

2. Next, use a hole spacer to mark starter holes that are perfectly spaced and ready for stitching.

3. A sharp awl is then all it takes to push holes through your leather and make it ready for hand-stitching.

WHIP STITCH

The easiest stitch to close the sides of your project, whip stitch also adds a decorative edge, and is especially good when used with colored leather cord. However, the stitches can slide a little so it's not the best choice for work that needs to stay rigid.

Use an awl to punch holes a little larger than your cord around the joining edges of the leather and then feed your cord or needle and thread through and back over the top, whipping over the join.

SADDLE STITCH

To give a really polished and professional finish to your leatherwork you'll need to learn saddle stitching. It's much easier than you would think. First prepare your leather for sewing following the previous step.

1. The secret is to use two needles, one at each end of your thread. Put one needle through your first hole so you have a needle either side of your leather.

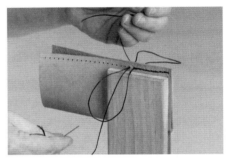

2. You now feed both needles through each hole in opposite directions, sewing a running stitch on both sides. It's a good idea to get into the habit of putting your needles through the same hole at the same time so that you don't split your thread. You'll find a rhythm that suits you.

3. To finish off, just backstitch a few stitches. Use a craft knife to trim your edges flush.

LEATHER TASSEL

A tassel is a fantastic punctuation mark on many different projects. Cushions and curtains, clothes and key rings can all be made to look just that little bit smarter with this easy-to-assemble accessory.

WHAT YOU NEED

- Leather scraps
- Scissors
- Pencil
- Tape measure or ruler
- Leather cement glue
- Leather thonging
- Wooden bead
- Wooden clothespins

WHAT YOU DO

1. Cut out a 5 x 7" piece of leather and mark a line ½" across the longer side. Then cut a fringe at ¼" intervals all the way along the line.

2. Fold your leather thonging in half and feed your bead onto it.

3. Run a line of leather cement glue along the top of your fringe section. Place the edge of your loop at the beginning of your glue line.

4. Carefully roll the tassel over the loop and secure with a wooden clothespin until dry.

5. You may want to add a decorative contrasting band of leather at the top. This also serves to hide any marks made by the clothespin. BONUS.

MAGIC BRAIDING

Learning how to magic-braid is a bit like cracking a code. At first you'll end up in a tangled mess, then suddenly it will make sense and you'll be braiding up bracelets, bag straps and belts in no time.

1. Measure out a length of leather. You'll need to allow for about 10 percent shrinkage. Using a sharp craft knife and a metal ruler as a guide, cut two parallel slits from top to bottom, leaving about 1" at either end.

2. Pin or tape your leather to a board to make it easier to work.

3. Take the bottom of your leather and feed it though the right-hand gap.

4. Yes, it will now confound you with its twistiness. Straighten out the three strands so the braid lies flat. The trick is to concentrate on the braid and not the mess that is happening underneath it.

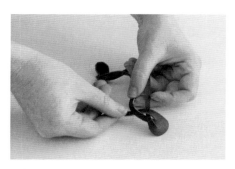

5. Take your left strand over the center strand, right strand over the center strand, then left strand over the center strand to create your first "braid."

6. Now take the bottom and feed it through the gap on the left side.

7. Repeat step 5, but this time start on the right and then bring the bottom up through the gap on the right side. This will magically unravel the tangle below.

8. After a bit of practice you'll get the hang of it. Braid left, right, left, then take the bottom up through the gap on the left, twisting it and so on.

9. Continue until you've braided to the bottom. Smooth out your braid. You can now add snap fasteners if it's for wearing.

RIVETING

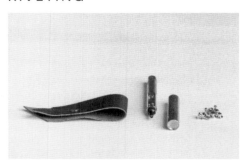

Riveting is great for adding handles to bags or as an all-over bedazzling technique. Rivet sets come with both fronts and backs. You'll also need an awl, rivet setter and hammer to get them into your leather.

1. Using the awl, create a hole big enough for your rivet front to go through. This should be quite snug; it's better to err on the side of smaller than bigger, or your rivet will come loose.

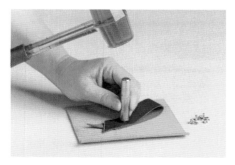

2. Next, use the rivet setter to hold your rivet back in position, then hammer it in place.

STAMPING

Stamping is an addictive way of personalizing leather projects. A monogram, a word, a decorative border or images can easily be added and make you look like a leathercraft superstar. It's super fun and super easy and marks the entry point into the world of traditional leather tooling. Stamp sets come in alphabets, words, patterns and images, as a single unit or with removable handles.

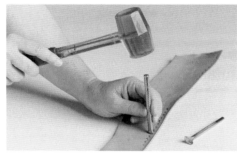

1. Dampen your leather first with a sponge moistened with water. This will soften the leather, making it easier to receive the stamp.

2. Use the handle to hold the stamp in place and give it a good whack with your mallet to make an impression.

STAINING

Upcycle leather bags and clothes that may be gathering dust in your parents' garage or basement from your biker phase. One quick way to do this is through staining.

Staining untreated leather is a cinch. If you're tooling or carving, the stain will pool in the depressions, giving you a stronger color in the grooves. Untreated leather soaks up a lot of dye, so it's best to buy top quality to ensure color vibrancy. You can also re-stain or dye old leather, although if it has been treated with a plastic coating the dye won't stain.

PROJECT IDEAS

→ There's nothing like a bit of summer camp crafting to reinvigorate your love of making. Leather is a great choice for easy projects such as a lanyard, bookmark or drawstring pouch, perfect for big or little campers. Get a vacation crafting kit together next time you hit the trailer park.

→ Nothing says old-school meets new-school like a nubuck leather carrier for today's technology. Make simple sleeves for smartphones and tablets, sewn with saddle stitch and embossed with hand-tooled monograms, or block-printed with metallic geometrics. A super-cool articulation of form and function in one neatly bound package.

→ Create a stunning bar stool by re-upholstering an existing one with a woven leather seat. By cutting two hides of soft but resilient leather into 1"-wide strips, you can flat-weave them together into a new piece of "cloth" big enough to successfully re-cover the seat. Just be sure to secure your weave by machine stitching around the edges before you get busy with the upholstery work!

→ Painting leather can transform or update tired bags, belts or jackets. Use several coats of watered-down acrylic paint for small areas. Try adding simple running stitches or folk-inspired floral borders. Flexing the leather between coats will prevent cracking.

→ Knitted or crocheted strips of soft kid leather make a durable and desirable fabric, perfect for anything from baskets to backpacks. Be aware it is tough on your hands and your needles, so keep your stitches a little loose and use metal knitting needles to avoid breakage — both them and you!

Glamazon Clutch

WHAT YOU NEED

- 8 x 20" piece of black leather
- 10 x 20" piece of gold leather
- Scissors
- Tape measure
- Black nylon or polyester sewing thread
- Sewing machine
- Needle
- Masking tape
- Pencil
- Leather cement glue
- Wooden clothespin

HOT TIP

If your personal styling is less Van Halen and more Mumford & Sons, you can switch up the look by using strips of raw-hide and nubuck, hand-stitching your side seams with saddle or whip stitch leather thonging, and adding wooden beads to your tassels.

We were lucky enough to snaffle a bag of leather scraps from a seconds sale that included a winning combination of metallic finishes and super-soft kid. This heady combo took us in two distinct directions, glam metal and glamazons, so we decided to mix up both, in a Sunset Strip meets supermodel mash-up.

WHAT YOU DO

1. Take the black and gold leather and cut it into strips. You need three black and two gold pieces 18" long and 2½" wide.

2. Place one black and one gold strip face to face; leaving a ¼" seam allowance, sew the strips together. Remember to backstitch at the start and end to secure your stitches. Sew the rest of the strips together in the same order until you have a single piece of leather to make up your bag body.

3. Place your pieced leather rectangle face down on a flat surface with one short end toward you. Fold this end up 6" to make your bag body, leaving a 4⅜" flap to fold over the top. Tape the bag body at the edges with masking tape to hold it in place. Then stitch the sides together, leaving a ¼" seam allowance at each edge. Remove the tape.

4. Cut a small slit into the central black strip, 2" in from the top, then fold the flap over and use a pencil pushed through the slit to mark the leather underneath. This is where you will need to sew on the tassels.

5. Cut one strip of black leather ¼" wide and 10" long, then cut two 4 x 8" gold leather rectangles. Use your new-found tassel-making skills (see Techniques) to make a tassel at either end of your strip.

6. Position your tassel strip on your mark so the tassels will hang at different levels, then securely backstitch the strip over the mark you made in step 4. Slip the top tassel through the hole to close the bag.

7. Fill your bag with party essentials and hit the club!

Rugs

◇◇◇

Floor coverings have been with us since the year zero. What began as an animal skin on the floor of the cave has developed into a worldwide tradition matched to the materials, technical complexity and style of its makers. As an example of the craft's antiquity, historians point to evidence that the ancient Egyptians employed a prodding rug-making method. However, many other cultures developed highly specialized aesthetic and technical customs, from the hand-tufted Tibetan rugs to the Paleolithic origins of the Berber carpets of North Africa. But it wasn't until much more recently that rug-making came into its own as a distinctive domestic craft in the West.

Tibetan rug-making is an ancient craft dating back more than 2,000 years to the Han Dynasty. These dense rugs were used in all aspects of daily life, from bedding to saddlery, and were made from the sturdy wool of Himalayan sheep. Fibers were dyed with plant material into rich deep colors and hand-tufted into intricate patterns of mythical and religious iconography such as dragons, clouds and lotus blossoms, which made them highly sought after for both practical and decorative purposes.

The kilims of the Middle East and Central Asia have been produced by both nomadic and village populations for centuries. Evolving off the loom, they use slit tapestry and soumak knotting to create weft-faced religious and totemic geometric motifs that are passed down through generations, with each weaver adding their own twist.

Tapestry and warp braiding were also the main techniques used in the creation of the Anatolian, Navajo and Pre-Columbian Peruvian rug-making traditions. Traditionally crafted on upright looms, they featured yarns from both indigenous plant material and trade and strongly symmetrical geometric patterning. You can almost chart the path of America's railroad through the changing color palette of Navajo rug-making as aniline dyes became available from the 1880s.

In the West the development of the shaggy rag rug as both floor covering and decorative object was very much part of the country craft culture of rural England. These early rag rugs utilized fabric scraps in a number of ways, from hooking to weaving, to provide warmth and much-needed cheer for snowbound hearths and homes.

The braided rug has recently been enjoying an Internet-led resurgence but has its roots firmly embedded in the dirt floors of colonial America. Fabric was an expensive commodity and pioneer women were canny upcyclers. Not a scrap of fabric was wasted in these homes. Instead, they were used in decorative ways as insulation against the elements. Strips of wool or cotton or a mix of both were braided together and then hand-sewn in a continuous coil.

Methods for D.I.Y. rugs vary from place to place and have moved in and out of fashion over the years. Latch hook rugs, made using a specialty tool and pre-cut pieces of yarn, were made popular from the 1940s right through to the early 1980s, as they came in easy kit form. Hooked rugs, made by pulling strips of fabric up through a closely woven fabric such as burlap, forming a solid mass of loops, have been an American tradition since colonial times. In Britain, prodded rugs are made by pushing short fabric strips up from the wrong side of the base fabric to form a shaggy pile. Rag rugs and braided rugs have made their way around the world as easy crafts despite their large scale and the many work hours they require.

There has been an increased interest in floor coverings in contemporary interior design, fueled by the speed with which aesthetic trends can travel via the Internet around the world. Old practices have been revitalized with new materials, as can be seen in the brightly colored woven plastic floor coverings of modern Senegal. Artists have taken the traditional patterning, techniques and cultural associations of the craft and twisted them into thought-provoking new works.

CONTEMPORARY ARTISTS

JONATHAN JOSEFSSON
Sweden

Jonathan Josefsson's roots in street art feed directly into his abstract sculptural rugs. These hand-tufted carpets swell and surge with rhythms similar to spray paint on a backstreet wall. Josefsson clearly revels in the dense tactile materiality afforded to him in this craft, as he works his color play and De Stijl-inspired graphic patterning into textural topographies as comforting to the eye as they are for the feet.

🖥 jonathanjosefsson.se

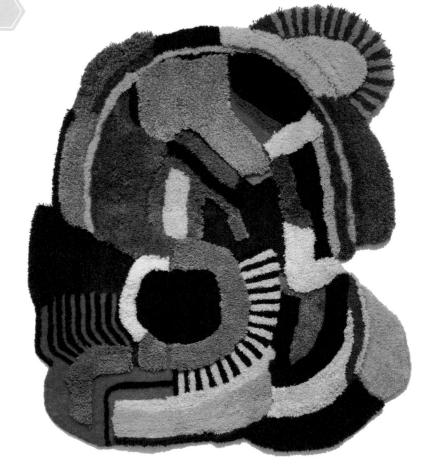

KATIE STOUT
United States

Katie Stout's multidisciplinary design practice re-imagines the domestic environment as a playground and playfully confounds form and function. She brings Liberace Vegas glitz to folk tradition in her braided gold lamé rag rug, and cleverly manipulates coiled construction techniques to incorporate 3-D "loungeable" shapes in her "ottoman" flooring/furniture range. Her collections of digitally printed landscape textiles, soft sculpture seating and molten geometric lights, made with clay artist Sean Gerstley, speak of dream house interiors in a truly literal sense.

🖥 katiestout.com

MYRA KLOSE
Germany

German fashion designer Myra Klose is the driving force behind the MYK label, the interiors collection that includes the playful Bommel range. "Bommel" means "pom-pom" in German, and Klose uses this ball base unit to create soft furnishings from poodle-shaped floor cushions to faux animal-skin rugs. Luxurious and whimsical, these perfectly handcrafted pom-poms are sewn together into guilt-free big game feature creatures that act as soft sculptures for the floor.

🖵 **myk-berlin.com**

KARL HUGO ERICKSON
United States

While primarily a video artist, Karl Hugo Erickson has made multiple interventions into craft-based process as a methodology to extend his sculptural work in both conceptual and material directions. His focus on the effects of language on human behavior and evolution find a sympathetic expression in pop cultural text, and the forms of motivational/inspirational dialects and spiritual doctrines of late-night evangelism. Melding these weighty concepts with the highly kitsch cultural and aesthetic sensibilities of latch hook work makes them all the more compelling.

🖵 **karlhugoerickson.com**

DESIGN NOTES

CAN YOU HANDLE IT?

There is no escaping the fact that if you are undertaking a rug project you're going to become intimately acquainted with your materials. Do not underestimate the toll this kind of handwork will have on your body, and think carefully about your choices. Big rugs are big projects, backing cloths can be very rough, and the in-and-out of a latch hook against its heavy-duty mesh can tear your fingers to pieces. Don't set yourself up for failure. Instead, be realistic about your commitment. There's no shame in your hall runner turning into a cushion cover!

YOU MAY ASK YOURSELF

Is it going to be in a high-traffic area? Are you going to want to wash it? Will it need a backing to stop it slipping? Rugs are big, time-consuming projects so you have to consider the boring stuff before you get started.

TAKE IT OUTSIDE

Rugs work just as well in outdoor locations. Whether you want to achieve decorative or functional impact, you can turn your hand to clever solutions by using unconventional water-resistant materials such as plastic bags, nylon rope or rubber. Apply all your rug-making skills to these common materials and glam up the patio or dress the deck to perfection. Better to make something beautiful than landfill, right?

RAGS TO RICHES

There is a rich history of rag rug-making as part of the pioneering "Make Do and Mend" philosophy. Not just a way of using scraps, rag rugs offer great "accidental" design opportunities from the mix and match nature of their raw materials. Save favorite clothes for deconstruction into raw supplies for braided, crocheted or woven floor rugs, or collect old t-shirts from your family and friends to make bathmats or doormats.

IF WALLS COULD TALK

If you catch the rug bug you may find you've invested so much time and energy into a project that the last thing you want is to have your masterpiece stood on by everyone from the toddler to the neighbor's dog. Many rugs employ beautiful, simple geometrics that make for some spectacular abstract art. Consider hanging them on the wall rather than laying them underfoot for maximum impact and minimum damage.

GET PERSPECTIVE

Designing for the floor is quite different from designing for the wall so you'll need to change your perspective. It can be very helpful to draw a plan and literally put it on the floor and position it and then stand back and have a look before committing to a particular project.

- **Sewing thread:** Choose heavyweight strong polyester or linen.

- **Latch hook:** A special tool with a latch for grabbing yarn.

- **Rug hook:** Similar to a crochet hook but without the latch, for drawing scraps or rug yarn through burlap.

- **Rug yarn:** Comes pre-cut in bundles, or cut your own from double knitting or bulky yarn. Acrylic works well for floor rugs as it is durable and easy to wash.

- **Latch hook canvas:** Stiff specialist open-weave fabric, which you can buy by the yard. It comes with blocks of squares marked on it, making pattern building easy.

- **Burlap**

- **Twill binding tape**

- **Hand-sewing needles**

- **Rotary cutter**

- **Scissors**

- **Cutting mat**

- **Crochet hook**

- **Scrap fabric strips**

BRAIDED RAG RUG

These classic upcyclers are constructed from long strips of fabric that are braided, coiled and then stitched together. Wool, woven cotton and old t-shirts work best. Sew long strips together so you don't have to stop and start too often, but not so long that you get knotted up. An arm's length is a good rule.

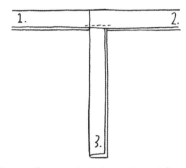

1. For an ultra-neat start, sew two strips of your chosen fabric together with three running stitches. Fold the strip over lengthwise, wrong sides facing. Place the third strip inside the fold. Secure it with a few more running stitches. This will make it much easier to sew the coil together when you form your rug.

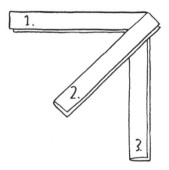

2. To start your braid, fold strip 2 into the center.

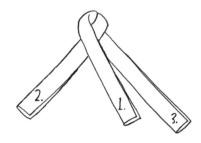

3. Bring strip 1 into the center, followed by strip 3 and so on. It's just like braiding hair.

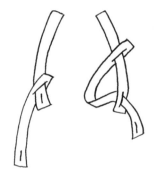

4. Join in new strips of fabric as you go, using the slit feed method: Cut a small slit into the end of the new strip, about ⅝" from the edge and do the same with the strip in your braid. Overlap the ends of your strips so the holes join up. Take the other end of the bottom strip and push it down through both holes, then pull it right through until it flips into a neat join.

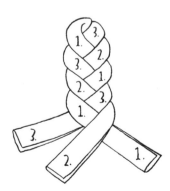

5. Continue braiding, alternating left and right until you have a long braid. You'll end up with a Rapunzel-like braid that you can now coil into a rug.

6. For an oval-shaped rug, take your braid and fold it over so that you have a short side-by-side length. The length will determine the shape of your rug.

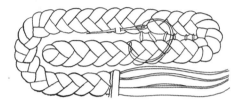

7. Take a double thread on a sharp needle and sew through one inside edge of the braid to attach it to the opposite inside edge of the other braid in your fold.

8. When you make it to the next round you can start threading your needle and thread through the loops of each braid. This helps to keep your rug flat and makes the work go much faster. Be careful, as it will bunch up if you sew too tightly.

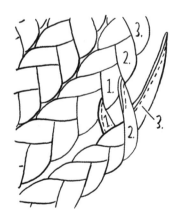

9. To neatly finish, take your three braid ends and fold, then stitch the ends into points. Tuck them under three consecutive loops and stitch in place.

HOOKED RAG RUG

Hooked rugs are made with strips of fabric hooked through a base to create a beautiful soft surface. Burlap, linen and specialty monk's cloth (which has a grid woven into it) can all be used as a base.

Any fabric can be cut into strips for hooked rugs, so look at your existing stash for pieces that can be put to good use. Keep your strips no longer than arm's length or you'll get knotted up. Match your strip width to both hook size and base fabric. Open weaves will need wider strips, and fine weaves will need narrower ones.

WHAT YOU NEED

- Base fabric: burlap
- Marker
- Embroidery hoop or specialist rug frame
- Rug hook
- Strips of fabric
- Scissors

WHAT YOU DO

1. Draw your pattern on your base fabric with a marker. For smaller projects an embroidery hoop can be used. For larger projects use a specialist rug frame to prevent the rug from distorting.

2. Hold your hook in one hand and rag strip in the other.

3. Push your hook through the burlap and use it to grab the fabric strip from underneath.

4. Draw the fabric up through the burlap, so it forms a loop on top.

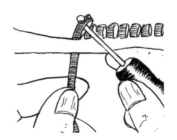

5. Keep drawing the fabric strips through the burlap, making loops on the top as you go and keeping them close together for a dense-pile rug.

6. To keep the height of your loops even, draw each one up taller than the adjacent loop and then pull it back down to match.

7. When you near the end of your fabric strip, pull the tail through so that it sits on the rug top. Start a new strip by pulling it up and through the same hole as your last strip tail. This will keep them both firm and they can be trimmed down when you've finished. Don't worry about the unlooped ends. By the time you've finished they will be invisible.

LATCH HOOK RUG

Latch hook is a slow but effective simple knotted rug technique. If you're into quick results, this may not be the craft for you. Yarn can be bought pre-cut, but you can cut it yourself in lengths of around 2½–3". Single strands of special rug yarn (a little heavier than double knitting) are normally used, but you can create interesting effects by using two or more strands of finer yarn, or even mixing colors.

However, you don't have to limit yourself to yarn. As long as it can make it through the latch hook canvas, it can work. Cutting strips of wool felt is time-consuming but will make up a beautiful and durable latch hook rug.

Latch hook canvas can be bought by the yard and usually comes with a printed grid, making it easier to keep track of rows if you are working to a pattern.

WHAT YOU NEED

- Rug yarn
- Latch hook canvas
- Latch hook

WHAT YOU DO

1. Fold the yarn in half around the latch hook shank, holding both ends of the yarn. Slip the hook under and through a set of the canvas's horizontal threads until the latch on the hook falls open.

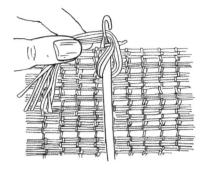

2. Wind the two strands up and around into the hook.

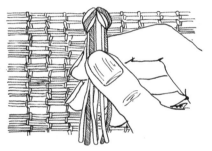

3. As you pull the hook back through the yarn loop and canvas, the latch closes around the yarn and creates a knot around the horizontal canvas thread. Tug on the cut ends to tighten. You now have completed the first stitch of many!

FINISHING TECHNIQUES

All handmade rugs can be hemmed with cotton binding for a neat and durable edge, and both latch hook and hooked rugs benefit from an additional layer of latex or felt as backing.

FRINGE

This simple fringe technique can be added to latch hook and hooked rugs. Make fringe from the same materials as your rug or contrast it with an alternative weight, texture or color.

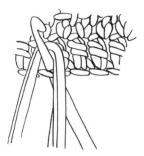

1. Using a minimum of four strands of yarn, cut double the length of your finished fringe. Thread a crochet hook through your rug edge at your starting point.

2. Fold your threads in half and, using your hook, draw them through, from the front of your rug to the back, creating a loop. Pull the strands through the loop to secure.

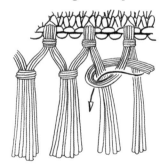

3. Keep your fringe knots evenly spaced as you continue along the edge of the rug. They don't have to go in every stitch. Every second or even third is fine, as long as you're consistent.

4. Once you've finished your single row of fringe, take half of your first fringe knot and half of the adjoining fringe knot and tie them together.

BINDING

You're not going to like this, but we recommend hand-stitching when attaching binding to a rug. It is almost impossible to wrangle a rug any larger than a bathmat through a sewing machine, so settle in and finish your piece off properly.

A wide woven twill tape works best for binding rugs, and you need to use a heavy linen or polyester thread such as upholstery thread for added strength and durability.

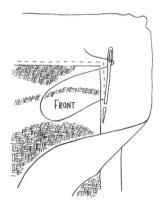

1. First, attach your binding to the front of the rug, using backstitch. This will look the neatest and provide extra strength, which is especially important if the rug is going on the floor.

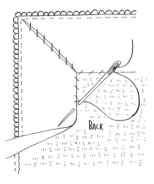

2. Now, fold the binding over to the back of your rug and pin it in place. Sew this side of the binding with a fairly loose stitch, to stop your rug from puckering.

PROJECT IDEAS

→ Old (clean) bed sheets softened by multiple washings make the best beginnings for rag rugs. Just be sure to check with any relevant parties before you take scissors to the linen. You don't want to be the one cutting up Grandma's wedding trousseau.

→ Latch hook rugs are a fantastic way to use up yarn scraps from knitting and crocheted fabrics. Keep a bag handy for these end pieces until you have enough to design a specific plan, or start a random latch hook rug project and let it evolve over time.

→ There are always secondhand or damaged rugs available for next to nix. Try finding some of these pre-loved gems and cut them into strips or squares. Re-assemble them with weaving or patchwork techniques for a modern twist on the rag rug tradition. Adding a bright binding or backing is a perfect unifying process that can bring it all together, or you could try dyeing the whole thing a brand-new hue.

→ Latch rugs made out of terry cloth or waffle-weave cotton make the greatest bathmats you'll ever know — soft and comforting underfoot, incredibly absorbent and easy to wash and dry. Be warned, there will be some initial "shedding" but they will settle into the perfect bathroom accessory with time and use.

→ Can't bear to part with your old Polly Pocket or Pokémon quilt cover but don't want anyone to know? How about those Star Wars curtains or your collection of band t-shirts you can't let go of? Maintain your teenage craze or childhood nostalgia by tearing your collectables into strips for a contemporary-looking braided rug — only you will know the secrets of its sentimental origins.

Color-by-Numbers Rug

WHAT YOU NEED

- 50 balls of double knitting wool or acrylic yarn
- Scissors
- 2 yard latch hook canvas
- Latch hook
- Twill tape

HOT TIP

For this project, we bought balls of an inexpensive wool-blend yarn and cut it ourselves. This takes more time than buying pre-cut yarn but is infinitely cheaper. We used 40 balls in five different colors (eight balls in each color) and 10 balls of our central pale pink. If you want to hang your work up, choose a binding tape wide enough to slip a dowel through so that you can easily make it "wall art" instead of insulation.

We used the printed grid of a latch canvas to build a repeatable design that would work over a variety of lengths, because this is an epic project. Make a bath mat if you get bored easily, or go for a full hall runner if you have the patience. Just remember, if you want to give this as a Christmas present, start in July.

WHAT YOU DO

1. Clear the dining table and start by cutting your yarn into latch threads in each color, so that you have enough to work on for a good couple of hours before stopping to stretch your back and cut more.

2. One of the best things about this project is that once you've mapped out your blocks you really are just filling in the boxes with your yarn, color-by-numbers style. It actually doesn't matter where you start, or how you work, as long as you follow the grid pattern. Match the blocks on the illustration with the grids on your backing and away you go.

3. Pick your starting point and work two threads per latch to fill the block. Keep doing this for about six months if you're working solo, or get yourself a few latch hooks and invite your friends around to have a crack at helping out. It's such a simple technique that it really lends itself to communal crafting.

4. Once you've finally finished (and hurrah for you), bind the edges as described in the Techniques section. We used a wide natural cotton band of twill tape.

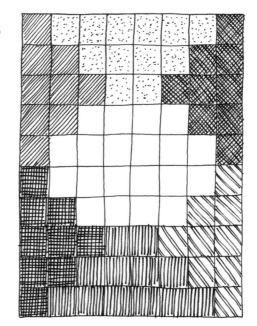

· Stitch ·

Embroidery

◇◇◇

Embroidery is a broad, sprawling family of textile crafts that spreads throughout time, geography and technique. What began as a method of connecting materials by stitches soon extended to embellishment and spread throughout the world in almost endless permutations for thousands of years.

We clothed ourselves for warmth and protection, developed mending techniques to extend the life of our garments and then refined the techniques into decorations for pleasure. Amazingly, there are remnants of hand embroidery that date back to 3000 B.C.E. and illustrative evidence that embroidery existed as a formal craft in China as early as 3500 B.C.E.

The simplicity and portability of embroidery has seen it develop simultaneously worldwide, sometimes in line with the movement of people and sometimes in complete isolation. It has been used to decorate the garments and décor of the ancient superpowers and great empires on every continent, at every stage. From the Persian and Ottoman empires, to the Catholic Church, European royal courts, imperial China, the Indian Raj, feudal Japan and the tribal nobility of Africa, all developed their own distinct embroidery traditions with variations in tastes and application.

Embroidery has long been a significant marker of wealth and status — the luxurious materials and labour-intensive work signifying access to resources and skill. The rise of the European merchant class, many of whom became rich off the back of the textile trade during the Renaissance, also led to their adoption of the visual trappings of wealth, so by the 17th century embroidery had been embraced within genteel society. Everything from curtains to christening gowns was embellished using a range of standardized stitches taught to young girls as part of their deportment and spiritual safety. The ridiculous belief in the proverb "idle hands are the devil's playthings" blended seamlessly with the equally daft idea that busy hands were a way to protect women from hysteria. In the 19th century, embroidery as a leisure activity received a boost when manufacturers began producing embroidery kits, pre-printed with images and patterns, which were sold to a growing middle-class market.

Given its cultural positioning as "busy work" for women, it's not surprising that stitch craft has long been used as a methodology to express social dissidence and feminist protest — from contemporary visual artists such as Louise Bourgeois, Jenny Hart and Tracey Emin, who use the craft to challenge gender, "taste" and cultural norms, to the wall hangings of revolutionary Zapatista, whose embroidered mantras mark Mexico's "Disappeared." The use of "subversive stitching" acts as both a powerful physical reminder of the labour and time dedicated to struggle, and a testament of honor to the lives lost in battle.

In the 1950s American custom tailor Nudie Cohn developed a brilliantly flamboyant rodeo style of embroidery and beading that was quickly adopted by musicians including Elvis Presley, Gram Parsons and Elton John, firmly cementing the craft into the pop culture lexicon in a relationship that is referenced to this day.

Embroidery is still created within the bounds of its rich and diverse history — as couture, craft and commerce — but more and more visual artists are taking up the needle and thread alongside their pens and paintbrushes to create amazingly detailed and tactile artworks, adding their own culture and aesthetics into the living continuum of the craft.

CONTEMPORARY ARTISTS

TAKASHI IWASAKI
Japan

Canadian-based Takashi Iwasaki has built a worldwide reputation for his hand-embroidered intergalactic abstract landscapes. In a kaleidoscope of super-saturated hues he painstakingly "paints" in satin stitch, bringing subtle, unexpected texture to the collection of tendrilled amoebic forms that inhabit his works. Both giddy and naïve, his pieces seem ready to spring to life.

 takashiiwasaki.info

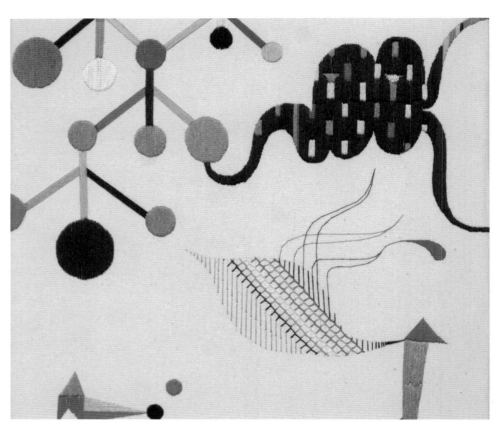

DANIEL KORNRUMPF
United States

Massachusetts-based fiber artist and painter Daniel Kornrumpf could be described as the Chuck Close of embroidery, such is the incredible attention to detail in his approach to portraiture. However, instead of Close's super-sized hyper-photorealism executed with paint, Kornrumpf uses embroidery floss to exquisitely render miniature snapshots of local hipsters.

danielkornrumpf.com

ANA TERESA BARBOZA
Peru

The work of Spanish artist Ana Teresa Barboza can be confronting. Described by some as animals behaving badly, her work combines highly detailed pencil drawings with appliqué and embroidery. In both flat and 3-D works, Barboza plays with perception and expectation, confounding both in pieces that perfectly align content and technique. Subjects include attack dogs, stray businessmen falling foul to jungle luncheons, and lustful lions devouring their loved ones.

 anateresabarboza.blogspot.com.au

AMANDA VALDEZ
United States

Brooklyn-based Amanda Valdez's bold graphic approach to embroidery adds dimensional depth to both the surface and content of her paintings. Brilliantly taking advantage of the nap of satin stitch, she creates areas that catch the light and create patterns that shimmer in and out of view as you move around the work.

 amandavaldez.com

NIKE SCHROEDER
United States

"Embroidery illustrator" is probably the best title for German-born, Los Angeles-based artist Nike Schroeder. She uses machine embroidery to create beautifully delicate portraits of friends, family and bystanders caught in candid moments. By allowing the ends of the threads to hang long beyond the frame, she evokes the melancholy of "the frozen moment" and gives her pieces a strange sense of transient movement, like seeing an image through a moving curtain or cut glass.

 nikeschroeder.com

JOSE ROMUSSI
Chile

Collage artist and embroidery whiz Jose Romussi is the perfect embodiment of contemporary art practice — interested in everything and constantly on the lookout for new ways to express his artistic vision. His collection of embroidered vintage ballet photographs quickly infiltrated the Web, making him, or at least his artwork, a household name in new media circles. Romussi's use of embroidery within his collage and collaborative portraits adds a simple graphic element that elevates the images from the 2-D plane.

 joseromussi.com

MARICOR/MARICAR
Australia

This Australian design duo take the sampler format to new graphic heights with their embroidered fonts. Working with an international client base, they fuse oddball humor and mad skills to create a lettering and illustration style wholly their own. Absolute genius.

 maricormaricar.com

LAUREN DICIOCCIO
United States

Lauren DiCioccio is a textile artist whose skill seemingly knows no bounds. In mind-bendingly intricate replicas of everyday-life detritus she draws attention to the tactile associations of these disappearing analog items and media, while reminding us of the many positives of digital technology. DiCioccio uses her simple needle and thread to ask complex, salient questions about what might happen to our species if we lose touch with objects as we exit the Industrial Age.

laurendicioccio.com

DESIGN NOTES

BASE NOTES

Your choice of base cloth can transform your embroidery. Consider washing raw linen or cotton with fabric paint or ink, or roughly painting on your design before stitching over the top. Block out areas of patterned fabric with single colors and create the illusion of patchwork. This kind of approach does dual service, giving the work more interest as well as creating a loose stitch guide. BONUS!

BEAUTIFULLY FLAWED

Stitch work tied to repair has spawned a rich array of decorative darning techniques. The Japanese art of boro features heavily patched indigo-dyed fabrics held together with heavy sashiko stitching, embodying the wabi sabi philosophy in a perfect marriage of form and function. Try visible mending techniques such as weaving with embroidery thread on the surface of fabric to turn flaw to feature.

REPEATING YOURSELF

Using repeat patterns is a simple but effective way of building a design. It's also fantastic for perfecting stitches. Practice really does make perfect! The power of repetition is undeniable and while all-over patterning is time-consuming it delivers maximum impact. If you're pressed for time, try a concentrated section of detailed repeats, such as a border of French knots.

THINK BIG

Embroidery motifs and patterns are traditionally made at a small scale; however, there is no reason you can't think big. Enlarge a single design element to a super-scale placement detail or amplify a traditional embroidery pattern across a large piece of fabric — the results will astound you.

BACKWARD GLANCES

The history of hand embroidery is full of variety. Whitework, blackwork, gold work, crewel work, ribbon embroidery and stump work have all come in and gone out of fashion, and are amazingly distinct and well worth mining for their aesthetic and technical variations. Do a little research and add some old-school knowledge to your new-school designs.

TRUE NATURE

Traditionally, embroidery artists have been inspired by nature, but urban dwellers can also draw inspiration from their own environments. The repetition and pattern found in skyscraper windows, cobblestoned alleyways, pavement cracks or even your kitchen drawers all have enormous potential for embroidery motifs.

GLITZ THAT FITS

There's no end to the embellishments that can be added to embroidery. You may be tempted to include everything from bows to crystals to ramp up the glam. However, we're going to look you in the eye and give it to you straight. If you can pull off the perfect pitch of Bob Mackie meets Rhinestone Cowboy, go for it — but be warned, you may end up bedazzling your work straight into pageant territory instead. We advise getting off the tinsel train before you reach kitschville.

TOOLS

Embroidery is essentially drawing or painting in thread. Just as an artist has their palette, brushes and paint, the modern embroiderer needs their own selection of thread, needles and fabric to stitch up great works of craft.

- **Needles:** Sharp tips and large eyes are the important elements of embroidery needles, but it is wise to use a blunter tapestry needle for more open weaves such as linen. Have a variety of needles on hand, and a good place to store them, and remember the golden rule: fine needle for fine thread, large needle for ribbon or yarn.

- **Embroidery hoops:** Embroidery hoops are made up of two interlocking circular frames made from wood, plastic or metal that hold your fabric taut while you stitch. The wooden ones are great as they can double as a frame for your finished work, and can easily be painted, decorated and hung. Some embroiderers prefer not working with hoops but we highly recommend it, especially for "in front of TV" embroidery.

- **Fabrics:** Most fabrics take well to embroidery, especially those with a visible weave structure. Cotton, wool and linen are the best, and felt (despite its density) is also a great base for all kinds of thread-based embellishment. You can also embroider existing garments and accessories. Shirt collars, skirt hems, pockets, totes, purses, tea towels and pillowcase edges are perfect starting points for your embroidery.

- **Transfer paper:** For years transfer paper was THE method of choice for conveying drawn ideas or patterns to fabric, but these days it's a lot harder to come by. As the name suggests, you place the paper colored side down, in between the fabric and the design, and use a sharp pen or pencil to trace around the design, thereby transferring the image straight onto your fabric as a guide.

- **Heat transfer pencil:** We love heat transfer pencils! You can draw any image onto tracing paper, turn it face down onto your fabric and then iron on the image. Remember that the design will be reversed using this method so take care with text, as you'll need to work in a mirrored image.

- **Disappearing-ink pen:** Disappearing-ink pens can be used to draw directly onto the fabric. The ink will fade with time or, in some cases, when you add water. These pens can be a little dubious to work with as you may need to redraw your design regularly while working to avoid losing it altogether. Best used for small projects.

- **Embroidery scissors:** Invest in these small, sharp scissors as they allow a great deal of control and precision when cutting. Under no circumstances are they to double as nail scissors. Trust us.

- **Embroidery floss (stranded cotton):** The most popular type of embroidery thread, floss comes in an array of silk, cotton, rayon, matte, pearl, gloss and metallic, in colors that are seriously drool-inducing. But not all floss is created equal. You can pick up really cheap, bulk packs of thread but this may end up costing you your sanity.

TECHNIQUES

RUNNING STITCH

The most basic of stitches. Used in many embroidery projects.

BACK STITCH

The needle is inserted backwards to meet the previous stitch, then brought up ahead. Great for solid outlines. Gives a robust, clean line.

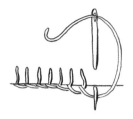

BLANKET STITCH

A decorative edging stitch that is fantastic for finishing textile projects. We love it for the edge of felt and knit work.

CHAIN STITCH

A versatile linked stitch that works well for filling in large sections as well as outlines. Gives a beautiful texture.

FRENCH KNOT

This little knot is easy once you master keeping the tension. Great for masses of expressive color or highlights.

SPLIT STITCH

Tricky to master but gives a great strong, solid line. Great for more illustrative embroidery work.

STEM STITCH

Perfect for curvy lines and floral shapes, and yes, stems. Important to keep the stitches close and even.

SATIN STITCH

This is made up of parallel stitches forming a satiny texture. Often used to fill small motifs. Also known as damask stitch.

LONG AND SHORT STITCH

Useful for filling areas too large for satin stitch. Great for gradations of color, creating more realistic images as you can make subtle changes in light.

PROJECT IDEAS

→ A mass of French knots in different shades of blue, radiating from dark to light, is labour-intensive but is undeniably appealing. Working with both repetition and texture, the surface patterning will result in a multi-dimensional ombré effect. You'll also get extra bonus points for becoming a French knot expert by the end of the project.

→ Mix geometry, nostalgia and embroidery together as a form of modern memory keeping. Take your own piece of personal ephemera (postcard, ticket, photograph) and, using needle or awl, punch holes in a simple geometric motif to stitch through. Complete the look by using color-coordinated thread.

→ Transform an unusual subject with the power of stitch work. Drill small holes into the back of a wooden chair and embroider a favorite lyric, whether intergalactic hip-hop or Norwegian black metal — you're only limited by your imagination and record collection.

→ Children's artwork is the perfect inspiration for embroidery design. Scan a favorite artwork and print it onto t-shirt transfer paper, iron onto canvas or linen and follow the image in stitches to turn the drawing into a textile masterpiece for framing, patches or soft furnishing. The coolest co-lab ever!

→ Embroidery has a strong tradition as a subversive form of protest. Radicalize your wardrobe with the symbols and speeches of revolution inside the collar of your favorite shirt or lining of a jacket, or wear your heart and politics literally on your sleeve.

Hooped Hipster Portrait

WHAT YOU NEED

- Embroidery hoop (10" diameter)
- Small paintbrush
- Black and white acrylic paint
- Masking or washi tape
- Spray varnish
- Approx. 1 yard of cotton fabric (to allow for mistakes), pre-washed and ironed
- Scissors
- Iron-on photo transfer paper
- Printer
- Iron
- White card
- Colored pencils
- Gray lead pencil
- Needle
- Embroidery floss/thread in a variety of colors

HOT TIP

We ain't gonna lie, transfer paper can be kind of mean. Read the instructions carefully. Make sure you pick a linen or cotton fabric so it can be ironed hot without damage. The extra material is to allow for mistakes with the transfer paper. Everything else is a doddle!

Create your very own embroidered artwork using a black and white photograph that has been heat-transferred onto fabric. Make one or make a series, use a couple for a perfect wedding or anniversary gift, or nerd up your favorite little person for a family portrait that even Wes Anderson would approve of.

WHAT YOU DO

1. Paint the outer ring of the hoop frame. Freestyle the stripes or paint white first, then mask off areas at regular intervals and paint black over the whole thing. When dry, remove tape to reveal stripes. Give your stripy hoop a light spray of gloss varnish to protect it and give it a nice finish.

2. Measure your cotton against the hoop and cut a section at least 2" larger than your hoop diameter.

3. Print out your portrait image in black and white on the transfer paper using your home printer, then, carefully following the manufacturer's instructions, transfer the image to the cotton.

4. Take some time to practice drawing and coloring bow ties using your card and colored pencils. Once you're happy with your bow tie, cut it out, position it on your transfer and gently trace around it using the gray lead pencil.

5. Using a simple satin stitch, fill in your bow tie with your chosen pattern. We chose balanced stripes for a rainbow effect, but spots would also work well, and a party hat or a mustache would also look ace.

6. Trim away the excess fabric from around your hoop. To hang your portrait, carefully screw cup hooks into the back or use the top screw bracket as an anchor for ribbon or string. Or you can just lean your portrait on a shelf and enjoy your handiwork!

THE ES●SENTIAL DAVID SHRIG

ARNASON

A HISTORY OF
MODERN ART
PAINTING · SCULPTURE · ARCHITECTURE

The Encyclopedia of
WORLD SEA POWER

Cross stitch

◇◇◇

Cross stitch has always played a significant part in the embroidery library. A simple counted stitch applied to woven fabric, it has been seen on garments, furniture and accessories since the 12th century. Not just a decorative stitch but also a practical one, as it strengthens the fabric, cross stitch spread along the Silk Road through China, Pakistan, Persia and Egypt, and it appears within the folk craft lexicon of nearly all these countries. By the time it hit Europe, the entire world was embellishing with this neat little stitch — from the Hmong people of Thailand to the Huayao of China, throughout Central Europe and the Americas, each continent adding its own chapter to the collective cross stitch library.

Before the Industrial Revolution gave birth to consumer culture, things were built to last. Using cross stitch on soft furnishings and garments served a dual purpose — showing off skill and status and lengthening an object's lifespan. But it wasn't just the strength of the stitch that built its appeal. Cross stitch's graphic simplicity readily lent itself to the easy creation and repetition of motifs, engendering a common design language among communities. These languages have since become synonymous with particular regions and cultures, and many of them remain unchanged, still practiced or "spoken" to this day.

In the West these kinds of patterns were maintained as samplers that could be kept with sewing supplies. These developed into simple templates, used to teach young girls stitching, numeracy and literacy skills. Throughout 18th- and 19th-century Europe, girls would have completed at least one major sampler piece as part of their education into the domestic crafts. Traditionally these included the alphabet, a row of numbers and decorative borders, but they often featured an image of the family home or county, their name and a significant date. In a world where women's ancestral lineage disappeared with marriage these samplers have become important genealogical documents.

Taking advantage of new print technologies and a hungry hobby market, cross stitch kits became popular in the 1920s. Simple charts were developed and included in women's magazines with wide distribution, and soon the resurgence of cross stitch as a domestic craft was complete. In the 1950s iron-on transfers became readily available, making it even easier to transfer the newly fashionable graphic designs of Scandinavia and floral and bird motifs of Chinese textiles directly into the suburban home.

In the context of today's craft culture, cross stitch is more than holding its own. Its graphic nature, simplicity of technique and association with language have seen it radicalized both in content and practice. Politically based craft groups, such as Radical Cross Stitch in Australia and Subversive Cross Stitch in the US, have used it to express feminist ideology, while makers such as Britain's Mr. X Stitch represent a new generation of men making the craft their own. Easily accessible and quickly learned, it's rapidly becoming a favorite again among artists and designers who are making use of its pixelated construction to fashion their own sampler images. Cross stitch could well be the perfect analogue technology for the digital age, as "X" most definitely marks the spot.

DIANE MEYER
United States

Diane Meyer makes us look and then look again. Taking seemingly innocuous photographs of people and places of personal significance, she painstakingly cross stitches sections over the image, changing the nature of the object from inane to interesting, or protecting the anonymity of the subject along the way, changing the viewer's interaction with the image. Nostalgia is pixelated, memory out of focus and hindsight providing only peripheral vision as some details are lost and others highlighted.

 dianemeyer.net

DAVE LIESKE
United States

Dave Lieske blows our minds. His work is a master class in how to seamlessly blend the old and new schools in the most literal of ways, using a combination of the aesthetic cues of domestic cross stitch samplers and the cultural references of graffiti and hip-hop's finest. Effortlessly rocking the embroidery needle like a grandmaster DJ does a 1200, Lieske creates work that is so rich with crossbred connections and subversive gender play it makes you wonder why no one has ever thought of it before.

daveygravy.ca

EVELIN KASIKOV
Britain

Evelin Kasikov's work is firmly grounded in a graphic design sensibility. Re-thinking the craft from an analytical and intellectual point of view led her to develop her CMYK embroidery technique, using these classic commercial printing building blocks (cyan, magenta, yellow, key/black) to create stitched fonts and images that have been used by both commercial clients and Kasikov for fine art and design projects. Kasikov has brought handworked elements, textures and processes back into increasingly digital design methodologies.

 evelinkasikov.com

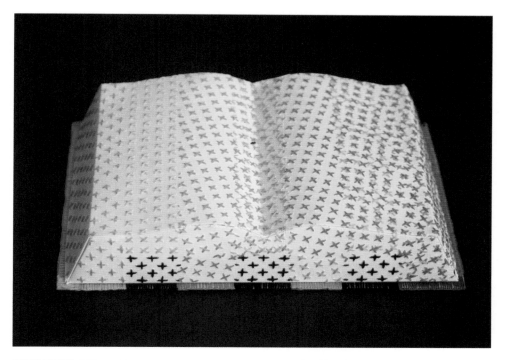

INGE JACOBSEN
Britain

High fashion meets feminist discourse meets domestic craft in the work of London-based artist Inge Jacobsen. Her cross-stitched covers neatly converge gender politics, contemporary media, cultural concepts of beauty and technical virtuosity in astonishingly complex pieces that deliberately challenge notions of complicity and commerce. Commissioned by high-end luxury brands and publications, she navigates an intriguingly complex world of contradictory positions and political posturing with assured aplomb and super skills.

ingejacobsen.com

DESIGN NOTES

X MARKS THE SPOT

Essentially anything that has regular holes on it can be cross stitched. And anything you can drill holes into can be cross stitched. We've seen chair backs, fly-screens, peg-board, garden lattice, fencing, outdoor furniture and rattan screens all successfully cross stitched. The key is even holes, because even holes equals even stitching. So don't limit yourself to fabric alone. As long as you can get a needle and thread through it, you can whip up a sampler on just about any surface.

GRAY SCALE

While tiny colored stitches are the accepted norm for working cross stitch, we're always in favor of flipping convention on its head. Approach your palette like a black and white photo for a simple way of renewing the aesthetic, or work up super-graphic patterns, contemporary handmade fonts, graffiti and tags. You'll be making the most of Middle European folk aesthetics while putting your own stamp on things.

SUPER-SIZE ME

Don't be afraid of up-sizing your projects from tiny stitches to wall-sized works. Big is sometimes better. Instead of cross stitching a cushion, why not cross stitch a whole couch? To make things easier on yourself, and maybe finish the project in your lifetime, super-size your stitches as well as your background.

PIXEL POWER

If you start feeling like you've slipped through a wormhole and landed in a Victorian parlor while you're cross stitching, fear not. Cross stitch is perfectly suited to the digital age because it's actually textile pixel art. Think one pixel per stitch and you'll be cross stitching a Minecraft landscape before you know it. Just beware of zombies and creepers.

GET THE MESSAGE

Cross stitch was traditionally used for creating samplers that featured text. Both historically and technically language translates really well into cross stitch, making it a pitch-perfect craft for lyrics, slogans and political rabble-rousing. Take time out to think about what you want to say and then commit it to stitch. "Home Sweet Home" might be classically stitch-worthy, but so is "I am the 99%."

LEARN TO COUNT

Cross stitch is perfect if you have a "math brain." But even if you don't, you can still follow a pattern, or work up your own. Take advantage of the blocks in graph paper to draw your design, then enlarge the patterns with a photocopier. This makes it easier to read in chunks and lets you tick off rows as you go. It may seem pedestrian but trust us, it will make it much easier to find your place if you get too absorbed in the latest episode of *Girls*.

STITCH IN TIME

You don't need to be tied to actual thread work to make use of the cross stitch aesthetic. So deeply ingrained is the craft in our collective creative histories that many artists use drawn or printed versions of cross stitch as a design device for everything from font development to textile repeats. Carve a simple cross into a rubber block and use it for borders, placement prints or wall-sized stencil art. Some may call it cheating but we call it creative "pattern-making."

- **Embroidery thread:** The most popular is embroidery floss, or stranded cotton, but there are many others, such as pearl cotton and Persian wool yarn. Use cotton or silk, or linen or wool if you're working on a cloth such as burlap.

- **Aida cloth:** Stiff, mesh-like cotton that's manufactured specifically for cross stitch. It comes in a variety of sizes based on how many stitches cover 1 inch (2.5 cm). 10-count Aida has 10 stitches per inch (2.5 cm). It traditionally comes in white or cream but can be dyed fairly easily.

- **Evenweave:** Loosely any fabric with the same number of warp and weft threads per cm or inch, but especially fine linen and cotton plain weaves produced specifically for cross stitch and other counted-thread embroidery. Stitches are worked over two or more threads, producing a more polished effect that on Aida cloth.

- **Waste canvas and soluble fabric:** Gives you the best of both worlds. Tack it to your evenweave fabric and then use it like Aida cloth. It will provide a clear gridded guide for your stitching. When you're done you can remove the waste fabric thread by thread; with soluble fabric, it just washes away. Great for putting cross stitch motifs on garments.

- **Cross stitch designs:** Either commercial or homemade.

- **Tapestry needles**

- **Sharp scissors**

- **Grid pattern paper**

- **Embroidery hoop**

- **Pencils**

- **Indelible marker**

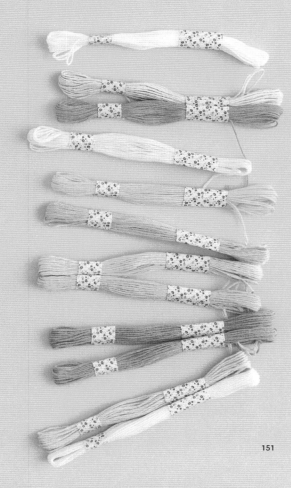

PREPARING THREAD

If you're using embroidery floss, there are usually six threads twisted into one, so you'll probably need to separate the strands and use just two or three, depending on your fabric. A kit will specify the number of strands, but if you're designing your own pattern, experiment on spare fabric to see what works best. Or you can try using a single thicker thread such as pearl cotton.

FINDING THE CENTER

To help you with placement, charts will often mark the position of the center stitch on the fabric. To find the center of your fabric, fold it into four and mark the fold point with a washable fabric marker. This is your center. Some cross stitchers also like to put a row of running stitches along the center line to keep track of it. We don't, but do whatever works for you.

HOW TO START

There is a general consensus that knots in cross stitch are bad news. They cause lumps and distort your work. However, knots have their uses. This technique is a great way to start as it helps anchor your thread without adding bulk or distortion, and is cut off the finished piece, leaving you knot free.

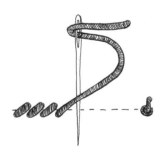

1. Knot your thread and feed it through your fabric so the knot is on the front. Carry your thread along the back and up through the fabric to the front. Then start stitching your row.

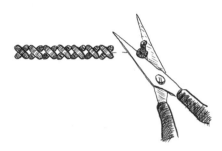

2. Once you have a few stitches in place, snip the knot off and you'll have automatically anchored your thread. Genius.

STITCHING ON AIDA CLOTH

There are two standard approaches to applying cross stitch to Aida cloth. They both get you from A to B. Figure out which one works best for you and stick with it throughout the project for consistency's sake.

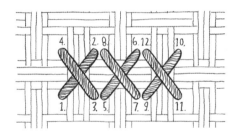

Method 1 — Complete each stitch one at a time across your fabric, using the numbers to guide you.

Method 2 — Sew a row of half stitches along the whole row, then go back and complete.

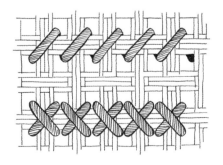

STITCHING ON EVENWEAVE

Just as with cross stitching on Aida cloth, the same principle applies to evenweave, although Method 1 is a bit trickier to pull off successfully. A quick way to check that you're on the right track is to look at the back of your work. Consistent stitching will be clearly evident. But don't panic too much if your first efforts are wonky; only the worst kind of people will judge you by looking at the back of your work. Ultimately, the best way to find what works best for you is to experiment with all base fabrics and stitch processes.

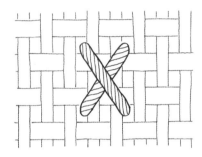

Method 1 — Take each stitch over two threads instead of one. Some find that this makes this method a little more challenging but it does produce a very neat stitch.

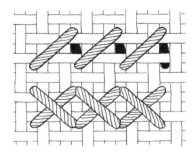

Method 2 — Create half stitches along the row. This can help make stitches more even throughout the work.

READING A CROSS STITCH CHART

Cross stitch charts are relatively simple as long as you remember that one square equals one cross stitch. Charts include a thread guide that shows what color embroidery thread to buy to match the design. If you suffer from poor eyesight take the time to enlarge the design on a photocopier first. It'll make your life MUCH easier.

Published cross stitch charts mean you don't have to make your own. This can be a great help when starting out but the options are fairly limited and mostly dated. Unlike contemporary embroidery and needlepoint kits, cross stitch designs (save those of the subversive stitch variety) are yet to be dragged into the 21st century. Thankfully, what has developed in the place of commercial designs is an endless array of brilliant new ideas, from Tardis to Tutankhamen, all easily found online.

WORK HINTS

Start simple, stay relaxed and keep a light and a close eye on your work. Stop tears and tantrums from ruining your day by reading the instructions carefully before you start. Cross stitch is all about rhythm. Keep a steady beat and you'll keep your stitches even. If you need to separate floss threads, do it one strand at a time to avoid twists and tangles. Use heavier threads or more strands of floss on darker backgrounds to ensure they stand out. Use only as much thread as you can pull easily. Longer lengths tend to tangle and you'll end up with embroiderer's elbow. A "wrist to elbow" length is ideal.

PROJECT IDEAS

→ Gingham is a traditional base fabric for cross stitch. We're particularly fond of an old-school gingham apron but if that's not your style you could plot out a chart for a tablecloth centerpiece or work a border around napkins or placemats for some vintage kitchen kitsch.

→ Buy or upcycle a set of plain dinner plates using ceramic markers to draw a cross stitch pattern food slogan. "Let's eat," "More please," "Where's the bacon?" or even "You do win friends with salad," would all be great mealtime conversation starters.

→ Change the scale of cross stitch by using gridded latch-hook rug canvas and soft stripped leather to cross-stitch a doormat or bedside rug. Geometric shapes are easy, while more complex patterns provide a decent challenge for experienced crafters.

→ Grab an old magazine and choose a full-page famous face for a cross-stitch makeover. Photocopy your image onto iron-on transfer paper and apply it to a unbleached muslin backing cloth. Then carefully cross-stitch over an important element using the photograph as a color-by-numbers guide. Stick to the picture or add in "special features" you think they should be sporting. (Yes, this includes mustaches and man-buns.)

→ Turn a tiny cross stitch pattern into a wall-size artwork. Blow up your pattern on a photocopier, match it against a bright piece of burlap and draw it in as a guide. Stretch your fabric over the frame and staple it in place so you can use it like an embroidery hoop to maintain tension. Use double knitting yarn to cross stitch your design. Voilà — instant art.

X Marks the Spot

WHAT YOU NEED

- Gingham garment ready for embroidering
- 9½" embroidery hoop
- Sharp embroidery needle
- 2 skeins of yellow cotton embroidery floss (stranded cotton)
- Scissors

Combining vintage kitchen kitsch with minimalist Mori style, we've made a perfect mash-up garment of our favorite things. This oversize t-shirt uses gingham checks as a grid for a super-sized, easy-to-achieve cross stitch feature.

WHAT YOU DO

1. Take your embroidery hoop and position it in the place you want your detail. We centered ours on the front panel 3" from the neckline. Remember to grab only the front of your shirt when doing this. You may want to put your garment on to double-check that your circle is in the right spot.

2. Tighten the fabric to obtain even tension right across your stitching surface.

3. Thread your needle with the embroidery floss using the wrist to elbow ratio. Starting from the bottom left, work a cross stitch on every second square.

4. Continue this process for your first row and then start the second row on the alternate square so you create a step pattern. We started on the black square and alternated it with the white squares to make it easier to see what we were doing. The edges of your stitches on both squares will start to neatly match up.

5. Don't be concerned if you can't get into the edges to make a perfect circle with the hoop on. You can easily even up your pattern once it's off the hoop. Remember, this is a gridded pattern on a large scale, so it will be a squared-off pixelated version rather than a seamless circle shape.

6. Once you've filled the circle, take the hoop off and fill in any extra squares necessary to make sure both sides are symmetrical, and you're done.

HOT TIP

If you're wondering where to place your circle, put your garment on and move your embroidery hoop around until it's in the right spot. Get a (close) friend to fit the other part of the hoop to the inside of your garment and you are ready to roll. We've chosen to do it on a large-scale check but the principle is the same no matter what size squares you're working with.

Needlepoint

◇◇◇

Needlepoint has long been popular as a domestic craft as well as a fashion and interior design technique. There is evidence of a similar technique being practiced in ancient Egypt, which just goes to show how much people can achieve without viral kitten videos to distract them. But it was in the grand houses of 16th-century Europe that needlepoint really blossomed into the multi-threaded beast we know today.

The terminology surrounding this kind of needlework is a bit of a minefield. In Britain it's traditionally been called tapestry because it was originally used to imitate true (woven) tapestry. In the US it has long been called needlepoint and now that term has started to colonize the rest of the world. Professional embroiderers, at least in Britain, still tend to call it canvaswork or canvas embroidery since it consists of stitches worked on canvas, usually covering the entire surface.

Needlepoint's first significant starring role was a heady mix of social status and skill. Artisans were employed by the aristocracy and wealthy merchant classes to create large-scale works depicting the family's noble deeds, both real and imagined. These textile billboards would adorn walls in much the same way as tapestries did, acting simultaneously as insulation and self-promotion. Their luxurious use of rare materials and specialist labour became a symbol of opulence, refinement and wealth.

More often, needlepoint was used to adorn smaller items such as furniture, purses, cushions and table covers. Designs were usually ecclesiastical or inspired by nature. It wasn't until the opening up of trade routes in the 17th century that the design influence of the world beyond European borders was reflected in needlepoint production.

The early 19th century saw the first needlepoint designs for home crafters published in Germany, and this quickly became the most widespread and popular engagement with the craft. These products were aimed at the middle class and scaled specifically for parlor craft. They represent the birthplace of the printed needlepoint

canvases that dominate the craft today, from Fragonard's seminally furtive *The Swing* to the classic 1970s stormy sea stallion.

As a domestic craft this kind of needlepoint is as much maligned as embraced by different groups within the craft community. These color-by-number projects are attempted and abandoned in almost equal measure, even among their most devoted supporters. Despite its simplicity, the commitment needed to complete larger works can sometimes get the better of people's best intentions. Contemporary crafters are reclaiming these discarded works to make new objects or re-thinking their context in new projects. In 2009 American artist and educator Mary Spull began purchasing unfinished needlepoints and completing them with white thread. Her ingenious "Society for the Prevention of Unfinished Needlepoint" was a witty and heartfelt project that spoke of the guilt associated with what we now somewhat optimistically call "works in progress."

It must be said that the domestic crafter can sometimes feel held hostage by commercial needlepoint kit designers and producers. It's a rare thing to take the time to design your own. With unprinted needlepoint canvases readily available, now is the time to break free of the constraints of existing patterns and designs. Take cues from contemporary artists who are re-embracing the technique to give the same rich, full surface coverage of a painting, and matching it with the lush, textured surface of a textile to translate ideas and visual language using needle and thread.

ANDONI MAILLARD
France

Conflating bucolic French landscapes with monster trucks is just a small part of the genius of Andoni Maillard. It would be easy to dismiss his low-brow interventions into traditional tapestry as the visual equivalent of the one-liner. However, the attention to detail in content selection and execution shown in his textile works really makes him one to watch. With his cross-stitched "soft" porn and skateboard decks he offers socio-political commentary and lateral pathways between the hobby culture of decorative "busywork" and less refined populist pastimes.

 andonimy-art.com

NICOLE GASTONGUAY
United States

Nicole Gastonguay has a terrific sense of humor and a keen eye for pathos. In addition to her crocheted work, she uses plastic canvas needlepoint to create a rainbow-hued world where toasters, boomboxes, cameras, pickles and gumball machines are all imbued with a very particular kind of urban neurosis. She transforms a much-maligned technique with advanced technical proficiency, amigurumi aesthetics and the judicious use of googly eyes, while gleefully mashing up a tasty variety of essential pop references and serving them hot.

nicolegastonguay.com

MICHELLE HAMER
Australia

Michelle Hamer's needlepoints are all about communication. They invite us to look into the mundane and quite literally read the signs. Taking inspiration from work symbols, road signs, graffiti and billboards, these pixelated photo-realistic textiles pull us up to the bumper at the dullest intersections and worst roadblocks. While stuck in this psychological traffic, we can take comfort in alternative meanings, even if the missive reads "slowing down won't kill you."

 michellehamer.com

JACQUELYN ROYAL
United States

As with so many contemporary textile artists, Jacquelyn Royal mines the rich associative culture and gender politics of the medium, subverting them through dissonant subject matter seemingly at odds with its historical interpretations. There is something completely traditional, however, in choosing the landscape as the subject of needlepoint, even when plugged into the aesthetics of urban decay. Royal's keen compositional eye and understanding of the rhythms of color, pattern and scale elevate the everyday and overlooked, translating them into refined moments of contemplation.

 jacquelynroyal.com

DESIGN NOTES

BEG, BORROW, STEAL

As cheesy as some needlepoint kits are, they are goldmines for motifs and images to plunder for your own original work. From rococo ladies in waiting to rose-clutching leopards, think laterally and you can find the perfectly ironic or just plain perfect design elements. Create a patchwork pastiche from multiple kits to make one wild new narrative or swap the indicated colors for monochrome or super-bright alternatives. Throw out the rule book, take the best and leave the rest!

CLOCKS TICKING

Needlepoint is an incredibly labour-intensive craft, and it takes a significant amount of time before you feel as though you're getting anywhere. Even after three hours of heavy-duty stitching you may step back and barely notice a difference. Don't be discouraged, but do plan ahead. Start projects with plenty of time in your kitty if you have deadlines to meet. The upside comes with the longevity of the outcome. Many hours will go into your work but you'll be making a textile to last a lifetime.

HAPPY TRAILS

There is a very good reason why so much needlepoint is done on open canvas or plastic frames. Anyone who's done a little of this craft will attest to the pain and suffering that comes from trying to pull your threads evenly through fabric that is too tight. If you're going off script (and off canvas), do a little testing and make sure your needle and chosen thread can travel smoothly through it repeatedly and evenly. Loose weaves in sturdy fibers such as linen or burlap are going to give you a lot more love than fine gauze — ignore this advice and you'll end up in knots.

SHUTTERBUG

The pixelated nature of needlepoint construction, where single stitches collectively build up a complete picture, has significant parallels with digital photography. Marry this textile technology with your own photography and you can create your very own color by numbers. Either print out simplified versions of digital images and hand-color your backing cloth, or print straight onto cloth for a pixel-perfect portrait.

IT'S ELEMENTARY

Needlepoint origins are just as tied to decorative repeats such as Bargello as they are to kitsch landscapes. Taking a single illustrative element and turning it into a stitched repeat can lend your work a hypnotic dynamism. Fill in around your singular elements with solid color to make them really pop up against tonal patterned grids that reference op art. Needlepoint is a useful, if often laboriously slow, way of re-imagining textile patterns in a new and tactile way that's perfect for high-traffic use.

PLASTIC FANTASTIC

There are now many plastic canvas shapes that are commercially available and which lend themselves perfectly to 3-D construction. Not only are they simple to stitch on because of their uniform rigidity, these lightweight, tough and inexpensive bases are also easily sewn into shapes that allow multifaceted viewing opportunities to showcase your stitching skills.

- **Plastic canvas:** This rigid canvas comes with gridded holes in a variety of different counts, which indicate how many holes there are per inch (2.5 cm) of canvas. The canvas comes in different shapes and large rectangular sheets that can be cut with a craft knife. Because of its durability, it is perfect for 3-D construction projects such as our Bangin' Bargello Basket at the end of the chapter.

- **Needlepoint canvas:** This comes in a variety of forms, all with their own pros and cons. Mono canvas is woven from single threads, with the most popular counts ranging from 7 to 18 threads per inch (2.5 cm). Interlock canvas is like mono except that its weft threads are actually double and are split around the warp threads to lock them in place. Double-thread canvas (delightfully called Penelope) is sized according to the number of holes between thread pairs per inch. Its threads can be separated and worked over individually for fine detail. We recommend starting with a 10-count canvas.

- **Embroidery frame (optional):** You may prefer to use a frame to keep your work from distorting but we like the portability of going without.

- **Needlepoint yarn:** It's easy to be seduced by the rainbow of delicious skeins of wool but be warned — it is a pretty expensive option. We've found using a good-quality pure double knitting wool yarn from the knitting aisle is a far more economical way to go.

- **Needlepoint thread**

- **Tapestry needles**

- **Scissors**

- **Needle threader (optional)**

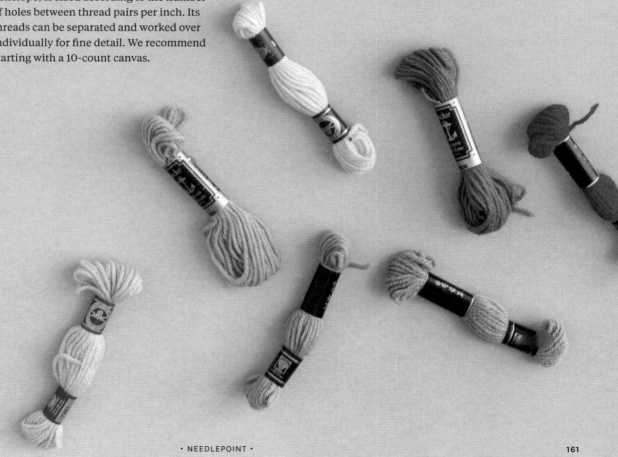

STITCHES

When it comes to needlepoint, there are enough stitch variations to fill this book a couple of times over. However, there are a few key basics that will quickly get you moving on your first needlepoint adventure. If you're starting a large needlepoint using a frame, it pays to start in the middle and work your way out.

HALF-CROSS STITCH

This is the most basic and economical of all diagonal needlepoint stitches. Draw your needle up through the first hole and take it up and across into the hole directly diagonal to your entry point. Come up through the hole below, next to your first hole and repeat the process across the face of your fabric. This will form a diagonal stitch in ordered horizontal or vertical rows.

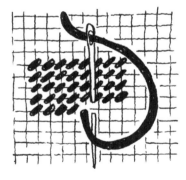

CONTINENTAL STITCH (TENT/HORIZONTAL)

Continental stitch looks almost the same as half cross stitch, but your needle goes through diagonally instead of vertically. Draw the needle up through your first hole and take it down into the hole directly diagonal to your entry point. Come up through the fabric next to your first hole and repeat the process across the face of your fabric. It uses twice as much thread as the half-cross stitch, so be aware of that when planning projects.

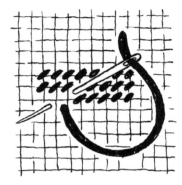

BRICK STITCH

Brick stitch is a filling stitch that forms a brickwork-style pattern across the canvas.

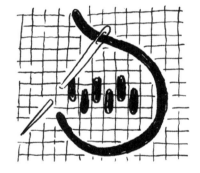

LONG STITCH

Long stitch is a super-fast stitch and is your best friend when it comes to filling in large sections of canvas quickly.

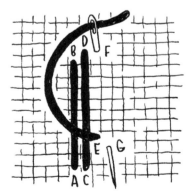

MOSAIC STITCH

Mosaic stitch produces a beautiful block pattern. Stitches alternate between short and long as you switch between taking the thread over one and two spaces.

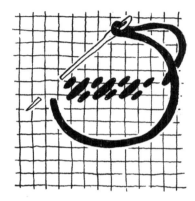

FLORENTINE STITCH (BASIC)

Florentine stitch is a classic zigzag pattern that forms the basis of many Bargello patterns.

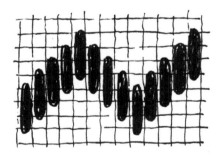

BARGELLO

Named after patterns found on the chairs of the Bargello Palace in Florence, this popular look can be found not just in needlepoint, but also in quilts, knitting and cross stitch.

Bargello needlepoint consists of rows of Florentine stitches in a repeated motif. One of the most well-known patterns is the signature Bargello flame style. The adjoining rows each use a different color but repeat the same pattern. Altering stitch lengths exaggerates the "flame" pattern into an almost dizzying optical illusion of movement.

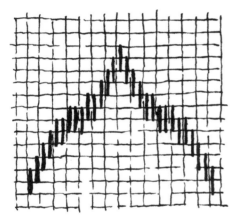

PROJECT IDEAS

→ Bring some needlepoint bling to your jewelry drawer. Plastic triangle needlepoint shapes make the perfect base for graphic, oversize earrings.

→ Bring a sense of play to kitsch needlepoint kits by switching the colors of one or two elements for something more surprising. Turn those cute kittens into different tones of pink and you get the idea.

→ You can bring your needlepoint skills to fabrics beyond those in kit form. A beautiful print can act as your "pattern." Overstitch the whole thing or just add a favorite motif for added texture.

→ Needlepoint is perfect for showcasing your favorite font. Make up an alphabet sampler or capture your favorite phrase in stitches. Sans serif fonts work best, but be warned — not even needlepoint can save Comic Sans.

→ Don't be afraid to go abstract. Let loose on some fabric with three, five or seven (we like odd numbers) of your favorite colored threads. Trust us, it looks amazing and it's novice-proof.

Bangin' Bargello Basket

WHAT YOU NEED

- Bargello pattern
- 10 balls of double knitting yarn, 2 for each color
- Scissors
- Tapestry needle (size 13)
- 4 A4-sized plastic canvas panels (7 count)
- 1 ball of double knitting yarn in black

HOT TIP

Remember to take your pot out of its jacket before watering. You can also add another panel to make a base and turn this planter into a super-fancy storage basket.

There is something decidedly retro about Bargello, so we stuck to the aesthetic of our childhood and used clashing colors of brick red, hot pink, burnt orange, sun yellow and grandma lavender to create the perfect decorative jacket for our favorite potted plant.

WHAT YOU DO

1. Take some time to look at the pattern. Our repeat pattern works five times across the 70 stitches that fill the width of your plastic canvas.

2. To begin, cut a double arm's length of red yarn and thread it through your tapestry needle to make a double strand. This allows you to make a thicker stitch, which will ensure you have a nice, dense surface.

3. Start at the lower-left hole of your plastic canvas, and take your needle up through it, leaving a tail of around 3" to thread back through the back of your work later. Work the first red row of the pattern across the width of your plastic canvas.

4. You will run out of thread before you reach the end of the row. To secure your new thread, take your needle through the back of your last three stitches. You'll be tempted to use longer threads to avoid this step but if you do you'll end up tied in knots. Work short and work safe.

5. Start the next color (pink) in the first hole on the far left of your canvas, directly above your red row. Work this row across in the same way as you did your red one. Continue following the pattern by adding each color in turn until you reach the top.

6. Because of the peaks and valleys in the pattern, you'll be left with spaces at the top and bottom. You can continue with the pattern as we have, or you can fill the first color (red) at the bottom and the last color (lavender) at the top.

7. Repeat steps 2 to 6 for the remaining three panels.

8. Once your panels are done, give yourself a little pat on the back. You're now ready to fashion your planter. To join the four panels together, use a whip stitch in black wool as a contrast detail. Lay the two long panel sides together, right sides out, and work your way up the edge.

9. Place your Bargello basket over your pot. Your plant is now ready for the best-dressed category!

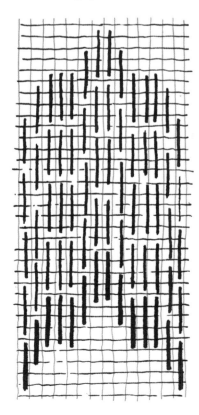

Sew

◇◇◇

Home sewing has the ability to liberate us. We don't have to be slaves to fashion — we can create our own. Armed with fabric, scissors, needle and thread we can make anything we turn our minds to. Well, maybe not a working space station, but certainly a soft sculpture version of one. Mind you, sewing does need a particular mindset. Concentration, patience and planning are all key qualities of the successful sewer. Add a machine into the mix and you'll need to be happy to take on quite specific technology that may involve a little swearing and frustration at first go. Don't worry, you'll get the hang of it soon enough. With that you'll be taking part in one of the most enduring and rewarding global crafts, and gaining lifelong and empowering skills in the process.

The increasing availability of the domestic sewing machine in the mid-1800s marked a revolution in domestic craft. With the ability to produce clothing and home wares with relative ease, there was new scope for creativity and design. Home sewers could buy patterns inspired by fashion, they could produce linens and furnishings and explore different fabrics and designs. Domestic creativity had reached a critical mass.

As mass production of clothing and accessories grew, cheap goods flipped the tables. Why make when you can buy? This concept was briefly put on hold with the advent of war. The British government's official "Make Do and Mend" policy during the Second World War created a way for those left at home to make a contribution to the war effort through their domestic sewing skills. The Queen Mother led the charge with her hosted sewing bees at Buckingham Palace. Brochures were produced with simple sewing instructions for government-issued patterns. Domestic sewers were encouraged to upcycle from existing textiles as clothing rations were put in place. It marked a time when people developed their craft skills because they had to. Necessity was the mother of invention.

This intense period of learning and skill sharing lasted well into the 1970s. The punk aesthetic created by fashion hero Vivienne Westwood encouraged people to have a more individualistic approach to what they wore. You could be your own designer as an act of defiance against homogenized and repressive conservative fashion. You could buy secondhand clothes and adapt them to your own taste. You could chop and change existing garments any way you liked, meaning you had complete control over what went on your body. Revolution through sewing.

Artists too understood the power of creating something from nothing with the aid of sewing. From the soft sculptures of Josef Albers to the hand-sewn clothes of Friedensreich Hundertwasser, sewing was used as a tool by artists to create objects, installations and wearable art. Recognizing the emotional pull and tactility of textiles, artists replaced the paintbrush with sewing to express themselves.

With the development of computer technology in the late 20th century, the ability to plug a sewing machine into a laptop and literally press "sew" saw attitudes and interest in domestic sewing rise again. As people turned away from mass-produced cheap goods in search of a more custom-made wardrobe, the stage was set for a renaissance of domestic designers. Endless tutorials in everything from pattern making to sleeve setting appeared online. Just as it began, sewing and the skills around it are shared freely as other makers encourage and support each other in a digital sense to harness the power of needle and thread.

THE SOCIAL STUDIO
Australia

Everything you need to know about The Social Studio is captured in their name. A collaborative space where new migrants to Australia can match their unique cultural knowledge with skilled design and ethical production, each piece is as much a prized one-of-a-kind as the people involved with its creation. The garments created in this groundbreaking enterprise carry an optimistic history perfect for citizens of the world.

 thesocialstudio.org

MEGAN WHITMARSH
United States

Megan Whitmarsh's career is built around sewing surprises. From embroidered disco yetis to soft sculpture trash, her work shows skill in both content selection and production. Continuing the feminist discussion begun by mid-1980s feminist art collective Guerrilla Girls, her reproductions of *Art Forum* magazine (aka "Art for Him"), serve to undermine patriarchy with tongue planted firmly in cheek. Knowing that only five of 99 covers have featured women, Whitmarsh honors these artists by using what is traditionally thought of as women's work while pointing out the continuing inequities that plague contemporary culture.

meganwhitmarsh.com

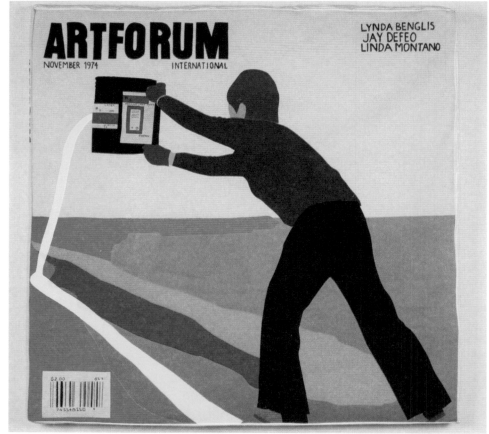

TERRY WILLIAMS
Australia

We continue to be amazed by the diverse output of Terry Williams. His prolific practice includes animation, drawing, painting, ceramics and soft sculpture, to which he brings his unique vision and preoccupation with UFOs and sci-fi cinema. His soft sculpture re-imaginings of domestic objects and machines are anthropomorphic but not of this world. Instead, they exist like extraterrestrial creatures from another dimension, ready to come to life with nefarious purpose.

 artsproject.org.au

ELENA STONAKER
United States

Elena Stonaker rocks our world. Her wearable soft sculptures, hand-embroidered and hand-painted with alchemical symbols, talismanic totems and supernatural cyphers, embody the energy and aesthetics of 1960s Californian craft and contemporary fourth-world mysticism. Through skillful fabric selection, color choice and manipulation, Stonaker allows the works to be simultaneously retro and futuristic, knowing and naïve, while her use of the works in live and video performance permits both wearer and viewer to engage in an overwhelmingly celebratory and transformative experience.

elenastonaker.tumblr.com

DESIGN NOTES

TOOLING AROUND

Different fabrics are going to require different tools — an obvious but often overlooked consideration. While most people will remember to use stretch needles and threads for stretch fabric, many forget that needle size, sharpness and head shape, machine tension and feet and the many vagaries of commercial threads can undo a plan quicker than a seam ripper. Do your homework. Match the right tools with the right materials and always sample first — it's seriously important.

HEART-SHAPED BOX

You don't have to be a master pattern maker to make great clothes. Commercial patterns offer domestic crafters key insights into construction that you can use for making your own clothes. Or you can take design cues from contemporary Japanese fashion and use simple boxy shapes to create elegantly draped garments. These simplified silhouettes use minimal oversize construction that can be incredibly forgiving to both novice sewers and "imperfect" bodies, while acting as brilliant canvases for showing off your screen print or dyeing skills.

TAKE IT SLOW

If you're like us then the speed of a sewing machine is the perfect antidote to endless hours labouring over projects, but true couture is built on the craft of hand-stitching for both accuracy and control. There's not much that exceeds the exquisiteness of a garment that has been slowly and methodically handcrafted to exact specifications. Besides the obvious eco-couture cred involved in the absence of powered machinery, the act of sitting quietly and slowly creating stitch by stitch might just be the perfect antidote to fast fashion.

ALTERED IMAGES

One of our favorite sewing jobs is customizing existing garments to fit our own specs spectacularly. Getting a commercially sized garment to match your body is about as easy as winning the lottery, but if you learn some basic alteration techniques you'll have a sure-fire fix for loose backs, baggy crotches and oversize sleeves with a few simple nips and tucks. Turn maxis to minis, add sleeves to the sleeveless, or a Peter Pan collar to a t-shirt. Re-make clothes in your own image and you'll ensure that your off-the-rack look is runway-ready in minutes.

LIBERTÉ! EGALITÉ!

Nothing is as liberating as being able to create your own wardrobe and homewares from scratch. Being able to find clothes, bed linen, curtains, cushions, hats, belts and bags in fabric you like or have made yourself is pretty much unbeatable in terms of creative and sustainable-production pay-off. Sewing skills, like gardening and cooking skills, are a gateway to emancipation. Whether you take your design aesthetics from pioneers or punks, take yourself off the grid and out of mass consumption. Your wallet and planet will thank you.

SOFT ARCHITECTURE

The key concept for designing sewn objects is moving from 2-D to 3-D. In this respect the pattern acts as a blueprint for soft architecture. Turn your clothes inside out and see how the pieces fit together. Break complex sculptural forms down into simple shapes and think seams instead of joinery. Start looking at your fabric as a builder looks at brick and timber. Once you've got your head around the basic techniques you'll be finding stitch-able construction lines in everything.

- **Sewing thread:** There is an ideal thread for every type of fabric and project. Cotton, polyester, metallic, invisible, upholstery, quilting and heavy-duty threads all have their place in the toolbox.

- **Fabric:** A small word for an almost endless world of excitement. We prefer natural fibers: cotton, linen, wool, wool felt, denim, canvas, felt and suede. When choosing thread to match it's wise to go one shade darker.

- **Sewing machine needles:** Universal needles are suitable for most projects but you should use ballpoints for knit fabric and specialist needles for leather and quilting. Be aware that some machines may require a specific brand of needle.

- **Sewing machine feet:** Like needles, they come in job-specific versions that make sewing better, so buy a range and swap them where needed. Buttonhole, zipper, Teflon and rolled hem feet are all great additions to your arsenal.

- **Dressmaker's pins**

- **Hand-sewing needles**

- **Seam ripper**

- **Point turner**

- **Acrylic grid ruler**

- **Tailor's chalk**

- **Disappearing-ink pen**

- **Tape measure**

- **Iron**

- **Ironing board**

- **Pincushion**

- **Beeswax**

- **Fabric scissors**

- **Pinking shears**

This doesn't even begin to cover the adventure you and sewing might embark on. We will guide you through the techniques that you'll find throughout the book and hopefully give you the confidence to design a project yourself. With every project, you learn something new. Sewing isn't just for Christmas; it's for life!

MACHINE WRANGLING

When you first get a machine it can be daunting. This may be the one appliance whose manual you do have to read. You have to learn how to thread the machine properly and gauge its tension. Each machine will have slightly different instructions on threading, but the end result will be the same: two threads, one traveling down to the needle and one coming up from the bobbin, which interlock like magic when you sew.

Even the most basic machine comes with different stitches, stitch length/width knobs and tension adjusters. It pays to spend an afternoon practicing and experimenting with your machine.

If a machine isn't for you, remember that all the sewing in this book can be done by hand.

HEMMING

You can machine-hem garments, it's true, but it will leave a visible hemline on the right side of your fabric, which is less than ideal. We prefer a simple hand-stitched hem method. Remember, hemming is a finishing technique so you want it to do your project proud. Hand-stitching is not as slow as you might think, but you do need to concentrate, so turn off the TV and put the radio or podcast on instead.

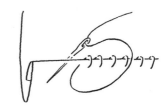

HEMMING STITCH

We use a simple hemming stitch. This all-rounder comes through a folded and pressed hem and just catches a few threads at the back of the fabric, making it invisible at the front.

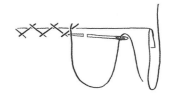

CATCH STITCH

Catch stitch is a little more complicated but does give a little stretch. You create a zigzag stitch with your needle and thread and catch threads on the reverse side only, so none show on the front.

You can also invest in a rolled hem foot for your machine, which creates a lovely finish on delicate fabrics such as silk.

SEWING MACHINE ANATOMY

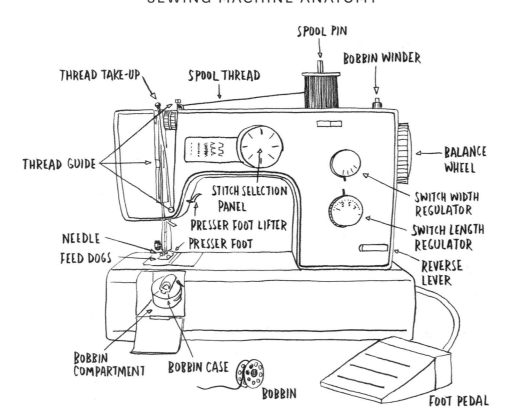

FRENCH SEAM

A French seam is like a magic trick that allows you to hide your seam within a seam, avoiding the need to invest in or learn how to use an overlocker. The downside is it does increase bulk in your seams so it works best on lightweight fabrics.

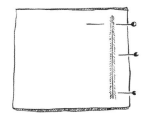

1. Pin your fabric together, wrong sides facing. The first time you do a French seam we'd advise marking a line with tailor's chalk, ⅝" in from the edge.

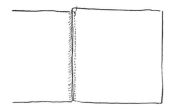

2. Sew your two pieces together with about a ¼" seam allowance and trim away the excess.

3. Open your fabric out. Now it's time to hide your seam.

4. Flip your fabric so that the right sides are facing each other.

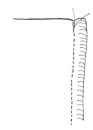

5. Using the chalk line as a guide, sew a second seam with a ⅜" allowance, being careful to keep your first seam locked in the channel. Now your edges are neatly hidden on both sides of your fabric.

CURVES AND CORNERS

These fall into the category of "things we wished someone had told us" when we first started sewing. From making a perfectly shaped softie head to creating a nice sharp point on a pillowcase, curves and corners are the sewing basics.

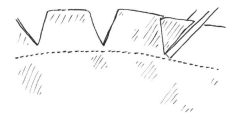

For a convex curve, sew the seam first and then cut out notches from the seam. This allows it to sit flat, creating a smooth curve that doesn't pucker.

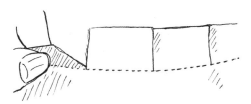

When dealing with a concave curve, instead of cutting notches out, just cut slits. This allows the seam to fan out, again giving you a smooth, pucker-free curve.

To create the perfect corner, first sew to the corner point of your fabric. Making sure that your machine needle is down, lift the machine foot and turn your fabric 90 degrees. Put the foot back down and continue sewing. Trim off the corner point, being careful not to cut your stitches.

ZIPPERS

Rest assured that zippers will not be your undoing — see what we did there? This basic zipper method is invaluable for finishing bags, cushions and purses.

First, let's talk feet. Invest in a zip foot for your sewing machine if you don't already have one. They allow you to sew nice and close to your zipper without busting needles and crying in frustration.

We find that the basic zipper works for nearly everything, but not all zippers are the same. Once you graduate from beginner to intermediate sewer you may want to sew an invisible zipper in your new skirt or trousers, which is quite a different process. There are a gazillion online tutorials to help.

1. Place your two pieces of fabric together with right sides facing and join the seam along the length of the zipper, using the longest machine stitch (called machine tacking). You'll be removing these stitches later. Press your seam open. Now pin or tape the zipper face down, centring the teeth over the stitching.

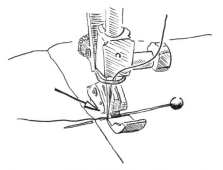

2. Turn your fabric right side up. Place a pin at the top of the zipper just above the zipper tab. Now swap your regular machine foot for your zipper foot. Make sure the needle is sitting on the side closest to your seam.

3. Change your stitch back to a regular straight stitch, backstitch to anchor the stitching and sew along the length of the zipper, close to the teeth.

4. With your needle down, lift up your machine foot, turn your fabric and put your foot back down to sew across the bottom of the zipper. Making sure your needle is still down, turn again to sew up the other side as far as the pin.

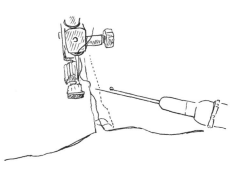

5. Here's a little finishing trick. Just before you reach the end, pause with the needle still in the fabric but your foot raised. Using the seam ripper, unpick the machine tacking stitches over the zipper tab, then pull the tab up so it's out of the way. Lower your foot and complete the stitching. Backstitch as before.

6. Flip your fabric and remove the machine tacking to reveal your zipper!

GUSSETS

If you want to go from flat to fat, you'll need to know how to make gussets. Gussets create volume — it's that simple. You'll have a light-bulb moment when you find out how easy they are, and your projects will look all the better for it. There are two methods. One requires you to sew first, the other to cut first. Both can be used for bags, purses and cushions. As simple as gussets are to make, you will need to remember to add extra length to your fabric to allow space for them. Whatever gusset width you choose you will lose in finished length — especially important when making totes or cushions.

SEWN GUSSET

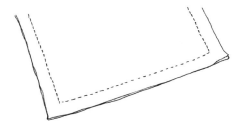

1. Using a ⅜" seam allowance, sew your two pieces of fabric together around three sides, creating a "bag."

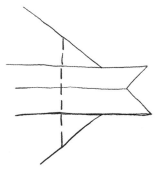

2. Now, open the "bag" up and press the seam open, creating a point on the corner.

3. Using tailor's chalk, draw a line from the top to the bottom of the corner. This line determines the width of your gusset.

4. Sew along the line, backstitching a couple of stitches at the beginning and end. Trim your excess pointy corner off and repeat the process on the opposite corner. When you turn your "bag" right side out, your gusset will have created a bottom panel giving you ... volume!

CUT GUSSET

1. Pin your fabric together, with right sides facing. Using a disappearing-ink pen or tailor's chalk, draw a square on each corner and cut them out. The size of your square determines the width of your gusset.

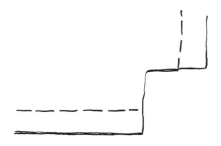

2. Sew your bottom seam and side seams only. Do not sew your cut square edges.

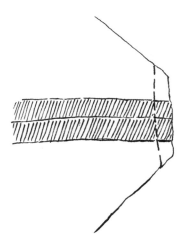

3. Open the seams up and iron them flat, aligning the seams. Sew across your end squares with a ⅜" seam allowance.

PROJECT IDEAS

→ Get meta and plan a few sewing projects around sewing. A machine cozy, needle book or pincushion gives you the chance to indulge in your favorite fabrics or use up scraps from other projects.

→ Sewing bees are an age-old custom ripe for reinvention. Invite one or many friends round for a sewing session, or plan a weekend away where you can all share expertise, materials and chocolate in equal measure.

→ If space is limited at your place, think about converting a freestanding cupboard into a sewing room. Create power access by drilling into the back and add castors for portability. Put hooks on the inside of the door for an ironing board and pattern blocks, and a pegboard on the back wall for holding threads, scissors and notions to complete a mini home studio.

→ Crafters are notorious hoarders. Organize your collection of essential equipment by whipping up reversible fabric baskets from your own hand-printed, dyed or marbled fabrics. Use sturdy canvas or denim as one of the layers to make sure they'll stand up, and your treasures will soon be both super-organized and super-stylish.

→ Play detective and see if you can work out how to recreate your favorite skirt or pants. Turn your garment inside out and see if you can make a pattern by following the construction lines. Use paper for your pattern and well-washed unbleached muslin for sewing, as it will probably take a few attempts before you crack their code.

Transit Tote

WHAT YOU NEED

- Dark denim fabric (19¾ x 47¼")
- Patterned cotton (19¾ x 47¼")
- Scissors
- Ruler or tape measure
- Sewing machine
- Heavy-duty thread to match your denim
- Cotton thread to match your lining
- Iron
- Pins
- Tailor's chalk or disappearing-ink pen
- Two brown leather straps
- Awl
- Hammer
- 12 rivets
- Rivet setter

A simple 60-minute project that will see you super stylin' on the subway and a boss on the bus. This denim bag has generous dimensions to hold everything but the kitchen sink. There's an inside pocket for your phone and an outside pocket for your tablet. With strong leather handles for durability, this bag is just what you need for the daily commute.

WHAT YOU DO

1. Take your denim fabric and cut out two rectangles, each measuring 16⅞ x 18⅛".

2. Cut two rectangles from your patterned cotton, each measuring 16⅞ x 18⅛".

3. For the outer pocket, cut a rectangle from your denim, measuring 9½ x 7⅛".

4. For the inner pocket, cut one rectangle from your patterned cotton, measuring 6¼ x 4¾".

5. Zig-zag stitch around three sides of your lining pocket to prevent it from fraying. Turn under and press a narrow hem on these edges. Turn under ¾" on the remaining edge, press and topstitch the hem in place.

6. Pin your lining pocket to one of your lining rectangles, then sew it in place. We placed ours around 4¾" from the top edge.

7. Repeat steps 5 and 6 for your denim outer pocket.

8. Pin your lining rectangles together with right sides facing and sew around these three sides, taking ⅝" seam allowance.

9. Make a gusset 5⅛" wide in the bottom using the sewn gusset instructions in the Techniques section.

10. Repeat steps 8 and 9 for your denim outer layer.

11. Turn under and press 1" on the top edge of your denim and lining bags. Slip the lining into the denim bag, aligning the top edges and the side seams. Pin the edges in place, then topstitch them together, stitching about ⅜" from the edge. Make sure to use the heavy-duty thread in the needle and the cotton thread in the bobbin.

12. Now it's time for the handles. Using your awl and hammer, punch three holes at each end of both handles. Line up where you want your handles to go and make a mark through the holes onto the tote.

13. Using an awl, make holes in your tote where the dots are to make it easier to rivet, then attach your leather handles using the riveting technique (see the Leather chapter).

HOT TIP

To ensure that your lining stays put, topstitch the two layers together along the side seams around a quarter of the way down. Use the denim thread in the machine and the lining thread in the bobbin. You won't see this stitching but it will help anchor everything in place.

Appliqué

◇◇◇

Appliqué is a brilliantly simple technique with enormous creative potential. It involves applying and securing cut fabric shapes to a base material, and its name comes from the French "appliquer" (to apply). While officially part of the patchwork and quilting family, it's deserving of its own chapter. Appliqué has a complex global history underpinned by people's drive to decorate, mend, strengthen and politicize textiles.

It's hard to accurately date the origin of appliqué as most pieces were used until they literally fell apart and the scraps were reconstructed into new quilts, canopies, tents and garments. Egyptian Queen Esi-Mem-Kev's funeral canopy is one of the earliest examples, dating back to 980 B.C.E. Aesthetic traditions diversified as different cultures utilized the technique for their own purposes — the stained-glass appliqué of Irish dance costumes, the distinctive "sacred geometry" employed by Arab tentmakers, the ralli quilts of Pakistan, the whitework of Rajasthan, the chintz broderie perse of 17th-century France and the traditional Hawaiian kapa moe.

Appliqué has played an important role in maintaining culture and community. The Kuna women of the San Blas Islands, off the coast of Panama, are a prime example. The colorful reverse appliqué of their blouses, called molas, is a vibrant expression of their culture. Many of the motifs were derived from the body painting practiced by the Kuna before the Spanish conquest, reinterpreted in the 19th century using vivid cotton fabrics acquired through trade. When, early in the following century, they won autonomy from the Panamanian government, the mola — which they still wear today — served as a symbol of their independent spirit.

Today appliqué is extensively used as an additional craft to embellish clothing, quilts and other domestic textiles. Contemporary fashion designer Natalie Chanin has built an empire by embracing traditional mola techniques and marrying them with a modern environmental philosophy, inventing her own signature "Alabama" style along the way. Avant-garde designers utilize the almost endless aesthetic possibilities within their couture collections, while visual artists are increasingly incorporating the technique into multimedia works to create texture or points of interest. Appliqué can be used either as a primary craft or in partnership with other textile techniques to extend visual language. So get your needles and thread ready — it's time to start applying yourself.

CONTEMPORARY ARTISTS

ALISON WILLOUGHBY
Britain

Textile designer Alison Willoughby is best known for her process-driven and elaborately patterned one-off A-line skirts. Willoughby's keen understanding and love of fabric are evident in the way she gleefully combines patterns, colors and weights in transformative works that are both history lesson and encyclopaedic resource for world textiles.

 alisonwilloughby.com

TONY GARIFALAKIS
Australia

Melbourne artist Tony Garifalakis is a multidiscipline compositor who uses the power of object and image juxtaposition to challenge socio-political, artistic and religious institutions in brilliantly articulate artworks. His "Mutually Assured Destruction" denim series showcases his deft handling of both heavy subject matter and historically loaded material and technique as he seamlessly (pardon the pun) combines hi-low cultural paradigms and technologies.

 tonygarifalakis.com

LUCKY JACKSON
United States

Lucky Jackson is as steeped in pop culture as her name would suggest. She approaches appliqué as collage and it plays a huge part in defining her embroidered figures against a patterned background. Movie stills and movie stars act as muse: Rob Lowe pops against a Liberty print, Bill Murray po-faces in front of seagulls, and Steve McQueen's cheeky mug shot sits perfectly on top of prison stripes.

🖵 **luckyjackson.ca**

GUNVOR NERVOLD ANTONSEN
Norway

Gunvor Nervold Antonsen makes use of appliqué technique in the construction of what he calls "fabric montages." These complex, large-scale installations skew traditional associations and applications, taking the craft out of the domestic realm and placing it front and center in contemporary art practice. Using fabrics in conjunction with drawing and painting, Antonsen brilliantly co-opts both their texture and surface patterning, as a collage artist would paper. In works that read like multi-layered 3-D illustrations he applies the technique to great compositional effect, using it to build large backdrops that reference flags or employing it as a material contrast to other "hard" mixed media.

🖵 **gunvornervoldantonsen.com**

DESIGN NOTES

APPLYING YOURSELF

When making functional work you'll need to consider the relative suitability of your fabrics in terms of consistent wash and wear. However, if you're not bound by these constraints then don't limit yourself to traditional textiles for appliqué pieces — plastic, paper and industrial felt can all work well if used with restraint and thought. Try using different textures and weights in reverse appliqué to create multi-dimensional effects.

KNOW YOUR PRODUCT

Different fabrics do different jobs and some will take to appliqué more easily — t-shirts and felt are a great start for Alabama or reverse appliqué projects as they don't fray. Finer cottons are easier to tuck under and sew but some fray easily so can't be overworked. Most fabrics are suitable for appliqué and it's a great way to use up scraps of fabric, particularly if you like working with small motifs. Collect your leftovers after major sewing projects for future use.

STITCHED UP

An important part of the appliqué process is the addition of stitching. Both functional and decorative, it's an important design element worthy of careful consideration. Stitches don't just hold your appliqué motif in place, they also sit on the surface of the work, so they need to complement your design. Simple running stitch, machine zigzag and blanket stitch are all good options, but each will change the look of the finished piece, so sample before sewing!

CULTURE VULTURE

When a craft has a long and interesting history, it is a great pleasure to dive into a little research. The Internet and, more importantly, books are laden with beautiful examples of San Blas molas, Hawaiian, Indian and Celtic appliqué styles, all rich with inspiring motifs, patterns and color combinations to help develop your own unique works. Don't copy, but do study.

SOFT COLLAGE

Consider appliqué as textile collage. Collect a load of different fabric options and lay them together to see how they work in different configurations. Which colors work best as accents? Which as grounds? Do you like clashing patterns together or more subtle gradient effects? Try using differently textured versions of the same color or consider stitching or beading for added interest. Once you've nailed the techniques, everything and anything is possible.

ON EDGE

The more traditional approach is to work an all-over design, but using appliqué as an edging embellishment or a single placement piece can work equally well. Think rows of appliquéd motifs added to the bottom edge of a quilt cover or appliquéd circles around the edge of a tablecloth; or cut animal shapes for cushions, t-shirts or bags.

You won't need many special items outside your regular tool kit to create amazing appliqué. However, there are a couple of key items that will make the process a little easier and add proper polish to your finished pieces.

- **Fusible webbing:** Without a doubt the quickest and most effective way to bond two fabrics together. Essentially it's glue in fabric form that bonds once ironed, and is washable, flexible and durable.

- **Scissors:** Small, light, super-sharp scissors will be your best friend, especially for cutting out tricky shapes over and over again.

- **Fabric marker**

- **Tailor's chalk**

- **Metal ruler**

- **Pins**

- **Iron**

- **Needles**

- **Needle threader**

- **Safety pins**

- **Bias binding**

- **Sewing machine**

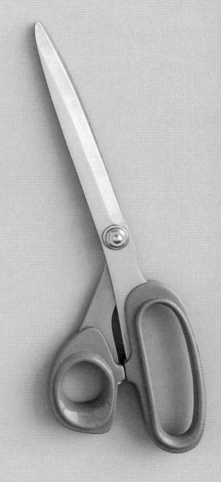

IRON-ON

Using iron-on webbing between your appliqué motif and background fabric is the most common technique of appliqué. The webbing ensures that the fabric won't fray or shift from its spot while you add decorative edges. This method is particularly useful when you are building an image from multiple elements.

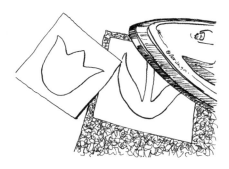

1. Draw or trace your motif design onto the webbing, then iron it onto the reverse side of your appliqué fabric.

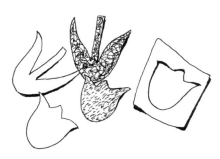

2. Cut out your motif. You'll see that the edges no longer fray when cut. Build your image using multiple elements with different fabric pieces.

3. Once your elements are in place, iron your appliqué motif right side up onto your background fabric. Leave as is or add a decorative stitch around the edges for added stability.

HAND

Hand appliqué is particularly useful for non-fraying fabrics such as felt or oil cloth that don't require iron-on webbing. Make sure to keep your hand-stitching neat so it isn't noticeable. If you do choose a fraying fabric such as cotton or linen, your iron needs to be set up and ready to press a hem around your motif before you begin to stitch.

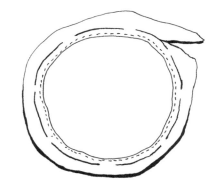

1. Draw your motif onto your fabric with tailor's chalk or a fabric marker, then cut around it, leaving a ¼" hem allowance.

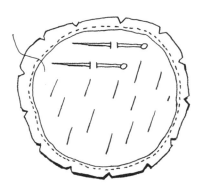

2. Cut notches into the curved edges to assist when turning this under. Pin your motif right side up to your fabric, then tack it in place with loose stitches, making sure that you steer clear of the edge to be turned under.

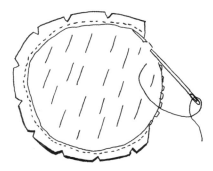

3. This is tricky, so prepare yourself. Using the point of your needle, push the hem allowance under the face of your motif and then secure with small slipstitches. Once you've made your way around the edges, remove your tacking. This process will take practice to master but gives you a really beautiful finish.

REVERSE OR MOLA

Reverse appliqué is probably one of the most difficult techniques to master. As many as five layers of fabric are stitched together, then a motif is cut from each successive layer, working from largest to smallest. Each opening edge is hand-stitched in place before the next opening is cut. The effect can be stunning and is well worth the trouble.

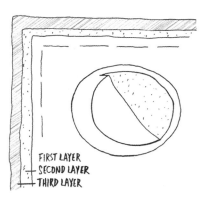

FIRST LAYER
SECOND LAYER
THIRD LAYER

1. Tack all your layers of fabric together, right sides up. In this example there are three. Mark out your cut lines with tailor's chalk or fabric marker and carefully cut through the first layer with sharp scissors, leaving ¼" for folding under. DO NOT CUT THE OTHER LAYERS.

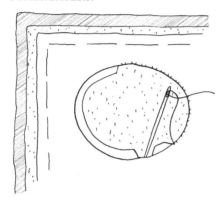

2. Turn the edges under (we cut notches in the curves of the circle to assist this process) and slipstitch just as you do in regular hand appliqué.

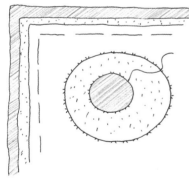

3. Mark out the next cutting line with tailor's chalk or fabric marker and very carefully cut through the second layer to reveal the third layer of fabric. Repeat the process of turning the edges under and slipstitching as with the layer above. You'll now see all three layers revealed in your design motifs.

PROJECT IDEAS

→ The simple things are often the best. Repeat one clean element to create a no-fuss graphic statement. Work with different-sized circles in a selection of fabrics sewn on a plain felt or linen background, and choose bright tones or monochromatic patterns to match your own style.

→ Use architecture as inspiration. Reduce the floor plan of your home to simple shapes, transfer them to various fabrics and appliqué them to a solid-colored base fabric. This can be transformed into a unique slipcover for a family album.

→ Nothing beats TV crafting. Take your favorite film and use it to create a palette and motifs for your very own cinematic appliqué homage. Work *Star Wars* faux-fur wookies; wood-grain logs and cherry pie straight outta *Twin Peaks*; or your very own Winterfell with metal thread, sword shapes and moody velveteen.

→ Celtic appliqué uses bias binding to make linear patterns that reference stained-glass work. Make like a modern-day Mondrian and give this technique a makeover, using single-colored bias tape and flat areas of colored fabric to make a super-clean graphic statement on homewares and clothing.

→ Combine screen printing and appliqué to create dimensional surface patterns. Stencil-print a variety of large graphic shapes onto a strong base fabric, then appliqué smaller versions of the same shape in the same color slightly off-center. Perfect for big items, from beanbags to beach bags.

Moon Phase Dress

WHAT YOU NEED

- 1.5 yard light raw linen
- Tailor's chalk
- Circle template, approx. 5⅞" diameter
- Dark linen dress
- Scissors
- Iron
- Pins
- Hand-sewing needles
- Cotton sewing thread to match appliqué
- Thimble (optional)

HOT TIP

Cutting circular templates for projects can be tricky. We've found that when in doubt, we head straight for the crockery cabinet. You'll find a ready-made selection of circles in a wide variety of sizes perfect for tracing around. For our sundress we used a noodle bowl, but you could easily scale up your appliqué by using a dinner plate, or micro-size it by tracing around a salt dish.

Appliqué is the perfect technique for transforming ready-made clothing and linen. We whipped up a simple linen dress to feature our moon-inspired motifs, but you could just as easily raid your wardrobe for an existing item ripe for lunar customization.

WHAT YOU DO

1. Lay your linen appliqué fabric out on a flat surface. Using your tailor's chalk, trace a row of circles using your template, leaving a 2" gap between circles. You can roughly work out how many circles you need by counting out how many times the template sits across the width of your dress with a 2" gap between each one.

2. Neatly cut out your circles. Leave one circle whole and cut the others in half.

3. Turn the edges under ¼" on all of your pieces and press the hem in place. Snip small v-shapes into the curves to help them turn under neatly. Be methodical and do this for all of your shapes. Yes, you do have to press them.

4. Working on the front of your dress, mark the center point and place your full circle over the mark so that its bottom curve is 4" from the edge of your skirt. Pin in place.

5. Take two of the half circles and place them with the curves facing the full circle, leaving a gap of around 2" between shapes. Pin these into place. Appliqué these three shapes onto your dress using slipstitch.

6. Pin the rest of your semicircles along at the same level, alternating flat edge to flat edge then curved edge to curved edge. Spread the elements evenly until the last two semicircles are facing each other at the mid back of your dress. Pin them in place and sew them on as you did the first three. This is not a quick-fix custom job. It is going to take some time to complete, so sit back, get comfortable and enjoy the process along with some music, movies or a favorite view.

Quilt and Patch

◇◇◇

Patching and quilting fabric together is a time-honored textile tradition that continues to enjoy global popularity. It's the perfect showcase for stitching skills, fabric design and composition, and results in the creation of a domestic object that's useful and beautiful. Quilts are historical artifacts that trace our culture in cloth. Composed of fabrics found, scrounged, recycled, coveted and bought, within their seams they carry both the story of the maker and of the craft itself.

THE ACT of patching small pieces of hide together to create bigger garments or blANKETS was once a necessity, so it's safe to say that patchwork techniques date all the way back to the Stone Age. As far as cloth quilts go, the actual evidence points to a small carved statue wearing a quilted cloak that sits in the British Museum and dates to 3500 B.C.E. A quilted floor covering discovered in Mongolia in the 1920s dates to 100 B.C.E., but aside from these rare remnants the fragility of cloth does not make for great archeological finds.

The oldest surviving whole quilt is the St. Tristian Quilt, made in Sicily around 1360. By the 14th century quilted armor had begun to appear in the form of doublet, tunics, jack and brigandine. These were handcrafted in homes and by specialist armories and were often padded with metal plate for added safety.

Throughout the Middle Ages quilts were a fixture of domestic interiors, providing warmth and comfort. Evidence of this is found in household inventories from the time. As trade opened up along the Silk Route, the quilting traditions of the Ottoman Empire and India started arriving in Europe, expanding both its aesthetic appeal and its technical execution. Quilts made from silk and ornately decorated became status symbols for the upwardly mobile during the Little Ice Age of the late Renaissance. By the 18th century, quilted clothing was popular throughout Europe and nothing was deemed more fashionable than a quilted silk petticoat revealed dramatically by a cutaway skirt.

In Japan quilting and patchwork were worn as village work wear, padded armor and *royal costumes*. There are many traditional applications, from the hand-tied futon mattress to the long nenneko jacket, a quilted haori worn over the kimono that kept mother and child cozy on outdoor excursions. Within the elaborate armor traditions of Japan, there were also many quilted protective undergarments, perhaps none so exquisite as the karuta sashinuki koto, a heavily stitched short jacket worn during the Edo period. "Boro" is the name given to the patched and mended textiles sewn in the 19th and early 20th centuries from rags of indigo-dyed cotton. Rich with stitches, these incredible patchworks act as an encyclopaedia of the hand-loomed cotton of old Japan.

As quilting moved from Europe to the "New World" in the late 18th and early 19th centuries, its development rapidly expanded. Quilts were an ingenious way of using up scrap material and insulating against the cold, as well as expressing creativity and ingenuity. In quilting bees, women met up to work on quilts in groups. This support network was highly significant in African-American communities. The small hamlet of Gees Bend in Alabama was originally a cotton plantation with a history of slavery and hardship. Women came together to create something for their own families, bringing in all the distinctive influence of their African heritage. The Gees Bend Collective is still thriving today. It's this communal spirit that sets quilting apart from most domestic crafts.

Amish communities, introduced to quilting by British Quakers, took to quilting like ducks to water. Their pared-back designs and sombre color palettes created a signature style that is still celebrated today. Basic square and rectangular quilts slowly evolved into more sophisticated works of composition and color.

The introduction of the sewing machine saw another leap in development — quilted fabric could now be manufactured commercially. Domestic sewers lucky enough to have access to a machine could patchwork at a faster rate than they could by hand-stitching. But machine quilting meant that the communal nature of the craft shifted. In recent years there has been a resurgence of interest in hand-quilting while machine quilting, matched with computer-aided design, continues to move the craft forward in leaps and bounds.

KATHRYN CLARK
United States

Kathryn Clark combines her former life as an urban planner with quiltmaking to create her series of "Foreclosure Quilts." Seemingly simple grid patterns are in fact stitched maps of home foreclosures, whole suburbs hardest hit by the American financial crisis. Crafts have long been used as a social record keeper, none more so than quilting. Clark's works are sombre, hand-stitched memorials of once prosperous neighborhoods, now ghost towns of the 21st century.

 kathrynclark.com

COLLEEN TOUTANT MERRILL
United States

Colleen Toutant Merrill explores the quilt as cultural and historical artifact. Taking existing handmade quilts, she engages in revolutionary acts by removing sections, re-stitching, layering, interweaving and leaving gaping open spaces. By then placing them as singular "articles" in a fine-art context, she makes us reconsider their role beyond the domestic. The object is no longer useful so the value system changes. The artist inserts her own handwork into the anonymous work of others, connecting the two across geography and time.

colleenmerrill.com

MADELEINE SARGENT
Australia

Madeleine Sargent of Made by Mosey takes patchwork into three lively dimensions. Sargent cleverly manipulates the sewn construction lines into a striking design feature, graphically piecing together flat areas of fabric in a stylistic mimicry of contemporary digital illustration. Exploiting bright tonal palettes and monochromatic detailing, her patched cushions, arrows, wall diamonds and fabric feather garlands conjure mid-century pop aesthetics married with storybook simplicity.

🖥 **madebymosey.com**

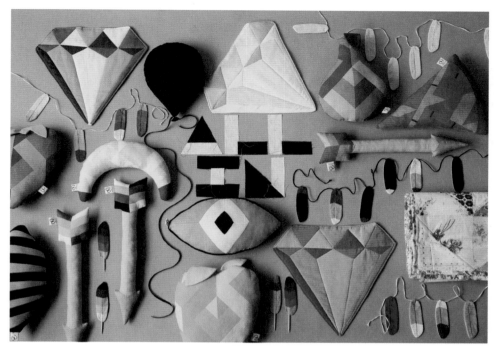

LU FLUX
Britain

It's a particularly British eccentricity, rich with literary references and bucolic wit, that informs the work of fashion designer Lu Flux. Her intricately complex and labour-intensive garments draw on the long history of English domestic textile production — from material selection to construction. Marrying *Alice in Wonderland* chic with minimalist modern shapes, Flux's folk glamour utilizes locally sourced fabrics and slow processes to create garments custom-made to order as part of her ongoing commitment to luxurious and sustainable fashion.

🖥 **luflux.com**

LUKE HAYNES
United States

Luke Haynes is a brilliant portraitist using patched quilt work to wryly comment on pop culture and subcultural personae. Folk hipsters, hip-hop heroes and drag queen superstars alike populate his large- and small-scale quilts, each artfully applied in freestyle appliqué atop intricate, more traditionally pieced grounds. Haynes seeks to reinterpret the associations of utility objects, drawing significant attention to the conscious aesthetic and construction decisions of the quilter as both architect and artist.

🖵 **lukehaynes.com**

PENELOPE DURSTON
Australia

Contemporary textile artist Penelope Durston has an encyclopaedic knowledge of the historical underpinnings of her craft. Drawing from their cultural and production origins, her sharp wit and keen eye skillfully manipulate the mundane into the profound. Discarded tartan woolen blankets become psychedelic log cabins and old jeans transform into modern designs referencing the best Amish minimalism. A strong advocate of "Make Do and Mend," Durston's reinterpretation of the classic Wagga quilt (the antipodean equivalent of the sack cloth quilt) are brilliantly considered color and pattern plays that honor our regional roots.

🖵 **misspenpen.blogspot.com.au**

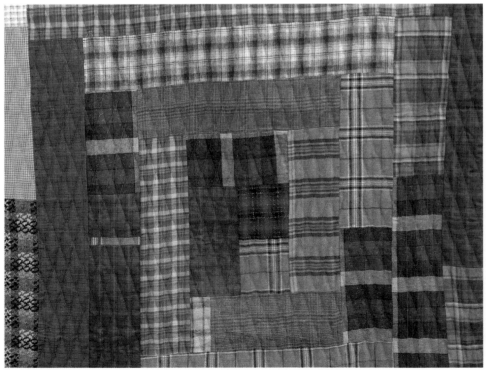

FOLK FIBERS/MAURA GRACE AMBROSE
United States

Maura Grace Ambrose has distilled the essence of quiltmaking to produce modern heirlooms under her Folk Fibers label. With a strong focus on the handmade, each piece is labour-intensive and unique. Ambrose pares the design process back, letting fabric, dye and traditional blocking do the work. Natural dyes create a very specific palette, hand-stitching gives her designs a particular texture and traditional blocking makes her work feel like it belongs to a craft continuum.

⌨ **folkfibers.com**

DEBRA WEISS
United States

Designer and artist Debra Weiss has undertaken a no-waste policy to create a series of hand-pieced and hand-sewn quilts that stand as abstract artworks, utilizing fabric scraps from her fashion label to create fabric collages writ large. Her core fashion practice serves her well as she deftly plays with composition and color from what was left on the cutting-room floor.

⌨ **rebebydebraweiss.com**

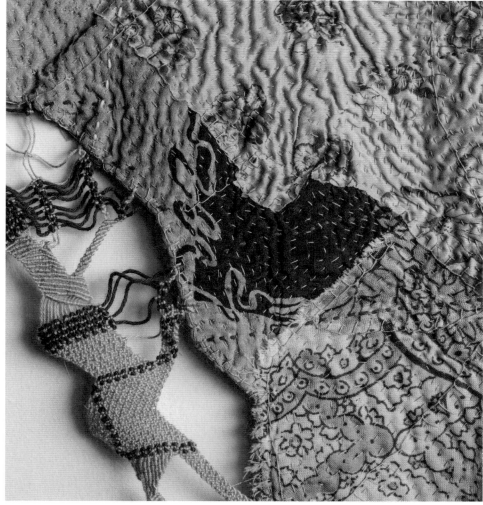

DESIGN NOTES

CHECKS AND BALANCES

The success of quilting is tied not just to the decorative patches but to the pattern of quilting stitches used for both embellishment and construction. The pattern of stitches you use will dictate the textural topography of the quilt, and the selection is as varied as the block patterns that go beneath them. In a Kantha quilt, the large simple blocks of fabric work perfectly with the detailed hand-stitching that binds them together, while decorative quilts with complex patchwork probably benefit more from a simple diamond stitch pattern. It's all about balance, so check before you wreck yourself and your quilt.

BLOCKHEADS

The established block forms of patchwork are a great place to start thinking about scale as a strategic design device. There's no reason why you can't take a single block and blow it up to become the entire design. One big star block would be simpler to sew and would pack some modern graphic punch as a quilt, or could be turned into a motif for the back of a jacket. If your temperament (and sewing machine) can take it, try miniaturizing blocks like digital image pixelation to convincingly bind hi-tech aesthetics with slow-craft technology.

MIX AND MASH

Mixing traditional quilt block patterns with non-traditional fabric choices is a quick way to change people's perceptions and make the old new again. Instead of homespun neutrals go with neon high-vis pinwheels, take a single color dyed in tones to make a super-graphic bear claw, or use gold and silver lamé in log cabin configurations to create your own "disco Amish" style. You'll see what we mean!

CELLULAR TECHNOLOGY

Traditional quilts employ patchwork as a kind of cellular technology that uses the power of repetition to create impact. While the traditional forms might seem staid, they're incredibly clever in design terms and make the most of color, form and scale. Spend time learning their tricks and you'll soon be switching it up and making your own. As with so many things, you've got to learn the rules to know how break them.

A STITCH IN TIME

Patchwork has a history tied as much to textile expediency and longevity as to decoration. The art of visible mending literally takes flaws and recasts them as features. Borrow from the Japanese tradition of boro and use simple running stitches and multi-layered patches to create beautiful imperfections.

TOUCHY FEELY

Mysteriously, fabric designed for quilting is more expensive than dress or décor fabrics, so don't feel compelled to use it and don't be afraid to mix things up. The most important thing is to LOVE the fabric you're working with. Backing fabric is traditionally a solid color or a small print so the quilt front can be the real showstopper. However, the backing cloth is also the side most likely to touch skin, so be wary of having too many seams or using rough fabric on that side. Having said all that, you might want a reversible quilt, in which case you'll have to do the hard yards and use soft fabric on both sides.

THE FINISH LINE

The majority of your design time will be spent on the quilt top but you also need to consider your backing, batting and binding options. Will the backing be a simple block color or a pattern? Will that pattern contrast with or complement the top? Will your binding be a feature or do you want it to blend with the quilt top? Would you prefer light polyester batting for ease of use and cleaning, or the more luxurious heavier bamboo, cotton or wool options?

TOOLS

- **Fabric:** Quilts are traditionally made from cotton, wool or linen fabrics, but the truth is you can use whatever takes your fancy. Fabric intended for patchwork comes sold by the meter but is more commonly bought in fat quarters (a meter cut into four), jelly rolls (narrow strips of different fabrics cut across the width) or layer cakes (squares of fabric, typically 9⅞ x 9⅞"). These are usually produced in a range of coordinating colors and designs.

- **Batting:** Cotton is hardwearing and warm, polyester is light and easy to wash, wool is more expensive but toasty, bamboo is super-soft and airy. Between us we prefer polyester (crazy, we know) and cotton for their practical qualities: cheaper to buy, easier to wash and easy to stitch.

- **Scissors:** You'll need a pair for fabric and a pair for paper.

- **Sewing machine needles:** Both universal and quilting needles, which are long and tapered to go through your three layers (top, batting and bottom).

- **Hand-sewing needles:** For general sewing, as well as quilting needles for going through all three layers, and embroidery needles for embellishing your quilt top.

- **Quilting pins:** These are longer and thinner than dressmaker's pins.

- **Seam ripper:** This little tool literally rips out stitches. Hey, everyone makes mistakes.

- **Wool yarn:** For tying quilt layers together.

- **Quilting thread:** Thicker than regular thread and traditionally used for hand-quilting.

- **Bias binding or wide twill tape:** For binding quilt edges.

- **Tracing paper:** For transferring designs onto fabric.

- **Iron:** Your best friend when you're doing patchwork.

- **Sewing machine**

- **Tape measure**

- **Steel ruler**

- **Craft knife**

- **Rotary cutter**

- **Cutting mat**

- **Safety pins**

- **Disappearing-ink pen**

- **Tailor's chalk**

- **Embroidery floss**

- **Pearl cotton**

QUILTING VS. PATCHWORK

First, let's get our terminology right. Patchwork is the technique of sewing pieces of different fabric together to make a larger piece. Arrange these in an ordered pattern or go wild freestylin'. Quilting is the process that brings a patchworked top, batting and backing fabric together, binding the three layers together with decorative stitches. Both can be done by machine or hand. They have a symbiotic relationship but can also fly solo. The shibori curtains in the Indigo chapter are a prime example of a pure patchwork project.

PREPARATION

You will need to become friends with your iron. You'll be pressing squares, strips and seams several times over within the course of patching and quiltmaking. There are some quilters who press seams to one side, and others who press them open. (We like them open, just sayin'.)

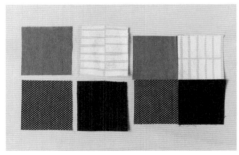

Cutting multiple identical patches may seem laborious but it is essential. Rotary cutters used against a ruler can speed things up and allow you to cut more than one layer at a time; however, when starting out you might want to take it slow and steady with scissors. Use a template to ensure that your pieces are the same size. Nothing is more frustrating than trying to align mismatched pieces of fabric. This really is a case of measure twice and cut once.

Besides pressing and cutting, the other most important consideration to get your head around is shrinkage. Laying out your cut pieces can fool your eye as work will appear much larger than it will end up once sewn together. Once you've added in the seams for each block you can be looking at an overall loss in size of up to 20 percent. Take this into account when planning specifically sized projects.

SEWING SQUARE PATCHES

Try to always sew your patches together in a logical order. Even the simplest projects are often made up of many parts. Be methodical and all will go well.

1. Pin two squares together with right sides facing, then sew together with a ⅜" seam allowance. Remove the pin and press your seam open. Repeat until all the single square blocks are double (rectangle) blocks.

2. Next, join these double blocks to another pair of double blocks. Be careful to align your seams before sewing and to press every seam open after you've sewn.

3. To make up the rest of the patchwork, systematically continue steps 1 and 2, joining your square blocks together into rectangles and then back into larger squares.

SEWING TRIANGLE PATCHES

You can't escape the appeal of the triangle. The easiest way to get your head around joining these pointy beasts is to follow the lead on piecing square patches and be methodical. It is essential to make sure all your pieces are the same size. Line them up in order, face to face, in a little pile and sew them together one by one along matching edges. To make triangles easier to deal with, you can piece them into square blocks and then sew the squares into strips.

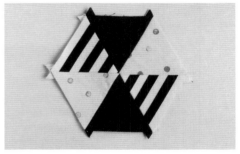

If sewing triangles together to make a hexagon, you need to match them point to point and pin them in place. If they don't quite match, you will have to live with it; if you try to stretch your fabric to fit, it will pucker and look even worse, believe us! This is tricky, but practice will make perfect. Learn this technique and you'll never baulk at tricky triangles again.

SEWING BLOCKS

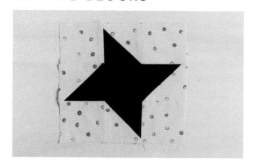

Blocks are at the heart of traditional patchwork and are always squares. They can be as simple as identical squares of fabric or be made up of many smaller shapes to create complex motifs and patterns.

Multiple parts make up one single block, which will be used repeatedly to construct the quilt. You'll notice that four of the nine squares above are in fact two triangles joined together. The four corner squares are what's known as a background solid and the center square is a foreground solid.

No matter how complex your finished quilt blocks are, they must all be exactly the same size before you sew them together — accuracy is everything. Make one bigger and your seams will never match up. Less than ideal.

The easiest way to ensure that all your squares are the same is to make a paper template of your square and pin it to each block as you sew, trimming any wonky edges and NEVER cutting smaller than your template. We know, epic, right? But definitely worth the effort.

STRIP

Strip quilting at its most basic is exactly what it sounds like. Strips of fabric are sewn into columns, then the columns are sewn together. Most often, the column seams are designed to create a step pattern (meaning the seams of each column don't meet), making it a brilliant option for novices.

LOG CABIN

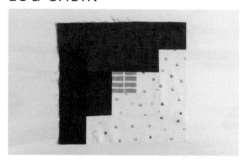

Without a doubt our favorite quilting block is the traditional log cabin.

1. The basic premise is this. You start with the patterned central square, then build ever-increasing fabric strips called "logs" around it to make a quilt block.

2. First cut out your logs, using the central patterned square to work out their size. The width of each log is the same as one side of the square. The length of the logs is one, two, three and four times the side of the square (for the lighter fabric) and two, three, four and five times (for the darker fabric).

3. Start off by adding your single square of the lighter fabric onto the side of your central patterned square, making a 1 x 2 strip.

4. Then add your second log in the lighter fabric onto the lower edge of this strip. This makes a new 2 x 2 square.

5. Add your first log in the darker fabric onto the left-hand side, making a 2 x 3 rectangle.

6. Alternate between adding light and dark logs until you have a 5 x 5 square.

QUILT ANATOMY

When a top, batting and backing fabric come together it's called a quilt sandwich. No, we're not joking. It's not a difficult process — if you can make a cheese toastie you can do this. But again, be methodical for best results.

1. Place your backing fabric right side down on a table, then lay your batting on top of it. Ensure your batting is around 3⅛ to 4" bigger than your quilt top to allow for shrinkage when you stitch through the three layers.

2. Starting in the middle of the top layer, use quilter's pins to pin the three layers together, then work your way out toward the edges to minimize distortion of your quilt.

3. Now that your sandwich is made, you are ready to start quilting.

HAND QUILTING

Hand quilting is quite an undertaking but gives a wonderful finish to the work. The techniques here all work to secure your three layers into a sturdy quilt. You can choose to use traditional quilting thread for fine stitches, however, we prefer to show our stitches off with a pearl cotton.

TYING

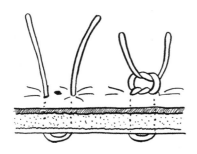

The easiest way to secure the three layers in your sandwich is to tie them.

1. Use tailor's chalk to mark where you want your ties to be, using the seam joins or block centers as a guide.

2. Thread a long embroidery needle (crewel needle) and push down through the quilt layers, then bring your needle and thread back through the top and tie a square knot to secure it. Remember, the knots are a design feature so choose your thread carefully.

RUNNING STITCH

We love the Kantha embroidery of India and Bangladesh. Masses of running stitches create a beautiful all-over pattern and are perfect for hand quilting. Whether you choose long or short stitches, keep them even throughout. Kantha embroidery looks most effective when you use a thread you can see, either heavier in weight or a contrasting color; pearl cotton is ideal.

MULTI-NEEDLING

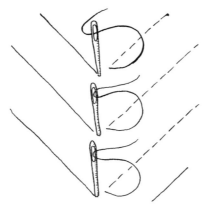

Quilts are unwieldy things, so when you're hand quilting it can help to have a few needles on the go at once. This will allow you to get a concentrated area completely covered before you have to shift around to the next section.

MACHINE QUILTING

Machine quilting is an art in itself. There are quilting machines that at the push of a button produce intricately patterned stitches. The best place for a beginner to start is with the "stitch in the ditch" method. This means following the seamlines of your quilt top, which creates a very neat look. If you can, invest in a "stitch in the ditch" foot for your machine. Remember, with machine quilting you will also have to buy special needles that can go through all three layers. If you love the look of machine quilting you'll find yourself wanting equipment upgrades fairly quickly.

The simplest versions of standard machine quilting are probably straight stitch sewing in diagonal lines across the entire quilt top or straight stitching in two directions to make squares or diamonds.

BINDING

This is the finishing touch to your quilt, so it pays to get it right. Binding creates a border that acts as a visual frame to your work. Bias binding works well as it has some stretch, so it can travel around curved corners. For your basic 90-degree angle, a wide twill tape or bias binding that matches your backing fabric is the easiest option.

The choice of width on your binding is a personal preference. If you are making your own binding, make your strips four times the desired visible width, as they are folded in half twice. Twice as wide will suffice on twill tape or pre-made bias binding. If you are making your own bias binding, sew enough strips together to make continuous binding to go around the quilt, plus a bit extra for good luck.

1. To start binding, trim any excess batting or backing fabric so that you have a neat edge around the quilt.

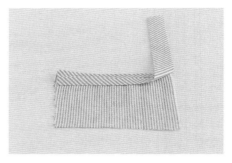

2. Press all your seams open, then press your binding in half.

3. Starting in the center of a long quilt side, pin the raw edge or cut side of your binding to the edge of your quilt. Don't start and finish in a corner because it will add bulk. Machine- or hand-sew your binding ⅜" in from the edge.

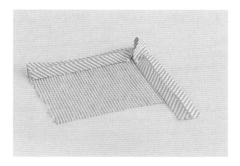

4. To make a neat mitered corner, sew your binding right into the corner of one side. Fold the binding up at a 90-degree angle and pin. Fold the binding back down and you'll now have a triangle-shaped flap. Pin the binding on either side of the flap. Continue sewing the binding on. The corner resolves itself when you attach the binding to the back of the quilt. Just like magic.

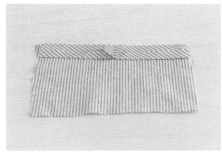

5. When your binding comes back to the starting point, hand-sew the two edges together and press your seam open.

6. To finish, turn your quilt wrong side up and fold your binding over, pinning it in place. You'll see your mitered corner has appeared on the front side (trust us) and you will have a small triangle to tuck under and sew on the wrong side in the corners.

PROJECT IDEAS

→ For a bite-sized patch project, try hand warmers. Small flannel-lined bags filled with rice, wheat or ceramic beads can be heated in the microwave and put in your coat pocket on frosty days to make the morning commute more tolerable. Alternatively, they can be put in the freezer to sooth a "too much screen time" head splitter.

→ Create a sketchbook of block ideas. Draw your block on the left-hand page and then experiment with it on the opposite page. Flip it, change the color, expand or contract the scale. It's a great way to sharpen your design skills for a larger project.

→ Find a pattern you like and change the suggested colors or fabrics. Some quilt pattern books fall into the "so bad they're good" category, while others are just plain bad, but you never know what hidden gems are lurking in those old books and magazines.

→ Give your bedroom an inexpensive makeover and practice your hand- or machine-quilting skills by turning a duvet cover or a couple of plain sheets into a new quilt. Place your batting between the sheets or inside the cover and add detailed quilting. Plain sheets will work well with a colored running stitch, while patterned ones will offer you plenty of design cues for machine work.

→ If regimented patchwork or quilt blocks aren't your thing, try a freestyle approach. Cut a large piece of paper into random shapes and assign a different fabric to each shape. Re-assemble your puzzle pattern and sew together for a stress-free selection process.

Foodie's Picnic Quilt

What could be better than using some of your favorite foodstuffs to custom-dye fabric for future food fun times? We used berries, cabbage and spices to make this strip quilt but you'll see in the Dye chapter that there are loads of other tasty options you could use.

WHAT YOU NEED

- 24 pieces of hand-dyed cotton, 11¾ x 23⅝" each
- Iron
- Scissors
- Needle and sewing thread
- Pins
- 2 yards of polyester filling
- 2 yards of black chambray
- Black pearl cotton (size 8) or crochet thread (size 10)
- 6.5 yards black and white striped bias binding, 1" wide

HOT TIP

To get the colors we used, try:
- red cabbage + alum = blue
- turmeric + ferrous sulfate = khaki
- strawberries + alum = pink
- turmeric = yellow
- turmeric + ferrous sulfate = pale green
- blueberries = purple

If you don't want to dye your own fabric, feel free to swap it for store-bought versions. Just remember, you need six different fabrics. You can tell from ours that the color results vary.

WHAT YOU DO

1. Iron each of your cotton pieces. You now need to turn them into 96 strips, which will form your quilt top.

2. Fold each piece in half so you have a square 11¾ x 11¾". Press the fold and cut through it. Fold each square through the center to make a rectangle 11¾ x 5⅞". Press and cut through the fold. Repeat this process until you have 96 strips, then sort them into their color groups.

3. Make six long rows of eight strips each, sewing short end to short end of each strip. Set aside.

4. Take three of your blue strips and cut them in half again, to make six 5⅞ x 5⅞" squares. These will go at the start and end of the next rows.

5. Your next six rows each use seven full strips and two blue blocks. Start sewing these, using the blue blocks at the start and end of each row and following your color order. Set aside.

6. Take one of each row and pin them right sides facing and sew a straight seam. Continue adding new strips, remembering to alternate as you go, until all 12 are sewn together. This will create the "step" pattern seen in our quilt. Flip it over and stand back to admire your handiwork!

7. Lay the chambray on a flat surface and place the batting over it. Lay the patchwork on top to make your quilt sandwich. Pin the layers together and trim the edges evenly.

8. Join all three layers with the black cotton or crochet thread, using the tying method. Place two ties in the center of each block, equidistant from the edges.

9. Once you're done, bind the edges of your masterpiece with the striped bias binding. Woo hoo! You did it. Now, chill the champagne and pack that picnic basket, ready for an outdoor celebration of your genius.

Notions

◇◇◇

Notions is a catch-all phrase for a vast range of ephemera attached to sewing projects — buttons, zippers, tapes, thread, pins, elastic, ribbon, needles, scissors, seam rippers and decorative trims. In medieval England a fabric store also sold birdcages, mousetraps and shoehorns, which may have been a little confusing if you'd just popped in to pick up some thread. While the term that describes their commerce is relatively recent, many of the items have a much older history as decorations, functional devices and currency.

Throughout the world, different cultures have designed notions items to suit their customs, fashions and access to materials — such as shells in islander communities, bone in Africa and mother-of-pearl in the royal houses of Europe. Wood, porcelain, and even paper have all been used to create buttons as far back as the Bronze Age. Ribbons, too, have strong ceremonial and symbolic cultural meanings both ancient (think maypoles and medals) and modern (think pink). The modern form of ribbon came into common European use during the Middle Ages as merchants made the most of exotic silks coming in via trade routes. The great demand for decorative ribbon instigated a highly specialized manufacturing industry that dates back to 11th-century France.

Tassels and pom-poms also have their own special history. Tassels have long been used around the globe as a practical and decorative finishing feature for textile work, and birthed the specialist field of passementerie in 16th-century France. These incredible artisans were required to undertake a seven-year apprenticeship and attain master status within their guild in order to create highly ornate fringes, cord, pom-poms and rosettes. It was a much more serious endeavor than the simple pom-poms we whip up with a fork at the kitchen table.

As contemporary artists have turned to domestic materials and techniques to examine, comment on and redefine traditional gender roles, they have also turned to a wide range of notions items to build, decorate and inspire their work. They have pushed conventional uses and nostalgic references in new and exciting directions, creating their own uniquely customized versions in surprising materials, scales and locations. Like Walter van Burendonk's super-sized pom-pom "walking sculptures," these familiar and mundane sewing-box items are being re-cast as extraordinary art. And while industrial and technical innovations have caused production to become overwhelmingly mechanized, there is still enormous appeal, not to mention eco cred, in creating your own notions items by hand.

TROY EMERY
Australia

Melbourne-based multimedia artist Troy Emery refers to his collection of trimming-festooned animals as "fake taxidermy." Using a range of pre-made kiddie craft objects such as pom-poms, tinsel and fringe in glorious candy-shop excess, he immediately pushes viewers into a challenging and dichotomous position. Using a barrage of conflicting associations (trophy comfort/reductive totem) and the visual traditions of plush toys, museum display and traditional decorative arts, he creates animal sculptures that are as much fairy floss dreamscape as they are animated nightmare monsters.

🖥 **troyemery.net**

MEGAN GECKLER
United States

Installation artist Megan Geckler uses mass-produced plastic ribbon, usually found on construction sites, to create site-specific works that sit deliciously somewhere between party streamer and super-sized string art. Transforming each location with her immersive geometric pieces, she offers new ways of both seeing and experiencing environments. Industrial-sized maypoling.

🖥 **megangeckler.com**

ELISE CAKEBREAD
Australia

Designer Elise Cakebread's playful interpretations of classic notions standards have hit a highly fashionable nerve. From her glorious dip-dyed ear tassels to her "soft hemispheres," she has elevated humble sewing kit standards into covetable works of art. Most compelling is Cakebread's artful combination of metallic threads, cotton and multicolored woolen yarns to create monumental pom-pom planets whose surface topography shifts with different color, density and texture.

⊡ **elisecakebread.com**

RAN HWANG
United States

Ran Hwang's approach to the button as material is as a building block. This Korean-born, New York-based artist creates intricate, highly decorative images of birds, buildings, Buddhas and blossoms by hammering hundreds of nails into gallery walls to hold button after button. Taking advantage of both the surface texture and refractive quality of pearly buttons, he slowly but surely builds rich, complex images on a grand scale in sharp contrast to their humble origins.

⊡ **ranhwang.com**

DESIGN NOTES

FINISHING TIME

Notions at its core is about finishing projects. It's the perfectly placed button, the hand-sewn fringe, or the invisible zipper on a dress that so often make the garment. So when using notions materials in your projects (art, craft or design), remember to look at the object as a whole and aim for a well-crafted outcome. The aim is to create harmonious and long-lasting works, so take the time to properly finish your projects on the inside (bias binding, we're looking at you), as well as on the outside.

HISTORICALLY SPEAKING

Period costume and regalia are rich with notions-based embellishment. For centuries, tassels, fringe, buttons, pom-poms, ribbons and cockades have been used as unifying decoration to denote hierarchy or to mark merit. Mine the history books for brilliant uses and style guides and whip up your own uniform. Think everything from super-sized cockades to gold-fringed epaulettes for your favorite jacket.

SUPER SAVER

We aren't ones to encourage hoarding behavior (not that we can talk). But notions is one of those areas where you will find yourself amassing lots of "bits and bobs" over time. This shouldn't necessarily mean regular trips to the trimmings department of your favorite craft store. Go with the old-school and create your own notions department. Salvage buttons from old clothing, keep ribbons and string from gift wrapping, and never underestimate the potential beauty to be found in your scraps stash. Store buttons and ribbons in clear plastic containers or glass jars if you want to display them. Sort fabric bits by color (or weight). A little organization and an eagle eye are all you need.

STRENGTH IN NUMBERS

Three safety pins on a cotton curtain would indicate a hole; 3000 safety pins would indicate a whole. If you are going to use notions items as a design tool, more is definitely more. Any single object amassed will seduce the eye. Even the most humble utilitarian object or material can be elevated to new heights when using the impact of repetition as a transformative tool.

PAUSE BUTTON

There are many examples presented here that talk about using notions items en masse. However, wise treatment of said items is key to getting a deliberate, focused result. Keep a critical eye on color and select material combinations judiciously. Even if you're using half a million gold buttons, sticking to one color helps keep excess in check.

MAKING OUT

We're giving you the keys to the kingdom, or at least the craft cabinet, by showing you a wealth of complementary customizing techniques throughout this book. Look through the chapters and you'll find loads of ways to make your own completely unique and complementary finishes for your projects. Want some super-sized birch buttons? Whittle them. Can't find exactly the right shade of ribbon? Dye it. Want to add a neon yarn fringe to your tepee? Twine it. Think laterally and creatively when it comes to hand-making your trimmings and you can really make your projects come to life.

- **Fabrics:** Start a collection of different plain and patterned fabrics, ready to be turned into buttons, ribbons and bias binding. Upcycle old clothes, keep sewing offcuts or pick up samples of super-luxe materials.

- **Bias binding maker:** This handy gadget allows you to turn any fabric into bias binding. They come in a variety of sizes, usually somewhere between ¼" and 2⅜" finished binding width.

- **Yarn:** Wool, cotton, silk, synthetic, hand-spun and commercial varieties.

- **Cardboard:** Seems simple but is a tassel- and pom-pom-making necessity. Keeping a stash of old cardboard boxes handy is a very cheap way to ensure that you can whip up a custom tassel or pom-pom at the drop of a thimble.

- **Ribbons:** Twill tape, grosgrain ribbon, decorative piping, seam binding, cord, fringe and rickrack, it's good to have a variety of ribbons on hand. Make your own and collect pre-made versions from secondhand shops or specialist suppliers.

- **Covered button kit:** Anywhere you use buttons you can use covered ones, with the added bonus of highlighting a beautiful fabric.

- **Pom-pom maker:** Homemade or store bought.

- **Needles**

- **Pins**

- **Thread**

- **Needle threader**

- **Scissors**

- **Buttons**

D.I.Y. POM-POM MAKER

While plastic pom-pom makers are readily available, you are limited by scale. If you want to make your own from scratch, this simple D.I.Y. cardboard kit constructed from upcycled boxes lets you make plain or patterned pom-poms like a pro.

WHAT YOU NEED

- Cardboard: a cereal or tissue box works well
- Pencil
- Scissors
- A ball of yarn
- Paper clips or masking tape

WHAT YOU DO

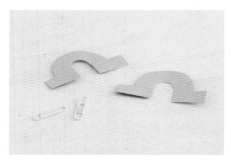

1. Draw and cut out four U-shaped templates from your cardboard. Your finished pom-pom will be the same diameter as the width of the widest part of your U shape.

2. Hold two templates firmly together and start wrapping on your yarn.

3. Continue to wrap your yarn around the cardboard template until you're satisfied with the amount of yarn. The more yarn you use, the denser your pom-pom will be.

4. Repeat the process on your other set of templates so you have two even U-shapes full of yarn. Put them together to form one circle and secure with paper clips or tape.

5. Cut through the yarn loops around the edge of your circle. You'll feel the little groove between the two pieces of cardboard as you cut.

6. Take a length of yarn and pull it through the gap between the two pieces of cardboard, tying it tightly in a knot.

7. Gently pull away your cardboard and trim your pom-pom into a perfectly round ball.

BIAS BINDING

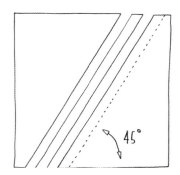

1. Using tailor's chalk, mark fabric strips at a 45-degree angle. Cut strips three times the width of your bias binding maker. For example, if you are making a 1⅛"-wide binding, cut your strip 3½" wide.

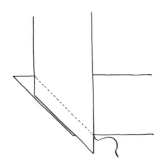

2. To make the bias tape long, sew strips together with right sides facing, at a 90-degree angle. Press the seam open.

3. Feed the sewn strip through the binding maker, pressing as you go. Pin the end to the ironing board to help you with this fiddly beginning.

SUPER-FAST TASSEL

This super-fast method will work with pretty much any material from silk embroidery thread to nylon rope — all you need is scissors, cardboard and yarn to match the scale of your materials and ambition.

1. Start by selecting your yarn and deciding on your tassel dimensions in both length and width, then cut your cardboard to the same length you want your tassel.

2. Wind your yarn around the card, but remember that it will be twice as thick as it looks on the cardboard facing you.

3. Cut a 4" length of yarn and use it to tie off your tassel at the top in a single knot. Cut through the looped ends at the bottom to release the yarn from the cardboard.

4. Cut another length of yarn, long enough to wrap tightly around the looped head of the tassel about eight times, about ¾" from the top. Tie a tight knot and trim the ends evenly. If you want a contrasting finish detail at this point, use a different-colored yarn instead.

PROJECT IDEAS

→ Tassels add instant oomph to curtains and cushions, but they're just as amazing when taken outside. Stock up on weather-friendly materials and you can gussy up your sun lounger or shade sail in an afternoon. Add beads, bells or mirrored detailing to the thread ends and you'll create a multimedia light and sound show for the whole back garden.

→ Banners and pennants are super cool. Whip up your own version by spelling out a name, commemorating an event or even celebrating a postcode on felt using pearl or matte buttons. Perfect for kids' bedrooms and hipster living rooms.

→ Fancy cord-making was one of the specialist skills of any passementier worth his salt. Making custom trims is the quickest way to ensure a unique project. Pursue the beautifully complex Japanese braiding technique of kumihimo or make cords from braided strips of stretch fabric to make edging for everything from cushions to coats. These decorative cords also quickly dress up the simplest brown paper package, which makes them a craft kit staple.

→ Fabric-covered buttons can transform a much-loved but tired cardigan or coat. Use a beautiful contrasting fabric and customize it by adding embroidered stitches, beads or drawn details for added decorative oomph.

→ There are not many craft projects or indeed outfits that can't be made better with the addition of pom-poms. If you want maximum impact from minimum effort, try making a large tennis ball–sized pom-pom and attaching it to a simple Alice band for a fashion-forward fuzzy fascinator.

Pom-pom Sweater

WHAT YOU NEED

- Cotton sweatshirt
- Scissors
- Tailor's chalk or a fabric marker
- 2 50g (2 oz.) balls of double knitting yarn
- Metal fork
- Cotton thread to match your yarn
- Waxed linen thread (optional)
- Sewing needle

We are big believers in the mighty power of the pom-pom, and as children of the 1980s we are also massive fans of an off-the-shoulder gray marl sweatshirt. Mix these together and what do you get? An awesome Flashdance-meets-kawaii polka-dot pom-pom sweater, that's what. We went with our favorite yellow and gray combo but any strong, contrasting color combination would work just as well. You'll also earn your pom-pom ninja badge by the end of the project. BONUS.

WHAT YOU DO

1. Cut the neck, wrist and hem ribbing off your sweatshirt, leaving the hem as a raw edge.

2. Using your tailor's chalk or fabric marker, map out the placement of your pom-poms and figure out how many you'll need. We went all over, leaving the underside of the sleeves pom-pom free for comfort and wearability. Once you know exactly how many you need, add another five to your list, just in case something goes pear-shaped. We made 50 for our oversize sweater.

3. Start making your little pom-poms by wrapping your yarn around a fork to the width you'd like your finished pom-pom to be — the more yarn you use, the denser your final pom-pom. Secure your pom-pom by taking your thread through the teeth of the fork and tying a double knot, then slide the pom-pom off your fork using a length of the same yarn, or waxed linen thread for a super-tight tie.

4. Use sharp scissors to cut through the edges. Once you're done, fluff and trim all your pom-poms to a regular circular shape and start sewing them onto your sweater one by one using a sturdy stitch, until they're all attached.

5. Put it on. You now look awesome.

HOT TIP

Use a stamp cutter to make small circles of colored paper that match your pom-poms and position them on the surface of your sweater to make it easier to get your placement right. If you want super-sized pom-poms rather than the mini versions we made, use your D.I.Y. cardboard pom-pom maker.

· Surface ·

Marble

◇◇◇

There is an element of magic involved in the craft of marbling. Whether on paper, fabric or solid objects, its appeal goes far beyond dusty endpapers in antiquarian treasures. One of the best aspects of marbling is that there is almost no failure rate — each piece is a one-off with its own unique charm that can spark the beginnings of innumerable craft projects. While you can spend years mastering the skills necessary to replicate complex patterns, once you've nailed the basics you can also be free and easy in your approach, making marbling a near perfect activity for children and novice crafters.

In 12th-century Japan, the Suminagashi (literally "floating ink") technique was developed to create decorative endpapers for handwritten volumes. Masters used a rudimentary but highly successful technique of blowing on the surface of the water to move the ink around. The muted colors and monochromatic palettes created simple but incredibly beautiful works imbued with an unassuming ease and restraint.

The style of marbling we are most familiar with today began in Turkey in the 15th century and was practiced throughout the Ottoman Empire, including the Deccan Sultanates and Mughal India. Known as ebru in Turkey or abri in India, this technique was unique in its inclusion of specific mark-making tools (rakes and combs) as well as the addition of a plant-based "size." Using this viscous solution meant that much more intricate and deliberate patterning was possible, extending the scope and possibilities for the technique and creating a process blueprint that exists to this day.

As part of the 17th-century European fascination with the East, the aesthetic of "orientalism" grew quickly, its exotic palettes and patterns seducing travelers' eyes. Buoyed up by this trend, marbled papers became highly prized in Great Britain, Germany and Italy as endpapers for books. Up until quite recently, these were the main vehicle for hand-marbling. Florentine artisans during the Italian Renaissance were particularly enamoured of the technique and embraced it with gusto, developing a highly popular signature style that remained popular right through the 19th and early 20th centuries and was used for everything from wallpaper to drawer linings.

Contemporary artists and designers are becoming increasingly engaged with marbling as both an end technique and a pathway to new works. Each print offers new possibilities, with almost endless room for experimentation. These makers are pushing the process in new ways that make use of the original technique but take advantage of contemporary materials from nail polish to shaving cream. New materials are opening marbling up to domestic crafters, while the scope of "ready colors" and pigment is so broad that your outcome can span soft pastels to psychedelic cascades. As with many old techniques, new designers are pairing hand-worked one-offs with digital manipulation and printing processes to enable large-scale repeats for mass production in fashion, applied design and homewares. Applied to everything from fine silk to timber flooring, this ancient craft is seemingly limitless in its scope and as seductive as ever.

ILANA KOHN
United States

New York City fashion and textile designer Ilana Kohn has crafted almost the ideal easy outfitting template for city dwellers. Using garments as a canvas, she applies bold patterning from fluid one-off marbled silks to graphic printed repeats. Her keen understanding of the complexities of color combining is key to the success of her marbled designs, keeping them as ice cool as the stone they reference. Restrained natural palettes and simple boxy shapes allow the beauty of the surface design to be the star of the catwalk.

⌨ ilanakohn.com

MILLY DENT
Australia

The apparent liquidity of the surface is what mesmerizes when holding the ceramics of Milly Dent. Using a slip-marbling technique in indigo blue on a snowy base, she evokes the openness of sea and sky. This, combined with her jewel-cut shapes, which she calls gems, makes the work a kind of treasure that can double as domestic ware.

⌨ millydentdesign.com.au

PERNILLE SNEDKER HANSEN
Denmark

Pernille Snedker Hansen has taken the most prominent feature of Scandinavian design — the wood floor — and created a marbled surface that brings it to life. From her Copenhagen studio she marbles everything from wood and wallpaper to fabric and paper. Cool pastels, whites and grays swim and dance in pools of color that sit well in modern spaces both domestic and commercial.

🖥 **snedkerstudio.dk**

MELIKE TASCIOGLU
Turkey

Multidisciplinary artist and designer Melike Tascioglu could be called a minimalist marbler. Her quiet studies are gentle pools of color that have had little or no interference with a marbling comb. They have a watery, dreamlike effect that, with the addition of the more graphic printed elements, becomes more retro space age and would not be out of place in a Kubrick film.

🖥 **meliketascioglu.com**

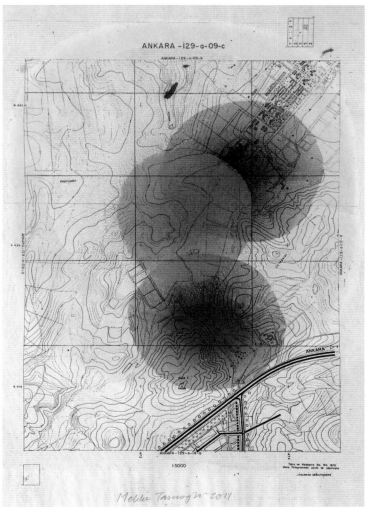

DESIGN NOTES

LAWBREAKER

Marbling has a long and venerable history full of aesthetic and technical rules and traditions. From straw-blown inks to complex comb-drawn chevrons, each definitely has its own pros and cons. As with many crafts it's worth mastering the old-school methods before becoming a lawbreaker and diving headlong into new territory. Once you've nailed these you'll be free to explore contemporary colorways and modern materials, and well equipped to develop your own unique style.

CONSIDER THIS

When it comes to marbling, not all fabrics are created equal. Different materials will create different effects, and surface texture, fabric weight, absorbency levels, fabric/paper color and coatings are all necessary considerations when choosing your ground. If using new fabric, make sure you wash it thoroughly to remove size, and choose opaque or metallic inks for dark-colored backgrounds. Whatever you choose, sample first, especially when working with expensive handmade papers or silks, and choose the right base for the job.

OBJECTIFICATION

Traditionally, marbling was a means of creating patterned materials for use in other objects. Why not flip this idea and add surface decoration to already finished products? If you can dip it then you can do it — think wooden boxes, silk bow ties, sunglass frames, beads and ceramic bowls.

MELTING POT

There is one important design element that is crucial to the success or failure of your marbled project. Remember that you are creating a fluid color palette, which will have to work harmoniously in order for the finished piece to really "sing." It sounds obvious but the technique itself can be so intoxicating that you can quickly forget color theory fundamentals — leaving you with muddy brown puddles rather than glorious pools of liquid gold.

AGAINST THE GRAIN

The process of mark-making within the marble bath makes a pattern akin to wood grain. There is a definite direction created that can be brilliantly exploited as an intentional design device. Create multi-directional movement in a single bath or patchwork together different marbled fabrics that feature strong, singular directions to create dynamism within your surface patterning.

BOUNDARY RIDERS

You'd be surprised by how often people prepare their marbling tray before ascertaining how large their fabric is. This one seemingly obvious principle guides the scale of your projects above all others. Your tray really DOES have to be larger than your project. It's also true that anything larger than about 11 x 17 inches is going to require an extra set of paws to help you lift the work in and out of the bath. We've used flat "under the bed" plastic storage boxes as baths for most of our work, but you can use anything from litter trays to a custom-built wooden frame lined with heavy-duty plastic. As long as it's flat and waterproof, it will work.

TAKING STOCK

Marbling paper or fabric is one of the nicest ways to spend an afternoon. Sometimes process really does take precedence over product and it's really okay to take a roll of paper or bolt of fabric and just go for it. Add your output to the craft cupboard for future use or give it to a crafting compadre as a special gift. And remember, even "mistakes" and scraps can go toward collages and smaller projects. Waste as little as possible.

- **Size:** Methyl cellulose is processed cellulose and carrageenan is a seaweed product. They are non-toxic thickening agents you add to water to create a more viscous surface that allows better control of your inks. We like methyl cellulose because it's super-fast to set.

- **Pigment inks:** These are by far the most effective and you get what you pay for. You can also use fluid water-based fabric paints or dyes for fabric.

- **Oil paints:** Watered down into a more liquid form with turps, these are a very good alternative to pigment inks for paper-based projects.

- **Turpentine (turps):** An oil-based thinner used to turn thick oil paint into a more usable inky consistency.

- **Ammonia:** Must be clear, not cloudy. Add it in with the methyl cellulose to help thicken the water.

- **Alum:** Often used as a pre-mordant for fabrics to ensure that color binds to the fabric permanently.

- **Trays or tubs:** You can buy specialist trays for marbling but they can be expensive, and let's face it, we'd all rather spend our hard-earned cash on inks, papers and fabrics. Any broad, shallow plastic tub will do. A kitty litter tray is perfect, an under-the-bed plastic storage box works for bigger projects and an aluminum baking dish is ideal for handkerchiefs or napkins.

- **Rakes and combs:** Use multi-pronged tools to create multiple line effects. Afro combs are great, or make your own from bamboo skewers cut short and taped between cardboard. Consider the direction of your patterns and make sure the length of your comb is smaller than your tray!

- **Eyedropper/squeeze bottle:** For controlling the inks as they go into the bath.

- **Metal spoons and measuring cups:** For making sure you get the quantities right.

- **Gesso:** For priming and sealing wooden or cardboard objects before they hit the bath.

- **Paper:** You can use any paper for marbling with varying degrees of success, but the best paper is size-free. Handmade papers and artist's rag paper work brilliantly but even uncoated copy paper is okay. You just need to ensure that the paper is not shiny and is a little absorbent.

- **Fabric:** Fine silk is the optimal choice and habotai in particular is brilliant, but any fine natural fiber will work, especially cotton sheeting. Look for dense weaves and high thread counts to get sharp results.

- **Clothesline and clothespins**

- **Iron**

- **Disposable gloves**

- **Drop cloths**

- **Bamboo skewers**

- **Whisk**

- **Drinking straw**

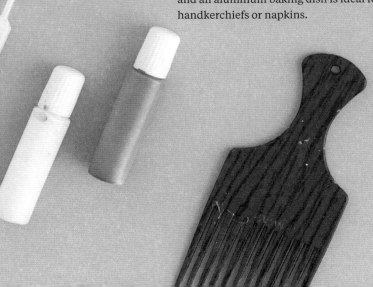

The chemical principle behind marbling is that oil and water don't mix. Traditionally, oil-based inks were added to a bath of water and were manipulated to create floating patterns. Today, the techniques remain the same, but the addition of carrageenan, ammonia and methyl cellulose turn the bath into a wobbly jelly that is much easier to work with.

BEFORE YOU START

As with all wet craft projects, set-up is key. Before you start, get yourself properly organized so you're not dragging things all over the kitchen or backyard and knocking stuff over on your way. Get your drop cloth down, utensils ready, bath on a steady surface and inks at the right consistency.

PREPARING YOUR BASE

While you can just wash and iron fabric before marbling, it's probably worth taking the time to pre-mordant it for a guaranteed set. To do this you need to wash the fabric to remove any starch or trace chemicals, then soak it in an alum bath of ¼ cup per gallon of water for around 90 minutes. Make sure your fabric is completely submerged. Dry your fabric without rinsing, iron and use it within two days, as the alum is corrosive.

Pre-mordant paper by spraying alum-water directly onto the surface with a spray bottle, wiping it gently to ensure you get a light, even coat. Make a small mark on the mordanted side so you know which one to use. Alternatively, you can just dampen the paper with plain water and marble while your paper is still damp, to aid the absorbancy of ink into its fibers.

PREPARING YOUR BATH

You can use either methyl cellulose or carrageenan to prepare a marbling bath for ink. Carrageenan will need 12 hours to rest before you can use it.

METHYL CELLULOSE

Add 4 tablespoons of methyl cellulose powder to 1 gallon of warm tap water and whisk for around 5 minutes until it's completely dissolved. Add 1 tablespoon of ammonia and keep mixing until it's clear. Pour the mix into your tray or tub and let it sit for around half an hour to set.

CARRAGEENAN

Add 2 tablespoons per 1 gallon of warm tap water and whisk for around 10 minutes until it's dissolved. Rest the mix for 12 hours before pouring into your tray or tub.

PREPARING YOUR INKS

1. Pour your marbling base into your tray. Skim off any air bubbles and dust on the surface by placing newspaper on the surface and dragging it toward you. Drop a little ink onto the surface to make sure your bath is set. If not, add a little more size. The bath is ready when the ink floats.

2. We find it helps to experiment a little to test which inks spread the most, as this will affect your design. Use the super spreaders first in your layering process. If you use them last, they'll push the other colors out toward the edges, leaving you with a splotchy mess instead of controlled pools of color.

3. Begin adding your colors by using either an eye-dropper or a squeeze bottle. Keep your dropper around 4" from the surface and work gently so as not to break the surface tension of the water. Some ink will drop to the bottom. Don't panic. Work your design from the background to foreground, with the most dominant color in your design going in last.

The blobby shapes that appear from your dropping process are called a "stone" pattern and are pretty cool as they are. If you like this design, go with it and move straight to step 5. If you want to make different patterns, now's the time to get to work with rakes and skewers.

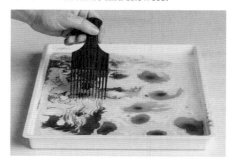

4. Create feathered or arched patterns by gently running your comb across the tray. Use a bamboo skewer to drag out the bottom of each blob of ink to make swirly patterns, or drag it through them in a wavy or straight line. Keep in mind that the more you agitate the surface, the muddier your colors will become.

5. Whether using fabric or paper, you need your base to hit your bath in one smooth, flowing motion. To do this, hold your fabric or paper between your fingers on two opposite corners in a U-shape, and let it hang. Gently lower it down toward the bath until the center lightly touches the surface. Slowly drop the sides down onto the bath surface in a rolling motion to ensure that there are no air bubbles underneath. This can be tricky if your fabric or paper is floppy, but persevere. Once you get it right, you'll have the hang of it forever. If you're working on anything larger than A3, phone a friend and get an extra set of hands to help you.

6. Let the fabric or paper lie on the surface, and tap out any pesky air bubbles gently with your finger. It will almost instantaneously pick up the ink, so once you see that it has absorbed (especially easy with rice paper and silk), gently lift it off. Paper can be rinsed under running water to remove any excess methyl cellulose, and fabric can be placed straight into a bucket of water for a gentle rinse, WITHOUT RUBBING. Hang it up to dry.

7. If you want to get another print or two out of the design, do it now — you can use either scrap paper or fabric. The prints will be less vibrant, but no less beautiful.

8. Once dry, iron fabric to heat-set. Wait a couple of days, then wash in a machine to be sure everything has set fast.

9. Clean the bath by using folded newspaper to gently skim off the remaining ink and push the rest to the bottom of the tray. Methyl cellulose baths can be kept safely for two to three days if they have an airtight cover. Baths can be rinsed down the drain or mopped up with newspaper and binned.

PROJECT IDEAS

→ Make marbled sheets of paper to use for origami projects. Work on large sheets and custom cut them into squares for unique gift boxes, mobile ornaments or garlands. Use your leftover strips for quilling or for making paper flowers, wrapping ribbon or paper chain decorations.

→ Take advantage of the enormous range of nail polish colors and make sets of kaleidoscopic cork coasters, each one in a tonal palette from super hot-pink to ice-cold blue. Perfect for Christmas presents or your next cocktail party.

→ Illuminating the random color patterns created by marbling is a great way of showing them off. Try dipping a section of a plain lampshade into your marble bath or covering a wire pendant light frame with your marbled paper or fabric for a fabulous room feature.

→ Turn a plain silk bow tie into the ultimate indie wedding accessory. Cut your own from pre-marbled fabric. Perfect for everyone from little ladies to big, bearded blokes.

→ Raw cardboard gift boxes get a lift when the lids are dipped into a marble bath. Give them a coat of white acrylic paint first to act as a sealant and make the colors pop. Perfect packaging for small gifts, and don't forget to marble a gift tag at the same time!

Lose Your Marbles Scarf

WHAT YOU NEED

- A kid's wading pool, at least 59⅞ x 48"

- Methyl cellulose

- Ammonia

- Warm water

- Black, white and yellow fabric marbling inks

- Bamboo skewer

- A friend to help you

- 47¼ x 47¼" piece of white silk satin, pre-mordanted with alum

- Bucket of water

- Clothesline

- Clothespins

We've combined a high-contrast palette and a super-sized bath in this project to really push the process. If you feel a little daunted by the size of this project, you can always start with a silk handkerchief or pillowslip and work your way up. You'll be working on the floor with this project so make sure you take care of your back!

WHAT YOU DO

1. Set up your wading pool. Make up your methyl cellulose mix (see Techniques) and carefully pour it into the wading pool to set. Once it's set, start adding your colors in concentric circles over the surface of your marble bath. Our order was white, yellow, black.

2. Make like an old-school master and use a bamboo skewer to lightly drag across the surface of your bath, moving the circles around into a pattern you like. Go with the flow and stop when you're happy with your pattern. Every marble print is a one-off, so it won't be exactly the same as the one in our picture.

3. Here's where your friend comes in. Each take two corners of the silk and lay it carefully across the surface, center first. Let the sides drop so that the whole scarf is touching the surface. You'll see through the silk that the ink has transferred almost immediately. Work together to gently and carefully lift the scarf out again and put it into your bucket of water for a rinse.

4. Hang it up to dry on a clothesline. Check it out! You've just made a monster-sized marbled masterpiece.

HOT TIP

There's no reason you have to marble entire pieces — marbling sections works just as well. Pillowcase edges, tote bag bottoms, baby footie pajamas and socks are all ideal candidates for a partial dip in the marble bath.

Indigo

◇◇◇

English textile designer William Morris once said, "Of blues there is only one real dye, indigo." One of the oldest dyes, and with a history as rich as the color itself, indigo has been used to dye fiber for at least 4,000 years. Its name is derived from *Indicum*, Latin for "from India." And although its most extensive use is tied to that region, it has been extracted from the plant *Indigofera tinctoria* right across Africa, Asia and the Middle East. Exactly where and when the method for producing this bewitching blue color was discovered remains shrouded in mystery, largely because it has been so widely cultivated for thousands of years. Nevertheless, someone somewhere managed to work out how to extract the active ingredient indigotin from the plant leaves and turn it into a soluble dye solution that has left a blue trail right across the globe ever since.

While the oldest continual use of indigo dye is most definitely located within the Subcontinent, there are examples of its use that date back to Mesopotamia, where a neo-Babylonian cuneiform tablet from 700 B.C.E. gives a recipe and instructions for dyeing lapis-colored wool by repeated immersion and airing. There is Egyptian woven fabric dyed with fine indigo borders dating back to 2400 B.C.E. and there are even Old Testament references to indigo traders from Sheba. Indigo has been used throughout China, India, Japan, Southeast Asia, Mesoamerica, Peru, Iran and Africa, with each area and population developing highly specific decorative techniques using resists as diverse as raffia binding to flour paste.

Some of the more recognizable indigo dyeing traditions include the family of tie-dye, such as plangi in Indonesia, bandhani in India, adire eleko and shweshwe picotage from West Africa, and the shibori of Japan. Wax resists have been used throughout Nigeria, China, India, Malaysia, the Philippines and Sri Lanka; however, the batik of Indonesia is probably the best known. Paste resist techniques have been developed throughout the world, making use of local materials such as flour in West Africa and rice in Japan, where the most common association with indigo dyeing is its link to Japanese shibori.

Vat technologies have been developed to match the decorative processes and geographic conditions. One of the most famous places for aizome (the traditional name for indigo dyeing in Japan) is the Awa area in Tokushima prefecture. Because indigo is insoluble there is a complex process of oxygen elimination that needs to be implemented, in order to convert the dye into a soluble form able to dye fabric. Pit vats, zinc lime vats, bio vats, chemical vats and natural fermentation are all processes that have been refined over thousands of years.

Indigo's intense color, light fastness and durability have made it a perfect dye for simple work clothes, evidenced by the emergence of denim everywhere from building sites to rock festivals. It has a strong association with the everyday, being used on workhorse fabrics from Edo period villages in Japan to California coal mines in the 1870s. From the sacred to the profane, indigo fabrics have been used to exalt and beautify, serve and protect.

The renewed interest in indigo dyeing and shibori techniques makes them more accessible to the domestic crafter than ever before. Kits with all you need to get your own vat going can now easily be obtained. Natural indigo, in particular, is experiencing an Instagram/Pinterest-driven renaissance. The combination of intense and seductive color with simple folding and knotting techniques makes for achievable and sophisticated results. Professional makers are driven more by the potency of indigo's long history and almost mystic qualities. This particular blue seems to spark imagination and meditation, a color with its own secret language and a process that allows you to unlock it.

ROWLAND AND CHINAMI RICKETTS
United States

Rowland and Chinami Ricketts are nothing short of a craft power couple. On their farm in Bloomington, Indiana, they grow indigo from seed, dye both yarn and fabric, and then transform the raw material using traditional techniques to explore contemporary art and design. Rowland creates striking art installations while Chinami weaves narrow-width fabric in the tradition of Japanese kimono and obi. Their mastery of indigo production adds defining layers of richness and detail, resulting in works as deep and culturally symbolic as the dye itself.

 rickettsindigo.com

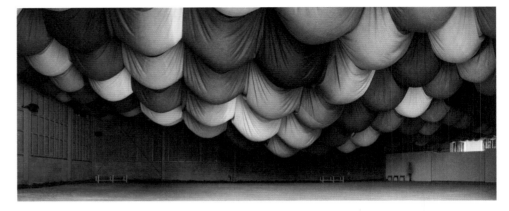

BONNIE SMITH
United States

Fiber artist Bonnie Smith's multidisciplinary practice has social and political commentary at its core. Her extraordinary installation works are created using lengths of dyed string, rope and planks of wood, reflecting childhood memories of farmers' work clothes, barn walls, America's complex history of slavery, and isolation through religious and class discrimination. Smith's works act as a redemptive metaphor, tangling and teasing out a mixture of memory and ideology and creating an alternative history through textiles.

bonniesmith.vpweb.com

ANTHEA CARBONI/YUNIKO STUDIO
Australia

Yuniko Studio's Anthea Carboni has had a long love affair with the color blue. Indigo features prominently throughout her practice — serving as both inspiration and material source in the creation of her beautifully raw domestic wares. Carboni draws from indigo's traditional use in the production of purposeful objects and garments tied to the rituals and duties of daily life, continuing the dye's long history in a functional context.

 yunikostudio.blogspot.com.au

IDO YOSHIMOTO
United States

Ido Yoshimoto is a self-described arborist, artist and tinkerer who revels in turning the commonplace into the extraordinary. Deeply connected to the cyclic narrative of nature, Yoshimoto honors his raw materials in the creation of new works that speak directly to the essence of their origins. It is little wonder that having honed his wood-crafting skills over many years he is now exploring the transformative magic of indigo to further develop his practice.

idoyoshimoto.com

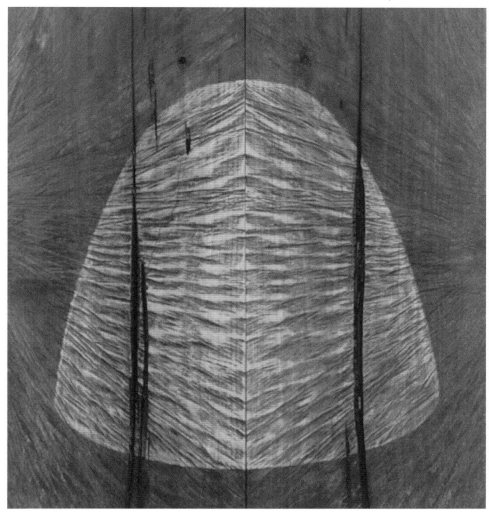

DESIGN NOTES

LAYER UPON LAYER

Think about experimenting beyond basic white when it comes to fabric color choices. Great results can be had from the vat if you dye pre-patterned fabric. Think checks, florals and geometric patterns as well as solid-colored fabrics. The vat chemicals will leach a little color from your commercial fabric, allowing some aspects of the pattern to be obscured while others become the star of the show. Use shibori or wax-resist techniques to keep elements of the fabric intact or dip-dye for a "surprise" result.

—

HARD TO RESIST

The itajime and ne-maki techniques traditionally use wooden blocks, pebbles, rice grains or beads as bound and clamped resists; however, there are now a multitude of modern materials that can be equally successful in technical terms while offering new scope for patterning. Kids' plastic toys, acrylic shapes, wire mesh, even bubble wrap can all be incorporated as resists with amazing results. Think laterally and collect an assortment of waterproof or water-resistant items for experimentation in your next vat.

—

GET THE BLUES

Indigo is for natural fibers only, but as a no-fix, no-fuss dye method it couldn't be simpler. While the number of dips will determine the depth of your color, essentially you are working within a single shade, so thinking about ways of getting the right blue for you is important. Different fabrics will react in different ways, so sample widely and often, and record your results in a dye notebook for the right results each time.

—

DESIGN TO DYE FOR

There is a reason why nearly every culture utilizes indigo. Complex patterning traditions have been developed throughout the world, yet the simple strength of the indigo blue is beguiling enough on its own for even the humblest process to yield extraordinary results. Instead of all-over patterning, why not try a small corner detail, or a center seam of folds? When it comes to indigo, less can definitely be more.

—

STYLE AND SUBSTANCE

As regular vatters know, as long as it is natural and porous, it will dye. Indigo's incredible coloring capacity means that a lot more than just fabric can go for a dip. The handles of wooden spoons, raw wooden beads, unglazed clay, even seashells are all good candidates for experimentation.

—

PICTURE THIS

Vat dyeing with indigo is a lot like developing a photograph. It's a reactive process in two parts — the fabric with the indigo, the indigo with the air. Remember this when folding, binding and stitching your fabric before dyeing. Carefully consider which surfaces will "touch" the dye the most, as they'll be the quickest to absorb the dye, get the most contact with air and dye darkest. Remember to adjust your design, your folds AND your fabric accordingly to ensure that you get the result you're after.

—

LIGHT AND SHADE

Indigo dye comes in both synthetic and organic granular forms, perfect for domestic use. Commercial dyeing is done with synthesized indigo because of convenience and scale — the color is consistent, readily available and usually cheaper. Plant-derived indigo can have some variances depending on the growing conditions of the plant itself, but devotees swear it has a darker, richer hue. We've had super dark and successful vats from both sources so take your pick depending on availability and personal choice.

—

- **Fabric or fiber:** Use cellulose and protein fibers only. Cellulosic fibers, such as cotton, linen, hemp and viscose, are those originating from plants, while protein fibers, primarily wool and silk, are those that come from animals. Either way, your materials need to be pre-washed and ironed before use.

- **Resist items:** Wooden blocks, plastic or acrylic shapes (square, oval, triangle, etc.), wooden clothespins, marbles, beads, rice, bubble wrap, twine, corded rope, ceramic tiles, chopsticks, rulers. Think laterally.

- **Rubber and disposable gloves:** Both small ones for untying with ease and long ones for reaching into a deep vat.

- **Spoons:** Metal measuring spoons, big wooden spoons for stirring and lifting.

- **Stainless steel bowls:** You'll need at least three: small, medium and large. Mixing bowls work well and are easy to come by.

- **Protective clothing and drop cloth:** It's a messy business lugging fabric in and out of the vat.

- **Lidded bucket:** For your vat and ideally deeper than it is wide. Plastic paint buckets are brilliant, but your project's scale will determine the size of the vat bucket you need.

- **Plastic pipe:** Plumbing pipe in different widths, used for arashi.

- **Clamps:** Metal or plastic, screw or spring.

- **Indigo powder (either natural or synthetic)**

- **Sodium hydrosulfite**

- **Soda ash**

- **Big plastic tubs:** For rinsing and soaking.

- **Vinegar**

- **Rubber bands**

- **Cotton or polyester thread**

- **Thermometer**

- **Measuring jug**

- **Kitchen scales**

- **Kettle**

Whether using natural or synthetic indigo, you have to change it from an insoluble state to a soluble one to release the magic blue hue into a workable dye. This is done by extracting the oxygen from the dye bath. This process can be achieved by natural fermentation using a bio or urine vat; through chemical fermentation in a zinc-lime vat; or through chemical reduction in a hydrosulfite or "hydros" vat. All vats are live chemical reactions and like yeast bread mixes they're gassy and stinky, but in a good way. The art of vat-making is both exciting and complex. We're giving you a taste with a quick hydrosulfite vat, but it's really worth checking out the other alternatives in specialist books or online.

MAKING A HYDROS VAT

In a hydros vat, sodium hydrosulfite is the agent that removes the oxygen from the dye bath while the indigo powder is dissolved in soda ash. The chemical reaction when the two combine changes the solution from blue to greenish yellow and adds a coppery sheen to the surface. These vats are quick to make and easy to use but are quite caustic and can't be stored long term.

Before you start, make sure to put protective gear on (face mask, rubber gloves). Soda ash and sodium hydrosulfite are chemicals you want to keep well away from your skin, eyes and nose.

This recipe will make a 3.6 gallon vat, enough to dye around 1 kg of fabric.

WHAT YOU NEED

- 34 fl. oz. of boiling water
- Metal mixing bowls: small and medium
- 5 oz. of soda ash
- 1.4 oz. of natural indigo or 1 oz. of synthetic indigo powder
- Long-handled wooden spoon
- Large plastic bucket with lid
- 2.8 oz. of sodium hydrosulfite
- Measuring cup
- Strip of fabric for testing

WHAT YOU DO

1. Pour the boiling water into a small metal bowl, then add the soda ash and stir with a spoon until it dissolves.

2. Mix the indigo powder with a little warm water in the larger metal mixing bowl to form a paste, then gradually add the soda ash solution. Thoroughly mix the two together with the wooden spoon.

3. Fill your bucket with 3.4 gallons of hot tap water and slowly stir the indigo and soda ash solution into it.

4. Sprinkle your sodium hydrosulfite over the vat, stirring gently with the wooden spoon. Put lid on the bucket and let it stand until the dye is completely dissolved (approximately 15 minutes).

5. When you take the lid off, it should be a clear greenish yellow with the requisite bronzy bubbles on the top.

6. Test your vat by taking a strip of fabric and dipping it into the solution. It should come out the same greenish yellow as the bath and quickly turn blue when exposed to the air.

DYEING TIPS

There are a few simple things to remember to get the most out of your vat.

- Before dyeing, soak all your fabric for around 20 minutes in a tray or bucket of water to make sure the fabric takes up the dye evenly. Even though you'll be super eager to get everything in the vat, do not forget this step.

- Pulling things in and out carelessly can oxidize your vat. Remember you're trying to keep the oxygen out of the bath. If your bath has started turning a blueish green color, sprinkle a little more hydros on the top to help reduce oxidization.

- When working with protein fibers, keep the vat at around 50 degrees Celsius for optimal results. We've dyed cellulose fabrics on cold and hot days with equal success. Mind you, dyeing on cold days is a chilly business.

- Indigo coats the fibers but doesn't dye the core. When denim jeans fade with wear that's the indigo layers being worn away with use. This means that unlike many other dyes, indigo only becomes darker with additional dips in the vat. Keep fabric in the vat for around 15 minutes, take it out and leave it on a drop cloth for another 15 minutes to oxidize. Repeat this process three or four times to build your color.

- An active vat is green; an exhausted vat is blue. Once exhausted it will no longer dye fabric and needs to be thrown away. You can dispose of small amounts in a toilet or larger amounts down a drain.

- Make sure you give your bound and clamped pieces a bit of a wiggle around the edges between dips to ensure that you are oxidizing the fabric. Don't undo your resists until you have finished dipping, no matter how tempting it is. Be patient and enjoy the great reveal at the end.

- Rinse dyed fabrics well in lots of cold water. Be sure to add vinegar to the water for protein fibers to counteract the destructive alkaline of the vat, which will eat into your delicate silks and wools if left unchecked. Vinegar baths also add the sheen back into your fabric, which is a nice bonus. Indigo does not need fixing or heat setting (YAY!) so once you've rinsed it you can wash it well with soapy water in your washing machine.

RESISTS

Japanese shibori has become synonymous with indigo dyeing and makes use of a variety of folded, stitched, clamped, wrapped and bound resists to create shapes and patterns. The blue indicates where the dye touches the fabric, while the white shows what is kept away from the dye by the resist.

No matter what technique you use, all bound fabric needs to soak in water for 20 minutes before going into the vat.

ARASHI

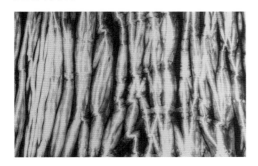

Arashi, or pole wrapping, is a fast, simple and effective method for creating beautiful rippling patterns by wrapping fabric around a cylinder, binding it with string and pushing it down firmly before dyeing. "Arashi" means "storm" in Japanese, and its lashing "rain" stripes can be manipulated with different folds to create directional lines that are completely unique.

1. Holding your plastic pipe upright, tape your fabric on a diagonal and wrap it around your pipe so it meets but doesn't overlap. Take a spool of heavy cotton thread and wrap the thread twice around the top of the pole, catching the top of your fabric. Secure your thread to the top of the pipe with either a tight knot or tape.

2. Place your pipe on its side on a table in front of you and wrap your thread around it by turning your pipe. Maintain a firm and even tension and continue wrapping, keeping your wraps evenly spaced for a stripe effect, or varied for a more free-form rippled pattern. Push your wrapped fabric down the pipe as you go. It will feel awkward at first but keep it up and you'll soon get into a groove. Once the fabric is in a little bundle at the bottom, tie off the thread tightly, cut the end and tape it to the pole, ready for dipping.

NE-MAKI

Ne-maki, or ringbound shibori, is a wonderfully ancient technique that involves binding small spherical objects into cloth with thread or rubber bands. It's a brilliant process for experimentation but can also create controlled formal patterns. Free-form designs can be made by using randomly placed objects of the same or different sizes; more formal patterning may require you to use a washable marker to plan out the spaces more carefully.

1. Lay your objects on the surface of your fabric. Make a small mark with a fabric pen where they will sit, then one by one put the beads in the spaces and wrap the fabric around each one, closing each end with a rubber band. Make sure the band is tightly secured and that the fabric is tight over your object. Repeat the process for all your objects and your fabric is ready for soaking and dyeing.

FOLDING

The fold is as important to shibori as it is to origami. Both use basic folds independently or in combination to create beautiful works. These basic folds can also be incorporated into almost all shibori resist processes and create organized repeat patterns either in designated sections or across the whole fabric. Accordion, square, and kikko (star) folds are three essential folds to get you started, but there are many more to learn from books or your own experiments. Use an iron to sharpen your creases as you fold, and record your folds as you go in case you come across something brilliant you want to remember!

ACCORDION FOLD

A basic "pleating" fold that starts at one end of the fabric and repeats one layer on top of another until you reach the other end. Use skinny pleats for skinny stripes. It is the first step for all of the following shibori patterns.

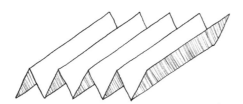

SQUARE FOLD

A square fold will give you a "full drop" pattern, meaning it repeats equally along both horizontal and vertical lines like a grid. First, accordion-fold your fabric into a strip, then start making another accordion fold down the length of the strip. You'll end up with a neat square parcel of fabric at the end, ready to tie or clamp with resists.

KIKKO FOLD

A kikko or star fold uses equilateral triangles to make a repeat like a kaleidoscope.

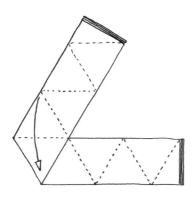

1. Start by making an accordion fold strip, then fold the strip in half on a 45-degree angle.

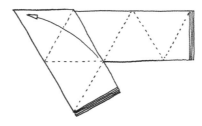

2. Fold the fabric back down again on the same angle, leaving the flat edge against the flat edge of your fabric strip; you'll see your first equilateral triangle start to form.

3. Keep folding these triangles from the point of the previous one, continuing along your strip, making sure your edges are flush. You'll end up with a neat triangle package with a half triangle on the back and front of your package. It's actually very simple, but if it feels too tricky at the beginning, try using a cardboard triangle template to help you get started.

ITAJIME

The combination of folds and shaped board placement give itajime its captivating trademark repeats. The resist is formed when two flat shapes are placed on either side of folded fabric and clamped tightly in place.

Patterns are altered depending on the size, shape and placement of your boards as well as the kinds of folds you use, and even the device you use to clamp the boards together. For sharp shapes, use clamps; for softer shape edges bind with string, thread or rubber bands. Experiment widely and record your results by noting your folding and board placements so you can repeat your favorites at a later date.

CLOTHESPINS

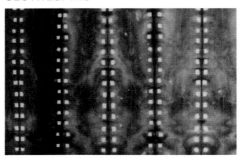

This technique uses a basic accordion fold and wooden clothespins as both resist shape and clamp to create dotted lines. Use the hollow of the clothespin to keep the edge of the fabric clear to ensure you get good dye coverage. Lower this one very carefully in and out of the vat so you don't lose your clothespins!

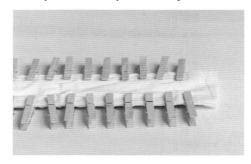

CIRCLES

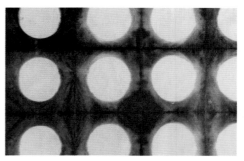

This pattern uses a square folded piece of fabric, two acrylic circles and two screw clamps. Make sure your folded fabric is larger than your resist shape and ensure that your clamps are not touching the sides of your overhanging fabric.

TRIANGLES

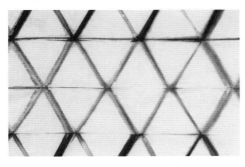

This technique uses a kikko fold, an acrylic equilateral triangle and three small clamps to bind the fabric. You'll see that there is only a very small edge of fabric left around the triangle shape, which makes the fine lines that define the negative (un-dyed space).

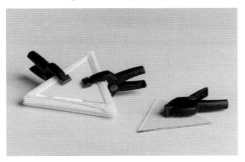

PROJECT IDEAS

→ Formal shibori techniques create predictable patterning results. But you can get amazingly beautiful outcomes from random resists. Try scrunching and balling up fabrics and use rubber bands, or wrap fabric around waterproof objects such as rubber ducks or toy figurines to really push the technique. The random results highlight the tonal diversity of this magical technique, offering almost otherworldly celestial patterns.

→ Crafting is always more fun with friends. Make up a vat or three and throw a "vat party." Get everyone to bring his or her own dyeable fabrics, yarns, music and snacks and get dipping.

→ Make amazing 3-D pleats, folds, bubbles and waves permanently on the surface of polyester fabric. Bind the fabrics as you would before dyeing but instead of hitting the indigo vat, put them into boiling water or a lidded bamboo steamer and steam for 30 minutes. Once set, the fabrics can be safely washed in cold water and the texture will remain. You can apply this technique to fine silk with less permanent results, although it's dry-clean only from then on.

→ Renew old or failed craft projects with the magic of indigo. Enliven bed linens by adding mokume stitch resist (simple running stitches across the face of the fabric pulled tight before dyeing) to create simple but stunning accents on pillowcases. Over-dye quilts, rugs and knits in blue to transport them from the "over it" pile back onto the much-loved list.

→ Use your fabric as a design device. With digital manipulation you can transform it into a whole range of repeatable objects. Scan your fabric and produce your own gift tags and wrapping paper.

Mood Indigo Curtains

WHAT YOU NEED

- 56 indigo-dyed samplers, all at least 13¾ x 13¾"

- 1 LP album cover (we used Chicago 5 but anything from Minor Threat to Mariah Carey will do)

- Tailor's chalk

- Tape measure

- Scissors

- Pins

- White cotton thread

- Sewing machine

- Iron

- Unbleached muslin (1.3 yard x 15¾"), washed and ironed. This will be used for the sleeve to hang your new curtains.

HOT TIP

To help you keep your corner joins neat and even, make sure your squares are all exactly the same size, make sure that the grain of the fabric runs the same way on all pieces and that you sew with the same seam allowance for each block.

If you're anything like us, you'll find indigo highly addictive and will quickly amass a large pile of samples, both good and mediocre. Joining these together into a patchwork is a great way to use up your leftovers in a style-savvy way. Independently they may not be solo worthy, but put them together and, like a choir, they sing. We used our finished fabric to make two full-drop curtains, but you could just as easily turn this project into a gorgeous double-bed quilt.

WHAT YOU DO

1. Take one of your samplers and, using your album cover as a template, trace around it in tailor's chalk. Add a ⅜" seam allowance around each edge and cut your square. Repeat this process for all your samplers until you have enough patchwork squares to cover your window. If you can squeeze two or three squares out of larger samplers, that's even better.

2. Divide your squares in two equal piles and start arranging them on the floor. Our curtains were each 4 squares across and 7 down, but you can adjust this to suit the size of your window.

3. Keep moving the squares around until you're happy with the arrangement, then get down and start pinning each vertical row together. Sew right sides together with a ⅜" seam allowance. Open up and iron your seams flat.

4. Once you've finished each vertical row, pin and sew the rows together to make up your curtain width, making sure that the horizontal seams line up. Sew right sides together with a ⅜" seam allowance, then iron your seams open.

5. Make sure to tie off or reverse stitch over both ends of sewing.

6. Press under ⅜" along the side and lower edges of each curtain and stitch these hems down, preferably with zigzag stitch to prevent fraying.

7. Cut two strips of unbleached muslin, each the width of one curtain and approximately 7⅞" deep. Pin a strip face down onto the top of each curtain, sew together and iron flat. Fold the unbleached muslin over to the other side of the curtain and fold a ⅜" seam allowance, iron flat and sew through all three layers.

Print

◇◇◇

Printmaking is a fine-art technique and also a craft and design technique with endlessly adaptive options for the domestic crafter. Where these techniques intersect is a complex and global story that takes in some of our earliest mark-making efforts and reactive subcultural stylings. From the Paleolithic hand stencils of Cueva de las Manos to Banksy's sprayed stencils on the streets of Bristol, print is seductive, subversive and definitely hands-on.

BLOCK PRINTing was used to print textiles before it was employed for books and paper. Wax resist and woodblock printing WERE used in ancient Egypt from as early as 400 B.C.E., and the oldest remnants of woodblocked fabric come in the form of a three-color print from China circa 220 B.C.E. Incas and Aztecs were keen printers and although examples of their work only date back to the Spanish invasion, it's fair to say the practice existed long before then.

Block printing was embraced by artists and artisans the world over and plays a significant role in both craft and design development. Textile printing has been practiced in Europe since the 12th century, first learned from the delicate Tarish (woodblock) text-printed linens produced throughout the Islamic world. By the 1630s the East India Company was importing Indian woodblock-printed cotton to the English market. In the mid-1800s, British textile designer William Morris used woodblocks to create incredibly detailed wallpapers and fabrics that remain a benchmark for the craft.

Stencil and silkscreen printing has a more convoluted history because it's directly tied to the production and availability of finely woven silk and sturdy paper. In China paper stencils were used during the Song Dynasty (960–1279 C.E.) and the technique quickly spread to Japan, where it continued to develop over the centuries. Evidence of stencil screen printing was first sighted in Europe around the 17th century when stencils were attached using silk thread or human hair. Yes, human hair — mind-blowing! Throughout the 17th and 18th centuries, as silk became more available in Europe, stencil screen printing gained some traction as a popular craft, although prior to the Industrial Revolution it remained a purely artisanal practice. It wasn't until the early 20th century, when photo-reactive chemicals were produced, that silkscreen printing really took off on a mass scale for both commercial publishing and textile applications.

Screen printing has taken on a kind of cult status as the craft of choice for subversive outsiders. With the advent of pop art in the mid-20th century, American artist Andy Warhol changed the perception of screen printing from industrial technique to super-hip social commentary, making image links between fame, high art and advertising. The liberation of low-fi D.I.Y. print production allowed limited runs of revolutionary ideas to be marketed en masse. Garage bands spawned garage printing. Posters, zines and t-shirts were printed up and distributed, and subcultures of all descriptions used screen printing, photocopying and sticky tape to spread their message and aesthetic sensibilities with ease.

With the advent of digital technology at the end of the 20th century, the production of printed fabric changed dramatically once again. Direct-to-garment printing allowed highly complex digitally manipulated imagery to be printed from desktop to fabric top using sublimation dyes. The aesthetic possibilities of this new process have been thoroughly embraced by designers and seen all over the catwalks and in the stores ever since.

Not surprisingly, as soon as we reached peak digital print, the pendulum quickly swung back to simpler traditional print methods and designs. A new generation of makers are diving back into the world of both block printing and hand-cut stencil printing, attending workshops in local craft centers or traveling abroad to learn skills from master artisans. Contemporary artists and savvy graphic designers are rediscovering traditional printing techniques such as lithography and letterpress while re-acquainting themselves with photo and stencil screen printing to produce eye-popping, limited-run publications and op art-inspired art. Print definitely refuses to be stamped out.

STUDIO HERETIC
Britain

Luke Frost, Jon Rundall and Therese Vandling are a London-based trio who operate under the moniker Studio Heretic. Their screen printing co-labs are jammed with op and pop art leanings, building print works from photographic images and old-school print patterns, supersonic collages, dripping with pop culture references and psychedelic color hits. Clever, funny, epic artworks that hurt the eyes and make the heart sing.

🖥 hereticheretic.co.uk

MARCROY SMITH
Britain

Marcroy Smith built his name creating screen-printed works that married low-fi zine sensibility with high-end digital imagery. His work recalled both 1980s kitchen table band posters and the infancy of fashion-forward mags such as *i-D* and *The Face*. Smith's love and commitment to the practice has determined his career path ever since. Founding a design agency in 2008 and the blog "People of Print," he's created an international platform to showcase the work of his favorite artists and foster the development of the best emerging talent. Smith continues to be a guiding light for contemporary printmaking, curating exhibitions and events worldwide and self-publishing a magazine wryly called *Print Isn't Dead*.

🖥 peopleofprint.com

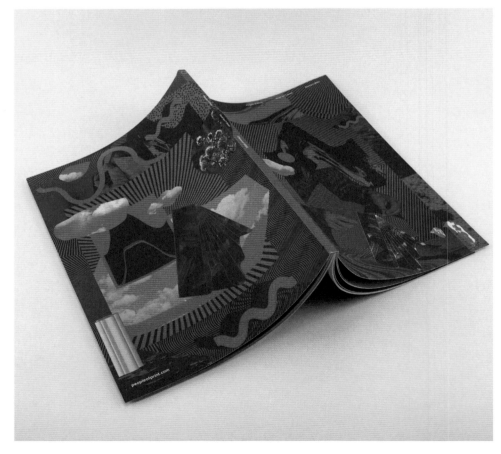

LILY AND HOPIE STOCKMAN/
BLOCK SHOP TEXTILES
United States/India

The designs of sisters Lily and Hopie Stockman are bold and graphic, and undeniably seductive. However, it's the way they have brought together their contemporary design sensibilities with the master printers of Bagru, India, to quietly create a brilliantly inclusive, equitable, ethically and environmentally sustainable business model that is truly worth celebrating. Exemplifying the best kind of fair trade partnerships, the master printers, broader Bagru community, Stockman sisters and end consumer all benefit from the creation of their beautiful block-printed scarves.

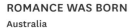 blockshoptextiles.com

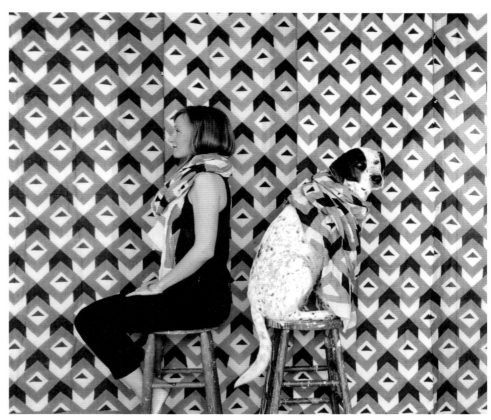

ROMANCE WAS BORN
Australia

If there was an award for best collaborative design crew as realized in digital print, Sydney duo Luke Sales and Anna Plunkett of Romance Was Born would win hands down. Their vision is absolute, uncompromising and intoxicating. Inspired equally by the best exponents of high fashion, the themes and aesthetics of superhero comics, Victorian busy work and mid-century psychedelia, their work manages to be simultaneously pure pop and properly crafty. The flexibility of the digital medium allows them free reign to bring to life the full scope of their peculiarly iconoclastic and gloriously eccentric viewpoint.

romancewasborn.com

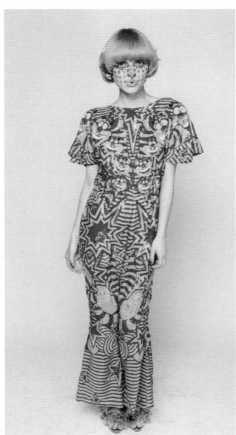

RONA GREEN
Australia

Rona Green's work is populated by a range of street-smart anthropomorphic tough guys. Rabbits, seagulls, dogs and cats come across as tattooed heavies who wear their life experience and identity on their sleeve. Using linocut and hand coloring to create a cast of characters, Green utilizes the most basic of printmaking techniques in the most sophisticated of ways, creating a unique and almost animated world.

🖥 ronagreen.com

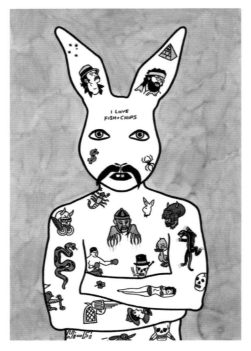

HANNAH WALDRON
Britain

Hannah Waldron carefully balances both weaving and printmaking, using strong graphic block shapes, architectural references, intricate line work and clever overprinting as signature features of her designs for fabric and paper. Waldron's reinterpretations of the traditional Japanese wrapping "furoshiki" come in smart geometric prints and a mixture of high-contrast palettes, in a seamless fusion of Japanese design traditions and her own personal aesthetics.

🖥 hannahwaldron.co.uk

PHILIPP HENNEVOGL
Germany

The linocut prints of artist Philipp Hennevogl stretch the technique to breaking point. This self-taught printmaker captures in high-volume realism everything from landscape to portraiture, with almost infinite detail in his large-scale monochromatic prints. By focusing in such a singular way on the linocutting process Hennevogl has mastered this technique, allowing him free reign to deliver his dystopian vision.

 philipp-hennevogl.de

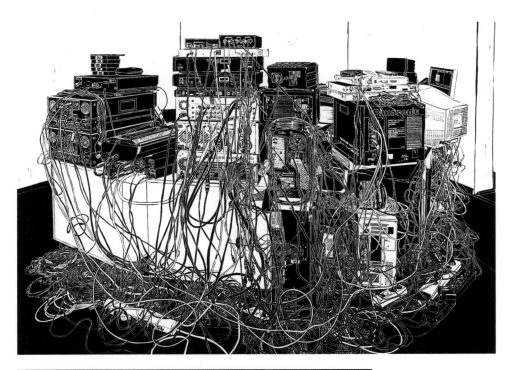

KATE BANAZI
Australia

Sydney-based screen printer Kate Banazi saturates her work with intense color and op art-inspired effects to create work that is simultaneously ultra-modern and totally retro. Banazi's work is knowing, sophisticated and confident, with visual and process references that span 1950s print ad aesthetics and post-war sci-fi genre cinema, all neatly tied together with a fearless approach to pattern play and graphic interaction.

katebanazi.com

DESIGN NOTES

REPEATING YOURSELF

Everything in nature is made up of multiple single units repeated to construct a whole. Perhaps this is the underlying principle that makes us respond so strongly to repeat surface patterning. Single elements can be reproduced in blocks, twisted and turned in order or at random, and complex interlocking repeats can be cut into paper and screen printed in seamless lengths. Consider the end use and choose your scale and coverage accordingly. The right repeat system can make or break a print. There are many established mathematical systems, but cutting out your elements and playing with them on paper or computer is a good place to start.

MIXED MESSAGES

Unless you're going to spend your life printing onto white paper or fabric you're going to have to come to terms with the impact of your "ground." Colored backgrounds can add instant impact but need to be handled with care, especially when printing on fabric. Opaque inks will give full coverage, ensuring sharp differentiation between print and ground, while pigment and ink will give a more translucent effect. Design your work with this in mind and use it to your advantage. White opaque ink on a black ground will give bold contrast while yellow pigment on blue will create green prints.

GEOMETRICENTRIC

It's no accident that so much ancient art uses simple graphic patterns. As a species we respond to the repetition of simple forms broken down to their most basic elements, and contemporary artists have known since cubism that geometric shapes will never let you down. When you are stuck for ideas or have grown weary of bird silhouettes, the humble circle, square, triangle, oval and hexagon will save the day.

DEVIL IN THE DETAIL

While you can fudge perfection in many crafts, nothing can hide sloppy printmaking. Mis-aligned screens, dirty paper, uneven printing, extraneous globs — you can tell yourself that they add character but you can't fool us. A dud is a dud. Even the most forgiving mono print can be ruined by a fingerprint smudge on your clean border because you couldn't be bothered switching to a clean pair of gloves. Proper set-up and attention to detail will ensure the right result every time. Some books may tell you to go with the flow on this point. This is not one of those books.

MAKE AN IMPRESSION

While there is an almost endless array of stamps available thanks to the burgeoning papercraft market, there's nothing more satisfying than carving your own. Creating patterns with stamps is one of the easiest ways of making both placement and repeat patterns, and today's materials, such as Speedy Carve, are incredibly simple to use. Take shape inspiration from the world around you, from plant forms to city streets, look to type and geometry for abstract ideas or transform your own drawings into repeatable blocks.

MOTIF MAGIC

A great way to get extra mileage from your printable motifs is to re-imagine them at different scales. Lateral manipulation of designs is a simple and effective way of getting the most from your work. Take a tiny cropped detail and blow it up. Use a photocopier or Photoshop to downsize a motif and repeat en masse. Mix large and small versions of the same motif to make an all-over pattern. Push yourself and see just how many different looks you can get from one idea.

TOOLS

- **Scribers:** You can use a knitting needle, ballpoint pen, comb or bone carver. In fact, choose anything that you can hold that will leave a mark when drawn across the paper.

- **Rubber blocks:** Look for smooth surfaces and quality feel, and experiment until you find the one that works best for you. You can also turn regular rubber pencil erasers into little stamps.

- **Pencils and pens:** For drawing on blocks or drawing designs. Use soft lead pencils for transferring designs.

- **Masking tape:** For taping stencils to screens.

- **Stencil brush:** For screen-free printing of small designs.

- **Silk screens:** You can make your own or buy a few in different sizes for different projects.

- **Rubber squeegee:** For pushing ink through the screen. Match them to your silk screen sizes.

- **Vegetable oil:** For cleaning up oil-based inks.

- **Plastic spatulas:** For mixing, applying and cleaning up print ink.

- **Spray hose nozzle:** Pressured water is best for cleaning screens, but a strong garden hose spray will do nicely for home printing.

- **Scrapers:** For putting print paste onto the screen and removing it during clean-up.

- **Print inks:** Buy the best you can afford; it will make a huge difference to your finished project. (See the Techniques section for descriptions.)

- **Paper:** Choose acid-free archival-quality art paper for permanency and clarity, or you can use rice paper, washi paper, drawing and flat watercolor papers. Weight, texture, absorbancy and surface finish are important considerations.

- **Fabric:** Finely woven or knitted fabric will always give you the sharpest results. Stick to natural fibers such as cotton, linen, bamboo, wool, viscose, felt and silk.

- **Assorted hard fruit and vegetables**

- **Glass or acetate sheeting**

- **Brayer**

- **Craft knife**

- **Scalpel**

- **Cutting mat**

- **Freezer paper**

- **Tracing paper**

- **Lino carving tools**

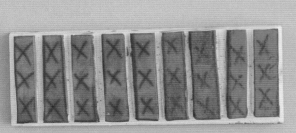

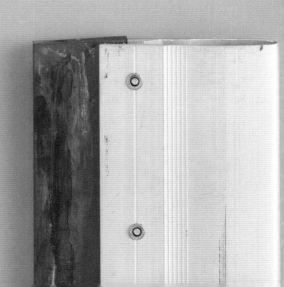

PRINT MEDIUMS

There are so many available options for domestic printing that it can be hard to get your head around what will work best. This list will give you an idea of how things work so you can match the right medium with the chosen process.

ACRYLIC PAINT

Acrylic paint can be used alone or mixed with fabric print medium. It's a good option for block printing on fabric and it is a cheap material that can be easily heat-set with an iron. Alone it can be lumpy to work with and dries super-quick. However, once mixed with fabric print medium, it transforms into a creamy consistency with enormous scope for color mixing. Use for mono and block prints, not screens.

BINDER AND PIGMENT

These work hand-in-hand to create custom-colored translucent printing ink by adding concentrated liquid pigment in drops to the white binder. Relatively cheap but kind of toxic, and colors are hard to match from batch to batch. Good on fabric and for block and screen printing.

PRE-MIXED WATER-SOLUBLE PRINT INK

Pre-mixed water-soluble print ink or paste is our number one choice for color, flow and environmentally friendliness. These inks are available in solvent-free versions in a huge range of colors (including intense fluoro shades, metallics and opaques), making them the all-round winner for every print situation. Opaque and metallic colors have a rubbery feel on the fabric. Most store-bought print inks will give you recommendations on temperature and times for heat setting, but you can do most of it at home with a hot iron and a bit of patience.

PROCION DYE

Procion dye is a cold-water fiber-reactive dye that can be screen-printed when mixed with a thickening agent (such as sodium alginate) and wetting agent (urea). Once thickened, these dyes are printed in exactly the same way as regular print ink. The dye permeates the fabric so the drape is maintained, which makes it a great option for light fabrics. Dyed fabric needs curing before washing. Good for block and screen printing on paper and fabric.

OIL-BASED INK

The traditional choice for prints on paper, oil-based ink is made with a linseed oil base. Intense opaque color options and sharp detailing make these inks perfect for block and monoprints in particular. They are a sticky mess and need to be washed out in light vegetable oil, but the results are well worth it.

REPEATS

You can extend the design options of even the most basic motif by using repeat systems. Think about how you put your motifs together to maximize their design potential. Experiment first with cut paper shapes to see how the repeats can affect your design.

FULL DROP

In full drop a motif is repeated evenly across the surface in parallel rows, both vertically and horizontally.

HALF DROP

Half drop repeat takes a motif and repeats it across the fabric vertically and horizontally but alternately staggers every other row or column.

REFLECTION

Reflection is literally a mirror image reflection of your motif.

ROTATION

Rotation is an incredibly useful and transformative process where a motif is rotated around a single point and repeated across the fabric horizontally or vertically.

COMBINATIONS

By combining two or more repeat processes, you can extend repeat patterns even further. This motif is rotated 90 degrees and put into a full drop with a mirror reflection.

RANDOM REPEATS

Repeated motifs are spread randomly. Elements can be spread out evenly or grouped together when working with single motif blocks.

MONOPRINT/MONOTYPE

Monoprinting or monotyping allows you to make one-off prints using acetate or glass sheet, paint or printing ink, mark-making tools and a roller. Acrylic paint lets you make loose lines but you need to work fast to stop the paint drying out before you make your print. Oil-based inks are sticky and messy but stay printable for longer and give great definition.

MONOPRINT

Paint your design directly onto your sheet of glass or acetate, then lay either dampened paper or fabric face down on top. Firmly rub over the back with your hand or a clean brayer to pick up the design.

MONOTYPE

Roll out a thin, even layer of printing ink onto your acetate sheet, then place your paper or fabric on top and draw your design on it with a scriber. It can be helpful to use a lead pencil instead to see the lines you're making. The pressure you apply while drawing picks up the print ink on the other side of the paper. Keep your hands off the paper as much as possible to eliminate excess ink transfer. Be aware that the print you create is a mirror image of the drawing on top, so factor this in if you're using letters or numbers.

BLOCK PRINTING

This is a simple contact printing process that uses relief cutting to create marks on fabric and paper. Print ink is applied to the block by brush, brayer, sponge or direct dipping, depending on the texture of the print ink. To transfer the image, either press the block directly onto the surface of your paper or fabric, or in the case of thin lino or wood cut blocks, lay the paper on top of the block and roll over it firmly with a brayer. Only the raised parts of your block will print.

RUBBER BLOCKS

Rubber blocks have the consistency of pencil erasers and can be cut with lino carving tools and craft knives with supreme ease.

1. Draw your image on the block. Remember, your print will be a mirror image of your drawn design. You'll need to reverse your numbers, letters and directional marks when designing.

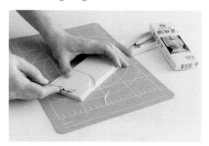

2. Carve away the areas you want to remain white and leave the areas you want to print. It helps to mark crosses into the cut-away sections so that you don't accidentally cut out the wrong section. Cuts shouldn't go deeper than halfway into your block.

3. Good prints come from well-coated blocks. To get the best print, first apply a little blob of ink onto glass and work a brayer over it in both directions until the brayer is evenly coated in ink. Then take your brayer and roll the ink right across the surface of your rubber block a couple of times until it's well coated with ink.

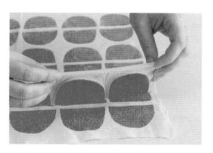

4. Lower your block face down onto your fabric or paper and press firmly with the palms of your hands. Hold the fabric down with one hand while gently peeling your block off with the other hand to make sure your fabric doesn't lift with the block.

5. Clean your rubber blocks well after each printing session, making sure to remove all inks. You can use a soft toothbrush for stubborn bits, pat with a cloth to remove excess water and let them air-dry before using them again.

TECHNIQUES

STENCIL CUTTING

One of the easiest ways to create sharp prints is with paper stencils. You can use virtually any paper for single prints. Amazingly, freezer paper can be ironed onto fabric to aid stenciling with a brush, while specialist stencil papers are purpose-designed for multiple use with screens and allow surprisingly intricate detailing.

Make a standard stencil by cutting away images in your paper, or a reverse stencil by cutting whole shapes, placing them on the surface of your paper or fabric and applying print ink over the top.

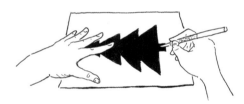

Standard stencils are most commonly used in screen printing, where only what is cut away is printed. Use an X-Acto knife for fine line work and graphic shapes, and circle cutters for circles — they're way too hard to cut freehand! Cutting against a colored cutting mat is a quick way of checking what your design will look like when printed.

SCREEN PRINTING

Screen printing works by pushing ink or dye through a fine mesh screen with gentle pressure created by a rubber squeegee. You can create wonderfully sharp details by masking areas not to be printed with tape, stencils, screen filler, masking fluid or photographic emulsion. Great for both placement prints and multiple registration color work. You can use the following technique on paper or fabric.

WHAT YOU NEED

- Mesh screen
- Masking tape
- Fabric or paper
- Pre-made stencil
- Print ink or paste
- Rubber squeegee
- Spatula

WHAT YOU DO

1. Tape screen edges front and back with masking tape to block any stray ink. This is really important as gaps result in ugly splotches on your print base that can't be explained away as "design features."

2. Place your stencil on the flat side of your screen, taping it in place lightly at the top and bottom and making sure that your stencil overlaps the tape around the edges. Don't worry about your stencil moving — the print paste will make it stick securely to the screen while you print. Trust us.

3. Before making your first print, pull the squeegee and flood the screen with ink. Flooding the screen is an important step and ensures you have an even coating of ink on the screen ready to make a sharp, clean print. Blob some print ink in a line across the top of the inside of your screen with a spatula. Be generous but judicious in your application. Hold your screen up off the fabric and firmly in the middle of the left side of the frame with one hand. Hold your squeegee firmly in the center with your other hand. Take your squeegee at a 20- to 30-degree angle and gently pull the ink down toward you, covering the screen with ink without pushing it through the mesh.

4. Lay the fabric or paper to be printed on the table and position yourself directly in front of it. Place your screen flat side down on your fabric or paper exactly where you want to make your print.

5. Place the squeegee back at the top of your screen and hold it at a 45-degree angle to the screen. The angle is really important, as it will push the ink through the mesh at a consistent pressure, ensuring a clean print. Firmly pull the squeegee down the screen toward you on the same angle, maintaining even pressure as you go. You'll see all the ink transfer from the screen through the mesh.

6. Lift off your squeegee, take it back to the top and make another firm pull down the screen. Two clean downward pulls should be enough to get a solid print. Check by looking through the screen at your print surface below to be sure. If there are still gaps, add a little more ink to the top of your screen and make another pull down the screen.

7. Gently lift off your screen and put it to the side onto some scrap paper or fabric. Make sure you don't put your screen down on a wet print or you'll end up with ink all over the outside of the screen, which will transfer to your clean fabric when you make your next print. To keep printing, add more ink and continue the process, making sure you work quickly before your screen starts to dry out.

8. Clean everything thoroughly once you're done. Using a spatula, scrape excess ink from the screen and squeegee back into the ink tub. Peel off your stencil carefully and gently wash it in water before hanging it up to dry. Take extra care to get all the ink out of your screen; if you don't have access to a high-pressure hose, use a garden hose and soft sponge. You need to get all the ink out before it dries and blocks the mesh, which would ruin your screen for future use.

PROJECT IDEAS

→ Never buy gift paper again. Instead, take rolls of brown craft paper and block print them with vegetable shapes for instant and unique wrapping. A great rainy day, bored kid activity, but just as fun for you.

→ Lino carving is a great technique, but you're limited by both block size and the dimensions of your print table. Buy several lino-carving squares or linoleum blocks and put them together as one. Then draw your design across the whole area. Carve each block separately, place them back together and print patchwork-style for a large-scale artwork.

→ A great way to quickly make repeat-patterned fabric without a screen is by attaching foam blocks to a rolling pin. Spice up your tableware by printing placemats using this simple technique. Either cut out your own design or attach pre-cut foam letters or shapes and get rolling.

→ Use the sun as your print assistant. You can buy light-sensitive papers and fabric as well as sun-sensitive fabric dyes, which come in a multitude of colors. The UV light develops the sun-sensitive fabric or paper, and objects placed directly onto its surface act as a resist to make patterns. It's a perfect hybrid of dyeing, photographic and print techniques.

→ Translate your print skills into other crafts to create unique detailing or all-over patterning. Simple eraser stamps printed in bright colors add pizzazz to a plain leather clutch. Geometric shapes can be printed through stencils on a warp before weaving. And metal can be digitally printed with squiggly repeats for super-cool jewelry.

Block Print Dog Bed

WHAT YOU NEED

- 3 x Speedy Carve blocks (4 x 6")
- Craft knife
- Carving tools
- Wool blanket
- Scrap newspaper
- Masking tape
- 1 yard of unbleached muslin
- Glass sheet
- Foam roller or brayer
- Screen print ink (we used black and hot pink)
- Ruler
- Scissors
- 1¾ yard of mid-weight denim
- Heavy-duty zipper
- Pins
- Black sewing thread
- Sewing machine
- Foam rectangle 27½ x 35⅜ x 3"

HOT TIP

If you have a smaller or bigger dog you can adjust the size of both fabric and zipper to match your dog. Fabric and zipper size are determined by the size of the foam insert. Print fabric needs to be 4" bigger than your foam on all sides, base fabric needs to be 7⅞" longer and 4" wider than your foam, and the zipper will need to fit across the width of the foam with 4" of fabric at either end.

If you're not into princesses or wacky bone graphics, it's very hard to find a comfortable dog bed that you can stand looking at on a daily basis. Our much-loved Muji is more inside lounger than outside scrounger, and he completely owns his corner of the lounge room. Inspired by tapa cloth, we made him a custom block-print cushion to keep him comfortable and save us from bad taste.

WHAT YOU DO

1. Copy our motifs onto blocks. The large arch is block 1, the striped row is block 2 and the half circle is block 3. Cut out each motif using your craft knife, then use your carving tools to carve away the background.

2. Set up your print space by laying out the blanket and newspaper, taping them to the table, then laying your unbleached muslin horizontally on top. Make sure it has no wrinkles and tape down the corners to hold it in place while you print. Set up your glass sheet, foam roller and print ink ready for rolling.

3. Using a pencil, lightly mark the mid-point of the fabric (across the width). Print from the mid-point out toward the edges in both directions to make a mirror image print. Start with a line of stripes across the fabric in pink, using block 2. Remember to re-ink your block as you go to keep the print quality consistent.

4. Ink up block 1 in black and, with the flat side facing the line of stripes, make a parallel printed row ⅜" away from your row of pink stripes. Repeat on the other side of your row of stripes so you have a mirror image row on either side.

5. Ink up block 3 in pink and, with the curved edges facing the curves of your arch, make another row of prints ⅜" away from the previous row. Repeat this row on the other side.

6. Take block 2 and make a row of black stripes ⅜" away from the flat edges of block 3. Then repeat on the other side.

7. Add another row of block 3, printed in pink, along the other side of your stripes, with the flat sides facing the stripes.

8. Make another row of block 1 in black with curved sides facing the curves, and repeat on the other side. Then leave your fabric to dry.

9. To complete your cushion, cut your denim in half and insert the zipper (refer to the Sew chapter if you need a refresher).

10. Pin your printed fabric and base denim fabric together with right sides facing and make a 4" cut gusset in all four corners, then sew up all four sides.

11. Turn the cushion right side out, insert your foam and call the dog — it's lie down time.

DYE ONLY

FROZEN
BLUEBERRIES
& ALUM

(EXHAUST DIPPED)

SILK DIPPED IN
THE
EXHAUST FROM
FROZEN BLUEBERRIES
WITH WATER (BOIL/
SIMMER)
1/2 CUP SALT (FIX)
NO PRE-MORDANT
1/4 TSPN ALUM
AS DYE MORDANT

SILK

COLD BATH
SAME BATH —
SOAKED IN DYE
COLD/SUN ONLY
FOR 4 HRS

SOY SOAKED
COTTON
(18 HRS)

(FRESH)

STRAWBERRIES
DIPPED IN 1/2
CUPS WATER
TSPN SALT AS FIX

BOILED/SIMMERED 1 HR
FABRIC IN WARM BATH
FOR 1/2 HOUR

FABRICS

SILK (HABUTAI)
SOY SOAKED COTTON
SALT BOILED COTTON
8 PLY ??????? YARN

COLD BATH W ALUM
WITH ALUM MORDANT 1/2 TSP
ADDED AND COLD SOAKED
FOR 4 HOURS

SILK

SOY SOAKED COTTON

BOILED COTTON

SILK

SOY SOAKED
COTTON
(18 HRS)

Dye

◇◇◇

Dyeing is both primal and magical. It's a truly universal craft; all cultures use staining of one kind or another to add variety and color to their textile traditions. Anyone who has spilled beet juice down their front or sat on a blueberry pie in their party frock (don't ask) will understand just how simple it can be to stain fiber.

Hardened dye made from ochre has been found from the Neolithic era around 8000 B.C.E. Ancient Egyptian hieroglyphs describe both extraction and application, and there is an unbroken history of over 5,000 years of dye practice in India and China alone. Nature provided the color palette until the mid-19th century, when synthetic dyes became available. Trial and error were employed by early civilizations. Key local ingredients became highly prized trading commodities. Plants, berries, bark, clay and even insects were utilized to create sought-after colors such as red, purple and blue. Dye materials and processes were heavily guarded secrets and different communities "owned" different colors. Threads or fabrics were often passed between communities, each one adding another color to create the finished work.

Each natural dye has its own story. Reds came from madder root and cochineal. Madder root, indigenous to central Asia, was cultivated there for centuries before it reached England in the 18th century and was used to dye the red coats of British soldiers. Cochineal, made from the bodies of cactus-feeding insects, was collected as tribute from the tribes conquered by Aztecs and, in turn, taken by Spanish conquistadors back to Europe. Woad was used for blue across Russia, China, Europe, Asia and the Middle East, before being superseded by the stronger indigo, its name derived from the Latin word *indicum*, meaning "from India." Green, ironically, was even harder to obtain naturally and required an iron mordant of yellow-dyed fabric or the expert combining of blue and yellow dyes.

In the 4th century B.C.E. Alexander the Great noted his admiration for the beautiful purple robes of the Persian monarchy. Called Tyrian Purple (one for *Game of Thrones* fans), the color was extracted from mollusc shells. More than 8,000 shells were needed to make one gram of dye, making it worth more than its weight in gold. To this day the reign of purple is still absolute. It remains a color associated with power, royalty and funky guitar riffs.

As dyes developed so did the techniques used to manipulate them into patterns on cloth. Almost every continent and culture brought its own unique approach to dyeing. Resists, such as ties, binds, clamps, pastes and waxes, were developed to stop dye from reaching fabric — shibori in Japan, batik in Indonesia, adire eleko in West Africa, blaudruck in central Europe, and tlalpilli of Mesoamerica and the bògòlanfini (mudcloth) of Mali. These processes remain relevant and relatively unchanged and their distinctive patterns continue to inspire makers and designers to this day.

Probably the most significant moment in dye's history came in 1856, when young English chemistry student William Perkin stumbled upon a synthetic aniline solution while trying to synthesize quinine. His purple — stable, reproducible and, most importantly, indelible — eventually became known as mauvine. Perkin patented his dye and with his father set up shop. This decision was impeccably timed with the mechanization of the textile industry formed on the back of the Industrial Revolution. The discovery of mauvine not only changed the fortunes of its inventor but ultimately created an industry of synthetic dyes and commercial dyeing.

In the mid-1950s the development of Procion (cold-water fiber-reactive dyes) was another great leap forward in dye manufacturing. Making it possible to bond pigment to fiber without boiling, Procion opened the door to modern dyeing and remains the most commonly used dye from industrial to backyard production. Known for their flexibility, color range and light fastness, fiber-reactive dyes are embraced by contemporary artists and designers alike.

As a considered approach to sustainable and small footprint textile production, there has been a resurgence in natural dyeing. People have once again taken to foraging for suitable plant stuffs in their own backyards and alleyways, rediscovering ancient methods and mixing them up with new technologies and techniques to create fabrics to die for.

JOANNA FOWLES
Australia

Joanna Fowles is a process-driven textile designer whose work fuses the unique irregularities of handcrafted mark-making with the uniformity of computer-aided design. Droplets, brushstrokes, watery washes and graphic lines intermingle in her experimental approach as she deploys the flexibility of dye as a design device through hand-painting, shibori and screen-print processes. Selecting interesting sections for further digital manipulation, Fowles adds a unique and richly textural provenance to her range of fashion prints and one-off homewares.

🖥 joannafowles.com

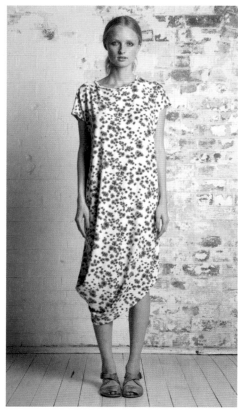

JESSICA LEE/WILLOW KNOWS
United States

It takes a particular kind of vision and restraint to create the dreamy, immersive textiles that are the trademark of Willow Knows. Lee works with natural, synthetic and foraged dyes to create delicate repeats from pressed petals, and astutely utilizes the soft palette and mark-making of vat processes in combination with the fluidity of silk fabric to create poetry.

🖥 willowknows.com

INDIA FLINT
Australia

If anyone embodies the essence of natural dyeing it is India Flint. Having spent the last thirty years honing her craft, she has created an aesthetic sensibility and technical proficiency that establish her as both a master-crafter and an exceptionally fine artist. One part botanist and two parts alchemist, Flint employs the plant, mineral and animal materials found in her immediate habitat to build highly complex designs, layer upon layer, through resist and direct dyeing techniques as the ultimate homage to the environment she inhabits.

🖵 **indiaflint.com**

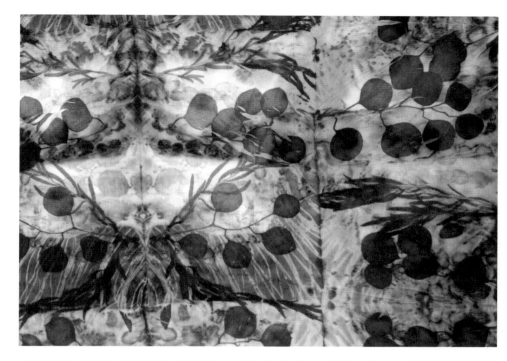

RAFAELLA MCDONALD
Australia

The immediacy of the bold mark-making found in artist Rafaella McDonald's House of RAF is a particularly riotous declaration that fashion should be not just fun to wear but fun to make. Drawing on the stylistic tendencies of the 1980s New Wave, but reinterpreted with the vivacity of youth, McDonald's designs are hand-painted directly on the fabric with the 3-D body in mind, and placement is everything. Her output also includes site-specific installations and paintings built around themes as esoteric as local swimming pools, while her wearable collections hang together as casual confrères, both unique and highly collectable.

🖵 **rafaellamcdonald.com.au**

DESIGN NOTES

NATURAL SELECTION

Natural dyes create harmonious palettes, which makes designing with them super easy. Everything from rainfall levels to soil quality can affect your foraged dye materials and dye bath, so you'll have to learn to go with the flow. The variable results that come with this dyeing process are one of its greatest strengths, so revel in the happy accidents and surprises that come with the territory.

—

'TIS THE SEASON

There are lots of pros to natural dyeing but one of the cons is that you are dealing with the vagaries of seasonality. One way of ensuring that you have access to colors and materials all year round is by dry harvesting or freezing your material. Try setting up your permanent collection of natural dyes like a spice pantry and use it to supplement what's in season.

—

DIP IT GOOD

Don't limit yourself to the dip dyeing of plain fabrics. You can create amazing custom combos by dipping either commercial fabric or your own patterned pieces. Dip the bottom of a store-bought skirt, the sleeves of a shirt or some bed linen to make them unique, or over-dye patterned fabrics and garments to create entirely new hues. This is a sure-fire way of unifying a wardrobe or a whole range of fabrics that can then work harmoniously in the same project.

—

DEAR DIARY

It is incredibly satisfying and helpful to keep records of your adventures with dye. Buy a great notebook or folder and invest time recording the details and outcomes of each bath. Cut out samples and note down quantities and locations of your ingredients, fabric preparation, mordants, dyeing times and fixing processes. You'll quickly find you have an amazing reference guide and inspiring color collection perfect for future project planning.

—

FADE TO GRAY

Keep using your natural dye bath until it's exhausted. Sometimes the most beautiful colors come from its last gasps. Use these tonal variants alongside their more vibrant brothers and sisters to create stunning monochromatic patchworks, mix similarly faded hues together or experiment with different fibers or mordants for your dye diary.

—

PRODUCT PLACEMENT

Yes, you can print with dye. It works particularly well with cold-water reactive dyes. With the addition of sodium alginate (a natural product made from algae) to thicken the dye to a paste, you'll be able to use it in the same way you use printing ink. Dye printing opens the door to repeat or placement designs using screen printing or block techniques while maintaining the drape of the fabric. Play with bold graphic shapes, multiple colorways and sharp, detailed surface patterning.

- **Resists:** Used to create a barrier between the dye and fabric. These can be as varied as rubber bands, beads, acrylic shapes, wax, wooden clothespins, marbles and clamps.

- **Dye pots:** Aluminum and copper pots impart a small amount of mordant into the dye bath, which is super handy for natural dyeing as it can boost a color during the process.

- **Procion MX dyes:** Cold-water reactive dyes that come in powder form in around 130 colors. Best to use on cellulose fibers, such as cotton, linen, ramie, bamboo, hemp and viscose.

- **Acid dyes:** Hot-water dyes used for protein-based fibers, such as silk and wool. These need to be dissolved in almost-boiling water to fix color, and lower pH dye baths. Cannot be used on synthetics.

- **Direct dyes:** Supermarket and craft store varieties, the most accessible but least colorfast. They work best when used with boiling water and salt. Best to use on cellulose fibers. Cannot be used on synthetics.

- **Synthetic dyes:** Specialty dyes for 100% man-made fibers like polyester. To get the best color results on mixed fiber fabrics, dye them in two batches, once in a natural fiber dye bath and once in a synthetic dye bath.

- **Mordants:** Used to assist dye uptake into fiber or change color tone and brightness. Potassium aluminum sulfate (alum), copper sulfate, ferrous sulfate (iron), rhubarb leaves (use outside only as the fumes are toxic), soy milk, soda ash and washing soda.

- **Additives:** Urea, sodium alginate, Calsolene Oil, vinegar, ammonia.

- **Bleach stop:** Used to stop bleach eating away fabric during discharge dyeing.

- **Natural dye materials:** Red and brown onion skin, willow bark, passionfruit skins, avocado pits, acorns, purple carrots, walnut hulls, red cabbage, oxalis, madder, cochineal, turmeric, eucalyptus, berries, coffee, tea, chamomile, beet, paprika. Not a complete list, but a useful start.

- **Buckets**

- **Disposable and rubber gloves**

- **Paintbrushes**

- **Small plastic tubs**

- **Kitchen scales**

- **Face mask**

- **Notebook**

- **Metal, plastic and wooden spoons**

- **Glass jars**

- **Measuring cup**

- **Bleach**

- **Bamboo steamer**

NATURAL DYES

Probably the best way to approach natural dyeing is to think of it as an experimental process, especially if you are using foraged materials. Unless you invest a great deal of time or are buying natural extracts in powdered form from a dye supplier, it's virtually impossible to get the same result twice. That being said, the kitchen alchemy that comes with using foraged finds to dye with is utterly intoxicating, often frustrating but overwhelmingly rewarding. We'll give you the basic principles and then you can go explore for yourself!

Instead of taking a measured approach, we prefer to use as much as we can cram into our dye pots. Plant matter can be stripped off branches, chopped into smaller parts, crushed, frozen or boiled to aid color dispersal. Once fabric has been added to the bath you can use further boiling, soaking and even solar energy to transfer color to the fabric. Each process will alter the result. Heat will ruin some colors while others can only be extracted in high boiling temperatures.

Natural dyestuffs are either substantive or advective. Substantives include onion skins, eucalyptus and turmeric, and these transfer their color directly into the fabric. Advectives are the dyestuffs that need a mordant to transfer their color.

The growing conditions, soil, season and storage of the plants you'll be using all have a direct impact on quality and color of the end result. The following colors are the most usual outcomes from the ingredients listed, but these can all be tipped in different directions by adding different mordants at different stages.

Be prepared for mixed results and enter with an investigative sense of adventure.

- Reds/pinks: avocado pits (pale pink), madder, cochineal, roses, strawberries, raspberries, cherries, red cabbage leaves, chokecherries, beet

- Greens: brown onion skins with iron, oxalis, cherry ballart, red onion with copper, tea tree, spinach, nettles

- Orange: paprika, eucalyptus leaves, red onion skins, pomegranate skins, sassafras leaves

- Black/gray: wattle seed, walnut husks, oak galls, carob pods (boiled)

- Yellow: turmeric, oxalis, dandelion flower, burdock, beet with alum, barberry, goldenrod, peach leaves

- Purple/blue: blueberries, red cabbage with alum and iron, dogwood bark, woad, indigo, cornflower, blackberry, grapes, elderberry, hyacinth

- Browns: brown onion skins, coffee grounds, red onion skins, dandelion roots, beet, black tea, walnut hulls, sumac leaves, juniper berries

There is a wealth of information out there in book and digital form, which is both enlightening and exasperatingly contradictory. It helps to allow yourself plenty of time to fully explore the successes and failures that come with experimenting — just remember to record everything in your dye journal for future reference.

MORDANTS

Traditionally these are metal salts that affect the acceptance of dye by the fiber or that fix the dye to the fiber. They can also change the performance of the dye, shifting it into different colorways or making it brighter and more intense. Mordants can be used before dyeing to make dye uptake better, during dyeing to change colors and after dyeing to fix color.

As a general rule, iron makes color darker, copper tips it green and alum makes it brighter. They can be used alone or in combination, and even within these guidelines you can still be surprised by what happens each time you dye. All three can be purchased from craft stores in granular form and added in tiny amounts (around ⅛ of a teaspoon) to dye pots to change colors during dyeing.

You can also use found items as mordants. Add rusty nails to your dye bath for iron, or use copper or aluminum pots for your dye baths and they'll act as mordants during the process. Whether using found items or commercial versions, keep yourself safe. Commercial versions are the least toxic option, but you should still make sure you avoid too much skin contact, and keep them out of reach of children. Label them clearly as poisons and avoid inhaling their fumes while you're dyeing.

All fabrics should be washed on a hot setting to remove any starch or trace chemicals. Before dyeing soak your fabric in a mordant bath to achieve better color results. There can be a big difference in the outcome based on the content of your fabric or fiber. Protein-based fibers such as silk or wool accept natural dyes best, while synthetics cannot be dyed at all. You can get good results from natural dyes on cellulose fibers (cotton, hemp, bamboo) if you "trick" the dye bath by pre-mordanting it in high protein soy milk overnight. Do not wash the soy milk out before dyeing.

ABOVE: Beet on wool, cotton, silk
BELOW: Red cabbage on wool, cotton, silk

FIXING

Unfortunately natural dyes are notoriously elusive when it comes to color fastness. It's really hard to keep them in the fabric permanently and they will all fade to varying degrees over time. If you are using commercially produced dye powders you will get much better color fastness than if you're playing with raw materials. It's best to keep your natural dye projects out of direct sunlight and avoid constant laundering.

COLD-WATER REACTIVE DYES

If you want guaranteed results when it comes to dyeing natural fabrics, look no further than Procion MX dyes — these are the bee's knees. There's a huge variety of brilliant and bright colors to choose from, they're completely color fast, and they can be used in a variety of ways, including hand-painting, printing and immersion dyeing. They're economical, non-toxic and very easy to use.

These dyes permanently bond with the fiber at a molecular level, and although they're designed to work best on cellulose fibers, they also work a treat on protein fibers such as silk and wool. Synthetic fabrics such as polyester, acrylic and nylon will not dye at all. However, synthetic–natural blends can be dyed with pale and patchy results, depending on the ratio of synthetic to natural fiber.

Most manufacturers will provide instructions for use, ratio guides for dye to fabric weight and recipes along with the dye. Generally speaking, however, all Procion dyes come in powder form and need to be mixed with either chemical water (see Additives below) or room-temperature tap water before use. Dyes can be used at full strength or watered down for lighter shades.

PRE-SOAKING

To get the most out of your dye it helps to pre-soak your fabric in soda ash. Mix 8 fl. oz. of soda ash to 4 litres of warm water. Always add the soda ash to the water and not the other way around or it will clump. We use a metal whisk to mix it vigorously. Soak the fabric in this mix for around half an hour for cotton and linen, although even 5 minutes can make a difference if you're short on time. A less robust fabric such as silk only needs around 5 to 10 minutes. Once you've pre-soaked, wring out the fabric so it's still damp but not dripping and ready for dyeing.

ADDITIVES

Some dye projects will require you to mix up additives such as urea, Calsolene Oil and sodium alginate into what are referred to as "chemical waters." If you're going to be doing a fair amount of dyeing, make this up in bulk and keep it in the fridge for up to a month, away from the food, in sealed containers.

Urea helps dyes dissolve and keeps fabric wet longer. Dissolve 5 g (1 teaspoon) per cup of warm water and let it cool before adding to dye.

Calsolene Oil helps break surface tension

and makes your dye uptake more even, and is especially useful for immersion and ombré dyeing. Add 30 drops (½ teaspoon) for every 4 litres of water.

Sodium alginate is made from seaweed. It thickens dye to decrease bleeding when hand-painting and turns it into a print paste for screen or block printing. Think of it as a sort of dye gelatin. Sprinkle between a pinch and a teaspoon per cup of water depending on how thick you want your dye. It will take around an hour to fully thicken so don't be tricked into adding too much or you'll have jelly instead of dye.

MIXING DYE

The amount of dye powder to water or chemical solution will depend on how much fabric you want to dye, but we advise mixing in small batches as the dye will not remain stable for more than a few hours, and may not give you the exact color you're after. As a gauge, $1/6$ oz. of dye per 4 fl. oz. of water is enough to dye one big t-shirt.

Using a spoon, mix the powdered dye with either room-temperature tap water or chemical water in a small plastic cup. Test your color on absorbent paper or scrap fabric and either water it down further if you want a watercolor effect or add more dye powder if your color isn't intense enough.

For direct dyeing processes, such as hand-painting and squeegee bottle tie-dye, this solution is ready to use. To turn your direct dye mix into printable paste add sodium alginate, or use this solution added to a large tub of water for immersion dyeing.

CURING

Procion dyes are best cured with steam and you can get great results by using plain kitchen equipment.

Line-dry your dyed fabric, then wrap it into a snake of unbleached muslin and seal it with masking tape.

Coil your snake inside, put the lid on and set it over a large pot of boiling water for 40 minutes. Once steamed, wash your fabric thoroughly in cold water until the water is clear and then hand-wash in detergent.

Alternatively, you can tumble-dry the fabric on high for 40 minutes, or air-cure for 24 hours (although your fabric will be duller and not as color fast). If you've used an immersion bath, the soaking time cures the fabric, so you don't need to go through this process. BONUS!

TURMERIC TIE-DYE

Turmeric is a great starting point for natural dyeing as you're guaranteed a good result.

We used kumo binding to make our tie-dye patterns. This technique involves pulling out a series of fabric "peaks," which you then bind with fine thread from the bottom to the top and back down again to form web-patterned diamond shapes.

WHAT YOU NEED

- Silk fabric
- 60 g turmeric powder
- 1 litre vinegar
- Polyester thread
- Scissors
- Bucket
- Wooden spoon
- Aluminum dye pot and a big saucepan

WHAT YOU DO

1. Tie your pattern into the fabric. If you want something simpler or more regimented, check the Indigo chapter for other options such as itajime and mokume.

2. Pour the vinegar and 3.8 litres of water into your aluminum dye pot and add your fabric. This is your pre-mordant soak to aid dye take-up. In the big saucepan, add your turmeric and ¾ gallon of water. Bring both to a near boil, then turn them right down to a simmer for around an hour.

3. Once your hour is up, drain the vinegar mix off your fabric and pour the turmeric dye bath over it. Keep this warm over a very low heat for around 45 minutes, using a wooden spoon or tongs to move the fabric around periodically to make sure it's not sticking to the bottom of your pot. Alternatively, you could leave your fabric in the dye pot overnight and turn off the power.

4. Take your fabric out and rinse it in cold running water to get the excess dye off. Carefully cut off your threads to reveal your newly dyed cloth, then rinse again. You're done! Just make sure that for its first laundry wash it goes in with the brights and NOT the whites.

SPACE DYEING

Space dyeing is an incredibly simple, intuitive process that allows you to create fluid random patterning with a level of artistic control.

WHAT YOU NEED

- Shallow dye tub
- Rubber gloves
- Pitcher
- Procion MX dye powder
- 30 g (1 tablespoon) soda ash
- Cotton or linen fabric
- Bucket
- Plastic sheet

WHAT YOU DO

1. Fill your bucket with boiling water and add the soda ash. Stir to dissolve, then add your fabric and leave it to soak for around 20 minutes.

2. Take the fabric from the bucket, wring out the excess water and lay it flat inside your dye tub, arranging it with your fingers so there are peaks (which will stay out of the dye), folds and valleys (which will allow the dye to pool).

3. Measure 10 fl. oz. of warm water and add ¼ teaspoon of dye powder, taking care to ensure that all the dye powder is completely dissolved in the water. Then carefully pour your dye into the folds and valleys of the fabric.

4. You can add other colors at this point but remember that as liquids they will mix together and create new hues, so consider your combinations carefully and design accordingly. Once you're done, cover your tub with the plastic sheet and leave it overnight for the dye to cure.

5. The next day remove your fabric from the tub and rinse it under cold running water until the water runs clear. Take a moment to marvel at your brilliance!

ICE DYEING

A freezer favorite that creates soft random patterning with a wonderfully cosmic feel, this is addictively fun and so easy it feels like cheating. Pre-soak your fabric as you do for space dyeing, and arrange it on a baking rack sitting inside your dye tub, using the same arrangement of peaks and valleys. Instead of adding liquid dye, add ice cubes to the surface of your fabric, and sprinkle them directly with Procion MX powder until all the ice is covered.

Put it safely out of the way of curious pets, small people and clumsy partners, and leave it for 24 hours so that the ice can melt, allowing the dye to take hold. Rinse it under cold running water to reveal your masterpiece.

PROJECT IDEAS

→ Dye is one of the best ways to resuscitate garments. Try using shibori resist techniques to highlight details and hide flaws. Alternatively, take a patterned fabric and over-dye it with a light color to reinvent the colorway. Blues dyed with yellow will turn to greens, while reds will turn orange.

→ Eco printing is a great way to use the principles of natural dyeing to create beautiful leaf- and petal-shaped patterning on silk using substantive plants like eucalyptus, roses, ferns, turmeric and onion skins. Lay your petals and leaves out on your fabric, then tightly roll up the fabric and bind it with string or rubber bands. Steam for an hour, then take your bundle out and let it cure for around four to six days. Unroll and wash with soapy water.

→ Update plain bed linen with hand-painted or printed dye techniques. Be bold and hand-paint your own gingham checks, or take your favorite vegetable and print up a large-scale repeat. This one's great for a gift.

→ Dip-dye thread or yarn in various colors for weaving or knitting. Pure wool takes dye better than nearly anything and will give you a unique palette to take your project to the next level. It's the craft equivalent of churning your own butter.

→ Don't limit yourself to fabric or yarn. Just about any natural fiber or material can be dyed — think about timber or leather as dyeable options ripe for experimentation. Cork placemats, chair legs, even plain tennis shoes painted or sprayed with dye can look amazing.

Spot the Difference Tee

WHAT YOU NEED

- Plastic sheet
- Rubber gloves
- 1 tablespoon sodium metabisulfite
- Bucket
- Cotton jersey t-shirt (we used navy but any deep color will do)
- Newspaper
- Glass jar
- Nylon bristle brush
- Half a bucket of bleach-stop solution

HOT TIP

You can use the discharge as an immersive dye or as space dye by pouring bleach over fabric in a shallow tub. The color revealed by the bleach will depend on your fabric's original dye: dark colors may reveal another hue; light colors may bleach to white. Choose sturdy fabrics to work with and if you can't make a bleach-stop solution, make sure the fabric gets a soapy solo laundering as soon as enough color has been removed. You don't want to end up with holes instead of dots.

Discharge dyeing involves the removal of color from fabrics by chemical reaction. It's pretty much the mirror image of regular dyeing and opens up a world of new colors and pattern options. Inspired by Japanese artist Yayoi Kusama, we gave the old-school D.I.Y. bleach option a new school makeover by hand-painting oversize polka dots directly on the fabric.

WHAT YOU DO

1. Lay the plastic sheet down on a flat surface outdoors or in a well-ventilated room, and put on the rubber gloves. Bleach is stinky and toxic so it's not an indoor activity — safety first, people.

2. Make up a bleach solution by adding the sodium metabisulfite to 2½ gallons of water in a bucket.

3. Lay your t-shirt flat on the plastic sheet, front facing up, and put 3 or 4 layers of newspaper inside. Pour some of the bleach into the glass jar and place it within arm's reach for regular brush dipping.

4. Dip your brush into the bleach and, starting in the center-top of your t-shirt, just under the neckline, paint your first polka dot. Dip your brush again and make your next polka dot 1" to the right, then repeat the process and make another one 1" to the left. Keep working on both sides until you have a line of polka dots painted across the front of your t-shirt.

5. Make the next row of polka dots around 1" underneath the first, staggering your dots with the first row. It will be hard to see where you're painting at first but the dye will quickly start changing the color of the fabric, making it easier to see where you are going.

6. Work quickly across the rest of the front of your t-shirt until it's covered in dots, then turn it over and do the same to the back.

7. By the time you get to the last dot on the back, the front will have completely changed, revealing the color underneath. Give it another 10 minutes to finish discharging before rinsing thoroughly in cold water.

8. Squeeze out the excess water and put your t-shirt into the bleach-stop solution. Leave it to soak for a couple of hours, then rinse again and hang to dry.

Collage

◇◇◇

Collage is an extraordinary technique for loosening up the creative muscle, providing new ways of seeing and composing. It's enormously liberating to be freed from the need to create images and patterns from scratch — and being able to work intuitively and arranging things by "feel" is a great way of building aesthetic self-confidence.

The term "collage" is derived from the French "coller" meaning literally "to glue," and involves the assemblage of different forms and materials to create a new whole. If you are the type of crafter who is also your toughest critic, collage gives you permission to play. Enormously beneficial in building color and design awareness, its principles can be applied to virtually all crafts. As more craft techniques seep into art and design, the use of stitching, beading, fabric and fiber within this graphic art form is increasingly common, blurring lines between disciplines and continuing to astound and confound.

While artists Pablo Picasso and Georges Braque were in a historical duel for the title of "Collage King" between 1908 and 1914, Weimar Dadaist Hannah Hoch was pioneering the technique of photomontage, breaking down gender roles and sardonically critiquing contemporary culture. Hoch's use of the material by-products of modern mass media (newspaper clippings, magazine photography and advertising) so convincingly lent itself to political commentary, surrealistic imaginings and ironic juxtaposition that it not only inspired a new breed of feminist cultural commentators, including Barbara Kruger, but remains the most common interpretation of paper collage to this day.

In recent times the impact of musical sampling, combined with the prevalence of hip hop's aural cut and paste techniques and fast-edit videos, have subliminally prepared a generation for collage as a default cultural aesthetic. Improved access to stock images and the technology to manipulate them, as well as tons of analogue materials, have led to collage being universally adopted by contemporary artists. While Photoshop is now as likely a tool as an X-Acto knife, there are still plenty of old-school purists rocking their paper and scissors.

JOCK MOONEY
Britain

Artist Jock Mooney uses collages to re-imagine his own illustrations in repetitive reconstructions that fool the senses and dazzle the eye. Brilliantly clever color use and pop cultural referencing make his wreaths as hilarious as they are beautiful.

🖵 **jockmooney.com**

RICHARD PEARSE
New Zealand

A master of pattern-making and placement, Richard Pearse's large-scale wood collages tap into traditions of abstraction, minimalism and constructivism without feeling weighed down by over-intellectualizing the process. Different surface textures from salvaged wood create points of interest and punctuation, colors dictate pattern, and composition brings balance. The work effortlessly straddles the sensibilities of both art and craft techniques.

🖵 **richardpearse.wordpress.com**

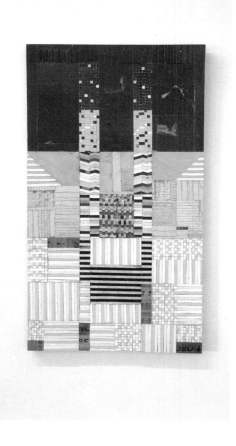

GRACIA HABY & LOUISE JENNISON
Australia

Gracia Haby and Louise Jennison create jewel-like collaborative collages that read like inverted historical society presentations. They are also keen zine and artist book makers who fill the pages of their brilliantly executed output with imagined worlds, where leopards rule kingdoms, birds wrestle with moral dilemmas and foxes have tea parties.

 gracialouise.com

JENNY BROWN
United States

The artful combination of drawn and found elements requires an extremely deft touch. Jenny Brown's ability to draw both aesthetic and literal inspiration from her pre-made base materials leaves the viewer in a chicken-and-egg conundrum of what came first in her whimsical, otherworldly collages.

 jennybrownart.com

AARON MORAN
Canada

The 3-D wooden sculptures of Aaron Moran exemplify all that is good about contemporary craft. Using foraged and found ex-construction/demolition site lumber, Moran reclaims, re-uses and reinvents these scraps into compelling new works. Moran's keen understanding of color and form is evident in his brilliantly balanced 3-D geometric forms and flat timber "collages." Pairing raw, patterned and pop-painted shard-like elements, he enlivens the surface, confounds the usual organic associations with eco-conscious art and astutely references the built environment.

 aaronsmoran.com

EUGENIA LOLI
Greece/United States

There is not much in the way of physical material or subject matter that escapes the eye of Eugenia Loli. From scenes of domestic discontent to glittering reinterpretations of worshipped women, her works are proof that when it comes to collage nothing is off the table. We love her witty incorporation of textile patterns such as lace and patchwork into her photomontages.

cargocollective.com/eugenialoli

MATTHEW CRAVEN
United States

Matthew Craven's works are a brilliant lesson in graphic and political history. Totemic pattern work is rendered in cut paper and fiber-tip marker against monotone and limited palette lithographic reproductions. With many of his core images plucked from antique texts of lost civilizations, the works tug at an almost primal response to decoration, managing to feel both prehistorically ancient and effortlessly modern.

 matthewcraven.com

EMIR ŠEHANOVIĆ
Bosnia–Herzegovina

The mysterious digital and hand-cut collages of Emir Šehanović elicit an almost visceral response. Both talismanic and disturbing, they appear to slide off the page and straight into the underworld. By repeating the same image over and over and skewing its position ever so slightly, the works start to "vibrate," shifting perceptions and evoking trance-like states of otherworldly possession.

 esh.ba

DESIGN NOTES

MAGIC HAPPENS

People have been assembling collections of objects to both decorate and make sense of the world forever. There is a dialogue that develops between seemingly random objects placed in close proximity that reveals itself almost magically. We are addicted to this process of discovery and never tire of the miraculous "ta-dah" moment when all the elements suddenly hang together.

LOOSEN UP

Try not to overwork or overthink the selection and placement of your elements, and let your gut guide you when you're starting out. Practice the age-old technique of free association — let your subconscious roam and see where it takes you. Discovering what "feels right" will help you create more complex pre-planned works further down the track.

MATERIAL BY-PRODUCT

If you can stick or stitch it you can use it in a collage. That said, paper-based materials are probably the easiest to work with. Re-use and recycle where you can. Op-shops and garage sales are full of magazines and books, and scraps of paper and materials from other craft projects and daily newspapers are a gold mine. Go to the local library and photocopy random selections off the shelves, keep your wrapping paper and envelopes, and empty out the junk drawer. Everything is fair game.

FEEL YOUR WAY

Including textural elements in a collage is a great way to add visual interest. Think of ways to incorporate materials that will add something to the narrative or aesthetic balance of your work — neutral papers with neon threads, black and white photos combined with patterned fabric, feathered cutting techniques or torn edges. Different textures are one of the real benefits of collage so don't be afraid to experiment.

COLOR AND MOVEMENT

Color and pattern can be used to great effect in even the simplest collages. While many artists combine photographic images to create altered realities or narratives, pure pattern play in monotones or high-contrast color can be just as effective in making compelling works. Take cues from fashion and combine dots, checks, florals and geometrics in a print-on-print effect, or use more minimal tonal palettes using texture and surface finishes to create interest.

ON REPEAT

Collage techniques are brilliant for trying out repeat patterns for printed textiles. Cut around hand-drawn motifs or shaped blocks of color and arrange them on a flat background. Use the elements solo, mix and match or add details in markers or paints until you find your groove. You can then either carve your motifs into blocks for printing or trace over them with stencil paper and cut them out for screen printing.

- **Cutting tools:** Finding the perfect cutting tool is like the search for the Holy Grail. Collage work involves a lot of cutting and your chosen tool needs to be sharp and comfortable to work with. Try an X-Acto knife or nail scissors for cutting clean lines and pinking shears, rotary cutters, decorative stamp cutters and circle cutters for more specific shapes.

- **Tweezers:** Especially useful to aid pick-up and delicate placement in small-scale work (or if you have Hagrid hands).

- **Milliner's cement:** Viscosity and slow drying time lets crafters slowly slide elements into exact positions before drying. Telltale glue remnants are easily rubbed off once dry. Our favorite adhesive.

- **Mod Podge:** Perfect for adding a tinted glaze to a finished product, or when using canvas or wood as a base. However, it is a very unforgiving adhesive. Once it grabs hold, it will never let go. We call it the emotionally needy adhesive.

- **Dimensional Glue Dots:** The "no mess no fuss" option. Glue Dots give you a depth of field that make interesting effects. Not our first choice but a handy option.

- **Papers:** Newspapers, magazines, postcards, butcher's paper, decorative paper, colored card stock, scrapbooking paper.

- **Brayer**

- **Paints, pencils, markers and ink**

- **Cutting mat**

- **Glue sticks**

- **PVA (white) glue**

- **Double-sided tape**

- **Masking tape**

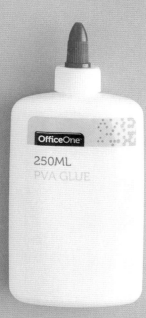

TECHNIQUES

DECOUPAGE

Probably the earliest collage technique, decoupage has been a decorative feature since the 17th century. It was initially an attempt to mimic the intricate Chinese lacquer work of the period, which was both highly fashionable and prohibitively expensive.

Furniture, lamps, screens, ceramics, even eggs can all get the decoupage treatment. There are specialist decoupage papers but wallpaper remnants, wrapping paper, scrapbook paper, magazine cut-outs or your own drawings all work well. Tissue paper is especially good at handling dangerous curves.

Make your paper more robust by pre-coating it with Mod Podge or PVA (white) glue. Once dry, your motifs will be much easier to cut out.

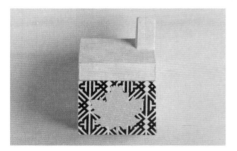

WHAT YOU NEED

- Sandpaper (if decorating wood)
- Damp cloth
- Cutting mat
- Scissors
- Decorative paper
- Low-tack masking tape
- Object to decoupage
- Foam roller
- Mod Podge or PVA (white) glue
- Rubber brayer

WHAT YOU DO

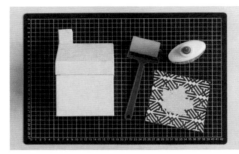

1. Clean the surface of your chosen object well. If it's wood give it a light sand and dust with a damp cloth.

2. Carefully cut out your motifs from the decorative paper. If applying more than one motif it will help to attach and position them with low-tack masking tape to your object surface. Take a phone photo of them as a guide for placement as you go. This way you can be sure to get your design right before you stick everything down.

3. Using your roller, give your object surface a light coating of PVA glue. If you're working on a large object, only apply to the section you're working on; otherwise it will dry before you get to stick anything to it.

4. Now lightly coat the back of your motif with PVA glue.

5. Carefully position the motif face up on the surface of your object. Gently smooth it out with your brayer to get rid of any air bubbles.

6. Once you've attached all of your motifs and they've dried, give the whole work a coating of glue and leave to dry overnight.

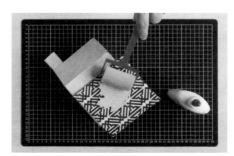

7. We like to give ours a second and third coat of sealer for good measure, leaving overnight each time. This can be painful but ultimately is well worth the wait, as you'll get a perfectly smooth and durable finish.

TRANSFERS

Most of us grew up sporting t-shirts that were printed in this way. It's a process often thought of in purely commercial terms but it's worth discussing the option of heat transfers as you can successfully use them to create both placement prints and repeat prints at home with an iron.

We recommend buying specialist heat transfer paper, available online for use with an inkjet printer, to ensure long-lasting durability that is wash-fast, soft to handle and free from plastic sheen. If you don't need to wash your design, however, and don't mind a plastic feel, you can just buy regular transfer paper sheets for use in a home printer. Both versions come in variants for dark and light cotton and cotton-blend fabrics.

You can easily create collaged heat transfer prints but there is a trick to it. You have to apply all your transfer elements at the same time. Otherwise you run the risk of ruining a section applied earlier with the hot iron.

1. Simply cut out the elements, leaving a slight gap between each one. They should never overlap; otherwise they will melt instead of transfer!

2. Tape them together on the reverse side with washi tape before ironing on to your fabric. Always follow the manufacturer's instructions; they are there for a reason (sigh).

PROJECT IDEAS

→ Use a super-simple collage technique to create a frame within a frame for photographs. Take a single piece of heavyweight colored paper the same size as your photograph and cut a geometric shape such as a triangle in the center of your paper. Place your colored "frame" over a black and white portrait image for maximum impact.

→ Photocopy or scan your collage works and make origami boxes, bringing them to life in 3-D. Work small, using 8½ x 11 paper, and hang them en masse for a brilliantly simple mobile; or scale up into 34 x 44 black-and-white photocopies to make a hanging light shade.

→ Double the fun and multi-purpose your output by wrapping a gift in a sturdy paper collage tied up with string. Take it a step further and have your collage translated onto fabric using a printing service or transfer paper to make a one-off furoshiki for a gift wrap that keeps on giving. Two gifts in one — BONUS.

→ Take collage off the page and make modern multi-dimensional wreaths. Work with thematically linked collections of cut-outs — delicate paper flowers, birds and butterflies, oversize faux leaves, or paint chips and painted cardboard layered flat in repetitive shapes.

→ There are obvious connections between fabric patchwork and collage but why not further reference textiles as part of your work? Use notions and trimmings such as lace, beads, pom-poms and ribbon to add dimensionality to paper collages, or photocopy your own textile works to include in paper collage.

Cut Copy Cushions

WHAT YOU NEED

- Collage elements photocopied onto transfer paper
- Scissors
- Ruler
- Washi or masking tape
- Iron
- Light cotton fabric for printing onto and backing your cushion — our cushion measures $23\frac{5}{8}$ x $15\frac{3}{4}$". You'll need to add at least 2" in both dimensions for seams.
- Pins
- Sewing machine
- Polyester filling
- Needle and thread

HOT TIP

This project is one you can ramp up to suit your skill level or accessorizing aesthetic. We've started super simple by making a "stuff and sew" cushion and customized it by adding a decorative pom-pom edging.

Custom cushions, or throw pillows, are the quickest way to update a tired living room. This project turns your 2-D artwork into 3-D décor in a matter of minutes. This super-simple technique is one of the fastest ways to extend your collage work beyond the frame.

WHAT YOU DO

1. Cut around the transfer paper collage elements, leaving a $\frac{1}{8}$" border round each one.

2. Arrange the collage elements into a design you like. You'll need to include about 2" of fabric around all edges of your design for a border and seams. Turn the pieces over and tape them together.

3. Cut out the fabric front and back pieces. Position the collage design on one piece and, following the manufacturer's instructions, iron your collage onto it.

4. Pin the front and back pieces together with right sides facing. Stitch around all edges, taking 1" seam allowance and leaving a gap about the width of your hand on one side for stuffing. It doesn't matter what shape your cushion is. In fact, the weirder the better!

5. Turn your cushion right side out and stuff it with polyester filling. Turn in the raw opening edges and slipstitch them closed. Fasten off the thread securely.

6. If you want to add some decorative edging, sew this around the edges of your cushion.

7. Yep, that's it — you've just made a cushion! WOO HOO!!! You are now armed and ready to artfully decorate your chair, bed, couch or swing.

Gild

◇◇◇

Gilding has been around for so long that it's mentioned in both Homer's *Odyssey* and the Old Testament, and anyone who's seen the iconic sarcophagus of Tutankhamen will recognize the seductive attraction of serious bling.

It seems that almost every culture has responded to the power of gold and silver by creating their own version of the craft — from ancient Egyptian gilded tombs and temples to Roman homes decorated with gold leaf. History is rich with examples of how humans have manifested the connection between precious metals (gold in particular) and supernatural or religious power. A classic example is the extensive use of gilding in the 13th century to create illuminated manuscripts and religious relics, with both pure gold leaf and paint pigment used to reflect and reinforce the valuable cultural and social currency of these documents and objects.

So strong has been the demand for golden objects that necessity has been the mother of invention, pushing highly sophisticated technical advancement in gilding techniques, many of which are the precursors of contemporary industrial processes. Pre-Columbian Mesoamericans developed a copper and gold alloy called tumbaga to create religious objects using an acid etch technique reminiscent of modern electroplating. Chinese artisans of the Qing Dynasty invented a process to embellish vessels and votives that quickly spread throughout Europe via the trade routes and remained in use for centuries. There has been long-term medicinal and culinary use of gold flakes and gold dust throughout Europe and Asia. References to edible metal leaf used to decorate Indian sweets also appear in ancient Sanskrit texts.

Gilding, while not necessarily on every crafter's "must do" list, has never really lost its currency. Gilded frames, objects and furniture are so deeply embedded within our cultures that we almost cease to notice them, but during intersections between high art and fashion a spotlight on the craft makes us rethink it in new ways. Gustav Klimt's "Golden Phase" (think *The Kiss*) brought the flat decorative gilding of Byzantine mosaics to a new European audience hundreds of years later. Today avant-garde fashion designer Martin Margiela uses blocked silver leaf foil techniques across garments and shoes, his designs drawn from historical references and re-applied in confounding new contexts.

While ancient craftspeople had to endure lengthy and often toxic processes in the creation of their works, thanks to the genius invention of imitation gold, silver and copper foil, this technique is now ripe for the picking for domestic crafters. Today new generations of designers and craft makers are as smitten as the ancients, re-engaging with traditional gilding techniques and creating new methods to match new materials and embellishing everything from cast concrete to cardboard couture.

SUSAN DWYER (UP IN THE AIR SOMEWHERE)
United States

Artist and designer Susan Dwyer's ceramic and papier-mâché vessels are inspired by the clean industrial architecture of her Chicago home. The sure simplicity of her forms is perfectly accented by the addition of gold and silver foil to create surface patterns and patina, resulting in domestic objects that are a heady combination of super luxury and utilitarian charm.

🖵 upintheairsomewhere.com

PEACHES + KEEN
Australia

Dynamic Melbourne-based design duo Lucy Hearn and Lily Daley have melded their respective skills in gold- and silversmithing and graphic design to corner the market in pop charm. Using a base of meltable plastic hobby beads and fine silver they have moved from peacock displays of pure color to new works which prominently feature the use of gold and silver leaf. Their use of both traditional and contemporary techniques, and their ironic juxtaposition of precious and plastic, are made even more obvious as their works morph from simple geometric shapes to flattened forms that reference more formal and ornate body adornment.

🖵 peachesandkeen.com

URBAN SOULE
United States

Seattle native Urban Soule (aka Kim McCarthy) is a pop-inspired artist with a keen eye for texture and surface decoration. While usually employing a cut-stencil approach to image-making, McCarthy's recent collection of cast concrete skulls and oversize diamond forms is inspired by graffiti culture and literally comes from the ground beneath her feet. By gilding them in gold leaf she brilliantly combines the ultimate utilitarian street material with the iconic hip hop allure of gold.

 urbansoule.com

LAUREN KALMAN
United States

Lauren Kalman has taken gilding to a new extreme. By attaching gold leaf and semiprecious stones to her body, she creates performance pieces that are both confronting and beautiful. Using the body as canvas, Kalman consciously challenges notions of image, value and consumer-culture — catapulting this rarefied craft into a place where gilding, adornment and art performance meet.

laurenkalman.com

DESIGN NOTES

FULLY FASHIONED

There's nothing that will take ready-to-wear to runway quicker than metal detailing. Even the most basic cardigan can be transformed into couture by the addition of fabric-safe gold, copper or silver leaf. Playing against type raises the stakes even higher, so consider seriously utilitarian fabrics such as canvas, denim or hemp, work-wear staples, sensible shoes and practical accessories as perfect items for a gilded makeover.

LIGHT AND SHADE

It sounds obvious but, when gilding, keep in mind where the light will catch the object. It is customary to gild whole objects but just focusing on one section is a more modern design approach. Embrace imperfections — use cracks in the gilt to reveal a painted surface underneath. Go traditional or choose super-brights, pastels or primary colors if that's more your bag — make time for happy accidents.

GILTY PLEASURES

Be warned that this is a highly addictive technique. You'll start to think that everything will look better with a bit of gold. Just between us, you may be right but there is an accepted design principle that less is more, at least to start with. Use your gilding power for good and try to highlight and enhance your work, drawing the attention to details without overpowering them. Also remember the adage that you can't make a silk purse from a sow's ear — you can't gild bad work and expect it to miraculously improve. Life doesn't work that way.

MIXING METALS

Once you get your skills up with the size (aka gilding adhesive) you can combine different metals for really dramatic effects. Imagine a papier-mâché egg starting as gold and then segueing into copper, or a silver-leaf tray with a chevron gold stripe, or a checkerboard pattern on a wooden box imitating parquetry techniques!

GLOSSING OVER

If you aren't using real gold your gilt will tarnish over time. You can call this "antiquing" and live with it or you can seal your work with a light spray gloss varnish to protect the shine.

Most of the tools for gilding can be found in your general tool kit — glue, brushes, trays, tape, cotton gloves. However, as with most crafts there are specialist materials and tools that can make your life a little easier if you want to move into the sphere of the expert.

- **Imitation leaf:** Copper, silver and gold are readily available in sheet form from art and craft stores and are usually very reasonably priced.

- **Imitation leaf flakes:** Leaf crumble that is brilliant for rolling into polymer clay.

- **Gold leaf:** More expensive but the result is amazing. Specialty jewelry suppliers usually have a range from 6- to 24-carat gold leaf available but we advise practicing with the faux stuff first.

- **Liquid gold leaf:** Can be applied with a paintbrush and is particularly handy for gilding narrow edges.

- **Gilding size:** A purpose-made adhesive that works best. Watered-down PVA (white) glue is an alternative but less than ideal.

- **Cotton gloves:** All imitation metal leaf contains copper, which will tarnish on contact with the oils on your hands. In addition to stopping this, the gloves will also help keep your sheets intact for longer while you work with them. BONUS.

- **Flat, wide brush:** Helps you pick up and lay down the leaf as well as brush off any excess without damaging your gorgeous work. Many gilding books recommend ox or horse hair but we've found that soft synthetic brushes work just as well, if not better.

- **Face mask:** When those metal particles are airborne, they can get into your lungs and cause long-term health issues and a short-term cough that will drive you crazy even if it doesn't kill you.

This basic technique will see you through applying any gilding leaf (gold, copper, silver) to most surfaces, including non-washable fabric. Gilding on fabric works on the same principle as on other surfaces: size to bind and leaf to embellish. It is definitely worth investigating further if you want to add some bling to wearable fabric. While we've used a cardboard box, you can use the same method to apply gilt to paper, wood, glass, and stone.

WHAT YOU NEED

- 2 paintbrushes
- Acrylic paint
- Painter's masking tape
- Size
- Cotton gloves
- Gold foil (imitation or real)
- Soft cloth
- Spray varnish (optional)
- Face mask (optional)

WHAT YOU DO

1. Give your object an undercoat of paint and allow it to dry.

2. Mask off the area you wish to gild. Apply size to the area in a thin even coat. Allow it to dry until it is "tacky."

3. Put your gloves on and, using a clean, dry brush, pick up a sheet of gold foil.

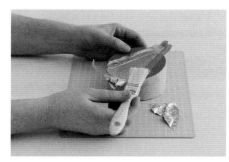

4. Use the brush to lay the foil gently over the sized area. Use the brush to gently tap the foil in place.

5. Allow the foil to set for 20 minutes before peeling off the tape and brushing away any excess foil.

6. Once your amazing creation has been revealed you can give it a gentle buff with a soft cloth and a coat of spray varnish to keep the imitation gold from tarnishing (skip this step if you splashed out on the real stuff).

LEAF ALTERNATIVES

Liquids, pastes, powders, paints and sprays are all worthy alternatives to the leaf process. Liquid leaf is particularly useful as it matches for shine and makes quick work of complicated jobs such as ornate wooden frames or edges where you want to get into every nook and cranny.

In order to get the best results you'll need to first prime your surface. It also pays to add a coat of polyurethane varnish or shellac when you're done to help keep things shiny and bright.

Gold embossing powder is perfect for fancy invitations. You'll need a heat embossing tool, which can be picked up at most craft supply stores, and a special clear size called embossing ink, which comes in both stamp pad and liquid form.

Using the ink, write your message, apply your design to the paper, then cover it with the embossing powder (move quickly as the embossing ink dries fast). Shake off the excess powder, then use the heat tool to "melt" the powder onto the paper, where it will magically turn to an iridescent gold.

PROJECT IDEAS

→ Try a minimalist mix of matte finishes and gilt. Try gilding the interior of a drawer, a bowl or a bookshelf for a subtle but effective result.

→ If you've got sturdy skin, get inspired and try a strip of gold leaf around your wrist as a faux bracelet or a touch of Cleopatra glamour around your eyes on your next big night out. Just make sure you check your size is skin-safe before you go all Goldfinger.

→ Clear objects are ripe for gilding and offer the benefit of a smooth food-safe finish without any extra effort if you gild the underside. Try using a thrift shop cut-glass platter and serve up something special at your next party.

→ Leather is a great base material for gilding, especially as you can cut and form it after the gilt has been applied. Try a wash of sizing across a square of soft colored hide and sew together on three sides to make a simple but glamorous sleeve for your phone or train pass.

→ Oversize raw wooden beads look fabulous when treated with gold, silver or copper leaf and a strong coating of shellac to protect their shine. String them alone, or combine with handmade polymer versions laced with gold leaf flecks to make your own modern-day Nefertiti-inspired neckwear.

Golden Mountain Headboard

WHAT YOU NEED

- Paper and lead pencil
- Plywood panel cut to size
- Painter's masking tape
- Foam brush
- PVA (white) glue or gilding size
- Cotton gloves and a face mask
- Gold foil (we used 2 full packs, 50 sheets in all)
- Dry-bristle brush
- Butcher paper or drop cloth
- Varnish spray
- Velcro tabs for picture hanging, strong enough to hold the weight of your plywood

Super-cheap and super-stylish, this golden headboard is a quick and easy way to give a bedroom an instant makeover without breaking the bank. Sweet dreams guaranteed.

WHAT YOU DO

1. Sketch out your mountain range on paper until you come up with a design you like.

2. Tape up the wood panel (we freestyled it but if you prefer, lightly draw your mountains on with a pencil first to help guide your taping).

3. Using a foam brush, coat the area to be gilded with a thin layer of glue or size and allow it to dry until it is tacky. Be careful to stay within your tape boundaries.

4. Wearing cotton gloves, carefully transfer a sheet of gold foil onto the size-coated area. Start from the bottom and move your way up.

5. Using your dry-bristle brush, gently tap the gold down (do not brush at this point or it will tear excessively).

6. Systematically work your way across the headboard, repeating steps 3 and 4. This took us about four hours. Don't try to rush — you need to take your time! Leave it to dry for 24 hours.

7. Once dry, place a sheet of butcher paper underneath and very gently use the bristle brush to remove any excess gold. Keep the brushed-off gold to re-use in other projects.

8. This is the fun part — pull away the tape to reveal your design. Give it a light spray of clear varnish to prevent tarnishing. We gave our headboard three coats, letting it dry completely between sprays.

9. WOO HOO! Your headboard is now ready to be hung, using stick-on Velcro tabs.

HOT TIP

If our mountain range design doesn't float your boat, rest assured you can mask off random areas to gild and still get a beautiful result. You could use letter stencils for text or more expressive brushstrokes for calligraphic flair.

• Form •

Clay

◇◇◇

The discovery that clay could be shaped into vessels and transformed by heat into pottery is one of those light-bulb moments in history that changed the shape of civilization. There are pottery shards dating back as far as 24,000 B.C.E., clear evidence that we have been exploring the medium for practical and aesthetic purposes for almost as long as people have been walking upright.

Significant technical developments happened quickly all over the world — in China (20,000 B.C.E.), Russia (14,000 B.C.E.) and Japan (10,000 B.C.E.) — and there is a continuous tradition of terracotta work in the Indus Valley dating back at least 5,000 years. These early examples used local clays and were pit-fired at relatively low temperatures, with rudimentary shaping techniques such as pinching and coiling. From the terracotta pots of Sudan and Ethiopia, and the clay sculptures of the Yoruba in North Africa to the Andean vessels dating back as far as 6000 B.C.E., no part of the globe has been left untouched by the development of clay work.

Pottery as an industry was in full swing from as early as 10,000 B.C.E., with tiles, bricks and vessels produced throughout India and Mesopotamia. By 8000 B.C.E. the Egyptians had started to use glazes, and there is evidence of the pottery wheel coming into use in Iraq by 3000 B.C.E.. The development of the wheel, paired with the invention of glaze technology and a variety of local versions of the updraft wood-fired kiln, changed the face of pottery production forever. Images on ancient Greek pottery depicted both kiln construction and loading techniques, and by the 1st century glazed pots had made an appearance throughout China, the Middle East, Europe, Africa, South America and Japan, with each region developing its own signature styles and practices.

Long and complex histories linked to ritual and to political and social change can be traced directly through the history of clay. As both raw material and finished object, its history reflects events and cultural developments of great significance. As pottery traveled through the world and the centuries, so did the desire for new potters to try

their hand at the new techniques. During China's Tang Dynasty, in the 7th century, green celadon porcelain made its way to the Middle East, beguiling potters with its lustre. The highly decorative surfaces and tin enameling of 9th-century Islamic pottery spread to Muslim Spain, where a similar type of pottery, exported to Italy, later inspired the development of Italian maiolica during the Renaissance. The glazed vessels of the Japanese tea ceremony inspired potters of the 13th century to try new forms and finishes. And so the list goes on, including signature styles such as Dutch Delftware and the instantly collectable jasperware of 18th-century Wedgwood, both of which refer back to the pottery of antiquity in form, technique and color.

Contemporary artists are mixing high-tech with lo-fi to push the medium to its technical limits, supersizing works, turning glazes into sculptures like hyper-color volcanic explosions and incorporating unexpected subject matter with traditional technology in modern museum mash-ups. As part of the slow craft movement, new potters are even going back to the earth and sourcing clay from their local area to create works as uniquely authentic as they are sustainable.

You can study ceramics at a local craft center, travel to Japan to learn the techniques of the master Raku potters of Kyoto, head to India to learn terracotta techniques as old as civilization itself, or begin a lifelong journey in pursuit of the perfect bowl. As a painter, printmaker or textile designer, you can find new surfaces for design and decoration, and as a sculptor you can experiment with shape, scale and form. From mud pies to fine china, pottery remains a craft with unending appeal.

BRIDGET BODENHAM
Australia

Bridget Bodenham's work is an effortless combination of nature and glamour. The country mouse/town mouse quality of her work is as user-friendly as it is beautiful. Organic hand-built shapes with bold surface design incorporate string graphic lines with touches of gold and silver that might highlight a handle or dress the curve of a cup. Vases have soft, round bellies and little feet, anthropomorphizing into bush creatures in fancy dress that reflect her connection to the country setting of her studio practice.

🖥 **bridgetbodenham.com**

IGGY AND LOU LOU
Australia

The "Driptopia" series, created by Irene Grishin Selzer (Iggy and Lou Lou), nimbly mixes current interior obsessions with mark-making and a knowing nod to Victorian mourning aesthetics. Using gravity to create accidental directional patterning alongside more conscious brush marks to build layers of quartz porcelain, the pieces are incredibly tactile. As the brush travels across the uneven topography of the vessels, these unique pieces cleverly offer further dimensionality.

🖥 **iggyandloulou.com**

MICHELE MICHAEL
United States

With a background in interiors, editorial and styling, Michele Michael of Elephant Ceramics has an intuitive understanding of what we want gracing our tables. Platters, plates and bowls come in organic shapes but are anything but boring. Indigo, sky, salt and sand make up her simple palette, drawing inspiration from the Maine coast where she is based. Brushing and dipping glaze gives the work a painterly quality, while subtly embossed surfaces read more like linen than clay.

 elephantceramics.com

KATIE JACOBS
Australia

The spirit animal takes on all the baggage of contemporary living in these oversize totems by Katie Jacobs. Notions of national and cultural identity are explored through the familiar iconography of sport, leisure, suburbia and backyard culture. Combined with highly detailed and emotive animal heads, all that is left for the viewer is to choose which team to cheer for.

katiejacobs.net

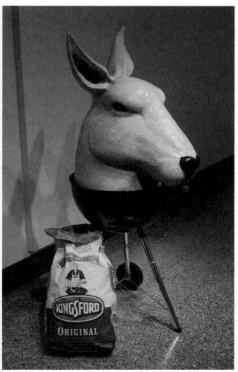

SUSAN ROBEY
Australia

Susan Robey's paper-thin clay house structures defy logic. On viewing they seem impossibly fragile, as if a gust of wind could take them out at any moment. However, with their weighted foundations and sturdy legs, they stand against the elements and march forward. They gather in "neighborhoods," communicating with a nod of their pitched roofs. Robey's architectural training, matched with her artistic eye, creates crumpled structures that multiply out like a strange urban planning experiment.

 susanrobeyceramics.com

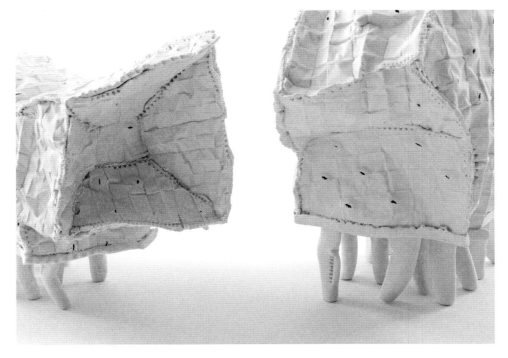

KIRSTEN PERRY
Australia

The weird world of multidisciplinary artist Kirsten Perry is littered with outsider objects that evoke universal emotions through motifs of endearing failure — vases that look like crumpled paper bags, maudlin support groups of coffee cups and wounded urns having bad hair days. Her hand-built pieces employ text, embossed textures and surface patterning, which makes them as rich in detail as they are in personality. She creates a world of flotsam and jetsam that is hilariously surreal, drawing from the best and worst of pop culture in equal measure. Her domestic works remain resolutely undomesticated, while her anthropomorphic approach to tableware means you'll never dine alone again.

kirstenperry.com

SEAN GERSTLEY
United States

The ceramic work of Sean Gerstley is refreshingly unapologetic. From the large-scale graphic abstraction of his gallery installations to the putty-edged modernism of his collaborative design objects, Gerstley's keen mind and skilled hands are gleefully present in the many nooks and crannies of his hilariously deft exercises in portraiture and primitivism. Knowing, biographic and resolutely fearless, his sculptural works showcase an audacious approach to mark-making and a remarkably broad range of glazing and firing techniques that allow him to fully realize the richly tactile surfaces of his wild and willful creatures.

🖥 **seangerstley.com**

BRIAN ROCHEFORT
United States

Brian Rochefort is taking ceramics in a new direction. His hollow-form "gloop" sculptures look like delicious globs of molten marshmallow but these seductive gelatinous forms are rock hard, fortified with automotive body paint in a "potter meets panel-beater" mash-up that is technically and conceptually confounding. Rochefort's masterful glaze knowledge and construction techniques give free reign to his imagination in tangible terms, while his radical approach to form places him at the forefront of a new vanguard of ceramic trailblazers.

🖥 **brianrochefort.net**

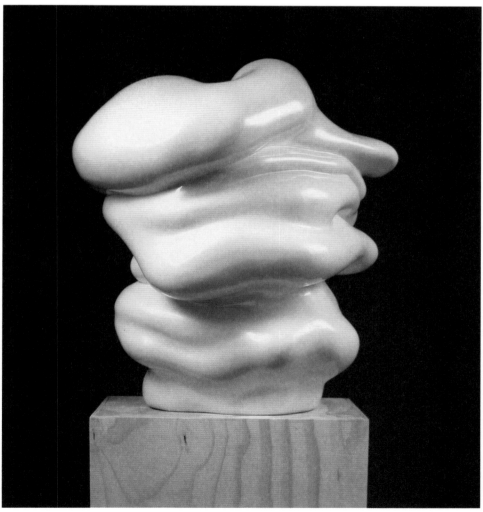

DESIGN NOTES

LIGHT AS AIR

Great results can be had with alternative "clay" materials. Air-dry clay, polymer clay, and precious metal clay are all brilliant choices for creating jewelry, small planters and vessels, with the added benefit of economy and convenience. The downside, of course, is that the work is neither food-safe nor dishwasher-friendly, which may limit your end-use options significantly.

—

CLEAR AS MUD

Your choice of clay can have a dramatic impact on your end product. There are both functional and decorative consequences of clay selections, so do your research and make sure you get the right one for the job. Porcelain is soft to work with, beautifully translucent and incredibly strong if high fired, but it's also floppy and unstable if you're trying to make large-scale objects. Gritty stoneware is harder on your hands and less "refined" but it has the perfect body to stand the weight of big-coiled or slab-constructed planters. Choose wisely and you'll save time and your sanity.

—

FEET OF CLAY

One of the most amazing things about working with clay is its incredible capacity for taking on and maintaining texture. Its soft surface allows you to emboss, mold, stamp, carve, squish, draw and cut into it to make decorative patterns or surfaces. If you're planning on firing, you can add another round of options, from glazes and marbling to metallic finishes that will catch the light and pick up the smallest details. Take your pick and take advantage — the options are almost endless.

—

HOT STUFF

Chances are you don't have a kiln set up at home (yet!) so you'll be "renting" space in a commercial kiln at the local pottery center or school. When thinking about the scale of your project, remember that it has to fit in that kiln, and if you're taking your work to market, it has to be worth the time and money involved to fire it. Kiln dimensions are an immutable rule. "Stacking for success" is key, whether you're going with one giant platter or six good soup bowls.

—

MIX IT UP

Once you've got your clay skills sorted out you'll find you start thinking more laterally about all the ways you can incorporate ceramics into other crafts, and vice versa. Buttons for crochet and knitting, and ceramic beads for macramé, jewelry and weaving are all fantastic fancy-pants ways of adding unique details to your work. Similarly, given clay's malleability, you can also bring many of those crafts into your ceramic work by leaving holes or grooves for additional detailing after firing.

LUCK OF THE DRAW

While they may be marketed to crafters looking to customize commercial ceramics, the new range of ceramic pens offer enormous scope for detailed decorating of your own work. Their fine tip and extensive color palette make them perfect for adding text or fine line-drawn illustrations and geometric patterning. Just make sure you practice on some "less successful" pieces before hitting your top shelf collection.

- **Clay bodies:** Earth-based clays including terracotta, stoneware, porcelain, paper clay and some air-dry clay, as well as synthetic compounds such as polymer clay.

- **Fettling knives:** Especially shaped to remove the ridges from cast work without leaving marks. They're also very useful for trimming slabs.

- **Cut-off wires:** Hardwood handles joined with wire used for cutting large lumps of clay.

- **Potter's needles:** Long, heavy needles set into wooden handles. Versatile for inlay and sgraffito mark-making, trimming, and scoring slabs and coils for joins when hand-building.

- **Modeling tools:** Made from wood and in all sorts and sizes. Extremely handy tools for mark-making and hand-building.

- **Plastic tubs:** Buy them with lids in a variety of sizes for storing clay and slip.

- **Sponges:** Both natural and synthetic are used for smoothing hand-built ceramics during forming.

- **Brushes:** Used for applying slip, under-glaze and glaze. Use natural-hair brushes, ideally ones that can carry water.

- **Slip:** Runny clay made from clay and water, used for joining; casting slip is used for molds and decorative slip for clay surfaces.

- **Underglaze:** Ceramic paint made from ground minerals and painting medium. A great option as it can be used like acrylic paint and comes in a range of different colors. Can be used on green and bisque-fired ceramics and is suitable for firing temperatures between 1,060 and 1,280 degrees Celsius (1,940 and 2,336 degrees Fahrenheit), but is also permanent after single firing.

- **Glaze:** Water-suspended glass that is applied to the surface of ceramics to add color, texture and waterproofing. You can make your own (tricky) or buy commercially prepared versions. Talk to experts and get advice before using.

- **Fine sandpaper**

- **Plastic protractor**

- **Hacksaw blade**

- **Plastic tablecloth**

- **Bucket**

- **Rolling pin**

- **Butter knife**

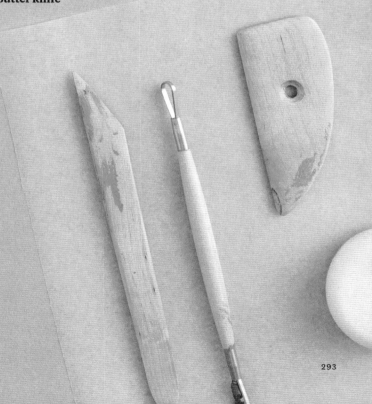

TECHNIQUES

CLAY BODIES

While you don't have to become an expert, it's worth knowing a bit about different types of clay and their firing temperatures so you can make better choices before designing projects. Naturally occurring clays are sedimentary materials containing various silicates that melt and bond when heat is applied. Prepared clay bodies are readily available through craft or pottery suppliers and are defined by the temperature at which the clay matures (bonds) during firing.

LOW-FIRE (950–1,100 DEGREES CELSIUS [1,742–2,012 DEGREES FAHRENHEIT])

These are all earthenware clays that mature at low temperatures before they can vitrify (become non-porous). Low-fired work remains porous and needs glazing to make it watertight. These clays can be worked by hand or wheel and include iron-rich dark-red and orange bodies such as terracotta, as well as newer white and buff earthenware made by combining a high-firing clay mixed with flux to lower the maturation temperature.

MID-RANGE (1,160–1,225 DEGREES CELSIUS [2,120–2,057 DEGREES FAHRENHEIT])

These clays vitrify before maturing in the kiln, which makes them stronger than earthenware and completely watertight. They include finer-grain stoneware and some porcelain with added flux to slow the maturation process. Glaze is used for decoration and to smooth the surface of the work for use. Clay colors range from gray to buff.

HIGH-FIRE (1,200–1,300 DEGREES CELSIUS [2,192–2,372 DEGREES FAHRENHEIT])

These are predominantly porcelain and bone china, both super-fine clays that are soft and malleable when wet, and incredibly strong, durable and translucent when fired. Amazingly versatile.

PAPER CLAY

Traditionally speaking, any of the clays mentioned with cellulose fiber added can be kiln-fired at low and high temperatures depending on the amount of cellulose the clay body contains. Paper clay is stronger at the greenware stage and is able to be joined when bone dry.

AIR-DRY CLAY

This is fine-grained natural clay that dries to earthenware strength after 24 hours. It cannot be used with traditional glazes or kiln-fired. It can be bought commercially or made at home. There are a multitude of alternative air-dry options created from everyday craft and kitchen ingredients. Look for recipes online.

POLYMER

This is a malleable non-clay chemical compound that hardens in a domestic oven. It can be bought commercially or made at home. You cannot apply heat to, or eat from, commercially available polymer clays.

DRYING AND FIRING

While you can dry your work anywhere, getting it fired is another story. Most pottery suppliers can let you know about communal kilns or kilns for rental, as well as providing expert advice. It's also worth noting that while all clays shrink in the kiln, they shrink at different rates. For example, studio porcelain shrinks around 12 percent from wet to fired, while white earthenware only shrinks 6 percent from wet to fired.

GREENWARE

This refers to dry but unfired ceramics. It helps to dry your work in a warm but not hot environment. As tempting as it might be to get the heater out, slow and steady is the way to go. Rapid drying can lead to cracking as different parts of the work dry at different times. Greenware is very fragile and needs to be treated with care. It can also be recycled back into workable clay with the addition of water.

BISQUE FIRING

This is the first firing for dried works that will be glazed. Work is low-fired to around 1,000 degrees Celsius (1,830 degrees Fahrenheit), enough to melt the particles in the clay while still keeping it porous enough to accept glaze. Bisque-fired work is very brittle and fragile, so treat it with care. It's incredibly important that work is completely dry when it goes in for firing because steam created by evaporating water will cause your work to explode. This will make you especially unpopular with your fellow potters if you are using communal kilns.

SECOND FIRING

This is the firing that will make stoneware and porcelain vitrify and cause the glaze to melt onto the ceramic surface. Ceramic work can skip the bisque firing and go straight to the second firing if it's unglazed or if you've used underglaze to decorate. We should also mention that you can keep firing and glazing work many times, so the second firing may be only the first step in a longer process.

WEDGING

All clay needs to be wedged before use. Wedging removes air bubbles, which can explode during firing. So commit to it as a necessary process. You'll get a hardcore arm workout as a bonus.

Wedging clay is a lot like kneading bread. Work with a big lump on a sturdy surface. Use your cut-off wires to halve it, then bring down one half hard on top of the other to force out any air bubbles. Press the clay down and knead it as you would bread dough, rolling forward and folding back up until the clay is pliant. This will take around 20 minutes. Cut it in half to check that all the air bubbles are out; if not, repeat the process. Invest the time to wedge in bulk and save time later.

PINCH

Using one of the easiest techniques, pinch pots are a great way of learning how to handle clay in the most tactile of ways.

1. Make a ball of clay around the size of a tennis ball and put it into the palm of one hand. Use your other hand to apply gentle pressure in the center of the ball with your thumb, then push it a little harder into the clay to make the hole deeper and wider.

2. Start rotating the ball in your hand while you continue to maintain pressure against the "walls" of the pot. Your ball will quickly start to open up into a pot shape. Continue to turn it in your hand while maintaining pressure against the side with your thumb as you turn it.

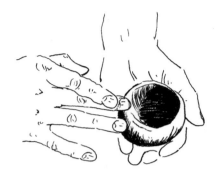

3. To thin the walls further, place your pot on your workbench and start pinching the sides between your thumb and forefinger. Starting from the bottom, work in an upward spiral around the pot until you reach the top. If the rim of your pot starts to crack it means your clay is drying out. Remedy this by using a wet finger or sponge to smooth it out.

4. Pinching can be used to make a variety of shaped vessels, from squares to triangles, by patting the sides into the required shape while forming. You can also easily turn pots into pourers by gently indenting one side and forming a spout shape. Add handles or feet by making them separately first. Score the joining surfaces on both with a potter's needle and stick them together with slip. Make a tiny clay coil to cover the joins and smooth this into the clay to secure it.

SLIP

Make your own clay slip for joining work in slabs or coils in its own container by taking a ball of clay and pushing your thumb into the center. Fill the hole with water and mix with a brush until you get a creamy, muddy slip. You can then use this to help your construction processes.

COIL

This ancient process lets you make pots and vessels of nearly every conceivable size.

1. First flatten a ball of clay or cut a slab base the same shape and thickness as the base of your intended vessel. Then put this piece aside.

2. Take a handful of clay and roll it into a sausage shape. Beginning in the center, spread your fingers and roll your sausage backwards and forwards, moving your fingers toward the edges as you roll. Keep your hands moist while you do this so the clay doesn't dry out.

3. Lay the coil on top of your base and coil it around the perimeter. Press it down into the base using your fingers until the two are well joined. Make a second coil and place it on top of the first, molding it to the first coil with your fingers. Apply a little pressure and work evenly around the inside and outside of the pot simultaneously.

4. Build your sides by making more coils and adding them to the pot one on top of the other, joining them together as you go. Some potters use slip to assist with the joining process but you can do it without this. Remove the coil ridges from the inside as you go by scraping gently with the round side of a plastic protractor, then smoothing with a damp sponge. As your pot grows you'll need to support the outside of the pot with one hand while you join coils with the other. If you're working on a larger piece, cover it with a damp dish towel in between work sessions, so it doesn't crack.

5. To shape your pot outwards, place each coil slightly to the outside of the one before. If you want to curve the pot inwards, place each coil slightly to the inside. Keep the placement even and you'll get a cylinder.

6. The easiest way to smooth the ridged sides of your pot is by raking over it in diagonal strokes with a hacksaw blade. Smooth these further with a flat knife blade — old bendy butter knives are great for this. Give it a final smoothing with a wet sponge.

SLAB

Slab construction is a fantastically versatile and quick method that allows you to build large- and small-scale architectural forms and vessels. You literally make flat slabs of clay, cut panels, and join them together to make your form. You'll need your clay to be dry enough to bend and manipulate without cracking, and strong enough to stand up and hold its form. This stage is called "leather-hard."

1. Think about the scale of your project and work out the dimensions of the pieces you need. If you feel so inclined, make a paper template to use when cutting your slab. You may need to make a few slabs to work with, depending on the scale of your project.

2. Take a generous lump of clay and turn it into a slab by rolling it out with a rolling pin — yes, it's that simple. Make sure it's large enough to cut your panel from and just a little thicker than your final wall width. (It will shrink slightly in the kiln.)

3. Put your paper template on your slab (or mark it out with a clay tool) and neatly cut it out. Repeat this process until you have all your construction panels. Cut your base a little wider than your side panels to allow room for the side panels to meet.

4. To assemble, first use a potter's needle to crosshatch the edges of your panels that will sit together, then apply a thick layer of slip with a brush. Start putting your vessel together, attaching one panel at a time to the base and holding the joins together firmly.

5. Strengthen your joins by pushing a thin coil of clay into the inside bottom joins of your vessel.

6. When all your sides are attached, use a sharp knife to cut the excess base edges off in line with your walls.

DECORATING

Applying surface decoration to your ceramic work adds dimension and uniqueness. Think of a piece as a 3-D canvas and you'll discover a whole new way of enlivening the surface of your work.

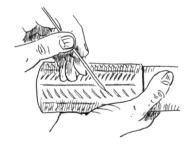

During construction you can use any mark-making or modeling tools to create patterns or relief detailing, or you can press work against textured surfaces. Once it's dry you can use underglaze to paint directly onto your work, or use sgraffito and inlay processes.

Sgraffito is a traditional technique in which colored underglaze is added to the surface and then scratched away to reveal the clay beneath. For inlay you use an indenting tool to scratch the surface, apply color over the marks, then wipe away the excess, leaving color only in the scratches.

GLAZING

Glaze is a thin layer of glass that sticks to the surface of ceramics, adding color, texture and waterproofing. Glaze can be clear but also comes in a large range of colors that are derived from metallic oxides. Some are food-safe and some are not, so it pays to check before using one. You can apply glaze by dipping your work into it or by brushing it onto the surface. Multiple colors may require multiple firings. For example, you might fire your colored glaze detailing and then dip your work into clear glaze and re-fire it to get a smooth, glossy surface.

Mixing and firing glaze is an art and science all its own that potters spend years studying and finessing. Thankfully, ready-made glazes are commercially available and conveniently come with firing temperature instructions. However, this is one area where we recommend that you talk to the experts at your local pottery supplier, or undertake further specialist study.

PROJECT IDEAS

→ Cookie cutters offer quick rewards and guaranteed results for shape-making in slab clay. You can turn out shapes en masse for garlands, mobiles, present toppers and Christmas tree decorations. Imagine how great a tree of terracotta gingerbread men would look.

→ The translucent qualities of porcelain make it a brilliant medium for illumination. Hand-build little vessels and half-fill them with soy wax, a wick and a drop or two of your favorite essential oil for a sweet-smelling house-warming gift.

→ No kiln? No worries! There are countless online resources for creating a fire pit or trash-can kiln at home. If that isn't going to fly in your third-floor apartment, oven-dry clay serves up a sweet alternative to kiln-fired work.

→ Once fired and glazed, all your ceramics will happily live outdoors. If you've got a green thumb as well as clay skills, you have a match made in heaven — think handcrafted pots, pavers and plant markers. Intentional drainage holes make you look like a professional but unintentional cracks can just as easily be utilized to turn your firing failures into garden features.

→ Dig your own clay. If you're a keen gardener you'll know if you have clay-heavy soil, but if in doubt, talk to a local surveyor, builder or even road worker, or look for places like river banks that get slippery after rain. If you're lucky enough to have some in your backyard, find a spot away from pesky tree roots and dig yourself a deep, narrow hole until you hit pay-dirt. If the clay can be coiled around your finger without cracking you've got yourself a clay mine.

Sake and Snack Set

WHAT YOU NEED

- A portion of prepared porcelain clay the size of a large orange
- Rolling pin
- Sponge
- Brushes
- Underglaze (we used black, pinkish red, yellow and turquoise)
- Access to a communal or rental kiln
- Fine grit sandpaper

Nothing goes better with a Kurosawa movie marathon than a handcrafted sake and snack set. Take color cues from kawaii and strong brush marks from sumi-e. Make one for yourself or a set for your friends, whip up some edamame, warm your sake and get ready for the *Seven Samurai*.

WHAT YOU DO

1. To make the plate, first make a ball of clay around the size of a tennis ball. Flatten it out using the palm of your hand until it's about 1½" thick, then use your rolling pin to roll it out into what will look like a clay pancake. Work from the center out and move around to keep your clay even and circular.

2. Keep rolling until your clay is around ¼" thick. Using your fingertips start gently turning up the sides around your circle so that you have a little lip around ¼" high. Set the piece aside somewhere safe and leave it to dry.

3. To make your sake cup, make a ball of clay around the size of a golf ball. Holding the ball in your left hand, use your right thumb to make a depression in the center of the clay. Start rotating the ball in your left hand, maintaining pressure against the sides of the pot to open it up into a cup shape.

4. Thin the sides further either in your hand or by pinching them from bottom to top on a flat work surface. Once they're about ¹⁄₁₆" thick, use a damp sponge to ensure that the top edge is nice and smooth. Remember, you're going to be putting this into your mouth! Once this is done, set it aside with your plate and leave it to air-dry for two to three days.

5. When your work is completely dry, use a damp sponge to smooth out any irregularities or tiny cracks that may have appeared while it was drying. If you don't cover a crack now it will only crack further in the kiln and not be usable for food.

6. Decorate both plate and cup with a brush dipped in your underglazes. You can water them down to create a translucent wash or keep them creamy and use them like acrylics, which gives you loads of design and mark-making possibilities.

7. Once your underglaze has completely dried, take your set off to the communal or rental kiln for firing at 1,220 degrees Celsius (2,228 degrees Fahrenheit). After firing, check the lip of your cup and, if necessary, give it a light sandpapering until it feels smooth to the touch.

Kampai!

Beads

◇◇◇

The history, geography and politics of the bead are intricately and inextricably woven into the development of civilization. Since Neolithic times beads have been used for adornment, currency, communication, protection and personal expression across all continents and cultures. The earliest beads were probably plant seeds; but elaborately beaded shell headdresses and complex lapis beadwork have been found dating all the way back to 2500 B.C.E. Yes, people, beadwork is seriously old-school.

Beads are incredibly valuable anthropological markers as their production tools, raw materials, designs and manufacturing techniques mirror the developing sophistication and movement of the cultures that employed them. Egyptians used turquoise, amber, quartz and ivory for embellishment. The Minoans of ancient Crete developed smelting techniques, which allowed them to create an extensive array of beads from precious metals, including gold, alongside precious and semiprecious stones. From Africa came intricate seed and shell work and the development of both brass beads and powder glass beads, which became a signature of Ghanaian craft. India, China, Australia, Asia and the Americas all hold archeological treasures of these earliest personal talismans.

Beads have been used for both the most pious and the most nefarious of purposes. During the Middle Ages a variety of beads were used for the finest ecclesiastical decorations, covering robes and Bibles with sanctified glitter. From the 14th century, complex patterned glass beads were being made in Murano, Italy, and they soon traveled the globe along trade routes. The beauty and availability of these beads eventually led to their use in acts of horrific oppression, whether used in the despicable sale of people — where they became colloquially known as "slave beads" — or dubiously employed by colonizers seeking to cheaply acquire lands or goods from native populations.

In the Elizabethan and Victorian periods, beads were used lavishly as decoration on the most fashionable garments and accessories. They were symbols of status and taste, a trend mirrored in haute couture today. The 1920s saw a resurgence in elaborate fashion beading as part of the Art Deco fringed flapper look. More recently, the beading style of the Native Americans of the Great Lakes region became hugely popular with the counterculture movement of the 1960s and 1970s and is still worn today by the Mardi Gras performers representing Indian chiefs.

Contemporary makers the world over are still drawn to the bead and its complex cultural associations to adorn, educate and protect. Visual artists and fashion houses remain tied to its rich history and geo-cultural traditions for design, technique and material inspiration. From hand-rolled synthetic polymers used to decorate new-school super-sized macramé projects to Pasifika reinterpretations of traditional cowrie shell work by urban Islanders, the bead still reigns supreme.

SARAH MALONEY
Canada

Visual artist Sarah Maloney has been working on her life-size "Skin" project on and off for almost nine years. Replicating the outer layer of a woman's body, this incredibly intricate work has been fully fashioned in the round from around 400,000 tiny glass beads and nylon thread. Serious amaze.

⌨ **smaloney.com**

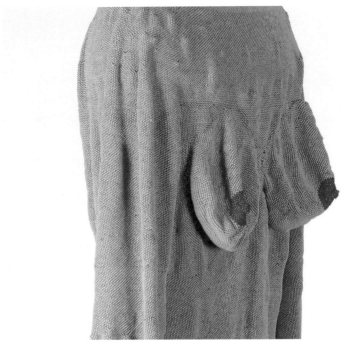

EDDY CARROLL
Australia

Eddy Carroll is a prolific contemporary artist who utilizes textile craft techniques (cross stitch, beading and printing) to create intimate and evocative pieces. She approaches her work with an open thoughtfulness that allows for happy accidents and detours as she takes her inspiration from the multi-layered experiences of travel. Amulets and charms, shrines and offerings, all encrusted with hand beading are created in slow and heartfelt meditation. Her work is imbued with magic, sadness and wonder at the real and the imagined world.

⌨ **eddycarrollwork.blogspot.com.au**

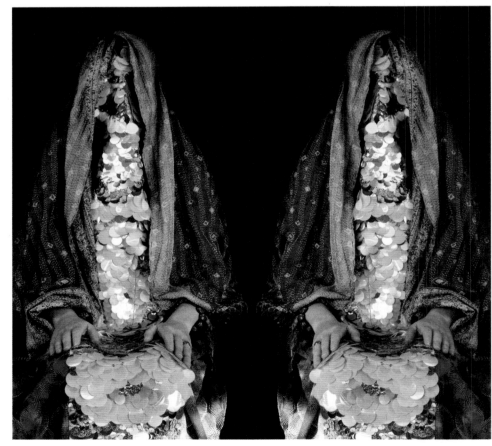

LEUTTON-POSTLE
Britain

Luxury knitwear designers and long-time friends Sam Leutton and Jenny Postle of Leutton-Postle are kind of mind-blowing. With an overwhelming arsenal of decorative textile tools and techniques at their disposal, they can justifiably be called the reigning queens of modern embellishment. So sharp is their eye, so clever their wit and so refined their skills, they effortlessly transformed the most humble of domestic kinder crafts into certifiable couture, mashing plastic beads with signature knits and prints in their stunning S/S 13 collection.

 leuttonpostle.com

KARLA WAY
Australia

Musician and fine jeweler Karla Way is a brilliant example of how creating your own beads can lead you to a unique and instantly recognizable aesthetic. Highly skilled in both high art and pop aesthetics, Way has created parallel versions of her signature animistic and organic forms. One makes use of precious metals and stones and the other plays with moody monochromes and neo-tribal handcrafted resin beads, affording her the opportunity to stretch herself creatively beyond the possible limitations of both.

karlajway.blogspot.com.au

DESIGN NOTES

SIZE IS IMPORTANT

The broad range of beads available gives free reign to crafters to make selections based on mood, aesthetic or project. Some techniques require specific beads but sometimes playing with scale can produce unexpectedly interesting results. Think large wooden beads for bead weaving or tiny seed beads strung and knotted into super-sized neckpieces, or mix tiny beads with super-sized options to create surprising new outcomes.

—

UNIQUE BOUTIQUE

Making or customizing your own beads is a great way to create unique beadwork. Polymer clay offers almost limitless options for color, size and shape. Wood can be dyed, painted or patterned with Sharpies, carving tools or wood burners, and gilding adds instant glam. Salvage old beads from neckpieces and garments in secondhand stores and garage sales and upcycle them in your own projects. If you can thread it, you can bead it. From foodstuffs to plumbing hardware — nothing is off limits.

—

LOCATION, LOCATION

Beads have long been used to create decorative focal points, but they can also be used to transform flaws into features, highlight the unexpected, or confound expectation. Think about using beads in places that are not traditional. Try the back of a top, the heel of a shoe or a darned elbow patch.

—

BEADY LITTLE EYES

Commercial beads come in a mind-boggling array of options, but the two most commonly used for embroidery and loom work are seeds (rocailles) and bugle beads. Seeds are small, smooth and round and come in opaque, translucent, metal or pearl finishes. Bugles are cylindrical and catch the light in a different and potentially more spectacular way. Both are enormously versatile.

—

HEAVY METAL

Think carefully about the wearability of what you're making and the context of where and how it will be used. A super-sized polymer and stone bead necklace on industrial rope will look fantastic but you may also need a wheelbarrow to carry it around. Metal beads on chiffon might be the ultimate hard/soft fashion dichotomy but it will probably tear the minute you try to put it on.

—

STRINGING YOU ALONG

Pretty much anything can be used to hold a bead — string, silk, fishing line, even shoelaces! If it fits through the holes, you can string your beads on it. However, if you're looking to create a weighty work or weave either on or off a loom you'll need to pick the right thread for the job. The last thing you want is your gorgeous neckpiece spread across the dance floor instead of your décolletage.

—

BEDAZZLED

Sequins and rhinestones have a dubious reputation, but they also impart high-voltage glam and super-kitsch awesomeness, which makes them a favorite for Mardi Gras, Día de Muertos, Carnival, and Vegas showgirls alike. We are of the "more is more" school, but if you are less inclined to work a Bollywood-meets-Grand Ole Opry style, be assured they're just as effective when used sparingly.

—

< TOOLS >

Different beading techniques employ different specialist tools but you can guarantee that the following will be needed for all projects.

- **Crimping pliers**

- **Needle-nose pliers**

- **Flat-nose pliers**

- **Wire cutters**

- **Needles for threading:** Either standard sewing or specialist beading needles for threading tiny seed beads.

- **Jewelry findings:** Jump rings, head pins, lobster clasps and chain.

- **Storage solution:** Specialist plastic sectioned boxes for beadwork are great but cookie and cake tins also work.

- **Beading mat or tray with sides**

- **Stringing options:** Memory wire, tiger tail, chain, ribbon, cotton, wool, elastic, leather, monofilament, silk.

- **Bead looms:** Bead looms are readily available online or in craft stores, in plastic, wooden and metal versions, and are used for creating flat expanses of beadwork usually seen in belts or bracelets. As these are specialist hardware we suggest first making your own simple version from cardboard before investing in the real thing.

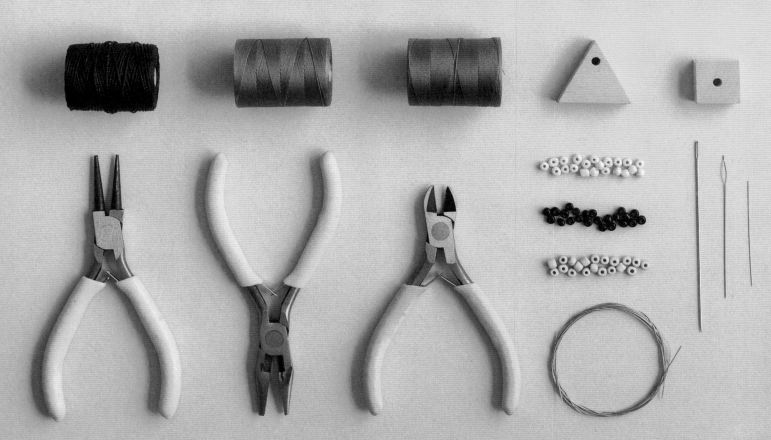

D.I.Y. LOOM

Weaving on a bead loom is a lot like tapestry weaving on a tapestry loom, so if you're familiar with that process you're already well ahead. If not, don't panic. It's much simpler than you think and the results are just amazing.

Bead looms are readily available and if you're looking to work on long or more detailed pieces, they really are your best option. However, you can make your own bead-weaving loom from a sturdy cardboard box, especially if you want to practice the technique without committing long term or just want to test ideas. Cardboard looms are particularly great for tubular Perler or Hama bead projects. Working on a bead loom is almost identical to working on any other loom with the threaded beads acting as the weft.

Make your own v-shaped grooves deep enough to hold thread along the short edge of the box spaced at $1/16$" intervals.

THREADING

1. To work out how many threads you need in the warp, count the number of beads across required for the first row of your design and add one thread to the outer threads to strengthen the sides.

2. Cut lengths of your threads 8" longer than the length of your cardboard box or loom and tie a knot at one end. If you're working with a box, rest your threads in the grooves and tape the knot to the outside of the box, then repeat on the other side.

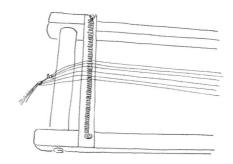

3. If you are working on a commercial loom, find the nail or screw on the tension rod at the end of the loom, then place the knot behind the screw so that it hooks in place. Spread the threads across the springs or notches on the loom. Keeping your threads straight so that they line up in the same spring loops or notches on both sides, wind the tension rod until your threads are springy and even. Then secure with a knot behind the other screw.

BEAD WEAVING

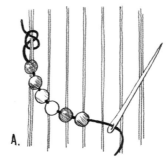

1. Knot the loose end of a long thread to one of the double outer threads of the loom, leaving a 3" length free for finishing. Count the number of spaces between the threads. You'll need as many beads as there are spaces. Thread this number of beads onto your needle and knot your bead thread around the outside warp threads.

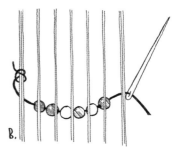

2. Pass your threaded beads under the stretched warp threads.

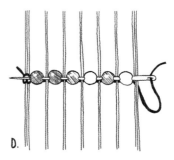

3. With your finger under the beads, push a bead into each space between the warp threads.

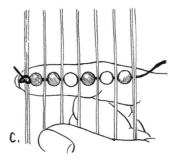

4. Holding the beads in position with your finger, tighten the bead thread to take up any slack and then pass the beading needle back through the center of each bead, going over the stretched warp threads. The beads are now held in position by two threads — one passing on top, the other underneath the stretched warp threads.

JOINING THREADS

Join threads by passing the new thread through the beads at the same time you would regularly pass one through. Yes, it's that simple! Once you've joined the new thread in, keep adding beads to your needle and keep on weaving as you were. You can sew in the thread ends when you finish.

FINISHING

Make sure you leave enough extra thread at the beginning and end of work so you can easily thread it onto a needle and pass it through the beads to ensure that you get a neat, secure finish.

WORKING A DESIGN FROM A CHART

If you're wanting to create a pattern within your beadwork — and why wouldn't you? — it's pretty simple. You just need to think ahead and reduce the pattern into a pixel-like diagram.

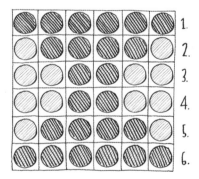

5. Using graph paper and colored pencils or markers to match your beads, draw your chosen pattern. If it's a simple repeating pattern you can just draw one instance of it, as in this example. Or you could use one of the more complex commercially available patterns.

6. Following your diagram, thread each row of beads onto the needle and weave it into the warp threads.

PEYOTE STITCH (EVEN COUNT)

Probably the most commonly used off-loom weaving technique is peyote. People around the world have utilized this simple process for thousands of years. One of its key strengths is that it easily lends itself to complex patterning in flat, round or tubular shapes.

The technique is now inextricably linked to the Native American beadwork that decorates objects used in traditional peyote ceremonies (hence its name) but the technique is such a winner that it works just as well applied to plastic beads as turquoise ones. Peyote can be used in odd or even numbers to create different patterns. However, trust us when we say that the even option is much easier for beginners.

We suggest starting with Perler or Hama beads as their tubular shape makes them easy to fit together.

1. Take an arm's length of thread into a beading needle. Tie a bigger "stopper" bead to the end of your thread to stop your beads from slipping off. You'll remove it later. Leave an end at least 5⅞" long on the knot. String an even number of beads onto your thread from left to right; we've used eight.

2. To make the next row, string one new bead onto your needle, skip the end bead on the far right of the row below and pass through the next bead along. Continue alternating in and out of bead rows in the same way, moving right to

left, until your thread comes out the end next to your stopper bead on the left hand side. You have now created rows one and two.

3. Start row three by stringing one new bead, then passing your needle through the first bead in row two. Continue left to right until you reach the end of the row, following the same over-and-under pattern to connect the new beads to row two.

4. These first four rows are the most difficult purely because of the small size of the work, but the more rows you add, the easier it gets. Trust us. Keep the faith and keep adding row after row, moving from one side to the other for as long as your pattern or thread allows.

CHANGING THREADS

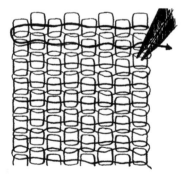

To end a thread, first take it through the last bead in the row (here ending at the right-hand edge), then thread it back through the beads of the two previous rows. Cut off the end.

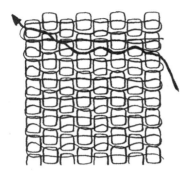

To start a new thread, re-thread your needle and insert it through an end bead below the bead where the old thread finished. Leaving an end at least 5⅞" long, weave the new thread back to the edge where you stopped weaving and start your next row.

FINISHING

Untie the knot on your stopper bead and thread the end through your needle. Weave it through rows 2 and 3 and cut off the end. Well done. You are now officially a bead weaver.

BEAD MAKING

Nothing could be simpler than making your own polymer beads. The trick lies in pushing yourself to make something unique. Do your research and look at traditional and contemporary bead forms and finishes from around the world. Think scale, shapes, patterns and additions, and mix your own custom colors. You can paint, gild or decorate after baking, but remember that polymer is sticky stuff and will pick up the tiniest crumbs. Working on baking paper is a great way of keeping your tabletop clean and wearing rubber gloves will prevent accidental color transfer between rolling sessions.

SHAPING

1. Knead the clay with your hands until it's malleable (like modeling clay).

2. Decide what shape you want to make, break off a piece of clay big enough to make your bead and start to shape it with your hands. Roll it into a ball, make long tubes or flatten with a rolling pin to create discs.

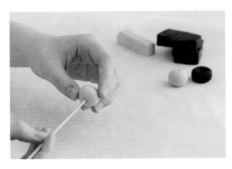

3. Make a hole through the bead with either a fine metal knitting needle, jewelry wire or a bamboo skewer, depending on the thickness of your string.

CARVING

1. Use an X-Acto knife to cut cubes and a needle to make holes in the center of each. Put your cubes into the fridge for around 10 minutes to make them easier to carve.

2. Cut off the corners of your cubes to form geo shapes. You can soften the edges with your fingers at this stage or keep them sharp and sand with fine-grade sandpaper once they're baked.

PATTERNING

To make spots on your beads, roll tiny balls of complementary colors and press them into your main bead. Roll this in your hand until the spots are integrated smoothly. Add another tiny ball slightly off center in each spot to create leopard print.

Torn flat pieces create terrazzo-style patterns, and tiny worms create interesting squiggles when applied using the same process.

To make marbled patterns, roll out thin, long ribbons in contrasting colors, twist them together and then roll them into one smooth, thick rope. Fold the rope in half again, then roll it all into a big ball. The marbled clay can be shaped using any of the carving or hand-shaping techniques.

To create texture just use any pointy-ended tool (knitting needle, bamboo skewer, clay tools, comb) to create dots, lines or hatching textures in soft clay. You can also recreate the surface of materials, from burlap to timber, by pressing soft clay against the grain.

BEAD STRINGING

To avoid headaches we suggest you make like a Boy Scout and be prepared. Whether you're using pearls or Perler beads, spend time getting everything safely laid out before you start, and work on a tray to catch beads that fall while you're stringing.

Regular beaders know that seemingly identical beads often have different-sized holes. Choosing an adjustable threading needle for fine beads ensures that you can get all your beads onto your thread every time. Or you can take advantage of the stiffness of tiger tail and wire to string beads without needles.

When working with multiple-sized beads, check that the smallest beads are bigger than the holes in the big beads next to them or they'll slide into obscurity under their larger companions as soon as you pick the work up. You can also try placing small spacer beads or knots between larger beads or groups of beads. This adds "flex" to your piece and helps maintain order.

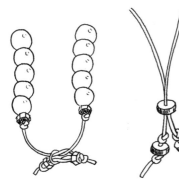

Finishing securely is key to a successful stringing session. To ensure that you end up with your piece intact, finish wire-strung beads with silver crimps, or see the Jewelry chapter to make a wire S-clasp attached to jump rings at either end of your work. Alternatively, you can use more simple knot pull closures such as the ones shown above.

PROJECT IDEAS

→ Take a super-subtle approach to couture embellishment. Highlight an element within a patterned fabric garment by embroidering clear beads over the top to give a shimmery 3-D op-art effect.

→ Create instant opulence by adding unexpected dimensional interest with stranded beads to a throw pillow.

→ Nothing is simpler or more striking than stringing a diverse selection of beads together into a statement neckpiece. Think outside commercial options. Found objects, shells and seed-pods are easily scavenged materials that can be turned into beads. Experiment with size, shape and color, or customize with permanent markers, dye or paint finishes.

→ Bead work en masse is a tried and true way of creating impact but why not mix this tradition with modern minimalism? Use the same bead repeatedly to create a wide monochromatic scallop in either bright yellow or moody indigo at the bottom of a raw linen curtain.

→ Humble basics can be quickly transformed into runway-ready with banging bling beadwork. Start from the ground up and transform a pair of tennis shoes with a collection of shiny beads, needle, thread and your imagination. Think all-over animal print or super-cute spots for starters.

Rumble in the Jungle Necklace

Oh no! It's Saturday afternoon and you've just been invited out to spend the night on the dance floor with the cool kids and you haven't got a thing to wear! Quickly update the most basic L.B.D. with this super-sized neo-tribal neckpiece and still have time to do your nails and hair before heading out the door.

WHAT YOU NEED

- 1 block of black polymer clay
- 1 block of taupe or gray polymer clay
- Baking (parchment) paper
- Rolling pin
- Sharp knife
- Size 11 knitting needle
- Toothpick or polymer-marking tool
- Baking tray
- 36" of tiger tail or fine wire
- 100 black opaque seed beads (around ⅓ oz.)
- Orange and natural wooden beads as shown (6 oval, 4 tube and 2 natural round)
- 1 sterling silver crimp
- Flat-nose pliers

HOT TIP

We find the quickest way to get a design right is to draw it before you pull out the polymer clay. Thinking through the elements and scale of pieces will speed up your process and ensure that you get a good result every time. Of course, there's nothing stopping you from mixing it up a little along the way if you get inspired. And when stringing different beads, use small jars or bowls to keep your beads separate and get a tray with turned-up sides to keep your beads off the floor and tantrums out of the craft room.

WHAT YOU DO

Making the beads

1. Preheat the oven to around 120 degrees Celsius (250 degrees Fahrenheit).

2. Using the patterning methods shown in Techniques, make two spotted gray and black balls around ¾" in diameter and another 1⅜" in diameter.

3. Flatten out the larger ball with your hands and place it between two sheets of baking paper. Roll it into a flattened circle around ⅛" thick, then cut off the top quarter and punch a hole in each top corner with your knitting needle.

4. Roll your remaining black polymer into four balls around 1" in diameter and decorate with surface patterns. Put holes in all your small balls.

5. Put all your beads and the flat pieces on a tray lined with baking paper and bake in the oven. Times vary according to the type of clay. It should take between 15 and 40 minutes. Check your packaging to make sure you get it right! Once they're baked, leave them to cool.

Stringing the beads

1. Work from the center out. Feed your tiger tail through the left hole of your pendant, across the back and out the right hole.

2. Add two black seed beads on each side as spacers before adding the natural round wooden beads, one on each side.

3. Start on the left-hand side and add in turn a spotted bead, two black beads, two orange wooden tubes and three small orange oval beads. Then start stringing on the seed beads using the tip of the tiger tail to scoop them up one by one. We used 50 on each side, but you can adjust the number to suit your own needs. Repeat this process on the right-hand side.

4. Carefully hold both ends (and we mean carefully) and hold the necklace up to your body to check the length. Shorten or add to suit, although if you're adding beads, remember to leave 2½" of bare tiger tail on either side.

5. Slide your tiger tail through the silver crimp one side at a time, pull it through until the beads are almost touching and close the crimp with a squish of your flat-nose pliers. Then take the leftover tiger tail and feed it back through the beads to give a classy, strong and invisible finish. Now, go hit that dance floor!

Books

◇◇◇

Books hold within their pages all that we are, know, believe and imagine. From the handcrafted versions of the Bible that took lifetimes to complete (and sent their artist monks blind in the process) to the democratization of learning that came with the invention of the mass-marketed paperback, books both mirror and spark the development of society, and follow a trajectory tied to technical and cultural innovation. Their complete integration within our culture makes them both subject and object of crafting activities.

The human imperative to record and communicate events and ideas is universal. Clay tablets and papyrus scrolls formed the first "books" produced by the Mesopotamians and ancient Egyptians, but China probably wins the day on both the invention of paper (around the 1st century C.E.) and as the originator of mass-production with the advent of woodblock-printed books during the Tang Dynasty (618–906 C.E.).

Today, in an increasingly "paperless" society, artists and makers are re-imagining the book, drawing inspiration from both its political/social context and its materiality — cutting, stacking, building, folding, carving

and molding existing tomes on both an intimate and a grand scale, indoors and out. Technological innovations are turning a new generation of writers, artists and photographers into book makers via instant access to digital print-on-demand platforms, while zine makers keep up the tradition of limited-edition publishing with super low-fi photocopy and staple living-room productions. Alongside this there is a growing number of contemporary artists reconnecting with the most ancient roots of the craft, studying the most complex hand-binding processes and creating their own highly conceptual "art books."

CONTEMPORARY ARTISTS

ALISON WORMAN
United States

What can't Baltimore-based book and fiber artist Alison Worman do? Combining two of our favorite activities in works that defy categorization, her output in both areas is outstanding. For us, however, it's when the two come together that the magic really happens. A terrific illustrator, pattern maker, printer, animator, weaver, and stitcher, her skill set is breathtaking. Her fabric art books are hilarious, surreal, clever and fun, while her sketchbooks are just about the perfect peek into the working mind of an artist. Book-worming that totally rocks.

🖥 **alisonworman.com**

PAWEL PIOTROWSKI
Poland

In a world where people obsessively snap photos of their food, graphic designer and photographer Pawel Piotrowski's Sandwich Book is a delicious piece of self-marketing. Playing fast and loose with our new obsession with image consumption, he's turned out a literal, literary page-turner, with each page showcasing both the ingredients stacked in order of appearance via a variety of paper art techniques and an extremely arch sense of humor.

🖥 **piotrowskipawelart.pl**

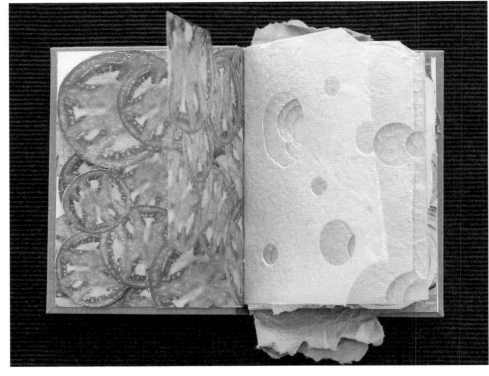

SONJA AHLERS
Canada

If only all scrapbookers had the keen self-referential honesty, critical social analysis, playful wit and pop culture antennae of Sonja Ahlers. Ahlers pretty much wrote the book (pardon the pun) on highly personal, bricolage-based girl power long before Tavi hit the blogosphere or newsstand. Intimate, animate, handcrafted and full of the kind of collected detritus that populates the memory boxes and private drawers of teenage girls all over, her limited-edition publications took the aesthetic and subversive spirit of low-fi zines and matched it with the new era of D.I.Y. print technology, creating the prototype for a new-feminist media, laden with both folk/craft nostalgia and seriously sharp edges.

💻 sonjaahlers.blogspot.com

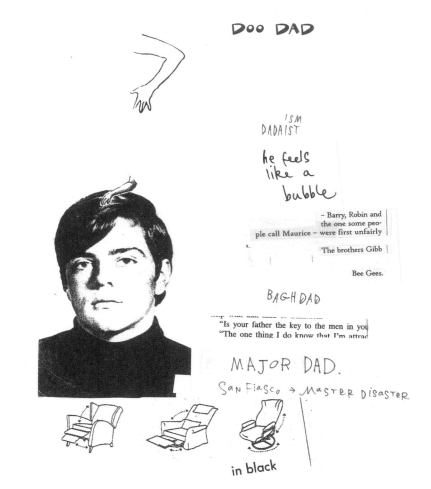

NICHOLAS JONES
Australia

Visual artist Nicholas Jones is a self-described bibliophile and cartography junkie. Wielding an X-Acto knife as sharp as the crease of his well-pressed trousers, Jones takes pre-loved vintage tomes and changes the way we "read" their text by carving, cutting and folding them into beguiling new works. Beyond the cultural horror of damaging or desecrating a sacred object, there's wonder and admiration as Jones charts new territory, transforming the common book into something of intricate beauty.

💻 bibliopath.org

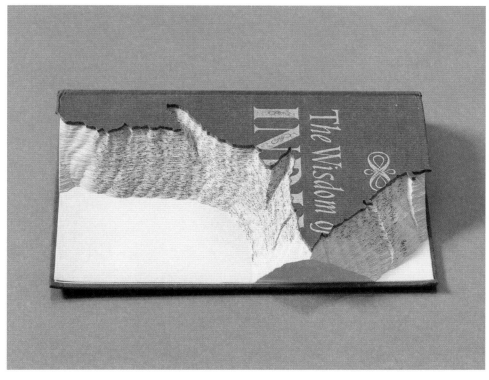

DESIGN NOTES

BETWEEN THE COVERS

We like to work green where we can, and when you consider that the average person uses about 700 pounds of paper a year (most of which ends up in landfill), it's worth thinking about alternatives before rushing out to buy new stuff. As the saying goes, one person's trash is another's treasure. Secondhand shops and garage sales are great sources of alternative papers. Think vintage books, magazines, wallpapers and sheet music, or make your own soft books for little ones from recycled clothing or bed linen.

OLD VS. NEW

Starting out with a well-thumbed paperback can be a lot less daunting than sitting in front of a pile of expensive handmade papers, binding glue and leather. So when starting out, try dusting off the book box hiding in the back closet or hit your local secondhand store or thrift shop.

SOURCE CODE

Think of the book as a brick, ready for building. Consider the color of the spine, look to end pages and illustrations for pattern inspiration, and use words and titles as themes for creative exploration. You can carve into a book to make an interior space, deconstruct it or work with books en masse to build new structures. Books are a seed waiting to be developed and germinated.

IT'S ALL GOOD

Traditional bookbinding can take a lifetime of learning, a fair degree of patience and considerable mathematical prowess. We say go for it if that's what floats your boat. But not every book needs to be a masterpiece. Good design is based on making the most relevant object for your own particular purposes. And thankfully there are no book police to say a single-fold staple notebook is any less useful than a leather-bound album or we'd both be under house arrest.

A WORD TO THE NERD

The old adage "Measure twice, cut once" is as relevant in book craft as it is with any other kind of construction. A little bit of foresight and structural blueprinting goes a long way toward achieving the desired end product. Whether embarking on an upcycle project or creating a new book from scratch, it pays to plan ahead. Once built, pages cannot be removed or redone without injury to the book and your self-esteem. Make like a Scout and Be prepared. Plot things out with care and assemble all your elements, materials and tools beforehand.

Whether you're starting from scratch, reworking an old tome or getting busy with a zine, you could make a long list of specialized items to aid your creation. You will most likely already have the basics in your general tool kit. However, there are a few specialist items worth getting if you think that this book-making business is for you.

- **Bookbinder's needles:** The higher the number, the shorter/thinner the size. You can get quite large ones that can go through multiple pages with ease.

- **Self-adhesive cloth tape:** For binding pages together in small books or as a decorative edging feature.

- **Weights:** Bookbinders use purpose-made weights to flatten books, but a brick wrapped in felt works just as well.

- **Book board:** A dense cardboard used to make book covers.

- **Book cloth:** To cover fiberboard. Any medium-weight cotton will work.

- **Endpapers:** To decoratively hide the binding process and add another design element to the book. Traditionally done with marbled papers.

- **Pencil**

- **Pencil sharpener**

- **Cutting mat**

- **Steel ruler**

- **Scissors**

- **PVA (white) glue**

- **Bone folder**

- **Bulldog clips**

- **Brayer**

- **Awl**

- **Waxed linen thread**

- **Ribbon**

- **String**

TECHNIQUES

PAMPHLET STITCH

This is an absolute standard that all crafters should be able to master. Make your own notebook using upcycled or handmade paper and use marbled paper, shibori remnants or stitched patchwork to bind it.

1. Fold your stack of paper in half. Ten sheets will give you a useful 20-page book and still be easy to manage.

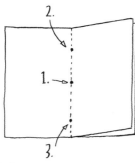

2. Mark the center point of the top sheet with a pencil, then two points evenly spaced from center to edges. Use your awl to make holes in all pages at these points.

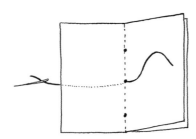

3. Erase the pencil markings. Pass the needle through the center holes, leaving 4" of thread at the end to tie up later, and take it from the inside to the outside of the notebook.

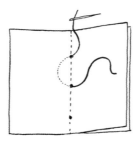

4. Bring the needle up through the top hole to the inside of the notebook.

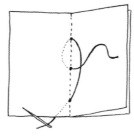

5. Carry the thread down to the bottom hole and through to the outside of the notebook.

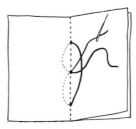

6. Bring your needle up through the center hole to meet the tail left in step 3. Pull tight and tie the threads together.

ACCORDION FOLDS

These are great for showcasing your work or a series of family photos. They are a breeze to make, and you can incorporate other craft techniques, such as embroidery, collage, origami, paper cutouts, painting and drawing, to make them really unique. If you can fold a map, you can make this book.

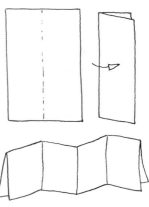

Fold a single sheet of paper in the center, then turn it 90 degrees. Fold again in half, then fold both edges back to the center crease.

ACCORDION BOOK COVER

For added finish a book board cover is ideal. This can be covered in decorative paper or fabric. Book board is just a high-density cardboard and is readily available in art supply shops.

WHAT YOU NEED

- Craft knife
- Book board
- Decorative fabric or paper
- Pencil
- Ruler
- Scissors
- Paintbrush
- PVA (white) glue
- Bone folder

WHAT YOU DO

1. Use your craft knife to cut your book board to size. It needs to be at least ½" larger than your book in all directions.

2. Place your board on your fabric, leaving a 1" border, and cut your fabric cover.

3. Trim the corners of your fabric diagonally, close to the corners of the board. Using a paintbrush, coat your board in glue and lay it face down on your fabric. Flip it over and use your bone folder to smooth out any air bubbles, then leave to dry.

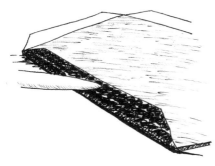

4. Once the glue is dry, lay your cover fabric-side down and coat each fabric edge with glue. Use your bone folder to turn the hem onto the back of the board and stick it down firmly. Leave to dry.

5. The cover is now ready to be glued to the first and last pages of your handmade book.

PROJECT IDEAS

→   Make yourself a swathe of small sketchbooks, right now. Even a quick-stapled notebook using some of your favorite papers, project leftovers or recycled office paper from envelopes will do the trick. Not only will you save loads of hard-earned cash, you'll also be amazed at how working on different patterned and textured papers changes your drawings and inspires new ideas.

→   Find an out-of-date school resource book (math and geography are great options) and carve a related symbol slowly and carefully into the book layer by layer. Think pi for math books or mountains for geography as a starting point.

→   Drill holes into a book cover pegboard style and cross-stitch a monogram. Repeat the process over a few books to make a 3-D word for your wall, or, if you're feeling particularly ambitious, get busy and do the entire alphabet.

→   The yellowed pages of old novels are the perfect backdrop for collages. Use them as a base or pull out phrases as inspiration for new works. Take a random line or favorite sentence and try to build an illustration around it. Or select an unknown character and imagine the clothes they might wear, or the interior of their home.

→   Write one. Don't be shy. If we can do it, so can you.

Cover-to-Cover Neckpiece

WHAT YOU NEED

- A fat paperback
- Cutting mat
- Craft knife
- Metal ruler
- Long, sharp, straight upholstery needle
- Linen thread
- Scissors

HOT TIP

While we've gone with a purist approach for our neckpiece, there is nothing stopping you from amping up the glamour. Try dipping the ends of your "rope" in gold glitter for a decorative finish, perfect for uptown book launches, or fluoro acrylic paint for downtown spoken-word events.

This is a project of transformation with the added bonus of zero waste. We suggest you pick a favorite tome to work with. Think cracking vacation reads, geeky series or literary classics. From the likes of King, Tolkien, Ellroy, Shakespeare or even Rowling, all are fair game in this project. After all, why wear something you wouldn't read?

WHAT YOU DO

1. Use your craft knife to remove the front cover.

2. Whatever book you've chosen, your aim is to break each page down into relatively equal squares of paper with zero waste. The ideal square size is around ½"–1". A nice idea is to maintain the reading order of the book, while deconstructing it into a wearable artwork. With this in mind you'll need to work methodically, starting with page 1 and working your way right through to the end. Get comfortable because it's going to take a while, but so does reading.

3. Gently tear your first page from the spine. Torn edges add a lovely deckle effect around the squares, producing a ropey texture in the finished piece.

4. Use your metal ruler as a guide to tear each page into strips. Fold these strips into squares and tear along the folds. Trust us, it's a remarkably easy process.

5. Thread your needle with linen thread to the length you want your necklace plus an additional 12" for finishing. Tie a knot at one end.

6. Feed your squares onto the needle, pushing gently through the center of each square, then push the squares off the needle and onto the thread.

7. If you want to ensure your pages stay in order, keep working methodically, tearing and threading each page in turn. If you don't care what order they go in, just tear up one chapter at a time and keep your squares in a tin or basket and thread them on randomly.

8. Once your entire book is on the thread in one long strand, knot the other end of the string. Tie a knot in the center of the piece, then tie the ends of the string together to finish your neckpiece.

Jewelry

◇◇◇

Our desire to adorn the body is fundamental to who we are. Self-expression, cultural representation, talismans, trade, ritual and royalty have all driven the desire and design of jewelry on every continent around the globe. The earliest evidence of jewelry-making stretches back 90,000 years to the discovery of perforated shells in Kenya and carved ostrich eggs in South Africa. Our pre-Homo-sapien cousins (Cro-Magnons) fashioned jewelry from bone, shells, seeds and stone, and as a species we've been banging on about bling ever since.

Both Norse men and women wore ornate silver and bronze jewelry, typically representing the god Thor's hammer. In 2011 an incredible archeological recovery of more than 200 pieces of Viking jewelry, dating back to 900 C.E., was uncovered in Lancashire, England. Known as the Silverdale Hoard, it included armbands, finger rings and brooch fragments. Armbands were used as both reward and trade, given in battle victory and in exchange for goods. This tradition of wearing your wealth is a common one, seen throughout the world from Gujarat to Ghana and from ancient times to the present day.

The first signs of organized jewelry production were found in ancient Egypt, where people attributed talismanic qualities to their jewelry pieces. With a passion for gold and an abundance of precious stones, they developed elaborate designs that included highly complex relief forming, stone setting and inlay techniques that demonstrated their opulent vision. It was the beginnings of jewelry as both status symbol and amulet. Jewelry was incorporated into funereal and other religious rites as a way of warding off evil spirits. This concept of the lucky charm continues in popularity to this day.

Jewelry's history has been recorded in high definition, not just due to the durability of its material composition but perhaps more importantly to the preciousness of its materials and its long associations with the upper echelons of society and aristocracy the world over. Crown jewels (fake as well as real) still play a major role in contemporary pageantry from beauty competitions to royal weddings, continuing to be a potent public display of wealth and power.

Contemporary art jewelry takes compositional cues from the rich multi-layered history of traditional production and turns them on their heads. While respecting and adhering to technical mastery, it draws material and aesthetic inspiration from innumerable and diverse sources. These new jewelers employ upcycling, personal history, environment, multimedia, and multi-craft practices that incorporate clay, leather or textiles for exploration and innovation. Makers engage in both practical and intellectual ways, fusing form and function with reference to architecture, fashion, philosophy and industrial design. The process of object making, the materials available and the positioning of those objects within culture all come into play.

This can seem overwhelming to art-jewelry outsiders. After all, you shouldn't have to get a Ph.D. to make a necklace, although some say that helps. This level of thought and investigation needn't be off-putting, especially if you consider it more a way of making meaning than as a fundamental part of your making. Our species seems hell-bent on decorating itself with anything from gold-sprayed pasta necklaces to the most complex filigree, proving that the desire to adorn is absolute and intrinsic to us all.

CONTEMPORARY ARTISTS

KATE ROHDE
Australia

Wearing the work of Kate Rohde is like having a key to the magic portal of a strangely fractal multicolored universe. Her resin cuffs, pendants, vessels and rings cross excessive rococo sensibility with a geeky hi-tech aesthetic born of B-grade sci-fi. Imagine giving Superman's crystal palace an 18th-century French makeover and you get some idea of the strange places her work can take you.

 **katerohde.com**

SETH DAMM/NEON ZINN
United States

If Odin held a wicked rave in Asgard you could bet the best Norse gods would be sporting the super-sized neckpieces of Seth Damm. Under his label Neon Zinn, Damm hand-dyes and deconstructs organic rope into sculptural forms that are incredibly tactile and spatially sophisticated. The process is hands-on and intricate, encompassing ornate braiding and knotting techniques and small-batch dyeing. Played out in graphic monotones and variegated color, Damm's pieces represent the best in new-school wearable art, so cool they manage to convincingly connect the Ancient Mariner with New York club kid in a seamless "old-salt tribalism." Anchors aweigh.

 sethdamm.net

ANNA DAVERN
Australia

Anna Davern's knowing acerbic wit is a defining feature of her work. A highly skilled gold- and silversmith, Davern is well equipped to willfully turn jewelry's historical and technical customs on their head. Combining new and traditional technologies, she makes clever aesthetic puns in surprisingly fearless ways. In particular, Davern's "Rocks" series deliciously subverts the elitism of luxury fashion by using sublimation technique to print oversize "photocopies" of precious stones onto the simplest metal. This hyper-faux glamour gleefully mixes 1980s television royalty with the "real thing," fusing them together as post-colonial, post-Dynasty jewelry for the 99 percent.

 **annadavern.com.au**

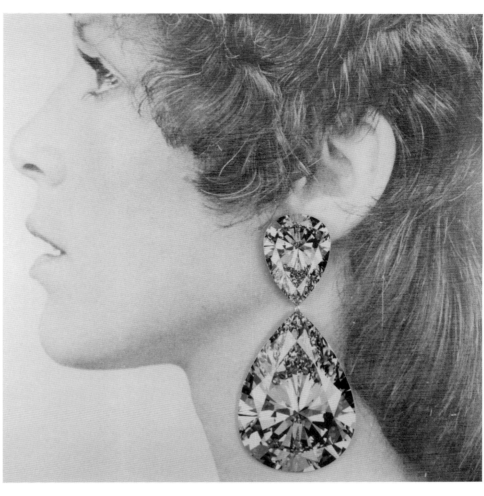

BIANCA MAVRICK
Australia

Combining both precious and non-precious materials, Bianca Mavrick brings all the gaudy goodness of Queensland to her oversize juicy pops of plastic. Referencing everything from 1980s pastel palette to hip hop's urban tribalism, her works skew scale and Australiana kitsch with trademark tropicana style.

💻 **biancamavrick.com**

DAVID NEALE
Australia

The natural world takes on a mystical quality captured in the quiet jewelry of David Neale. There is a lot to be learned from his confident distillation of form, stripping back the form of flora and fauna until all that remains feels essential. While still using precious materials, the work remains decidedly non-elitist. The inclusion of text is more than just statements of fact, providing titles of artwork to be worn for a lifetime. He is the perfect example of jeweler as artist.

💻 **davidneale.com.au**

NATALIA MILOSZ-PIEKARSKA
Australia

Contemporary jeweler Natalia Milosz-Piekarska has developed an international reputation for her strikingly bold work. Her commitment to creating key elements from scratch has created a highly personal talismanic language that draws heavily on both her family traditions and the natural world. Her unique approach sees her reference food, sea and plant life, using rich color combinations and a multitude of textures and materials in audacious works that often look good enough to eat.

💻 **ahhness.com**

MEREDITH TURNBULL
Australia

Simple shapes and humble materials belie Meredith Turnbull's deep understanding of contemporary craft and design. A circle, a square, a crescent become symbols drawn from a distinctly urban environment, providing minimalist signposts. A simple string of hand-painted square wooden beads that would look more at home in a toy box is elevated to sophisticated status when worn on the body. Changing scale, moving effortlessly between adornment and object, and engaging in ambitious public participation make Turnbull's cross-disciplinary practice far more complex than the simplicity of her shapes and materials.

🖵 **meredithturnbull.com**

DENISE J. REYTAN
Germany

Denise Reytan's craftiness is deliberate and expressed in far more than just technical terms. She creates bright mixed-media wearables that may at first appear like a bowerbird grab bag of baubles. However, under closer inspection it becomes obvious that the harmonious balance of each work demonstrates superior design nous, significant material understanding and methodical planning. Playing with ideas of preciousness and taste, Reytan questions the cultural conventions of adornment in audacious works that explode off the body like costume jewelry fireworks.

🖵 **reytan.de**

DESIGN NOTES

SHOW OFF

While traditionally jewelry is meant as adornment that explicitly interacts with the body, many contemporary makers are taking it off the body and putting it on the wall. Removing the wearable concerns of function allows you free reign to super-size your scale and materials. Imagine wall-sized pendants, bulky boating "beads" strung as outdoor bunting or oversize chandelier earrings transformed into mobile sculptures.

SURPRISE!

If you're making wearable pieces, think about the whole body as the canvas for your work. While traditions may dictate the scale and placement of works to fit ears, wrists and necks, there's nothing to say you can't change these to make bold new statements. Super-sizing or shrinking a conventional work is one way to add impact, but unexpected placement can make even the most mundane magnificent.

WEARABLE SHAREABLE

We've said it before but we'll say it again. If you are going to wear something, you really need to pay attention to your finishing and materials. Nothing turns a masterpiece into landfill more quickly than a scratchy clasp or pantyhose-tearing catch. Check bought findings for allergic potential as well as sturdiness, file off sharp edges and flatten hair-catching coils before wearing the piece yourself or sharing it with others.

NUTS AND BOLTS

While there is something special about heading to a specialist jewelry store for your materials, it's even more satisfying walking the corridors of a hardware store and discovering the perfect chain or bead for a necklace. Don't limit your expectations when it comes to materials — from tackle box to stationery store, there is an amazing range of unusual supplies that can easily be transformed into wearable artworks with a little imagination.

COLOR BY NUMBER

Enameling is a beautiful but complex technique that requires both skill and kiln. You can, however, achieve similar effects by using enamel hobby paints. Little pots of flat and metallic color are readily available and perfect for small jewelry pieces, while big cans are easily sourced at hardware stores. Mix and swirl together 1970s-style, paint in patterns or color block solid areas of silver, copper and brass. Just be aware that the paint will wear away with time and contact.

UP DO

Raid secondhand shops, garage sales and even your own drawers for long-forgotten jewelry that can be reclaimed in some way. By breaking the pieces down into their elements (beads, stones, findings, chains) you'll be able to reinvigorate old work or create new pieces while saving both the planet and your bank balance.

TOOLS

- **Pliers:** For the wire work in this chapter, you'll mostly use round-, flat- and needle-nose pliers.

- **Wire cutters:** Flush cutters achieve the cleanest cuts.

- **Rubber or rawhide mallet:** Helps to form shapes without marking metal.

- **Ball peen hammer:** Has one flat face and one rounded face. It's a great all-purpose hammer for flattening and shaping metal, removing dents, and driving chisels, punches and stamps.

- **Handheld brûlée torch:** For burnishing and melting the ends of wire into balls.

- **Metal wire:** Comes in many metals, finishes and degrees of pliability (called its temper). Its thickness is measured by gauge, with higher gauge numbers meaning finer wire. We recommend dead soft and half-hard wires. Use round 0.9 mm (19-gauge) silver for earring hooks and 1.02 mm (18-gauge) for jump rings. Copper and brass are good for forming practice, but not for ears.

- **Metal sheet:** Available in base metals such as copper, brass and bonded alloys such as silver/copper plate as well as fine silver and gold. All are sold by millimeter and either standard or custom sheet size.

- **Metal chain:** A huge range of options are available online, sold by continuous length or finished with clasps attached.

- **Dowels:** Available in a variety of sizes for winding wire and making jump rings.

- **Crimps:** Tiny metal rings used for finishing strand ends and holding beads in place. Silver, gold and a variety of alloys are available.

- **Bench clamp and work vise:** An extra hand for holding work and dowels and to harden wire for use in findings.

- **Findings:** Pre-made findings come in sterling silver, gold, various alloys and stainless steel (a wearable option for people with metal allergies).

- **Small needle files**

- **Large files**

- **Fine sandpaper**

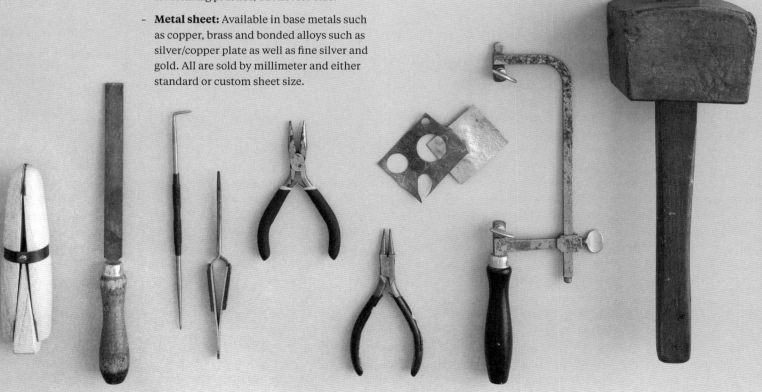

While the basic techniques we explain here are easily accessible for beginners, some processes are better off taught in person, particularly those that require specialist equipment and dangerous materials. It's worth taking a short (or long) course to learn gem setting, lost-wax casting, filigree or enameling. Expert advice and tutelage is a must if you want to ramp up your skills to match your ideas. Learn from the masters.

SAFETY FIRST

Jewelry making can be a risky business, even if you're not getting into the toxic chemicals and hot techniques such as casting and soldering. Follow these helpful hints and you'll live to craft another day.

- Wear safety glasses when cutting metal and filing. You'll look like a mad scientist but you'll save your eyes from nasty cuts and scratches.

- When cutting wire, hold it on both sides of the cutters to stop it flying off into the path of unsuspecting bystanders such as pets and small children. In fact, try to keep both out of your way and out of your tool kit. Sharp stuff is dangerous, people!

- Focused crafting tends to lead to hunched backs. It's easy to lose track of time and end up stuck in one position for hours. Try to regularly stretch your body to stop your neck and shoulders from getting stiff, and stop every hour or so to do finger exercises or you will start cramping up.

TEMPERING AND STRAIGHTENING WIRE

We've recommended using dead soft and half-hard wire for its malleability; however, this tends to both crimp easily and lose its shape if not hardened. One of the easiest ways to harden and straighten wire is to make a little bend at one end and put it into a bench vise. Hold the other end with sturdy pliers and give it a hard flick up and down. You'll see it straighten and feel it harden almost immediately. Before starting out on any of the processes below, remember to temper and straighten your wire.

LOOPS

These little loops are essential to learn, easy to master and endlessly useful.

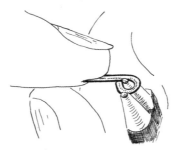

To make a p-loop, hold your round-nose pliers in your right hand, insert your wire into the pliers from the left and using the plier tips, roll the wire toward you until you have a loop that literally looks like a little "p" bending toward your straight wire.

To turn this into a centered loop for use in beading and clasps, just hold the straight wire beneath the loop with needle-nose pliers and bend the wire to one side until it's centered on the wire.

JUMP RINGS

These little rings may seem humble, but they are essential items to connect elements, allow movement and form chains. They are one of the backbones of jewelry making. While you can buy them (and to be honest that's often the easiest option), knowing how to make your own allows you to switch scales, mix metals and create custom shapes for unique and dynamic designs.

WHAT YOU NEED

- 6" of 10.2 mm (18-gauge) tempered wire (makes 6–10 jump rings)

- Dowel ½" in diameter

- Flat and needle-nose pliers

- Piercing saw and blade

- Fine-grit sandpaper

- Brûlée torch (optional)

WHAT YOU DO

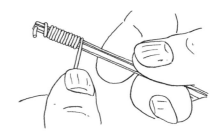

1. Using your thumb, press one end of the wire against the top of your dowel. Wrap the wire firmly around the dowel. Then turn the dowel to keep wrapping the wire, until you get to the end. Use your needle-nose pliers to press the ends firmly against the dowel. The wire will spring out a little so it's always worth picking a dowel slightly smaller than you want your ring to be.

2. There are a couple of ways to cut through your rings. You can cut them with a saw once you've cut them off the dowel, or you can use wire cutters instead and just make sure you file the ends well so they close properly.

3. Use the saw gently and slide it up and down through the metal; you'll feel it move smoothly and see the rings pop off as you cut. It's a very satisfying feeling.

   Note: While sawing might look daunting, you can get the hang of it pretty quickly. Drop your shoulders, relax, remember to breathe and let the saw do the work. Hold it too tight and you'll get a jerky motion, broken blades and flowing tears.

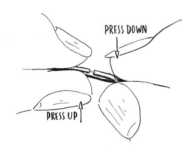

4. To get your rings to close, you'll first need to get your wire ends flat. Hold the jump ring between the fingers and thumbs of both hands, and gently twist the ends back and forth, so you can easily slip in your sandpaper and file it until the edges are smooth.

5. To close your ring, use your flat-nose pliers to hold the ends and move them back and forth again, pushing them closer together and then a little over each other as you do this. You'll feel a little snap when they meet properly. Ingeniously, this process also serves to further harden the metal to make sure it stays in shape.

6. To link jump rings just wiggle them sideways with your fingers (if they're small and soft enough) or with pliers (for thicker wire). Slip the next one on, close the first with flat-nose pliers and continue with the next.

EAR HOOKS

Knowing how to create your own ear hooks immediately opens the door to a world of amazing options. You'll be able to design hooks that suit the object, its movement, and placement in relation to the body. They do take a bit of practice, but once you've got the rhythm of making them you will be able to whip them up quite quickly.

There are lots of different versions of ear hooks you can make. Try varying your dowel width to make more circular versions and lengthening the front to make long, elegant hooks. Add jump rings to the front loops to create more movement in your earrings, and remember to keep the back end longer than the front, so gravity can do its work and keep them in your ears and not on the dance floor.

WHAT YOU NEED

- 2 x 2½" lengths of 0.9 mm (19 gauge) round dead soft wire

- Round- and flat-nose pliers

- Plastic yarn needle

- Dowel ½" in diameter

- Needle file

- Fine-grit sandpaper

WHAT YOU DO

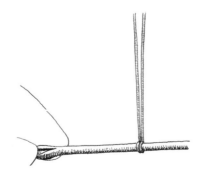

1. Use your round-nose pliers to create a p-loop at one end of your wire. Repeat for the other wire. Then slide the needle through both loops and roll the wire slightly to turn your p-loops into little circles.

2. Hold your dowel parallel to the needle, leaving a space the same length you want the front of your hook to be. While holding the needle and dowel in your right hand, use your left to exert pressure to curve the wire over the dowel to make the top bend of your hook. Continue this motion until you have curved the wires around the dowel so it nearly meets the loop at the front.

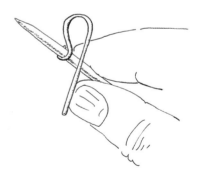

3. Slide out your dowel so that you can see your hook on the needle and check that it looks the same from the side and front angle. Slide it off the needle and if you need to straighten it, place it into the jaws of flat-nose pliers and gently press down.

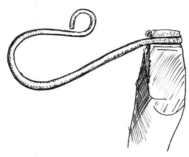

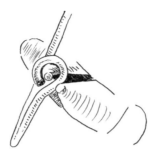

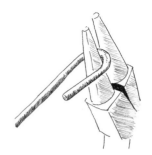

4. Using the same flat-nose pliers, take the long end of the hook and make a slight curve that kicks backwards away from the hook. Use your file and fine sandpaper to file off any burrs left from your wire cutter on the end that goes into your ear, and you are done.

p-loop that sits horizontally from the wire hoop, around ¼" from the end.

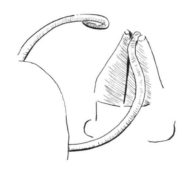

1. Cut your wire three times the length of the size you want your clasp to be. Mark the center with a permanent marker. Make your first bend by inserting needle-nose pliers midway between your center point and the end of the wire and then turn the end toward the center until they almost touch.

EAR HOOPS

Hoops give you a whole new range of design options, and they're simple to make. The width of your dowel will determine the diameter of your hoops. Use the same tools and 0.9 mm (19 gauge) round, dead soft wire as you did for hooks. This technique will let you make matching pairs.

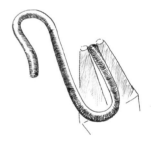

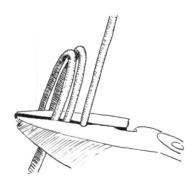

1. Take your wire and wrap it around your chosen dowel three times, using a medium tension, then let it spring back into looser tension so you can slide it easily off the dowel. Using wire cutters, cut through the loops with the flat, long ends facing toward you, then file the edges with sandpaper or a jeweler's flat file if the edges are stubborn.

2. Use your round-nose pliers to make a

3. Take the straight end of the wire and smooth it with fine sandpaper, then use your needle-nose pliers to bend it up at the very end — ⅛" should do — so it will fit securely through the loop without scratching your ear when it's on.

S-CLASPS

Now that you have learned some bending techniques, you will quickly be able to make this super-simple clasp, which will allow you to finish off neckpieces or bracelets beautifully. They are made from straight wire bent at both ends to form the letter S, hence the name. As with hoops and hooks, the tools remain the same. Because S-clasps are used as closures, you need to make sure your wire is strong enough to hold your work.

2. Turn your wire 180 degrees and repeat the same process at the other end so you have an S-shape. Take your pliers and make a little kick-away bend around ⅛" from each end. This will make it possible to feed one clasp into the other easily.

3. To make use of this clasp you need to make a permanent attachment at one end and keep the other open to hook over a jump ring or loop. To secure one end, open your S-bend, slip it through a p-loop or jump ring and close it tightly shut again with pliers.

4. Use a handheld brûlée torch to melt the ends of fine-gauge silver wire into balls for a decorative and body-friendly finish.

PROJECT IDEAS

→ You can create an infinite variety of works by combining one or more simple basic shapes linked together in different ways. Start with cardboard and play around until you find the right arrangement, then recreate it using metal or acrylic sheet, with jump rings as connectors.

→ Square-cut or pear-shaped, the traditional rocks of royalty might be out of reach, but you can take inspiration from their gems and settings to create a tongue-in-cheek take on high-end bling. Think geo-cut polymer "diamonds," gilded wood bead "pearls" and sequins instead of sapphires, and you'll soon have your own crown jewels.

→ Ramp up the daisy chain of your childhood by creating a wearable work sourced directly from nature. Seed pods, shells, bones, wood, feathers and stones are all beautiful starting points for a woodland- or beach-based project.

→ Transform copper or silver metal sheet into an armored amulet. Cut out a large semicircle and use a nail point to hammer in textured surface detailing. Drill through holes at opposing ends and add jump rings and a bulky chain for some old-school shieldmaiden glam.

→ We can't think of a single chapter in this book that can't be used for jewelry inspiration. Challenge yourself by opening it up at random and utilizing the technique or material you land on as a starting point for creating unique neckpieces, earrings, bangles or brooches.

Third Eye Earrings

WHAT YOU NEED

- Pencil
- 1 plank of ⅛"-thick balsa wood, at least 4" wide
- Craft knife
- Paintbrush
- Black and white acrylic paint
- Tin sheet
- PVA glue
- Ruler or tape measure
- Tapestry needle
- Pliers — round, needle nose and flat
- 2 x ⅓" silver jump rings
- 2 silver ear hooks (handmade, of course)

HOT TIP

This is one of those great projects where you can easily change the shape, color or scale to suit your own taste. If balsa ain't your thing, you could use upcycled plastic, metal sheet or fired porcelain to construct your teardrops.

The teardrop earring is a classic style most often seen in hand-wrought silver or gold, but we're here to tell you that you can turn cheapskate materials into upmarket bling with a little imagination and your own handcrafted silver findings.

WHAT YOU DO

1. Draw a teardrop shape on your balsa wood with a pencil, scaling it to fit comfortably between the bottom of your earlobe and your shoulder.

2. Cut out your shape using a craft knife and use it as a template to draw your second earring, then cut this out too. Use the knife to cut the pointed tip off so you have a nice flat edge at the top of your earring shape.

3. Draw two half circles on the balsa wood, just big enough to sit inside the bottom of your teardrop shape and cut them out with the craft knife.

4. Paint your teardrop shapes black on both sides, and the half moons white, then leave to dry.

5. Cut two cat's eye shapes from your tin and set them aside.

6. Once your balsa pieces are dry, glue the white half circle onto the black teardrop, and the tin cat's eye to the white half circle.

7. Using the tapestry needle, gently pierce a hole in the top center of your teardrops, around ¼" from the top.

8. Open up your jump rings and insert them into the holes you've just pierced, then attach the earring hooks and close the jump rings.

9. Put the earrings on, delight in your gorgeousness and proudly hit the streets with a sassy spring in your step and new-fangled dangles in your ears.

Origami

◇◇◇

Paper-folding traditions are almost as old as paper itself, but the craft we know as origami began with the introduction of paper to Japan via China around 610 C.E. Over the next 1,000 years it continued to evolve, crystallizing with the publication of *A Box of 500 Folds* in 1728. Origami is a literal translation of both material and practice — "ori" means "paper," while "kami/gami" means "folding." Strict rules mapped out its construction system; practitioners were required to fold forms from a single sheet of paper and without the aid of glue. These principles exemplify the common philosophical underpinnings of many traditional Japanese craft practices. Objects must simultaneously be harmonious, practical, decorative, aesthetic and intellectual.

Artist and educator Josef Albers, famous for color theory and minimalism, taught origami at the Bauhaus in the 1920s as part of his professorship. Origami offers both children and adults a hands-on methodology to explore and understand mathematics in three dimensions; it feels more like play than required learning. Origami makes abstract concepts such as fractions and physics more "real" while also flexing creative and problem-solving muscles.

There are various types of origami — action, modular, wet folding and pureland. Action involves creating forms that can be animated, from the blowing up of playground "water bombs" to the traditional flapping bird form. Modular origami is a variation on regular origami that dispenses with the single paper concept while adhering to the rule of using no glue or thread. In this form, complex structures are created through the joining of separate modules that interconnect through tensioned flaps and folded pockets. Wet folding takes advantage of the molding possibilities offered by damp paper to create sculptural forms that move beyond the purely geometric. The most recent addition, pureland style, was developed by British origamist John Smith and utilizes only mountain and valley folds, making the craft more accessible to both mobility-impaired and novice folders.

Origami's continued relevance is perhaps a testament to the purity of the craft in terms of both conception and process, but there is also something magical and bewitching about it. Deceptively simple yet infinitely complex, it has provided an almost unending source of aesthetic and intellectual inspiration to scientists, contemporary artists, fashion designers, architects and industrial designers. From lighting to superstructures, and from couture to space exploration, it would appear that origami continues to offer new perspectives and lateral insights wherever it's applied.

MADEMOISELLE MAURICE
France

Mademoiselle Maurice is a French urban
artist who fell head over heels in love
with origami while living in Japan. Moving
beyond the limited scale of her studio,
she has taken the craft to the street,
creating unique outdoor origami graffiti
works that push the form of both to new
levels. Using paper in public spaces,
she plays with notions of ephemerality,
legality, communication and display
while offering colorfully transient
meditations for everyday life.

🖥 **mademoisellemaurice.com**

JULE WAIBEL
Britain/Germany

Jule Waibel uses the transformative
capabilities and geometric aesthetics
of origami-folding techniques to create
garments and objects that change shape
as they interact with the body. Unusual
pairings of base material and end use
confound expectation in witty responses
to the constant flux of contemporary
living. Her project "Entfaltung" ("unfold/
expand/develop") used Tyvek, a
lightweight, tear-proof and waterproof
paper, to re-imagine both clothing and
accessories, while new "raised works"
feature heavy wool felt and more
monumental construction in a range of
collapsible seating structures as clever
as they are fun.

🖥 **julewaibel.com**

KOTA HIRATSUKA
Japan

The origami mosaics of Kota Hiratsuka are brilliantly constructed modules that take full advantage of the 3-D aspects of his craft. Playing with light and shade, his works seem to shift across the plane depending on your viewing position. Hiratsuka also shares his love of the craft by providing all his geometric modules in downloadable patterns from his Web site, accompanied by wonderfully engaging instructional videos.

 origamimosaicworks.com

MORANA KRANJEC
Croatia

The paper fashions of Morana Kranjec confound the senses and defy logic. Breathtakingly complex, her folds obscure all clues of visual construction, playfully distorting volume and shape while also playing up the female form hidden beneath. Referencing traditional dress forms from Elizabethan ruff to samurai armor, her capacity to transform the limitations of paper into convincingly wearable garments showcases both extensive historical knowledge and absolute technical mastery.

moranakranjec.com

DESIGN NOTES

PROCESS MAKES PERFECT

It is said that origami is more about the journey than the destination, which is a mantra that can apply to most crafts. But let's face it, we all like to have something at the end of that journey. As a method of meditation origami works wonderfully, but only if you first commit to perfecting your skill. Origami can also be an exercise in frustration of epic proportions, so prepare to commit to developing the art of patience and non-attachment alongside your folding skills as you deal with effort after effort looking more like a scrunched-up shopping list than a perfect paper crane.

TEAM WORK

Origami, while being a meditative craft, is also great fun in a group or with kids. Most big urban centers have origami groups that welcome newcomers, and aside from the minor risk of a paper cut this is one of the safest kids' crafts around. There are so many simple fold techniques that children as young as five (or a living room full of tipsy adults) can tackle it, which makes it a perfect choice for a rewarding kids' crafter-noon or a fun bridal shower.

BIG AND SMALL

The 6 x 6" paper square is the building block of all origami. However, there is no reason why you can't challenge this, as long as you stick to the square shape. Oversize origami pieces look great but can be tricky as you usually use much thicker paper. But that's not to say they cannot be mastered with the right materials, skills and location. An easier option might be to consider going small. Origami star paper earrings, perhaps?

FREEFOLD

Use old envelopes, magazine pages, newspaper, paperback novels, old school books, notepads. Take advantage of random patterns, words and associations to create new works, or use these materials as 3-D "sketchbooks" to practice more complex patterns before moving on to expensive papers.

FOUNDATION STUDIES

Origami is the perfect end point to any number of paper-based crafts. Think about turning your own 2-D output into 3-D sculptures — from block prints to boxes, screen-print to star. Or you can use sheets of hand-decorated paper mimicking animal skins or patterned surfaces such as marbling to create more complex animal forms. Alternatively, work the same idea in reverse and use simple geometric origami shapes as blank canvases for painting or drawing.

MULTIPLE CHOICE

Try to think laterally about what you've made and how it can be applied to as many different projects as possible. A simple pinwheel can be just that — a pinwheel. But make 15 of them in different colors and they are a garland or a bouquet. Make them in different materials, such as leather or oilcloth, and they become accessories for body or home. Make them in miniature and they become beads. One design form has almost endless possibilities if you think laterally.

SINGULAR VISION

Traditionally origami uses a single sheet of paper to create its forms, and it's this philosophy that has intrigued and inspired architects and fashion designers to manipulate metals and fabric into amazing new structures. This approach is brilliant for stretching your own creative problem-solving capabilities as it creates a simple conceptual envelope to push against when developing new forms or applying origami to alternative applications and materials.

- **Origami paper:** The most common paper used. Very fine squares of pre-cut 6 x 6" paper can be found in generous packs at craft and stationery stores, and sometimes at Asian specialty markets. There's also a plethora of suppliers online. Traditionally colored on only one side, papers colored on both sides are now becoming more common.

- **Chiyogami paper:** This beautiful Japanese paper comes printed with traditional woodblock designs. A great choice if you're incorporating your origami pieces into card-making or wrapping projects.

- **Washi paper:** A Japanese paper that has a luxurious soft surface. It is also known as mulberry paper and is soft, fibrous and hard to tear, all properties that make it fantastic for wet folding techniques.

- **Scissors:** Small and sharp are best.

- **Bone folder:** For heavier paper stock.

While there are thousands of origami patterns out there, the basic folds remain quite simple and are easily learned. If you can fold a piece of paper in half you can learn origami. These three patterns — pinwheel, box, and water bomb — will teach you the basics as well as giving you some useful objects for other craft projects. Keep your edges together and your folds sharp, and you can't go wrong.

PINWHEEL

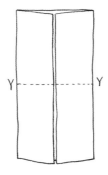

1. Take a square of paper and fold it in half both vertically and horizontally. Unfold and then fold the two edges to meet in the middle.

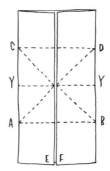

2. Fold the bottom half of your rectangle up to meet the center crease (Y–Y), making a new crease, A–B, then unfold. Fold the top half down to make the fold C–D, then unfold. Fold diagonally A to D, then unfold and fold diagonally B to C.

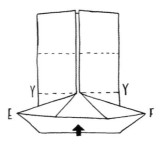

3. Pull up E and F and fan them out to meet the center crease, taking the bottom of the paper with you to create a boat shape. Fold in place.

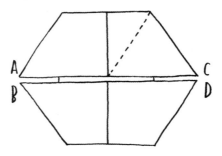

4. Repeat step 3 for the other side, folding down to meet the center crease. This is called a boat base fold. Your paper will now look like the above image. Make a diagonal fold as shown above, so that point C becomes the top point of your shape.

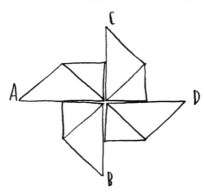

5. Repeat this diagonal fold with point B, folding it down to become the bottom point of your shape. You now have four sails. Gently open them so they will catch the wind. Stick the pinwheel onto a pencil with a thumbtack and take it out for a spin.

BASIC BOX

These boxes are great for gift giving. Create a matching lid to fit on the top of your box by increasing the size of your square by 1". Make sure all your creases are extra sharp, as they will form the guidelines for your box during the tricky business of turning it from 2-D to 3-D.

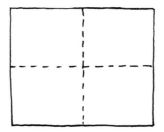

1. Place your paper decorative side down and fold it in half vertically and horizontally, then unfold.

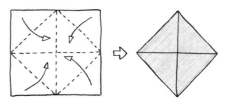

2. Fold the corners into the center. The decorative side is now on top.

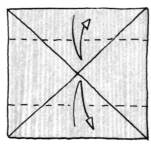

3. Fold the horizontal edges to the center crease. Unfold these edges.

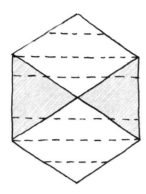

4. Unfold the top and bottom triangles.

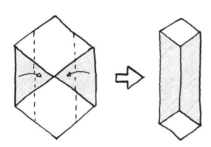

5. Fold the vertical edges into the center, to make a column shape.

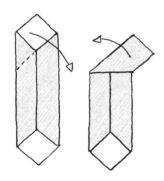

6. Fold the top corner down to the right, making a crease as shown above, then unfold. Then fold the top corner down to the left to make a mirror-image crease.

7. Your paper should now look like this.

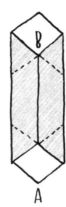

8. Repeat step 6 for the bottom corners. Then take point A and fold up to point B, to make a crease for the bottom of your box. Unfold and repeat on the other end of your column.

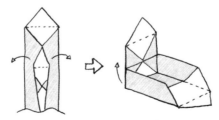

9. Here's where we start making the box shape. This bit is a little tricky but it gets easier once you've done it a couple of times, and your sharp folding will guide you on your way. Use your thumbs to lift the center out and form two sides of your box, while using your fingers to push up the back.

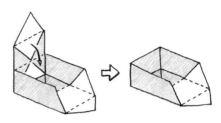

10. Take the upright flap and fold it down into the center of your box. It will naturally follow the shape of the walls, and you'll start to see how the triangular points meet in the middle of the box and the sides lock into place.

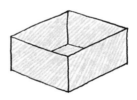

11. Turn your box around and push the open sides together to lift the other edge of your box. Then fold the top flap down, just like the first side to finish it off. While the action is fresh in your mind, quickly make a couple more so you get the hang of it for next time!

WATER BOMB

These little cubes are great units for building bigger projects like lanterns, mobiles or our chandelier project. Or you could of course fill it with water and throw it at somebody.

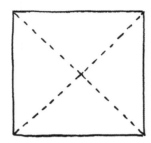

1. Fold your square diagonally to create a triangle, then unfold. Turn it over and fold another triangle in the opposite direction, then unfold.

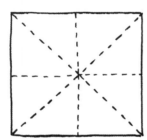

2. Turn your paper over and fold it in half to create a rectangle. Unfold and turn your paper 90 degrees clockwise and make another fold.

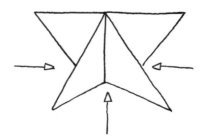

3. Turn your paper over and push two sides in so that they collapse into a triangular shape.

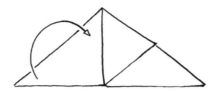

4. Holding the flat face toward you, fold up the outer corners into the center to make a square, then turn your paper over and repeat the process on the other side.

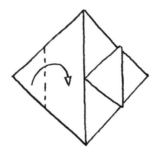

5. Take the right corner to meet the center and fold. Do the same for the opposite corner, then turn over and repeat the process on the other side.

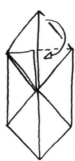

6. Fold the top of both corners at one end into the center, then turn over and repeat the same process on the other side.

7. Now, here's where it gets tricky. Carefully open up the triangular folds formed in step 5 and use your fingers to tuck the pointy corners into these little pockets. Repeat the process on the other side.

8. Turn the shape the other way up. Firmly blow into the hole at the point until it puffs up into a little cube.

PROJECT IDEAS

→ Try making multiple versions of one simple 3-D design (for example, a box or pinwheel) and suspend them from a rod to create a photo backdrop wall — the ultimate party accessory.

→ Fashion designers have been inspired by origami for decades, for both construction and decorative purposes. Dramatically change a basic elastic-waist skirt into a wearable work of art by incorporating pleating, embroidery or folded darts to change the entire silhouette, or create a tactile surface decoration.

→ Playing with scale is an age-old design trick that works particularly well with origami. Try up-sizing for dramatic effect and make a sculptural centerpiece for your dinner party, or a collection of oversize forms as hanging outdoor decorations for your next BBQ.

→ Seasonal decorations are an obvious but enjoyable choice for showcasing origami projects that the whole family can help to make. Try an origami-laden tree, garland or wreath. Decorations can be spray-varnished, painted, glittered and gilded for an even more festive look.

→ Take a playful approach to simple origami folding that is perfect for highly personalized card making. Print or cut out a photo image that you like, make a judicious fold and watch the transformation from an ordinary scene to one of hilarious surrealism.

It's My Party Chandelier

WHAT YOU NEED

- 120 sheets of double-sided standard origami paper (ours was backed in silver and gold)
- Stripy paper straws
- Scissors
- Straight upholstery needle
- 27 yards of fishing line or cotton thread
- Child-size hula hoop
- Long gold tinsel strands (enough to go around the hoop)
- Double-sided tape
- S-hook

HOT TIP

If you don't want to use commercial paper you could always cut your own marbled or painted paper into squares. Similarly, if you want to scale up your cubes, you can just increase the size of your paper squares accordingly.

This project takes party decorations to the next level. Origami water bombs make the perfect centerpiece for a special occasion. Inspired by the traditional Polish Pajaki mobile, it's simple but oh so time consuming. Speed up the process by getting the whole family, friends and kids involved as a social activity beforehand and unveil the completed masterpiece at the event.

WHAT YOU DO

1. Fold 120 water bombs using the pattern provided on page 344.

2. Cut your straws into 1" lengths.

3. Thread your needle with fishing line and sew chains of 20 bombs, alternating a bomb with a cut straw. Continue until you have made six chains.

4. Tie off the ends of your fishing line, leaving enough line at each end to tie to the hook and the hoop.

5. Attach your chains to the hula hoop, making sure they are evenly spaced.

6. Attach your tinsel to the outside edge of the hoop using double-sided tape.

7. Tie the top ends of your chains together then feed your S-hook beneath the knot. Now hang the S-hook from a beam or a light fitting.

8. Get a friend to hold your hoop up, allowing the chains to drape through to create the chandelier shape. Then use fishing line to secure the hoop to the S hook.

9. Trim your tinsel to a satisfying length and get the party started!

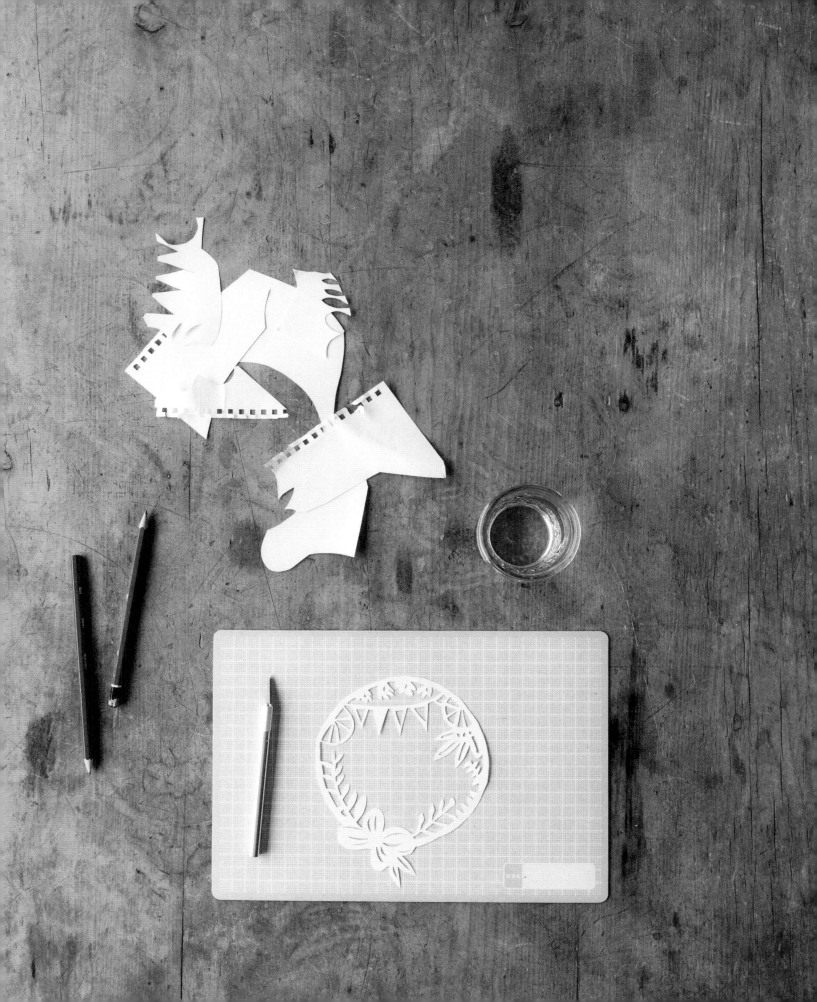

Paper

◇◇◇

People have always wanted to make their mark. From cave drawings to hieroglyphs, we've searched for ways to visually communicate our stories to each other. Around 2400 B.C.E. Egyptians pressed and dried papyrus, a common fibrous plant that grew along the Nile, to create a basic material that could be written and painted upon. This was a major improvement on the rudimentary clay tablets that had previously been used and allowed for the easy transportation of important information and the keeping of records in scroll form. But the official story of paper as we know it today starts in China with one man.

In 105 C.E. Tsai Lun, an inventor and official within the Emperor's court, experimented using both mulberry and bamboo fiber, mixing them with water and then draining them through cloth. He discovered that cellulose materials naturally knit together and when dry create a lightweight, economical writing surface. He reported his discovery to the Emperor, so although recent archeological findings point to paper's existence in China some 200 years earlier, Tsai Lun owns the day as the first official paper maker.

Paper making didn't spread out from China to the rest of the world until much later. It initially began a nomadic journey to Vietnam, Tibet and on to Korea, and by the 6th century to Japan. By the 8th century the technique had made its way to India, where it began its push west, first through the Middle East before entering Europe in the 12th century.

Up until this point European scribes, almost exclusively monks, used parchment fashioned from animal skins, a costly and complicated process. Paper making became widespread with the invention of water mills, which offered a mechanized way of producing paper, most commonly with rags of linen, cotton or hemp. Even when the far simpler methodology of paper production was introduced, it would not be until the 15th century that paper would be considered a really accessible product for all. The fate of paper manufacturing is then inextricably linked to the 1456 production of the Gutenberg Bible, named after Johannes Gutenberg, who also invented the moveable type used to print it, which heralded the beginning of mass communication and the modern printing industry. Combined with other mechanized production and distribution systems of the Industrial Revolution, paper could now be made more accessible and finally became part of everyday life.

Crafting with paper has developed into rich and varied traditions around the world. Paper cutting has been around since at least the 6th century in China, Japan, India, Mexico and Thailand. Silhouette portraits cut from black paper in the 18th century remained popular family keepsakes right up until the early 20th century. Bookbinding, marbling, printing, scrapbooking, papier-mâché and collage are all crafts that developed in tandem with the widespread availability and affordability of paper.

Once seen as ephemeral, papercraft has seen a massive resurgence in contemporary fine art and design. The firm Confetti System almost broke the Internet with its glammed-up party props and large-scale papercraft installations. Artists such as Banksy have taken the once-lowly material to the streets in paste-up artworks that have redefined fine art practice. Graphic designers and video directors have embraced 3-D papercraft, remaking objects from Instamatic cameras to full-scale room interiors to stage their work. Cheap, fun and full of possibilities, paper is so seductive that even the arcane art of quilling has poked its nose up on the cover of magazines. Get out your scissors and glue; papercraft is most definitely back.

PAIGE SMITH/A
COMMON NAME
United States

Paige Smith transforms our ideas of preciousness in her ongoing "Urban Geode" project. Paper seems an unlikely base material to use for work that spans geography and time, but Smith transforms it into gem-like geodes that nestle into their urban spaces around the globe. Whether wedged in a brick façade or filling up a public telephone booth, they appear to have been uncovered rather than placed. Rigorous photographic documentation means her work takes on a permanent preciousness.

 acommonname.com

MICHAEL VELLIQUETTE
United States

The multi-layered and immersive paper fantasies of Michael Velliquette inspire a kind of devotion in his legion of fans that is easy to understand. Beginning with the holy trinity of papercraft (paper, scissors, glue), he creates dense, detailed pieces that can swallow a room and the viewer whole. Velliquette reinvents the traditional craft of paper relief by working in prismatic hyper-color and monotone metallics, delivering a universe of mythical beasts, mad machines and totems to navigate the modern age.

velliquette.com

CARLY FISCHER
Australia

Carly Fischer's mastery of mimicry is breathtaking. Fischer's critical eye focuses on the hidden narrative of what is discarded, brilliantly turning the medium into the message and using paper as both conceptual and mechanical tool. She plays with the tradition of model making and flips it, using the "real" items as the starting point and the model as the finished work, producing works so convincing that they raise all kinds of chicken-and-egg conundrums for the viewer.

 **carlyfischer.com**

AMY BOONE-MCCREESH
United States

The paper works of Amy Boone-McCreesh look like the material aftermath of a fantastic opening-night party exploded against the gallery wall. Both celebratory and melancholy, her feathered, crimped, folded and molded constructions reference the rich decorative displays and cultural traditions used throughout the world to mark important familial and calendar events.

 amyboonemccreesh.com

DESIGN NOTES

SCRAPPY DO

Scrapbooking is a highly personal craft despite what the Internet might tell you. A huge part of it is industry driven, and it can often feel more like shopping than crafting. That said, journal- and memory-keeping are steeped in tradition and your stories of family, friends, adventures and dreams can't be put in a virtual shopping cart or downloaded as a pdf. You may love all the gorgeous papers, ribbons, embellishments and sticky letters but you certainly don't have to. Use the paper detritus of your everyday life to add authenticity — the inside of envelopes, old books and magazines, used wrapping paper and your notions drawer can all provide the materials needed to produce great craft that will more eloquently tell the story of you.

KNIFE'S EDGE

From super-detailed paper poetry to bold simple shapes, this graphic technique is a brilliant way to re-imagine your drawings. Paper cutting takes a steady hand, a keen heart and a sharp blade. Paper cuts are all about negative space. It's what you remove that reveals the image so you need to reverse your mind's eye a little in order to get the best results.

WHY D.I.Y.?

Paper making is a craft unto itself and definitely worth investigating. It does take a bit of specialist equipment and a lot of water but there are benefits to custom-made, especially if you are using paper for a particular purpose (invitations, gifts, artwork). There are dozens of tutorials online to help you on your way and kits are available both online and in stores. It is a bit fiddly and very messy but in terms of upcycling and eco cred it's great. Being able to control the outcome completely is brilliant — especially if you're going to use your output for other paper-based activities such as bookmaking, marbling or origami.

STAYING GROUNDED

While the lightness and pliability of paper might fool you into thinking you can trick physics, all kinds of buildings need to adhere to the basic construction principles to stay upright. Don't ignore good foundations. If you're after freestanding sculptures, ground them on something steady such as cardboard or wire armatures, add weights or an anchor to them, or they will fly off the shelf at the first sign of a breeze.

PAPER TIGERS

Paper is complete genius as a material. Bend, shape, tear, crimp, form, build, fringe, fold, glue, paint, dust, sew, glitter, wash, dye. Its capacity for making is virtually limitless, so be brave and a little ambitious. An easy way to start is to look to other craft techniques and outcomes and use paper as a material. There's a long history of artists using paper for everything from jewelry to fashion to draw inspiration from. Experiment boldly and often, push the envelope literally, and play hard and fast with everything but the rules.

STICKY FINGERS

Papier-mâché can be the stuff of both dreams and nightmares. Many a clumsy volcano and last-minute Venetian mask has been whipped up with wallpaper paste and balloons with mixed-to-appalling results. But do not be fooled — this low-fi children's craft technique can deliver sophisticated results if you keep your shapes simple and your palette clean and contemporary.

- **Mold and deckle:** This is essential for paper making. The mold is a frame with mesh stretched over it that is used to catch paper pulp and drain excess water. The deckle is the frame that sits on top and creates the edges of your paper.

- **Card stock:** Usually acid free, it comes both flat and textured in size 8½ x 11" size in endless colors, and is great for folding and building. Larger sheets are especially useful for bigger projects.

- **Cotton rag:** Specialist artist's paper that is expensive but well worth it. It's superior for nearly every purpose, and especially brilliant for painting or printing.

- **Scrapbooking paper:** Usually acid free, it comes in handy 12 x 12" squares, is available in a multitude of finishes and is often double-sided.

- **Tissue paper:** This is perfect for paper flowers, pom-poms and tassels. It comes in a large range of colors and is inexpensive, although delicate.

- **Crepe paper:** Stretchy, strong and lightweight, our favorite is double-sided. It does double duty as a dye when used with water.

- **Vellum:** For tracing and overlaying. It's great to print on and for transfers, but it doesn't take too well to folding.

- **Origami paper:** Foldable and durable, this paper makes a colorful and inexpensive option for nearly all papercrafts.

- **Wallpaper:** Thick and often boldly printed, it comes in rolls and samples. It can be pricey but can also be found for next to nothing in op shops. Textured versions can be transformed by paint and ink.

- **Quilling strips:** This comes pre-cut in a wide range of colors, and is great for paper weaves, construction and collage.

- **Kraft paper:** Cheap and readily available, it can be bought in reams or rolls, lined or plain. Just make sure you choose the right weight for your project. Highly versatile and a great base alternative to white paper.

- **Floral tape:** This magical waxy tape has the ability to stick to itself and is used to attach buds, stamens and petals to the wire. It's readily available in a variety of colors. Essential if you're going to make paper flowers.

- **Scissors**

- **Pinking shears**

- **Fringe scissors**

- **X-Acto knife**

- **Craft knife**

- **Double-sided tape**

- **Glues:** PVA (white), glue sticks, dimensional glue dots, paste.

- **Decorative stamps, cutters and punches**

- **Adjustable hole punch**

TECHNIQUES

PAPER FLOWERS

There's an endless variety of ways to make paper flowers. We love using crepe paper (our favorite being the double-sided kind). Tissue paper also yields beautiful blooms. Use them as wrapped gift toppers, wedding bouquets, garlands, table centerpieces, birthday bunches, wreathes and on headbands. The following are simple instructions for our three favorite flowers and a couple of foliage options. We've used all of these in our Paper Flower Wreath project (see page 356).

Choose your materials wisely, as not all crepe papers are created equal. Cheaper stuff can be thin, floppy and easily torn. Choose thick floral crepe with a bit of stretch and buy good-quality, waxy floral tape as it's key to successful flower making. Use it to attach buds, stamens and petals to your floral wire. Millinery stamens are worth seeking out as they add bling, realism and high-end finish to your work.

Cut your shapes by feel, with the visible grain running vertically. If you're not too confident, you can find loads of printable templates online. As always, we advise you to be brave and try. After all, there are no straight lines in nature.

WHAT YOU NEED

- Tape measure or ruler
- Scissors
- Crepe paper
- Wire cutters
- Floral wire
- Floral tape
- Fringe scissors
- Millinery stamens
- Pinking shears

GARDEN ROSE

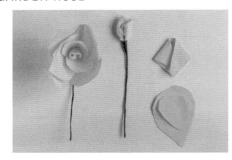

1. Start with the bud center by taking a 2½" square of crepe paper and folding it into a triangle, and then folding the far points into the center. Scrunch your triangle slightly to create the bud shape. Attach the bud to the top of the wire using floral tape and wrap the entire wire with floral tape.

2. To make the bloom, cut out three 2" long teardrop shapes and five 3⅛" long teardrop shapes.

3. Using the floral tape, attach the three small petals around the bud center, then attach the five larger petals in the gaps left between the small petals. Once complete, gently curl the edges of each petal outward for a more rose-like appearance.

CHRYSANTHEMUM

1. Cut three lengths of crepe paper measuring 3 x 12" and fold each one in half, and half again lengthwise. Use fringe scissors to cut three-quarters of the way down the paper to create a fringed edge.

2. One at a time, attach your three fringes to the wire stem with floral tape.

3. Starting at the base of your flower, wrap the entire wire stem with floral tape, then fluff out your fringe to create the signature puff-ball shape.

FIVE-POINT PETAL FLOWER

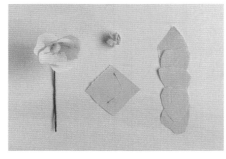

1. Start with the bud center by cutting two 2" square pieces of crepe paper, scrunching one into a ball and covering it with the second piece. Attach your bud to the wire using floral tape, and continue to wind the floral tape around the wire until it's entirely covered.

2. Take four stamens and gently bend them in half. Attach them to your stem at the base of the bud. Spread your stamens out so that they evenly work their way all around the bud.

3. Cut five equal-sized petal shapes out of crepe paper. Ours are 2½" long. Attach each petal one at a time around the bud. Once all are attached, gently curl your petals out for a more realistic appearance.

THREE-POINTED LEAF

1. Use pinking shears to cut out three elongated leaf shapes and scrunch them together at the bottom points.

2. Place wire in the center of your leaves and use floral tape to attach them to the top of the wire. Continue wrapping the entire wire stem with floral tape.

LEAF BRANCH

1. Cut five leaf shapes out of crepe paper, then cut five short lengths of wire — ours are 4". Using your floral tape, attach a leaf to each short length of wire.

2. Attach your leaf stem to your main branch stem with floral tape, adding a leaf stem alternately to each side as you go. Once all are attached, bend your branches out and gently stretch your leaves into shape.

PROJECT IDEAS

→ Piñatas are a party must. Go wild with gold and silver tissue paper fringing for a wedding-worthy version, or get your kids to think up a z-grade blockbuster chimera and whip them up their very own sharktopus for their next birthday.

→ A paper kite makes for a great statement piece on a child's bedroom wall. Incorporate your recipient's artwork into the kite panels for a special suprise or get them to customize the paper before you start. Add bows, pom-poms or paper streamers for a super-cool tail.

→ Use coiling, weaving or papier-mâché techniques to transform scrap paper into a brilliantly functional scrap paper basket or plant pot. Paint it or keep it au naturel to show off its recycled roots. Decide if you need indoor assistance or all-weather wear — water-based sealants are definite insiders while solvent sealants love the great outdoors.

→ Masks aren't just for Carnival or Halloween. Fold, crimp, paste and cut yourself a wearable self-portrait or alter ego. Get your friends to make their own for your next dinner party — just don't go all *Friday the 13th* and terrorize the neighborhood.

→ Go big or go home! Paper is as light as a feather so it gives you great scope to make oversize crafts that can be hung from the ceiling without stress. Everything from the beautiful Polish Pajaki chandeliers to garlands of handmade blooms can transform any living room into celebration central.

Paper Flower Wreath

While traditionally speaking these are seasonal decorations, we believe that wreaths are for life, not just for Christmas! This beautiful paper version uses all the greenery and blooms from our paper flower Techniques section, making it a perfect sampler project.

WHAT YOU NEED

- 14" embroidery (quilting) hoop
- Gold spray paint
- Ribbon or picture hook
- Crepe paper (we used pink, peach, dark pink, dark green, and silver)
- Green floral tape
- Floral wire
- Ruler or tape measure
- Scissors
- Fringe scissors
- Millinery flower stamens (we used gold-tipped white)
- Pinking shears
- Wire cutters
- Hot glue gun + extra-hot glue sticks

WHAT YOU DO

1. Spray paint your embroidery hoop gold and allow to dry. This will be your wreath base.

2. Attach your ribbon or hook to the back of your base.

3. Following the instructions in the Techniques section, make six roses in pink crepe paper, six chrysanthemums in peach and 16 five-point petal flowers in dark pink. Feel free to mix up these blooms to suit yourself.

4. Then make eight branches in dark green crepe paper and six three-pointed leaf sets in silver, following the instructions in the Techniques section.

5. Using your hot glue gun, begin attaching your foliage to the wreath base. Start with the branches, making sure they travel around the hoop in the same direction. Keep a bowl of ice water nearby in case of glue burns. Stick your hand straight into the water and the glue will instantly harden and easily fall off your skin, preventing serious injury.

6. Attach your three-pointed leaf sets. Imagining the wreath as a clock face, place three between 10 and 11 o'clock, and three between 4 and 5 o'clock.

7. Evenly distribute your eight green branches around the hoop.

8. Take your roses and evenly space them around the wreath starting at 12 o'clock.

9. Attach your chrysanthemums next to your roses.

10. Use your five-point pretties to fill in the gaps.

11. The final step is the most satisfying. Work your way around the wreath and give your crepe paper petals and leaves a bit of a stretch into place. This will make them come to life.

HOT TIP

Balance is key to successful wreath making, so work your elements accordingly. If you don't like peach and pink you can make the same flowers but turn up the volume with kaleidoscopic hues, or go gothic in basic black for Halloween — wreath making should be fun and intuitive so shake it up depending on the occasion (or what's left in your craft cupboard).

Mobiles

◇◇◇

While it's true that people have been hanging treasured objects since the dawn of time, the invention of the modern mobile can be traced back to one man — Alexander Calder. Mobiles are a great end use for any number of other crafts such as origami, papier-mâché, needle-felt, whittling and polymer clay. If you can make it, you can make it into a mobile.

Influenced by the abstract work of Miró, Arp and Mondrian, Calder began creating kinetic floating sculptures way back in the early 1930s. Although the term "mobile" was initially coined by Duchamp to describe Calder's mechanical sculptures, it soon became synonymous with the free-moving works we now recognize today. Just as mobile makers choose objects that represent their own aesthetics and culture, Calder's mobiles embodied the optimism of the industrial age. His flat, brightly colored steel and clean abstracted shapes were both architectural and scientific.

Mobiles are constructed to take advantage of the forces of equilibrium and are reliant on the hanging objects balancing each other perfectly to maintain their form. While Calder had the benefit of both a background in mechanical engineering and mathematical flair, you don't have to be a rocket scientist to achieve the delicate balancing act necessary to make a mobile. From simple cross beams to more complicated multi-tiered formations, the rules remain the same. You don't even need to be tied to the idea of circular motion to create an effective kinetic artwork. You can take advantage of both material and environment and get brilliant, mesmerizing mobiles.

Contemporary mobile makers (and there are many) are now exploring the outer reaches of materiality, subject matter and scale in their work while still paying homage to the fundamental principles of the form. Other makers are creating both wall-bound and free-floating hanging sculptures that rely more on material and pattern design than on movement, and which are just as seductive as their kinetic first cousins.

KIM BAISE
United States

Los Angeles-based artist Kim Baise is a perfect example of someone who has taken their personal aesthetic into three dimensions. Using papier-mâché and painted twigs, her geometric constructions and figurative assemblages embody the energy of her mark-making. While referencing traditional cartonería (Mexican papier-mâché), her ice-cream trucks, banjo-playing cats and crying eyes reveal her own hilarious take on the everyday.

 jikits.blogspot.com

MELISSA HRUSKAA
United States

Himmeli are probably the definitive geometric mobile. A traditional good-luck decoration in Nordic homes, their name literally translates as "sky" or "heaven." Melissa Hruskaa's beautifully elegant interpretations of this traditional form evolve from a few basic building blocks into complicated multi-tiered masterpieces, reinterpreted again in different materials that extend the life of the work even further. Crafty design in every sense.

hruskaa.com

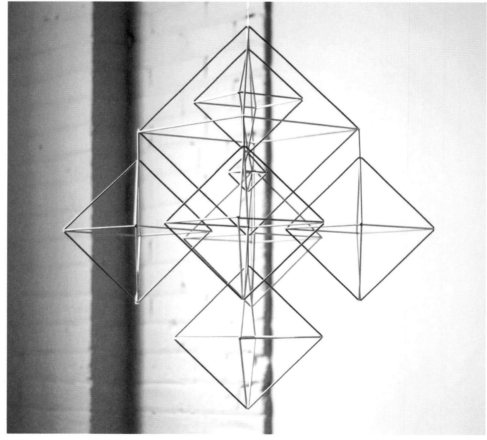

DEAR PLASTIC
Australia

Japanese-born and Melbourne-based design duo Dear Plastic have a knack for elevating (pardon the pun) the simplest of materials. Using scale, hand-painted color, repetition and form, their paper gems, mountains and rainbows are elemental and often monumental. Their playful, inclusive approach is disarmingly engaging and shows a lightness of touch in keeping with their choice of material. Super-fun stuff.

 **dearplastic.com**

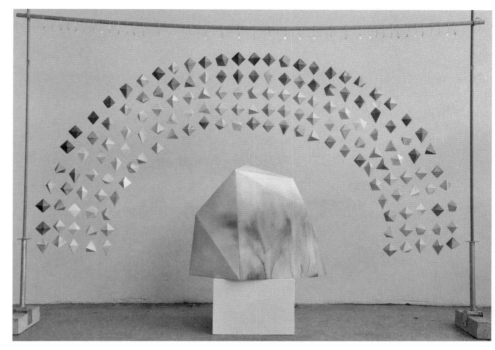

LADIES & GENTLEMEN
United States

There is an interesting song that the mobiles by design studio Ladies & Gentlemen perform. Combining ceramic, wood, plastic, copper and brass, each movement, no matter how slight, creates new music. Both playful and minimalist, these kinetic sculptures provide a soundtrack to the cool interiors they no doubt inhabit.

ladiesandgentlemenstudio.com

DESIGN NOTES

VISUAL MUSIC

The combination of Calder's random metal shapes and hypnotic air-driven movement created free-form rhythms that inspired generations of avant-garde and jazz musicians from Frank Zappa to Earl Browne. It's worth keeping this musical reference in mind while working through your design ideas. Think of the rods as musical measures and the hanging elements as notes. Both structure and object choice will dictate the final "sound" of your own mobile arrangement. Do you want to "listen" to punk rock or reggae, hip hop or folk, new wave or new age?

BALANCING ACT

Traditionally a kinetic mobile consists of a balanced "anchor" beam from which weighted objects and other beams hang. It is important that these beams are kept relatively horizontal and spaced widely enough to move freely without touching each other. They should be able to rotate around with minimal prompting. While traditional "family tree" configurations are easy to manage, what you choose to hang and how you hang it is up to you. Just remember, light objects are the simplest to assemble and move most easily in the air, while heavier things will need more serious construction and are more likely to stay still.

TIES THAT BIND

Whether embroidered birds or laser-cut acrylic dodecahedrons, all your pieces need to be secured safely and appropriately. Depending on whether this is fishing line, wire, chain or thread, the best solution could be tying, clipping, threading, drilling, gluing or even riveting. While in some work you might want your connector to "disappear," you can also use it as a design element — think baker's twine, pearl cotton, neon bricklayer's string and oversize plastic gold chain, or bump it up even further by adding a variety of beads or pom-poms to your threads.

OBJECTS OF YOUR AFFECTION

Collecting or making objects for hanging is officially the fun bit. One of the great things about mobiles is that pretty much anything can be turned into a mobile, which can quickly lead to thoughts such as "seventeen glittered dinosaurs hanging above the dining table would be complete genius!" Mobiles can be as simple as found shells strung from driftwood or as complex as industrial steel and LED lights that fill three stories of gallery space. We say go for it. If you can hang it, you can use it — nothing is off the table.

LOCATION LOCATION

Babies are naturally attracted to moving objects so nurseries are an obvious placement choice. However, any room in the house can stand to benefit from the inclusion of a kinetic artwork; look up and you'll find a whole new plane to decorate. Stairwells, dark corners, windows, patios, even trees are all perfect final destinations for your hanging masterpiece.

THE HOOK-UP

There's no point in creating a mobile masterpiece if you don't have somewhere safe to secure it. Ceilings are often made from different grade material from walls, and not all areas of the ceiling are created equally when it comes to heavy-duty lifting. For light mobiles, commercially available adhesive products with purpose-built hooks will be more than adequate and usually come with relatively guaranteed weight and usage guides. However, more elaborate, heavy works will most likely need a screw-in hook, so make sure your ceiling can take the weight of your masterpiece before you install it!

The tools for making a mobile largely depend on what you're choosing to make it from. That being said, your basic craft tool kit should pretty much cover what you need. Below are some of the other items that will let you work like a pro.

- **Variety of beams:** You can use wire, driftwood, thin dowel, metal pipe, plastic tubing and paper straws.

- **Adjustable hole punch:** Every crafter's dream accessory, as it puts everything from leather to plywood on the mobile menu.

- **Shapes:** Balsa wood, cardboard, small toys, foam sheets.

- **Connectors:** You can use thread fishing line, woolen yarn, crochet cotton, embroidery thread, fine-gauge wire, ribbon, baker's twine and even fine plastic or metal chain.

- **Craft knife:** For card cutting.

- **Drill and drill bits:** For making holes in your objects.

- **Pliers:** For bending wire.

- **Wire cutters**

- **Scissors**

- **Double-sided tape**

- **Super glue**

- **Hot glue gun**

- **Glue sticks**

Mobiles can be incredibly simple or infinitely complex. There are a few technical concepts but the most basic principle is balance. All mobiles use one or more anchor beams and connectors. Learn how to identify and balance them and you'll soon be making your own mobiles from scratch.

MOBILE ANATOMY

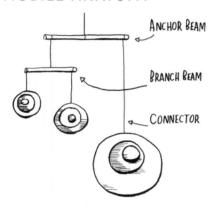

ANCHOR BEAM

The anchor is the stable base from which the branch beams hang. It's the first horizontal beam in a tree-style mobile. Anchor beams literally and figuratively anchor your work. They can be as chunky as driftwood or as fine as medical-grade wire.

BRANCH BEAM

Traditionally this beam is the horizontal "branch" from which objects and subsequent branches are hung in a tree configuration. In simple hoop or cross-beam mobiles there are no branch beams.

CONNECTOR

"Connector" is the formal term used to refer to the stuff you use to attach single objects to beams, beams to your anchor, and beams to other beams. Obvious choices include cotton, string, wire and fishing line. All serve the same purpose of allowing objects to hang in space.

BALANCING A MOBILE

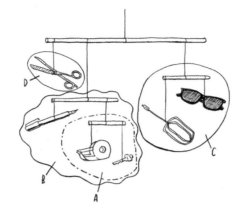

Balancing a mobile is as easy as ABCD! Follow the image above and recall a little of your high-school algebra. A = B = C = D. It doesn't matter what hangs from the branch beams, but it does matter that the contents of each branch beam are equal in weight and spaced evenly across the beam to maintain balance. This simple system works right across the spectrum, whether you are using a hoop, cross beam or tree formation.

CROSS BEAM

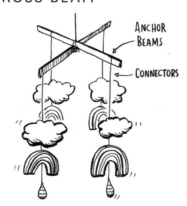

The cross beam is one of the most common formations for simple mobiles. Take two horizontal beams and secure them in the middle by binding the beams with string or yarn. This cross creates four beams and one central point at the cross connection to hang objects of equal weight.

HOOP

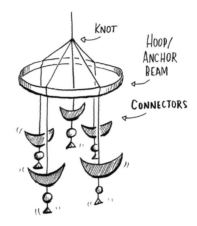

Possibly the simplest mobile construction, a hoop acts as the anchor beam from which all the objects are hung. Your hoop could be constructed from a pre-made or handcrafted circle. Any closed round shape will work, from an embroidery hoop to cut plywood, or even reshaped wire clothes hangers.

1. The easiest way to get it to hang straight is to take two threads of the same length — around 28" for a large embroidery hoop — lay them side by side and knot them in the middle. Take the four ends of your threads and tie them at four evenly spaced points around the hoop.

2. Take another, longer thread, tie it around the center knot of the four threads and lift. You've got a hangable hoop ready to attach your mobile objects to. Hang as many connectors as you like from it. Just remember that you'll need to keep them evenly spaced or equally balanced to make sure it hangs well.

TREE FORMATION

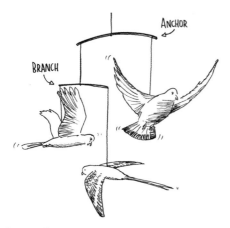

The tree formation is used to create mobiles with free-flowing movement. It can be as simple as this three-tiered example, or as complex as a room-sized behemoth.

1. Start with a sturdy anchor beam and tie a thread around its center point for hanging the mobile up.

2. To make a three-object tree, tie one connector to a second-tier branch beam and the other to a single object that weighs the same as the combined contents of the second tier branch beam to keep the mobile evenly balanced.

PROJECT IDEAS

→ Hang shells, sea glass, driftwood or plastic sea animals as individual collections or combined to create everything from beachside chic to trailer kitsch.

→ Stones, seedpods, feathers, branches and leaves are all easily applied to mobiles. Think paint-dipped leaves or stones, or keep it natural and take advantage of the inbuilt color and texture of the elements to bring the outdoors in. Collect a range of found elements and link them together through form and detailing.

→ Balsa wood is the ultimate mobile material — easy to cut, light to hang, and perfect for painting, printing or gilding. Cut one large shape and two smaller ones and customize them with painted stripes in contrasting colors. Use a tree formation to hang them up for a quick but high-impact mobile.

→ Why not use your crochet skills to whip up mini amigurumi creatures, or your sewing skills to make little stuffed soft toys? Hang them from a large embroidery decorated with pom-poms or fringe for a unique soft-sculpture approach.

→ Traditional Scandinavian mobiles called Himmeli use real straw, but drinking straws made of paper or plastic are perfect for creating a successful non-traditional version. Light, cheap and accessible, they come in a brilliant range of colors and patterns, which makes them a dynamite option for bringing geometric line drawings to life in 3-D.

Diamonds are Forever

WHAT YOU NEED

- Cutting mat
- Pencil
- Ruler or tape measure
- Plank of ¼"-thick balsa wood
- Craft knife
- Wire cutters
- 1 yard of ⅛" bendable wire
- Round-nose pliers
- Paintbrush
- PVA (white) glue
- Fine holographic silver glitter
- Small dish
- Tapestry needle
- Scissors
- Clear fishing line

HOT TIP

Because all of the pieces are the same weight, the mobile will balance irrespective of what lengths of fishing line you use to hang your diamonds. This gives you free reign to experiment if you feel like the diamonds need to be hung at different heights.

Nothing lifts a decorating "dead spot" like a mobile, especially one covered in sparkles. Inspired by the mid-century stylings of early Bond movies, we used geometrics, blonde wood and holographic glitter to give you a hit of ice-cool, space-age glamour.

WHAT YOU DO

1. Draw nine diamond shapes on the balsa wood plank 4" high and 2½" at the widest point.

2. Cut the diamonds out using the craft knife and cutting mat and set them aside.

3. Using the wire cutters, cut one 16" length of wire and three 8" lengths.

4. Take the round-nose pliers and put them in the middle of the first 8" length, bending the wire around the curved tip to make a small loop. Turn the wire so the loop is on the bottom and turn up each end with the pliers to make another small loop. Repeat this process for all of the other pieces of wire.

5. Sparkle time. Take your first wooden diamond and paint one side of the bottom half with a thin layer of glue. Sprinkle with glitter until it's well covered, then tap excess glitter off into the small dish and set it aside to dry. Repeat for the remaining eight diamonds. When dry, repeat the process on the other side, until all your shapes are glitterfied.

6. Use the tapestry needle to poke a hole through the top of each glitter-free section of the diamonds to thread the fishing line through.

7. Next step, assembly. Lay the pieces of wire out on a table with the longest piece at the top as the anchor and the three shorter pieces as the branch beams below. Cut three lengths of fishing line around 12" long and tie one end into each of the three loops on the anchor beam. Tie the other ends to the middle loop on each branch beam.

8. Cut nine more lengths of fishing line and tie each one to the top of your wooden diamonds, then tie them onto the loops of each branch beam. You should now have three diamonds attached to each branch beam.

9. Cut one long piece of fishing line and attach it to the top middle loop of your anchor ready for hanging.

10. Lift it up from this point and check out your handiwork. Hang this baby up in any location for an explosion of instant awesome.

Upcycle

◇◇◇

The process of taking what is essentially waste and creating something new is at the heart of upcycling. With a combination of lateral thinking, clever design and a commitment to a lighter footprint on the world, writer and entrepreneur Gunter Pauli, known as the "Steve Jobs of sustainability" coined the term "upcycling" in 1996 as a new way of approaching waste. It was the recognition that we needed to shift our focus from seeing waste as an end product of manufacturing to seeing it as a starting point for something new.

Upcycling is an economic imperative in poor countries such as India where nothing is wasted and everything must be re-used. But in the industrialized West, consumerism matched with prosperity means that waste is produced on an almost unbelievable scale. Upcycling differs from recycling in the sense that it is not about breaking down the material to its basic form. Instead you are re-fashioning it into something new — going up rather than going down.

The concept was perfectly aligned with concerns about our impact on the health of the planet and trickled down from large-scale enterprises to the individual. This commitment to reducing our impact one footprint at a time saw upcycling being embraced as fundamental to craft practice.

Upcycling as a term is relatively new but is an age-old practice for makers. From the salvaged grain sacks of early American quiltmaking to Britain's wartime motto of "Make Do and Mend," and the Japanese art of boro, upcycling has been a constant with crafters the world over. Today, in increasing numbers, we see vintage jewelry reset and reinterpreted, furniture built from salvaged wood, yarn sourced from old sweaters, shirts and t-shirts, and mosaics from broken china in new works that all utilize base materials that many assumed had outlived their purpose.

Upcycling encourages makers across all craft practices to see things in a new way. Materials can be utilized in multidisciplinary ways that can both challenge and invigorate the design process. There is an intellectual engagement even before the making begins. Questions need to be asked: Can this be useful? Can I create something beautiful? And, conversely, am I just creating more waste?

CONTEMPORARY ARTISTS

LOUISE RILEY
Britain

Discarded, used mattresses are not the first objects that come to mind when thinking of embroidery grounds, but so impressive is the work of British artist Louise Riley that you wonder why no one has done it before. Riley embroiders incredibly detailed, intimate figures with an almost photographic attention, creating unnervingly realistic portraits of humanity at its most vulnerable.

🖥 **louiseriley.blogspot.co.uk**

GUERRA DE LA PAZ
United States

Collaborative artists Alain Guerra and Neraldo de la Paz create large-scale sculptural works, utilizing contributed raw materials, post-consumer waste and the industrial scraps of fashion production. En masse, piles of fabric speak of consumerism, waste and human labour, with some works taking a decade to complete. They are unapologetically political works that comment on everything from the environment to world conflict and sexual politics. Using a material destined for landfill, the pair elevate waste into engaging and highly charged art.

🖥 **guerradelapaz.com**

BEN VENOM
United States

Venom's focused use of upcycled band
t-shirts pairs an outsider's D.I.Y. attitude
with the "Make Do and Mend" ethos of
this traditional textile craft. His blending
of the metal fraternity's subcultural
signifiers with the craft of traditional
quilting may seem counterintuitive.
However, there are a multitude of
fundamental threads that connect
these seemingly disparate aesthetics
and societies. Serious crafters and
metal-heads both adhere to universally
accepted design forms, foster an
appreciation for the craft's history and
genealogy, and display dedication to
the acquisition of skill through practice.
Venom's authentic appreciation of
both allows him an unapologetic foot in
both camps.

 benvenom.com

CAL LANE
United States

Cal Lane likes a bit of contradictory
compare-and-contrast. Using lace
pattern-work she creates a kind of
industrial doily effect on discarded metal
tools and utilitarian objects. Oil drums,
wheelbarrows, car bodies and shovels
are all given a Victorian overhaul that not
only provides an obvious juxtaposition of
masculine and feminine, hard and soft,
ornament and function, but reveals our
more deeply held relationships with the
ritualistic use of lace to ceremonially
mark birth and death as she brings new
life into rusted metal carcasses.

callane.com

CONTEMPORARY ARTISTS

PENNIE JAGIELLO
Australia

Pennie Jagiello's bowerbird eye for shape, color and collection provide source material as varied as the junk we let slip into our oceans without concern for the environmental impact. Discarded electrical wire, lost flip-flops, fishing lines and plastic in all its forms — beach detritus is given new life in both object and wearable form. Jagiello acts as a modern-day archeologist of our oceans and the Australian urban environments that cling to their edges.

 penniejagiello.com

LYN BLAZER AND TONY PERKINS
Australia

Lyn and Tony have a deep connection to the spectacular natural forms and dangerous beauty of the Australian landscape that inspires the photographs and objects they create. Strong color, weighty stones, twisted leather and chunky metals combine to create bold accessories that could be described as elemental amulets for glamazons. These aesthetic and spiritual sensibilities are manifest in their collection of upcycled denim pieces. There is a knowing, simple poetry in creating a high-fashion accessory from a low-fashion remnant.

 lynandtony.com

TEJO REMY AND
RENÉ VEENHUIZEN
The Netherlands

Design duo Tejo Remy and René
Veenhuizen have built a reputation on
re-thinking and re-using materials to
create something new. Their blanket
rug, constructed from turned strips of
densely stitched upcycled blankets,
takes on an organic free-form shape that
is both visually and texturally inviting. It
is a perfect example of the sort of lateral
thinking that good design can offer.

 remyveenhuizen.nl

ROWAN MERSH
Britain

The scope of Rowan Mersh's unique
talent is breathtaking. A thoughtful
multidisciplinary maker, Mersh
effortlessly straddles the arbitrary divides
between hi and low art, craft and design.
His mastery of tactile technique —
folding, twining, stripping, sewing — is
both the tool of his trade and the defining
feature of his practice. Transforming
mundane materials in astonishing ways,
Mersh creates bewitching works that act
as potent visual statements to promote
responsible and sustainable design.

rowanmersh.com

DESIGN NOTES

THE THREE RS

You know us well enough by now to realize we are fans of recycling, reinventing and re-using. Resources are finite and we want to encourage you to think about your craft footprint in terms of waste and consumerism. That being said, there is no point making more useless stuff out of useless stuff. Our rule of thumb is if it doesn't have a function (yes, decorative counts), it doesn't get made.

MAKE DO AND MEND

This British wartime slogan has greater currency today as we stare down the barrel of global warming, peak oil and oceans that contain more plastic than marine life. There is nothing more satisfying than utilizing basic mending skills. It sounds so obvious but in a culture where even furniture is virtually disposable, we encourage you not just to darn your socks but perhaps re-upholster your sofa too.

ALL IN ALL

The scope for upcycling is limitless and we encourage you to make it your mind's first port of call when embarking on any craft, design or interior project. We know not everyone is going to want to build a mud brick house, or want reclaimed wooden furniture as much as we do, but there isn't a single craft that can't utilize upcycling in some way. Responsible crafting is clever crafting, not to mention thrifty!

GRAND DESIGNS

Redesign is always at its most interesting when you confound expectation. Pushing an object into a new place is a great way of re-imagining it. Packaging is a product that is readily available, often waterproof, highly malleable and, with the right treatment, beautiful. Apply the object's best design characteristics to a different purpose and you'll be adding value rather than landfill.

BE KIND, REWIND

There is a wealth of material available for the canny crafter in the half-completed or discarded craft projects of others — needlepoint, crocheted blankets, knitted sweaters, tooled leather, beaded bags and all manner of jewelry. Needlepoint can be pieced to make cushions, bags or coin purses; blankets and sweaters can be unwound to make balls of yarn for new projects; tooled leather can be re-fashioned into new items; beading can be unstrung and re-sewn; and the fastings and features of other people's jewelry can all be re-used. Honor the unknown crafter and make something fabulous.

GAME CHANGERS

So many objects that are otherwise considered useless make amazing tools for other crafts. It's just a matter of changing your mindset to re-think form and function. Corks make great tools for stamping or batik printing, wood scraps can be used in shibori dyeing or carved into block stamps. Plastic bottle caps are terrific starting points for jewelry, and fabric scraps that are too small for projects can be kept as stuffing. Start saving your leftovers and scraps in a box and think of it as your own personal reverse rubbish store!

TOOLS

- **Paper:** Newspaper for papier-mâché, magazines for collage, wrapping paper, gift cards, paint chips.

- **Plastic:** Plastic bottles and containers often come in great colors and even textures that can be used in anything from jewelry projects to block printing.

- **Fabric:** Turning t-shirts into yarn, scraps from one project saved for the next, linens torn into strips for rag rugs — fabric gives you an almost endless source of upcycling possibilities.

- **Wood:** Anything from old furniture to driftwood can be given a new lease on life. Fallen branches, project scraps and side-of-the-road finds can also yield treasure.

- **Glues:** PVA, wood glue, super glue, 2-minute epoxy.

- **Storage tubs**
- **Sewing machine**
- **Scissors**
- **Ruler**
- **Tape measure**
- **Iron**
- **Craft knife**
- **Rotary cutter**
- **Hand saws**
- **Hammer**
- **Nails**
- **String**

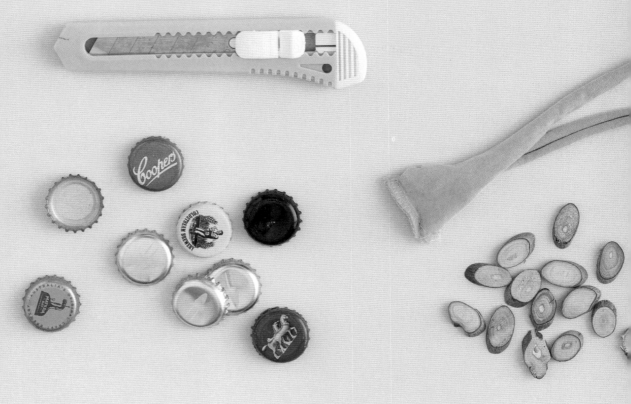

TECHNIQUES

PAINT CHIP GARLAND

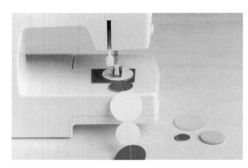

Paint chips Or swatches provide a beautiful gradient palette and sturdy construction paper, which makes them super-versatile for upcycling. Use them for gift tags, garlands, bookmarks, paper flowers and punched shapes to use in scrapbooking or collage projects. Circles and triangles work particularly well en masse or mixed up in different shapes and sizes.

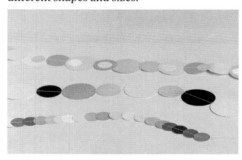

1. Using a medium tension setting on your sewing machine, a sharp needle and ordinary thread, slowly start feeding the paint chips through one at a time.

2. Once you've done the first few, keep your stitching even and continue along your row until you reach your target length or run out of paint chips.

FUSED PLASTIC FABRIC

Plastic bags. We all hate them, right? This clever upcycling hack can turn plastic bags into waterproof yardage that can be cut, sewn, pieced, knitted, woven, crocheted, worn, and adorned.

WHAT YOU NEED

- Plastic bags
- Scissors
- Baking paper
- Iron

WHAT YOU DO

1. Cut off the bag handles and bottom seams so the bags lie flat. If they are printed, turn them inside out to stop the ink running everywhere when you iron. Using about six bags, place them on top of each other and sandwich them between two layers of baking paper. Make sure no plastic is peeking out or you will ruin your iron.

2. Set your iron to the dry rayon/polyester heat setting. Keeping the iron moving, apply pressure and pay attention to the edges to ensure they fuse really strongly. After about 20 seconds flip your sandwich over and iron on the other side. Have a peek to see if your layers are fused. Careful, it's pretty hot! If it's ready you can peel off your baking paper to reveal your plastic fantastic fabric.

PAPER-WEAVE BASKET

This simple technique takes time and patience but the result is a sturdy and useful basket. By working with paper, you'll learn the basic principles behind woven baskets and develop some of the skills needed to work with sturdier materials such as veneer or wicker.

WHAT YOU NEED

- Newspaper (amount variable)
- Scissors
- Box (same size as desired basket size)
- Double-sided tape
- Stapler (optional)
- PVA glue (optional)

WHAT YOU DO

1. Prepare your strips of paper. You'll need a lot, even for a small basket. Cut the spine of your newspaper to give you approximately 40 sheets of paper. Fold each page lengthwise in half; repeat this process until you have a strip approx. ¾" wide. Repeat this process with the other sheets until all your strips are made.

2. Make your base by weaving strips over and under into a cross. This is where the box comes in handy for working out how many strips to use. Securing the occasional strip with glue or staples will make this process easier; staples can always be removed later.

 FORM

376

3. When the base is finished, place your box in the center and turn up the strips to create your basket sides.

4. Time to weave in your weft strips. Don't be alarmed if it feels chaotic as you try to fit your strips into the first row. Judicious use of glue can help, as does leaving your shaping box in the center so you have something solid to work around. Don't start or finish a strip on a corner or you'll get holes where you don't want them.

5. Once you reach the top, make sure your ends are secure by binding the edge with a strip. You can use double-sided tape, staples for a utilitarian look or a sewing machine stitch and colored thread for a decorative finish.

6. You're done. Leave your masterpiece as is, or coat it with either spray varnish or PVA (white) glue for extra durability.

PROJECT IDEAS

→ Mismatched socks have a multitude of uses beyond sock monkeys. Sew them into lavender sachets for the closet or draft excluders for the front door, fill with catnip for pet toys or stuff with polyester filling for baby-safe balls.

→ Transform an old wooden crate into a wall-mounted notions or spice cupboard by adding a shelf and hinged doors. Strip the crate back for painting or wax it to keep its original roots on show. If you're all out of wall space, screw wheels into the bottom corners of your crate and make it a moveable storage unit.

→ When is a t-shirt not a t-shirt? When the bottom is cut off to make an infinity scarf. When it is sliced into strips to make t-shirt yarn. When the bottom is sewn shut and slits cut in the top to make a stretchy shopping tote. When strips are woven into a chair seat. Or when an oversize one is dyed, printed or stamped to make a super-chic summer muumuu.

→ Maps, street directories and public transportation pamphlets (especially old ones) are a great source of material for upcycling into any number of paper projects — matte boards for travel snaps, covers for albums, scanned and printed on fabric, woven into baskets, or even découpaged onto wooden furniture for travel-themed style.

Plastique Fantastique Terrarium

WHAT YOU NEED

- Clear plastic soft-drink bottle
- Craft knife
- Gravel
- Free-draining potting soil for succulents
- Succulents
- Sand or decorative stones
- Assortment of small toys

Rainy day inside and need something to keep yourself or your young person busy? Been drinking too much soft drink and feel like you need to hide your secret shame so the neighbors can't see? Well this project is for you!

WHAT YOU DO

1. Strip your bottle of its label and give it a good wash in hot soapy water to remove any glue residue. Rinse and allow to dry.

2. Slice your bottle in half. We cut ours at the middle point, at the "waist" of the bottle. Lay the bottle on your work surface and pierce it with your craft knife, then roll it away from you while cutting.

3. Spoon gravel into the bottle, taking it up to the first ridge.

4. Add your soil, taking it up to the halfway mark, then plant your succulents.

5. Add a layer of sand, decorative stones and a dinosaur attacking a car. That's right — bring on the drama!

6. To take care of your terrarium be very sparing with water. It shouldn't need any more than a teaspoon once a week.

HOT TIP

We've utilized the bottom half of our bottle, but you can just as easily use the top half as an upside-down hanging garden with the addition of string, an S-hook and some plants. Strawberries and tomato plants work particularly well, but try out others and see how they fare.

Veneer and Wood

◇◇◇

Wood is good. It's a naturally occurring, easily shaped material that's been a feature of the craft lexicon forever. Used for shelter, tool making, transport and decoration, wood can be manipulated in many ways to express our creativity or make our lives easier. Wood continues to be one of the most loved and practical materials because of its almost endless array of applications.

While the use of wood on a grand scale is well-documented — think construction, shipbuilding and defense — its context within ancient domestic craft is often overlooked. Handcarved wooden vessels, furniture and tools were integral to the development of household rituals and farm-based settlement.

The ease with which timber could be sourced and worked made it a favorite of early civilizations. Well-preserved examples of wooden toys and automata have been found in the tombs of ancient Greeks. Egyptian tombs have yielded wooden chairs and chests. Figurative and totemic wood-carving are found universally from the Pacific to North America, Japan, China, India and Australia; and are humble examples of how wood was incorporated into the everyday.

Scandinavia and northern England provided the perfect location for the development of woodcraft. With an abundance of materials and highly skilled crafters, the Vikings and Celts created a wealth of detailed wooden carvings, furniture and architecture during the Iron Age. They developed complex joinery systems and iron tools, from lathes to drills, that laid the foundations for modern woodcraft.

The development of finely wrought furniture, however, was not common outside the Church and the royal courts until the 14th century. Carpenters' shops were under the control of monasteries, and thrones were the most ornate of any furniture fashioned at the time. Simple benches in food halls or rustic chiseled log beds were as complicated as it got outside the castle walls. In Europe it was not until the 16th century that wood furniture and its design became more sophisticated: first among the aristocracy and wealthier merchant classes, then eventually in workers' homes.

Wood has been integral to the artistic, religious and architectural practices of Japan for centuries. With more than 70 percent of Japan's land under forest cover, no part of Japanese life is untouched by timber. Japanese carpenters not only focus on knowledge and technical skill but also have an ongoing commitment to respectfully understanding the "personality of the wood." In a system that mirrors the Japanese tradition of eating from the mountain to the sea, carpenters pay close attention to the location and position of the tree and match these with the final construction. The intrinsic elegance of Japan's nail-free joinery and the exquisite beauty of its fine veneer and lacquer techniques continue to influence woodcrafters the world over.

The use of veneer developed as the desire for wood in decorative domestic use increased. To this day, woodcraft and veneer remain wedded for design purposes. Veneer has been used widely since the 17th century to adorn floors (parquetry), furniture (marquetry) and objects (inlay). Slices thinly cut from logs such as mahogany, walnut and ebony served a dual design purpose: disguising cheaper wood such as maple and birch and creating a beautiful surface. The design flexibility these processes offered enabled them to become arts in their own right, with highly complex geometric patterns created by cutting and mixing different woods for floors, and furniture becoming an ongoing part of both woodcraft and interior design language.

Wood's inherent beauty and idiosyncratic patterning connect us directly to nature. Our growing awareness of the cost of irresponsible forestry has made consumers more circumspect about timber goods. Both designers and crafters are expressing themselves in more sustainable ways by turning to upcycling and salvaged woods along with timbers farmed responsibly without degrading virgin wilderness. Inspired by examples as diverse as the handcarved demons of Indonesia and the whittlers of Appalachia, artists are returning to handcarved traditions to render improbable figures from fast foods to b-boy freestylers. Whether carved, cut, constructed or inlaid, wood and veneer crafts continue to thrive and develop around the globe.

RON VAN DER ENDE
The Netherlands

The pieced bas-relief works of Ron van der Ende are like lumber trompes l'oeil. Constructed from found wood cut into ⅛"-thick veneer, his works are both materially and conceptually connected to the contemporary use of veneers to trick the eye through dexterous mimicry. Van der Ende neatly folds three dimensions into two in monumental wall works that perform a kind of visual alchemy as fine shards of salvaged lumber are meticulously hammered together to convincingly replicate rusted metal car bodies, out-moded technology and monolithic stones.

🖵 ronvanderende.nl

CLEMENS BEHR
Germany

Clemens Behr uses wood as a form of abstract marquetry, employing a wide variety of wood shards and veneers to create collaged abstracts in 2-D and 3-D. In lesser hands this composite of material and color could be a hot mess. Behr, however, deftly finds balance in what could be construed as almost random placements of elements. The interplay between shape, grain and color results in harmonious wall works and objects that hold a sophistication and lightness of touch that belies their original material state.

🖵 clemensbehr.com

AJ FOSIK
United States

The glorious wood sculptures of AJ Fosik
pry at the most primitive parts of our
souls. Multi-headed beasts of claws
and teeth are fastidiously rendered
in carved and tiled wood, creating a
particularly ambiguous symbology,
both familiar and foreign, that recalls
Motorhead iconography as easily as it
does traditional Bhutanese mask culture.
The jewel-colored psychedelia of his
palette and mandala-like construction is
hypnotic and draws you into his universe
of nightmare creatures frozen in flight,
their compelling power crackling at the
edges of this world.

TOBY POLA
Australia

Toby Pola's balsa-wood sculptures
are wryly wrought musings on outer
suburbia. Pola's use of wood flips hard
and soft material paradigms in a skillful
mirroring of the high/low, harmful/
harmless dichotomies that fill the world
of the average Joe. Baseball caps, fugly
sweaters, band t-shirts, porn mags and
junk food are meticulously carved and
elevated onto plinth or gallery wall, both
inside joke and uncomfortably familiar
reminder of the power of tribal hegemony
beyond the gallery.

☐ instagram.com/unskilledlabour/

DESIGN NOTES

FINISHING LINE

Finishing wood with wax or oil is not just a way of keeping it safe and maintaining its integrity. Waxing does double duty by providing a waterproof layer that helps deflect scratches while adding a gorgeous soft lustre perfect for light-colored woods such as beech, oak and pine. Lacquer and resin-based sealants are brilliant over-painted surfaces, while oils are particularly useful for adding a protective sheen that also brings out the wood's natural grain on either raw or stained lumber. Match your aesthetic outcomes with end use and you'll win on all fronts.

LIGHT OF MY LIFE

The innate pliability of veneer can be manipulated brilliantly to create objects in the round, and as it's so thin, it's also beautifully translucent when lit from behind. Combining these factors is just one of the reasons veneer is so abundantly used in lighting design. Let the piece of wood guide you to make the right decisions about where to showcase the grain with back lighting and where to bend it to hide flaws.

MIX AND MATCH

Although veneer is often used to create the illusion of large, flat surface cut from one kind of wood, there's no reason why you can't combine different woods in one project. All sorts of exotic and sustainable timbers are available, often at a reasonable price, along with other fibrous material such as bamboo. This allows you huge scope to artfully combine light and dark woods, both natural and stained, and different grain directions, to create a timber patchwork.

TOOL TIME

Think of timber beyond the traditional end use and you'll discover a wealth of other craft options for your own project scraps or foraged finds. Use the grain for rubbings to make patterned paper, cut into shapes for block printing, use as a resist for shibori, or glue on your hand-cut rubber stamps to make them easier to grip.

ADVENTURE TIME

From super-sized totems to tiny hand-held miniatures, there's almost no end to what you can explore when it comes to carving. Despite what the local lumberjack might tell you, size does matter so choose the right tool for the job, be it chisel or chainsaw, and match it with the right grade of lumber to save on time and doctor's bills. It's softwoods for porch whittlers and hardwoods for extreme carvers. Don't get these confused — believe us, it won't end well.

FAKING IT

Traditionally, veneer was used to mask what was hidden beneath or to trick the eye into seeing something "real" that was in fact fabricated. With this in mind, you can apply the concept of veneer more laterally and use commercially manufactured faux materials such as Laminex to get metallic, marble, stone and timber finishes for projects, as well as making your own. Faux bois is a brilliant approach to fakery that can be applied to paper, fabric, ceramics, plastic and glass by drawing, carving, printing or even knitting a wood grain into the surface — creating authentic cabin charm without the splinters.

STRIP SHOW

Stripping back old wood can give you a unique material history or offer you a clean slate to write a new one. Mix distressed woods in washed-out hues with raw lumber to create surface patterns that draw on parquetry traditions. Strip back old teak bowls and boards to make perfect canvases ready to carve, paint or burnish with your own illustrations or graphic designs. Let your wood do the talking and you'll have half the design work done for you.

<⬡ TOOLS ⬡>

- **Workbench:** You don't need a specialist woodworking bench but it's important to have one that is sturdy, level and will take hard hammering and sanding vibrations.

- **Wood planer:** Used for shaping wood, reducing timber thickness and giving a smooth surface to rough wood.

- **Sawhorse:** Just like a trestle leg, use two to support lengths of lumber while cutting.

- **Jigsaw:** Fine-bladed vertical power saw, good for cutting curved lines.

- **Circular drop saw:** Power saw with a rapidly rotating toothed disc that makes cuts. Extra-versatile, it makes neat, straight edges that can be matched with a miter corner, which eliminates the need for a specialist miter saw.

- **Orbital sander:** A round electronic sander, which vibrates in tiny circles: great for ultra-smooth sanding.

- **Power drill:** We prefer a cordless model as these offer the most flexibility for work.

- **Sandpaper:** Comes in a variety of grades. Start with the coarsest and work your way up to fine for a smooth finish.

- **Basic claw hammer**
- **Assortment of nails**
- **Spirit level**
- **Craft knife**
- **Wood-carving knife**
- **Chisel set**
- **Clamps**
- **Block plane**
- **Handsaw**
- **Safety goggles**
- **Hearing protection**
- **Paint stripper**
- **White oil**
- **Furniture wax**
- **Screwdrivers**
- **Pencils**
- **Notebook**
- **Vacuum cleaner**
- **Rags**

SPOON CARVING

We cannot begin to tell you how easy and how fun it is to carve your own spoons. We are huge fans of cooking and of whittling on the back porch, so this particular project ticks a lot of our boxes.

WHAT YOU NEED

- Piece of hardwood

- Pencil

- Spoon to use as a guide (optional)

- Jigsaw or bandsaw

- Spoon gouge

- Clamp (optional)

- Carving knife

- Sandpaper and rasp

- Food-safe oil (we love coconut oil)

WHAT YOU DO

1. With a pencil, draw a spoon shape on your wood. You may want to use an existing spoon as a guide. Cut out the basic shape with a jigsaw or bandsaw.

2. Using your spoon gouge, slowly work out the bowl of your spoon. Take it slowly with the gouge. The trick is not to take too much at once. You may find it easier to clamp the spoon to a table while you work on it, although we prefer just to whittle on the back porch — true story!

3. Once you've established a good spoon shape, mark the back shape of your spoon with a pencil.

4. Use your carving knife to work on the back of the spoon. Leave the handle until last, as you'll want it to stay as strong as possible while you carve. You'll be tempted to over-carve your spoon as it takes shape. Spoons are actually much shallower than you think. Check your depth against another spoon to avoid ending up with just a stick.

5. Once you're close to your desired shape on the head of your spoon, get to work on the handle. Work carefully, only taking out small strips at a time. Use the rasp to help you round out the shape.

6. Starting with your roughest-grit sandpaper, smooth out your spoon, concentrating on the "bowl" first. Use increasingly finer sandpaper until it's completely smooth. Oil your spoon and leave it to cure for a day or so before using.

MAKING A BOX

This simple box can be sized up or down depending on your needs. Drill a few holes in the base and it becomes a planter box, add a hinge and an extra panel and you have a lid. These boxes use a simple butt joint, which makes them a great first project. We used a circular saw to make sure our cuts were straight and joined perfectly.

WHAT YOU NEED

- ⅛–⅜"-thick pine plywood

- Saw

- Wood glue

- Clamp (optional)

- Finishing nails

- Hammer

- Sandpaper

- Paint, wax or oil

- Paintbrush

WHAT YOU DO

1. Cut your wood to the required size. For a simple square box you'll need five panels.

2. We love the look of ply and more often than not leave it unpainted. It's important when cutting wood to take note of the grain direction so that your grain runs the same way on all sides of your box.

3. Using wood glue, attach your two short sides to your base and allow to dry.

4. Attach your longer sides with wood glue and allow to dry.

5. You may want to use a wood clamp at this point to give the box extra stability. Drive your finishing nails an equal distance apart at your joins.

6. Give your box a good sand all over before applying paint, wax or oil.

PROJECT IDEAS

→   The wooden pallet is a ubiquitous "side-of-the-road" find that can be upcycled into anything from couches to vertical gardens. Try sanding, painting and adding legs and casters for the perfectly proportioned, moveable coffee table.

→   You don't need a rocking chair and porch to have a whittlin' party. While you do need to concentrate, you can still converse while carving your salad servers or bird whistle. Set up a bonfire in the backyard and get your friends to bring over their balsa, tools and maybe a first-aid kit.

→   Pegboard is an all-time favorite. Its natty repeating-dot pattern adds great minimalist detailing to white walls as well as providing a wealth of hanging options for frames and trinkets. If you don't want to use the commercial variety, why not use a drill and grid paper to create your own version cut from the lumber of your choice?

→   Old floorboards can often be picked up for a nice price at auction, or at lumberyards. Wide planks make a perfect table (three plank widths for a sideboard, five plank widths for a dining table), while trestle legs make for an easy (and storage-friendly) build.

→   Wood veneer is so light it makes a fabulous mobile material. Use found twigs or an embroidery hoop as your base and hang cut-out forest folk, leaves and trees for a woodsy-themed display without the weight.

Tetris Tea Caddy

We love a modular storage solution, don't you? This one has the added benefit of being small and light enough to grace your kitchen wall. With the addition of painted panels you'll be color-coding your Earl Grey and your Constant Comment in no time.

WHAT YOU NEED

- ⅜" pine plywood
- Circular saw
- Wood glue
- Sandpaper
- Soft cloth
- Clamps
- Masking tape
- Acrylic paint in 5 different colors
- Wood wax
- Flat wall hooks or brackets

WHAT YOU DO

1. Cut your plywood pieces or enlist the help of your friendly hardware store to pre-cut them for you in the following dimensions.

   The depth of all your boxes will be 4¾".

   - Box 1: 8 x 8"
   - Box 2: 4 x 6"
   - Box 3: 8 x 6"
   - Box 4: 8 x 4"
   - Box 5: 4 x 6"

2. Assemble your boxes using the box instructions in the Techniques section.

3. Give each box a light sand and wipe down with your soft cloth. Arrange them on a flat clean surface.

4. Glue your boxes together one at a time, leaving them to dry completely before adding the next box.

5. Use your clamps to hold the boxes steady during the drying process.

6. Tape off the side and back edges of each box and paint the top of the floors, one color for each box.

7. Once the paint is dry, give the whole thing a good wax to seal it.

8. Use flat wall hooks or brackets to hang. Take into account the weight of your caddy and the weight of what you're putting in it.

HOT TIP

The beauty of this design is that it can also be freestanding and you can stand it on any side. Put this boxy brilliance in any room of the house. Use it to showcase your robot collection, model cars or Pokémon figurines, or at the front door as a mail and key cubby. Make a couple and use them as tool storage for a kid's craft corner.

Zakka

◇◇◇

In 2001 an article appeared in the Style section of the *New York Times* reporting on a new fashion trend coming out of Japan known as zakka. Described as where "savvy meets the mundane," it was a style aesthetic that combined retro kitsch, Scandinavian design, the Japanese passion for ritual, and an overarching desire to create a world within the domestic sphere that represented who you were and how you felt about your space. It was fashion and interior design meets craft and personal style at the contemporary kitchen table.

As with so much contemporary Japanese culture, zakka became a lifestyle choice, complete with a subcultural support structure that included books, magazines, clothes and websites dedicated to the concept and how it could be made manifest. It was a movement of sugar-free sweetness, an authentic celebration of the everyday. This highly personal but connective craft movement's mixture of savvy and sweet has allowed zakka to thrive well beyond its initial consumerist tag.

So how do you know if something is zakka? What qualifies? While there was strict coding in the style's infancy, today the term is what you make of it. Zakka's period as a commodified design label has long passed and it has now settled into diverse methodology with a common goal of creating craft for the home from the home. In many ways zakka's appearance in Japan is as important to the development of today's cool craft crusade as the renegade craft emerging from the Riot Grrrl movement was in North America. Although almost perfect counterpoints in style and concept at their core, both were about making things by hand in a way that was relevant to contemporary culture.

So pervasive has the mix of Scandinavian clean with Japanese cute become that many young designers and artists now reference it unconsciously. Zakka's mash-up style has made blending cultural markers with nostalgia and knowing winks an almost universal approach for some, while others have taken the importance of softening industrial production with handcrafted customization as a metaphor for re-thinking everything from fonts to furniture design.

Of course, zakka is a new name for something we've all known for quite some time. It doesn't matter if it's a high-rise apartment building, an inner-city warehouse or a family home in the suburbs. It doesn't matter if it's you and your extended family of 16 or just you and a goldfish. The investment in hearth and home as a place of personal expression, optimism, beauty and functionality is and always will be at the heart of domestic craft.

CONTEMPORARY ARTISTS

HELLO SANDWICH
Japan

Ebony Bizys of Hello Sandwich is the perfect embodiment of the zakka philosophy applied to commercial design. Ribbons, stickers, washi tape, crepe paper, confetti, vintage cards, metallic paper, tickets and postage stamps are all the tools of her trade. Artfully combined with her own hand-designed papers, they explode off the page in Japanese pop aesthetics and retro style. With a background in both visual art and publishing, Bizys displays serious design skills paired with contagious enthusiasm for domestic crafting that has allowed her to build an indie empire from the comfort of her Tokyo home studio.

 hellosandwich.blogspot.com.au

JOEL HENRIQUES
United States

Without doubt Joel Henriques should be wearing the paper crown for being the world's funniest dad. Using common household materials, he set out to entertain both himself and his children with a series of homemade toys and activities. Henriques then became an online phenomenon as he shared his downloadable templates, instructions and patterns with an eager audience. Mid-century dolls' house furniture, paper cities and cool coloring pages are both playful and egalitarian, allowing families of all skill levels and economic status to create useful and beautiful toys at home.

madebyjoel.com

KITIYA PALASKAS
Australia

Optimism, playfulness and popular culture all intersect in the papercraft creations of artist/designer Kitiya Palaskas. Piñatas are downsized to miniature fruits and then up-sized for giant wedding rings. Lost technology, kaleidoscopic pom-poms, pizza slices in cushions, embroidered patches and cardboard sculptures are all motifs that make up the fantastically fun lexicon of what Palaskas terms "craft-based design."

 kitiyapalaskas.com

SHINO TAKEDA
United States

Shino Takeda's ceramics speak directly to the zakka philosophy of seeing the potential cleverness in the most mundane. Covered in unctuous colored glazes applied in loose brushstrokes, these simple stoneware forms turn the most everyday utensils into objects of real beauty. Spoons, bowls, cups and planters humbly offer up function and charm in a particularly mindful way, minimizing superfluous consumption and ensuring that each daily ritual is made as pleasant as possible.

shinotakeda.com

DESIGN NOTES

HAPPY HOME

The moment you customize a domestic object you are entering the zakka zone. It may be as simple as running stitch on a blanket, decorative stamps on a hand-written note, or a crocheted cozy for your coffee cup. It's worth remembering that zakka design is not judged against a level of competency or complexity. Instead, success is measured by how much happiness the addition of "signature style" brings to your home.

—

MIND MELD

Imagine zakka as the magical space where Scandinavian chic meets Japanese mori style. Natural lighting, simple forms, muted palettes and a predilection for humble utilitarian fabrics make for an effortless "easy to live with" style. When designing, your material cues are clear: think gingham, yarn-dye stripes, ticking and small print florals as perfect choices for material mash-ups and patchwork projects. Cotton, raw linen and felted wool provide sturdy, natural choices for clothing.

TO THE STREETS

It might sound like we're drawing a long bow, but we have come around to the notion that yarn bombing is a kind of guerilla zakka. This public act of domestic craft is used to "soften" urban landscapes, acting as political commentary on the nature of public/private spaces and drawing attention to failed urban planning by adding individuality to the everyday. Once you've mastered the requisite skills at home, why not make things a little more comfortable in your own neighborhood? Bus shelters, bike racks and park benches are all brilliantly customizable starting subjects.

—

RITUAL OF THE HABITUAL

Creating beautiful craft around daily rituals is an easy way of entering into the spirit of zakka, and as far as we're concerned there's no better ritual than eating! If you consider the many steps of food preparation and service, you'll find a cornucopia of crafting options from stovetop to tabletop, ripe for zakkafication.

—

HARD AND SOFT

Nothing says zakka like a cozy. By definition it embodies all the warm fuzzies that domestic crafting is supposed to be about. Today, artists are utilizing the cozy concept to cover everything from houses to army tanks, but you can play with this hard/soft dichotomy within the comfort of your own home. Make use of sturdy insulating fabrics such as felt to soften hard edges from table corners to coffee cups.

—

DOMESTIC BLITZ

While this style is a modern take on decorative kitsch cornerstones, you don't really want to end up with a house full of dust-collecting tchotchkes. Basic functional items such as aprons and potholders all offer perfect starting points for zakkafying your life. And remember that while everything can be customized, it doesn't necessarily need customizing. If, however, you want to whip up personalized tissue box covers, who are we to argue!

—

TOOLS

Zakka tools come from every craft chapter and have a particular poetry to them. Most of the items in your regular craft kit will get a good workout in zakka, whether you're making textile crafts, ceramics or even candles. The list below is by no means exhaustive, but it will keep you in the zakka zone.

- **Candle-making supplies:** See Cup Candles in the Techniques section.

- **Button jar, filled with assorted wood and novelty buttons**

- **Fabric:** Felt, wool, cotton and linen in cute kitsch, retro patterns mixed with muted block colors. Stick to natural fibers and nostalgic prints and use all your scraps from other projects.

- **Wool yarn**

- **Embroidery thread**

- **Rubber stamps**

- **Ink pads**

- **Plain and decorative papers**

- **Washi tape**

- **Pom-poms**

- **Scissors**

- **Sewing needles**

- **Pins**

- **Sewing machine**

- **Ribbons**

- **Patterned bias binding**

Zakka is not so much a technique as an attitude and aesthetic. As we've mentioned, you can take all the techniques you've learned in this book and turn them into objects for your home that fit under the zakka umbrella. That said, we think there are three particular items that pretty much sum up all that is zakka: homemade candles, handcrafted pot holders and block-printed napery.

CUP CANDLES

Nothing casts a sweeter light than a candle poured into a handmade or vintage vessel. We made our porcelain pot following the techniques from the Clay chapter but you could just as easily find a lonely teacup at the back of the cupboard to breathe new life into.

WHAT YOU NEED

- Waxed wicks
- Handmade ceramic or vintage cups
- Ice pop sticks
- Saucepan (big enough to sit the pitcher in)
- Soy wax beads or sheets (we prefer soy wax as it is slow to burn and doesn't smoke)
- Heatproof glass pitcher
- Essential oils

WHAT YOU DO

1. Place your wick in the center of your cup. If you have a wider vessel like ours you might want to use two wicks placed as shown. Use a couple of ice-pop sticks resting across the cup to keep the wick upright.

2. Half fill your saucepan with water and bring to the boil. Lower the heat, put your wax in your glass jug and place in the simmering water to melt. NEVER melt your wax over a direct flame — it can catch fire and be quite the drama (don't ask).

3. When the wax turns clear, add your essential oils. Carefully take the pitcher out of the water, being careful to wipe excess water from the outside.

4. Gently pour the wax into your cup three-quarters to the top and leave it to harden. This will probably take a few hours so use that time to either bake a cake or jazzercise! Once your candle is opaque, cool and hard, you can trim the wick. Now put on some Barry White and get that mood lighting happening!

POTHOLDER

Nothing is more ubiquitous to the aesthetic of zakka than the potholder. Humble and homey it is a classic domestic craft object. It appears in nearly every craft book published in the past 60 years and with it holds the history of the homemade. Think of the potholder as a small padded cloth that encapsulates your own personal style as well as an overarching life philosophy and you'll be ready to give it pride of place in your kitchen.

WHAT YOU NEED

- Linen or cotton fabric scraps
- Scissors
- Cotton thread
- Sewing machine
- 10" square of wool felt
- 10" square of cotton batting
- Pins
- 1¼ yards of bias binding

WHAT YOU DO

1. Make your patchwork top first, remembering that you need to end up with a 10" square block. See Quilt and Patch Techniques for instructions on patchwork.

2. Place the batting on top of the felt, then place the patchwork on top, right side up. Pin the layers together to secure them while stitching. Hand- or machine-quilt together using the Techniques in the Quilt and Patch chapter as a guide.

3. Trim any excess batting or felt so that you have a neat square. Attach your bias binding following the Techniques in the Sewing chapter. You can make a square or curved edge. When you hit the last corner, instead of cutting off your binding tail, use it to create a loop for hanging.

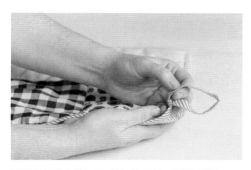

VEGETABLE BLOCK PRINT NAPKIN

One of the quickest ways of customizing your kitchen apparel and one of our favorite afternoon crafts, vegetable-printed napery is just about the perfect table accessory. Regular spuds are the most common choice, and are easy to carve shapes in, but we also like the natural shape of carrots, parsnips and rutabagas. As long as your vegetables are hard you can use them to print.

1. Cut your vegetables in half with a sharp, flat knife, then pat the cut side with a paper towel to ensure your surface is dry. Paint the cut side with a foam brush, then simply stamp your fabric. Try out some of the instructions for repeat motifs in the Print chapter to create continual patterns or keep it simple with a decorative border and contrasting running stitch.

2. Print a set for a perfect housewarming gift!

PROJECT IDEAS

→ By now you'll have a ready arsenal of skills to help you on your way to a handmade home, so start with the most important room: the kitchen. Coil a porcelain pourer, hand-dye a tablecloth, weave a fruit basket or whittle your salad spoons and make mealtimes much more meaningful.

→ Kids love pockets and zakka loves kids. Make a wall hanging with lots of little hand-stitched secret pockets, perfectly sized for little kids' cars, marbles, pencils or special treasure collections. It will keep them amused and save you from having to continually pick stuff up off the floor.

→ Get busy with a guerilla project that pays it forward. Make some soft patchwork cushions from scrap fabric to leave at a bus stop or on a park bench. You'll be beautifying the landscape while also making things more comfortable for commuters.

→ Make yourself a set of postcards using photographs and ephemera from your local haunts and start sending them out to friends and family in faraway places. Not only will you make someone's day, you'll also get to practice your collage skills and (hopefully) start finding things besides bad catalogs and bills in your mailbox!

→ Start collecting food packaging for use in rainy-day, toy-making projects with your kids. Cereal box cities are brilliant for budding urban planners, toilet tissue tubes make great finger puppets, and everyone needs to make at least one egg carton crocodile before they reach adulthood. Keep it simple and fun and you'll soon have a home of happy little crafters.

Cool Clay Cutlery

WHAT YOU NEED

- Rolling pin
- Porcelain clay
- Kitchen knife
- Cutting mat
- Sponge
- Underglaze in a variety of colors
- Paintbrushes
- Access to a kiln
- Sandpaper (optional)
- Clear glaze (optional)

Hand-building your own spoons is a beautiful way of personalizing a dining experience, and nothing could be more zakka than that. From salad servers to salt spoons you can manipulate scale, color, and surface design to match your food and your mood. Dinner is served!

WHAT YOU DO

1. Work out the size and number of spoons you're going to make. Using a rolling pin, create a slab of porcelain big enough to accommodate all your designs.

2. Cut a rough outline of your intended shape from your slab with a knife and then start forming the stem using a pinching action.

3. Make the bowl of your spoon by starting to pinch from the center out, forming the sides of your bowl in accordance with your design. You can pinch it until it's super-fine, or leave it chunky, depending on your chosen style.

4. Pay particular attention to the shoulder section of your spoon. This bit can be tricky to make and awkward to look at if not handled right. You're aiming for a smooth transition that won't snap when the bowl hits the foodstuffs.

5. Once you've turned your slab into spoons, leave them to dry for 48 hours in a warm, but not hot, spot. Turn any leftover clay back into a ball and store it in an airtight container ready for crafting another day.

6. Once your work is dry, use a damp sponge to smooth out any rough edges or tiny cracks that may have appeared during the drying process. Decorate with liquid underglaze using sgraffito, inlay or brush-dipped techniques. You can water the glaze down by up to 20 percent to create a translucent wash or keep it creamy and use it like acrylics. See the Clay chapter.

7. Leave the spoons to dry, then take them off to the communal or hire kiln for firing at 1,220 degrees Celsius (2,230 degrees Fahrenheit). Once fired, check the edges and if necessary, smooth them further with light sandpapering.

IMAGE CREDITS

FELT

Sonya Yong James p. 16
Anthropod, 2010, photographer: Louis Cahill

Kiyoshi Mino p. 17
ODLCO, (Three-toed Sloth), 2013,
photographer: Kiyoshi Mino

Cat Rabbit p. 16
Wintery Rabbit, 2013, photographer: Cat Rabbit
Turtle in a Turtleneck, 2013, photographer: Cat Rabbit

Felt Mistress p. 17
Trunk & Loggins, 2013, photographer: Felt Mistress
(Louise Evans and Jonathan Edwards)

KNIT

Freddie Robins p. 26
Craft Kills, 2002, photographer: Douglas Atfield
One Letter Apart, 2013, photographer: Douglas Atfield

Mandy McIntosh p. 27
Beige Crystal, 2004, photographer: Mandy Mcintosh

Tracy Widdess p. 26
Idol, 2013, photographer: Tracy Widdess

Isabel Berglund p. 27
Floating Island of Pearls, 2014,
photographer: Christoffer Askman

CROCHET

Jo Hamilton p. 38
Shine Reclining, 2013, photographer: Jo Hamilton

Nathan Vincent p. 39
007, 2007, courtesy of the artist and Emmanuel
Fremin Gallery

Phil Ferguson aka Chiliphilly p. 38
The Burger Hat, 2014, photographer: Phil Ferguson

Cécile Dachary p. 39
La Ville, 2012, photographer: Cécile Dachary

WEAVE

Jess Feury p. 50
Untitled, 2013, photographer: Ashley Batz Photography

Hiroko Takeda p. 51
Blue Note, 2003, photographer: Hiroko Takeda

Justine Ashbee/Native Line p. 50
Native Lines group shot, 2014,
photographer: Justine Ashbee

John Brooks p. 51
The Object in Flux, 2012, photographer: John Brooks

Caroline Rose Kaufman p. 52
SS15 Collection hand woven look, photographer:
Caroline Rose Kaufman

Summer Moore p. 53
Vazo Necklace, 2014, photographer: Summer Moore

Maryann Talia Pau p. 52
Mo Lo'u Tama (Samoan), 2009, photographer:
Steven Rhall

Lucia Cuba p. 53
"United states of..." part of the project "Articulo
6" by Lucia Cuba, 2014, art direction: Lucia Cuba;
photographer: Erasmo Wong S.; model: Stefania Merea

TAPESTRY

Sola Fiedler p. 66
Vancouver, 2014, photographer: Amanda Skuse

Margo Wolowiec p. 67
Due North, 2014, image courtesy of Anat Ebgi Gallery

Erin M Riley p. 66
Nudes 17, 2014, photographer: Erin M Riley

Daniel Edwards p. 67
Giles, 2010, photographer: Jenna King

MACRAMÉ

Sally England p. 78
Macramé Fort, 2014, photographer: Carson
Davis Brown

Natalie Miller p. 79
Yellow Field, 2014, photographer: Natalie Miller
Natalie Miller Image 3, photographer: Natalie Miller

Eleanor Amoroso p. 78
Eleanor Amoroso AW12 Look Book, 2012,
photographer: David Sessions

Sarah Parkes p. 79
Avido Wine Bar, Sydney, photographer: Will Reichelt

YARN

SPIDERTAG p. 90
Madrid, 2013, photographer: SPIDERTAG

Ivano Vitali p. 91
Detail of Tape-stry 11, 2008, photographer: Ivano Vitali

Nikki Gabriel p. 90
Triangle Knitting Projects Construction No.4, 2013,
photographer: Anthony Chiappin

Jay Mohler p. 91
Peaceful Mind, 2014, photographer: Jay Mohler

BASKETS

Tim Johnson p. 100
Woven Costume 2, 2011, photographer: Tim Johnson
Woven Costume 1, 2011, photographer: Tim Johnson

Doug Johnston p. 101
Family, 2011, photographer: Michael Popp

Michele Morcos p. 100
The Infinite, 2014, photographer: Michele Morcos

Cordula Kehrer p. 101
Bow Bins, 2012, photographer: Frederik Busch

LEATHER

Claire McArdle p. 110
Koala, 2014, photographer: Claire McArdle

Una Burke p. 111
RE.TREAT, 2009, photographer: Diego Indraccolo

Simon Hasan p. 110
Industrial Makeshift Bottles, 2010,
photographer: Emma Wieslander

Atsushi Kitazaki p. 111
Carving geta (Fujin Raijin),
photographer: Atsushi Kitazaki

RUGS

Jonathan Josefsson p. 122
Rug #81, 2011, photographer: Jonathan Josefsson

Myra Klose p. 123
Snow leopard, first developed in 2011,
photographer: Jan Illmann

Katie Stout p. 122
Pink Rug/Ottoman, 2013, photographer: Andre Herrer

Karl Hugo Erickson p. 123
Julian Cope's Left Eye, 2008,
photographer: Karl Erickson

EMBROIDERY

Takashi Iwasaki p. 136
Fishbonbon, 2012, photographer: Takashi Iwasaki

Ana Teresa Barboza p. 137
Untitled, 2011, photographer: Juan Pablo Murrugarra

Daniel Kornrumpf p. 136
Austin Texas, 2009, photographer: Daniel Kornrumpf

Amanda Valdez p. 137
She's mine, 2014, courtesy of the artist and
Denny Gallery

Nike Schroeder p. 138
Berlin_3, 2011, photographer: Anja Schäfer

Maricor/Maricar p. 139
Macho Distrust, 2011, photographer: Maricar Manalo

Jose Romussi p. 138
Rainbow, 2013, photographer: Rocio Aguirre

Lauren Dicioccio p. 139
Composition Book, 2009,
photographer: Lauren DiCioccio

CROSS STITCH

Diane Meyer p. 148
The West I, 2011, photographer: Diane Meyer

Evelin Kasikov p. 149
Screen/Book, 2012, photographer: Evelin Kasikov

Dave Lieske p. 148
East vs. West, 2011, photographer: Davey Gravy

Inge Jacobsen p. 149
Beyoncé Front Cover of Dazed and Confused July
2011, courtesy of Sharif Hamzafor, Dazed and
Confused Magazine

NEEDLEPOINT

Andoni Maillard p. 158
Breizh, 2013, photographer: Ludovic Zeller

Michelle Hamer p. 159
Two way traffic, 2013, photographer: Marc Morel

Nicole Gastonguay p. 158
Lo Mein, 2008, photographer: Oliver Dalzell

Jacquelyn Royal p. 159
Barcelona 1B, 2011, photographer: J. Szot

SEW

The Social Studio p. 168
TSS LookBook spring/summer 2014, photographer:
Paul Philipson; creative director: Gidi Creative

Terry Williams p. 169
Terry Williams Not titled (Stereo) 2011, photographer:
Penelope Hunt, courtesy the artist and Arts
Project Australia

Megan Whitmarsh p. 168
Artforum/Lynda Benglis, 2014,
photographer: Megan Whitmarsh

Elena Stonaker p. 169
Sacred Sacred Wedding Dress and Alter (custom
made for Carly Jo Morgan), 2013, photographer:
Shelby Duncan

APPLIQUÉ

Alison Willoughby p. 180
Skirt 265, 2006, photographer: Alison Willoughb

Lucky Jackson p. 181
Richie's Tent, 2011, photographer: Lucky Jackson

Tony Garifalakis p. 180
Mutually Assured Destruction, 2013, Installation view
from "Melbourne Now," courtesy of National Gallery
of Victoria

Gunvor Nervold Antonsen p. 181
Installation view from the exhibition "Spring Burial,"
2013, photographer: Øystein Thorvaldsen

QUILT AND PATCH

Kathryn Clark p. 190
Modesto Foreclosure Quilt, 2011,
photographer: Kathryn Clark

Madeleine Sargent p. 191
ALL IN, 2014, photographer: Madeleine Sargent

Colleen Toutant Merrill p. 190
Rope Piece, 2012, courtesy of Colleen Merrill

Lu Flux p. 191
Missouri patchwork dress from the Gee's Bend
collection, 2013, photographer: James Champion

Luke Haynes p. 192
[Iconography #7] Rags to Riches, 2012,
photographer: Brad Farwell

Folk Fibers/Maura Grace Ambrose p. 193
Quilts for Terrain, Winter 2012,
photographer: Wynn Myers

Penelope Durston p. 192
Vintage wool suiting "wagga" style quilt, 2013,
photographer: Penelope Durston

Debra Weiss p. 193
Layers of a Life, 2010/2011, photographer: Dan Stack

NOTIONS

Troy Emery p. 204
Wild Thing, 2009, photographer: Michael Myers

Elise Cakebread p. 205
Soft Hemispheres – Venus and Mars, 2014,
photographer: Michael Quinlan

Megan Geckler p. 204
Every move you make, every step you take, 2010,
photographer: Megan Geckler

Ran Hwang p. 205
Dreaming of Joy, 2008, photographer: Sung-Ha Cho

MARBLE

Ilana Kohn p. 216
Marble Scarf, 2012, photographer: Miguel Gomez

Pernille Snedker Hansen p. 217
Marbelous Wood _ Refraction, 2013,
photographer: Kirstine Autzen

Milly Dent p. 216
Marbled Gem Plate, 2014,
photographer: Octavia Rogers

Melike Tascioglu p. 217
Untitled, 2011, photographer: Melike Tascioglu

INDIGO

Rowland and Chinami Ricketts p. 226
I am Ai, We are Ai – Warehouse Installation, 2012, photographer: Rowland Ricketts

I am Ai, We are Ai – Returning Indigo; Omiya Shrine, 2012, photographer: Rowland Ricketts

Anthea Carboni/Yuniko Studio p. 227
Indigo Wash Ceramics, 2013, photographer: Angelita Bonetti

Bonnie Smith p. 226
Indigo Mound, 2012, photographer: Bonnie Smith

Ido Yoshimoto p. 227
Indigo on cypress from the series "Astral Planes," 2014, photographer: Randall Fleming

PRINT

Studio Heretic p. 238
Spectral Sandwich, 2013, photographer: Studio Heretic

Unreality Rehearsal Preset, 2013, photographer: Studio Heretic

Lily and Hopie Stockman/Block Shop Textiles p. 239
Hopie & Dolly in Mosaic Marigold & Black, photographer: Lily Stockman

Marcroy Smith p. 238
Print Isn't Dead, Element #002, 2015, courtesy of People of Print/Marcroy Smith and Studio Heretic

Romance Was Born p. 239
Cheshire Cat – Mushroom Magic Spring/Summer 2013, photographer: Daniel Boud

Magicland Jumpsuit – Mushroom Magic Spring/Summer 2013, photographer: Pip and Pop

Rona Green p. 240
Chips, 2008, photographer: Aaron McLoughlin
The Duke, 2008, photographer: Aaron McLoughlin

Philipp Hennevogl p. 241
Studio, 2010, Philipp Hennevogl

Hannah Waldron p. 240
MAZE furoshiki design, photographer: Hannah Waldron

Kate Banazi p. 241
Astronaut, 2012, photographer: Kate Banazi

DYE

Joanna Fowles p. 252
Joanna Fowles fold dress, 2011, photographer: Damien Van Der Vlist

India Flint p. 253
Ecoprint Silky Merino, 2014, photographer: India Flint

Jessica Lee/Willow Knows p. 252
Willow Knows Dye Fall collection, 2014, photographer: Jessica Lee

Rafaella McDonald p. 253
Painted Structures, 2013, photographer: Theresa Harrison

COLLAGE

Jock Mooney p. 264
I Surrender to the Spirit of the Night, 2010, photographer: Jock Mooney

Gracia Haby & Louise Jennison p. 265
As inclination directs, 2013, photographer: Gracia Haby & Louise Jennison

Richard Pearse p. 264
Mount, 2011, photographer: Richard Pearse
Cowshed, 2011, photographer: Richard Pearse

Jenny Brown p. 265
Fruit of the Sea, 2012, courtesy of Jenny Brown

Aaron Moran p. 266
Huron Church, 2014, photographer: Aaron S Moran

Matthew Craven p. 267
Body Werk, 2014, courtesy of Matthew Craven

Eugenia Loli p. 266
Spring Crop at the Rosseland Crater, 2014, credit: Classic Film: www.flickr.com/photos/29069717@N02/ and SwellMap: www.flickr.com/photos/94207108@N02/

Emir Šehanović p. 267
Sihir, 2011, photographer: Emir Šehanovic

GILD

Susan Dwyer (Up in the Air Somewhere) p. 276
Peach and Gold pot, 2013, photographer: Ben Syverson

Urban Soule p. 277
Gold Skull, 2013, photographer: Urban Soule

Peaches + Keen p. 276
Golden Peaks Botanical Circle, 2014, photographer: Peaches + Keen

Lauren Kalman p. 277
Hard Wear (Tongue Gilding), 2006, photographer: Lauren Kalman

CLAY

Bridget Bodenham p. 288
Untitled, 2013, photographer: Kara Rosenlund

Michele Michael p. 289
Seafoam and White Platters, 2011, photographer: Michele Michael

Iggy and Lou Lou p. 288
Driptopia Bud Vase Group of 3, 2014, photographer: Irene Grishin Selzer

Katie Jacobs p. 289
Installation view of Australia Head (Sydney Swan) and Wolf Head, 2014, photographer: Natasha Holmes

Susan Robey p. 290
Bigmouth/Zigzag, 2014, photographer: Chris Sanders

Sean Gerstley p. 291
Easy G, Draft Dodger, and Paint Can, 2014, photographer: Carlos Avendaño

Kirsten Perry p. 290
Grid Jug, 2014, photographer: Kirsten Perry

Brian Rochefort p. 291
Pink Sculpture, 2014, photographer: Brian Rochefort

BEADS

Sarah Maloney p. 302
Skin – detail 1, 2003–2012, photographer: Morrow Scot-Brown

Leutton-Postle p. 303
Peutetre, model: Chris Arundel, photographer: Natalie Malric

Eddy Carroll p. 302
Sovereign unto oneself, 2014, photographer: Lesley Turnbull

Karla Way p. 303
Cosmic Grounds neckpiece, 2013, photographer: Karla Way

BOOKS

Alison Worman p. 314
Two, Then One, 2012, photographer: Alison Worman

Sonja Ahlers p. 315
Fatal Distraction, 2004, published by Insomniac Press, Toronto, Ontario

Pawel Piotrowski p. 314
Sandwich book, 2010, photographer: Paweł Piotrowski

Nicholas Jones p. 315
The Wisdom of India, 2013, photographer: Matthew Stanton

JEWELRY

Kate Rohde p. 324
Hybrid Geology Crystal Cuffs, 2012, photographer: Andrew Barcham

Anna Davern p. 325
Rocks earrings, 2009, photographer: Anna Davern

Seth Damm/Neon Zinn p. 324
Some Royal, 2014, photographer: Akasha Rabut

Bianca Mavrick p. 325
Surf Earrings, 2013, photographer: Lisa Brown
Comb Necklace, 2013, photographer: Lisa Brown

David Neale p. 326
Tree Climber Earring, 2010, photographer: David Neale

Meredith Turnbull p. 327
Block necklace, photographer: Andrew Barcham, courtesy of Pieces of Eight Gallery, Melbourne

Natalia Milosz-Piekarska p. 326
From the Deep Neckpiece, 2010, photographer: Natalia Milosz-Piekarska

Denise J Reytan p. 327
Burnet, photographer: M. Fischinger

ORIGAMI

Mademoiselle Maurice p. 338
Urban Installation, 2014, photographer: Mademoiselle Maurice

Kota Hiratsuka p. 339
7 Flowers Mosaic, 2013, photographer: Kota Hiratsuka

Jule Waibel p. 338
Image courtesy of Jule Waibel

Morana Kranjek p. 339
Untitled, 2011, photographer: Sandra Vitaljić

PAPER

Paige Smith/A Common Name p. 350
Geode #3, DTLA, courtesy of Paige Smith

Carly Fischer p. 351
We are one but we are many, 2012, photographer: Matthew Stanton, image courtesy of Carly Fischer and This Is No Fantasy Gallery, Melbourne

Michael Velliquette p. 350
Summer God, 2012, photographer: Michael Velliquette

Amy Boone-McCreesh p. 351
Divine Minnie, 2014, photographer: Amy Boone-McCreesh, image courtesy of Hamiltonian Gallery, Washington DC

MOBILES

Kim Baise p. 360
Pretty Flamingos Mobile, 2014, photographer: Kim Baise

Dear Plastic p. 361
Rainbow Mountain, 2013, photographer: Dear Plastic

Melissa Hruskaa p. 360
Himmeli in Brass, photographer: Melissa Hruskaa

Ladies & Gentleman p. 361
Aura Wind Chime, 2013, photographer: L & G Studio

UPCYCLE

Louise Riley p. 370
Joined at the Hip and Bent Over Backwards, 2008, photographer: Louise Riley

Ben Venom p. 371
In to the Sun, 2013, image courtesy of Ben Venom

Guerra de La Paz p. 370
Tribute, 2002–2012, photographer: Guerra de la Paz (Alain Guerra & Neraldo de La Paz)

Cal Lane p. 371
Oil Tank map of the world, 2008, image courtesy of Art Mûr

Pennie Jagiello p. 372
De Pendant neckpiece, 2011, photographer: John Lee

Tejo Remy and René Veenhuizen p. 373
Accidental Carpet, 2007–2008, courtesy of Tejo Remy and René Veenhuizen

Lyn Balzer and Tony Perkins p. 372
REworked Denim Choker, courtesy of Lyn Balzer and Tony Perkins

Rowan Mersh p. 373
WWF sculpture, 2012, photographer: Jim Naughten

VENEER AND WOOD

Ron van der Ende p. 382
Akai-VT100 (open reel portable video recorder), 2006, courtesy of Ron van der Ende

AJ Fosik p. 383
Transpanthanation, 2010, courtesy of AJ Fosik

Clemens Behr p. 382
Paravan and Luster, 2013, photographer: Clemens Behr

Toby Pola p. 383
Loser blames their parents, failures blame their kids, 2013, photographer: Jeremy Dillon

Thrasher magazine, 2012, photographer: Jeremy Dillon

ZAKKA

Hello Sandwich p. 392
Image courtesy of Hello Sandwich

Kitiya Palaskas p. 393
Piñatas, 2013, courtesy of Kitiya Palaskas

Joel Henriques p. 392
Paper City Paper City Vehicles, 2010, photographer: Joel Henriques

Shino Takeda p. 393
Horizon, 2014, photographer: Shino Takeda

INDEX

ACKNOWLEDGMENTS

A project of this magnitude is truly a team effort. First and foremost our thanks go to our publisher, champion and friend Paulina de Laveaux. What began as a search for macramé instructions resulted in the book you now hold in your hands. It has been an honour and a pleasure to work with you!

We'd also like to thank our production team — designer Spencer Harrison, who created something truly wonderful, and above and beyond our expectations. Oslo Davis, whose illustrations brought so much humour and light to the book — excellent work Captain, you're officially crafty. Photographer Hilary Walker and her assistant Rochelle Seator who define 'grace under pressure'. Our in-house intern Hope Lumsden-Barry for the many, many hours spent in our papercraft department. Margaret Barry, for spending four months at the dining table with the latch hook rug, an amazing contribution. Michael Larobina, our heavy machinery maestro and in-house lumberjack. Bobby Ly for his gophering assistance and support throughout the project. Our extraordinary technician Shula Hampson whose prodigious skills in and out of the studio provided ongoing assistance as one-woman cheer squad, agony aunt, taxi service, support staff and eleventh-hour seamstress. And finally, Tahlia Anderson, and the crew at Thames & Hudson Australia — your tireless work and support have been invaluable.

Our models: Mym Den Elzen, Emma Greenwood, Paulina de Laveaux, Maxwell Larobina, Finian Larobina, Hope Lumsden-Barry, Thomas Barry, Bobby Ly and Muji the most excellent dog. What a gorgeous bunch you are!

A special thank you to Gemma Jones for her generosity and foresight in recommending us for this project, and our enormous gratitude to all those makers who shared with us their knowledge and skills. You gave us the confidence to write this book: Rachel Hine, Emma Greenwood, Penelope Durston, Anna Davern, Kirsten Perry, Ilka White, Claire McArdle, Nicky Hepburn, Lara Davies and Jess Wright, Joanna Fowles, Vicki Mason, Paperlab, Popcraft, Victoria Pemberton, Sophie Moorhouse Morris, Maryann Talia Pau and everyone we had the privilege of working with at Craft Victoria.

RAMONA WOULD ALSO LIKE TO THANK: My beloved Alan Blease, your unwavering support makes anything possible. To my gorgeous children Hope and Thom, the best things I ever made. My lovely mother Margaret, who stuck a pen in my hand and said go for it. To all my friends who cheered the project on from start to finish, especially Andrew and Jackie Coates whose faith in me many years ago set me free. Most of all to my best friend, co-author and collaborator Beck Jobson. Your drive, creativity, energy and talent as a writer and a maker are a constant source of inspiration. Love your work.

BECK WOULD ALSO LIKE TO THANK: My secret winged keel, Michael Larobina and beautiful wild boys Max and Finny — you three make everything better! My Nana Lily, who gave me my first craft book and open access to her supplies. Mum and Dad for teaching the importance of music, nature, politics, curiosity and silliness. Matt and Simonne for being the bomb, always. My style heroes David Bowie, Yayoi Kusama, Sun Ra, Stevie Nicks, Zandra Rhodes, Black Sabbath, Parliament/Funkadelic and Prince — I owe you everything. David Band for teaching me to keep it simple. My extended family of beloved friends and colleagues — 'I love youse all'. And, finally, my super-skilled crafting compadre and pal without peer, Ramona Barry — without you I wouldn't have had the will or wherewithal to undertake this crazy adventure. You rule.

ABOUT THE AUTHORS

Ramona Barry is a Melbourne-based artist, writer and curator specializing in craft and design. She has a background in printmaking and illustration and was Chair of Craft Victoria, Australia's leading contemporary craft organization.

Rebecca Jobson is a Melbourne-based textile designer, artist, writer and curator with twenty years' experience in the craft and design industry.

Together, they co-write their blog handmadelife and present a specialist craft programme on Australian radio.